Students and External Re

4 5 6 11

Greater London

AN AGRICULTURAL ATLAS OF
ENGLAND AND WALES
by J. T. Coppock

THE CHANGING USE OF LAND IN BRITAIN
by Robin H. Best and J. T. Coppock

LONDON 2000
by Peter Hall

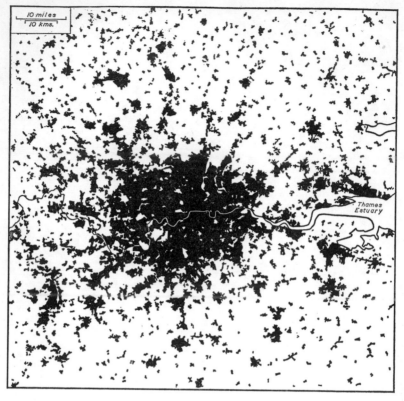

FIG. 1   The built-up area of London *c.* 1960
Based upon Ordnance Survey one-inch maps.

'. . . the great cities of the twentieth century look like something which has burst an intolerable envelope and splashed.'

H. G. WELLS: *Anticipations*

GREATER LONDON

edited by

J. T. COPPOCK

and

HUGH C. PRINCE

FABER AND FABER LTD

24 Russell Square

London

First published in mcmlxiv
by Faber and Faber Limited
Printed in Great Britain by
Ebenezer Baylis and Son, Ltd
Worcester and London

GP5810
600251

© *Faber and Faber Limited 1964*

Architecture
. 600251

TO
OUR COLLEGES

Contents

CONTENTS

Plates

(between pages 224 and 225)

11

Maps and Diagrams

MAPS AND DIAGRAMS

MAPS AND DIAGRAMS

Tables

TABLES

Preface

London is so vast and complex that any book about it must be highly selective. The theme of this book is the growth and character of contemporary London, as seen through the eyes of a group of geographers. Its authors are, with one exception, members of the teaching staff of the University of London and they have all been engaged over a number of years on investigations into various aspects of London and its environs. The idea of the present volume germinated during preparations for the XX International Geographical Congress, London, 1964, when it became apparent that there was no contemporary book dealing with the major features of London's geography.

The book falls broadly into four parts. Chapters 1 and 2 are concerned with the physical environment of London, although the first chapter has been extended, for the benefit of those unfamiliar with London, to provide a general summary of its growth and character as a framework for the more detailed studies which follow. The next four chapters have as their theme the growth of London since the beginning of the railway age, the third section, comprising Chapters 7, 8, 9, 10 and 11, deals with three principal aspects of London's economy, while the focus shifts in the last section from the built-up area to the surrounding countryside.

London is not only vast but difficult to define; certain conventions have therefore been adopted. London (unqualified) refers to the built-up area, now roughly co-extensive with the Greater London conurbation as defined by the Registrar-General (Fig. 9). Where a precise definition is intended, capitals are used; thus, the Central Area consists of those boroughs and parts of boroughs shown in Figure 31, but central London refers in a general way to the City and Westminster and the area immediately surrounding them. Inner and Outer London similarly refer to the county of London and the rest of the conurbation respectively, but inner London and outer London are less precise, being broadly equivalent to Victorian and inter-war London. No general location map has been provided; for London, Geographers' Atlas of Greater London is probably the most useful source and for other areas, the Ordnance Survey special ½-inch map of Greater London.

The authors and editors are indebted to many people for help in the production of this book. Most of the illustrations have been drawn in the Department of Geography at University College by Messrs J. Bryant, M. Nash, Kenneth Wass and M. Young, without whose skill this book would not have appeared in its present form. Illustrations in Chapters 3 and 9 have been prepared by Mrs K. King of Birkbeck College and those in Chapter 10 by Mrs S. Weston of the London School of Economics, while the drawings in Chapter 7 have been compiled by Mr D. F. Stevens. The quotation from H. G. Wells' *Anticipations* is made by kind permission of his executors. Numerous people have provided illustrations or information and the individual acknowledgements appear in the appropriate chapters. Special thanks are due to Dr Marion Ward for preparing the index at great speed. We are also indebted to Mr M. Shaw for his patience and skilled guidance in seeing the book through the press. To all those who have helped to make this book possible we express our grateful thanks.

J. T. COPPOCK
HUGH C. PRINCE

University College London

1

A General View of London and Its Environs

*

J. T. COPPOCK

'What a Monster must London be, extending from the farther End of Chelsea, West, to Deptford-Bridge East'. When Defoe wrote these words London was little more than one-hundredth of its present extent; for although it was then, as it had long been, by far the largest city in the country, it is from the beginning of the nineteenth century that London's greatest expansion dates.[1] This book is about the growth and character of modern London and the summary description of its setting and growth in this chapter is intended to provide a framework for the more detailed discussion which follows.

The Physical Setting

The present built-up area, which corresponds broadly with the Registrar-General's Greater London conurbation, lies wholly within the London Basin, a broad synclinal depression bounded by the scarps of the North Downs and the Chilterns (Fig. 2). The Thames, which bisects the conurbation, does not follow the axis of the basin, but has migrated southwards in post-glacial times; consequently the built-up area extends almost to the crest of the North Downs, but nowhere reaches the southern margin of the Chilterns. Similarly, while to east, west and north London's sphere of influence is largely contained within the London Basin, to the south it extends well beyond the bounding scarp. The terrain on which London and its satellites have developed is very diverse; indeed, in L. D. Stamp's

19

opinion, 'few, if any, of the great cities of the world are so situated that there can be found within a radius of 25 miles (40 km.) such a variety of land and soils'.[2] Some idea of this variety is essential to an understanding both of London's development and of the problems which it has posed.

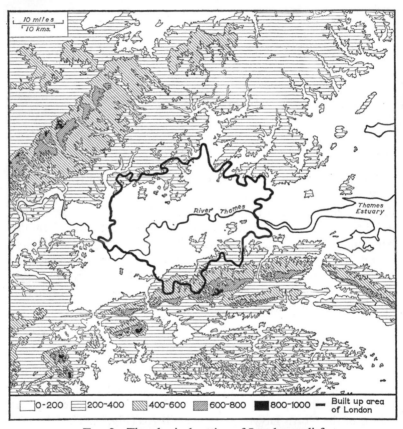

FIG. 2   The physical setting of London: relief
Heights are shown in feet. Metric equivalents are: 200, 60m; 400, 120m; 600, 180m; 800, 240m; 1000, 300m.
The heavy line marks the limit of the continuous built-up area of London.
Based upon Ordnance Survey maps.

The central feature of Figure 3 is the gravel tract formed by terraces of the Thames. It lies mainly north of the river and is at its widest between Maidenhead and Tilbury. Although there are differences within the tract, particularly between the Flood Plain terrace and the higher Taplow terrace, the gravels provide level, well-drained land and easily-worked soils of high quality, especially where they are overlain by brick-earth. Where it has not been built over or worked for gravel, such land is often used for market gardening. Downstream from London Bridge there are wide expanses of alluvium, once marshy and flooded at high tide, but now embanked; the alluvial belt upstream is much narrower, although the risk of flooding has often

FIG. 3   The physical setting of London: surface rocks

Key: 1, alluvium; 2, terrace gravels; 3, other gravels; 4, boulder clay; 5, clay-with-flints; 6, London Clay; 7, chalk; 8, sandstones; 9, other clays; 10, other materials; 11, chalk scarp; 12, Lower Greensand scarp; 13, City of London; 14, limit of the continuous built-up area of London.

Based upon maps of the Geological Survey.

21

discouraged house building along the banks of the Thames. The river terraces are mainly bounded by very different terrain on London Clay, which is most extensive in Middlesex and Essex. In the south of these counties the clay forms a gently undulating plain, broken here and there by low hills. Further north, in the South Hertfordshire Plateau and the South Essex Uplands, where much of the higher land is capped with gravel, the relief is more marked and the scenery more varied.[3] A bastion of this higher ground, the Northern Heights, extends southward to Highgate and Hampstead. To the south of the river the London Clay is less extensive and its topographic expression more varied. In south-east London it overlies the pebbly beds of the Blackheath Plateau, between Richmond and Wimbledon it forms a low, gravel-capped plateau, while west of Croydon it forms a narrow vale. Most of the London Clay outcrop provides poorly-drained, heavy land of medium quality; outside the built-up area it is now mainly used for mixed farming.

Beyond these clay outcrops the terrain is even more varied. To the west of London lies the Bagshot Plateau, an area of coarse sands and poor soils, much of it under wood and heath, with extensive tracts used for recreation and military training. To the north-west, separated by the Thames valley and the Vale of St Albans, are the Chilterns, a dissected chalk cuesta which is mainly covered with clay-with-flints. In the western Chilterns the land is not of high quality and is mainly used for mixed farming, but the abundant woodland and steep-sided valleys make for attractive scenery. Further east soils are better but the relief is less bold and the scenery correspondingly less striking. The East Anglian Plateau, east of the Hitchin Gap, is lower and the soils developed on the calcareous boulder clay provide good arable land; but the scenery here is probably less diverse than in any other part of the area under discussion. This sector has been little affected by the growth of London and the land is mostly used for agriculture.

The North Downs offer greater internal contrasts than the Chilterns. West of Croydon the dip of the Chalk increases and the outcrop narrows until, in the Hog's Back, there is only a low, steep-sided ridge. To the east the cuesta is broader; the upper slopes are covered with clay-with-flints and have many affinities with the Chilterns, while along the northern margin the Thanet Sands and loam deposits overlying the Chalk give rise to a belt of good agricultural land, much of it under fruit and vegetables. Like the Chilterns, the North

22

Downs are well-wooded but the quality of the agricultural land is generally better.

The scarp-foot belts of the Chilterns and the Downs provide sharp contrasts in both soil and scenery. The scarps themselves have thin chalk soils and are covered with wood, scrub or rough grazing; below the scarp is a belt of good arable land developed on the Lower Chalk, which is in turn succeeded by heavy, low-lying land underlain by Gault Clay. Both of these tracts are much wider to the north of the London Basin than to the south.

The area lying north of the Chilterns has, as yet, been little affected by the growth of London. It is largely a clay lowland and almost entirely in agricultural use, although east of Bletchley the low cuesta of the Lower Greensand introduces a note of variety with its heaths, conifers and, further east, market gardening. The country south of the North Downs is more varied and has come more strongly under London's influence, both as a dormitory area and as a place of re-creation. Here sandy formations are as abundant as clay and dominate the relief. The bold Lower Greensand cuesta, which overtops the Chalk west of Dorking, reaching nearly 1,000 feet (300 m.) in Leith Hill, provides some of the most attractive scenery around London; it is mainly under heath and wood, for, apart from the outcrop of the Bargate Beds, the soils are generally poor. Around Maidstone, however, the pattern of land use is very different; for here the Lower Greensand consists in part of alternating limestone, Kentish Rag, and loamy sand, giving rise to more fertile soils, largely under orchards. The Low Weald, a broad clay lowland mainly underlain by the Weald Clay, separates the Lower Greensand cuesta from the sandy terrain of the High Weald, formed of the Ashdown Sands and the Tunbridge Wells Sands. The Weald Clay is largely in agricultural use, although it makes poorly-drained land of indifferent quality, but the High Weald, like the Lower Greensand outcrop, contains much heath and wood. To the south, beyond the narrow Vale of Sussex, lie the open chalklands of the South Downs and the coast of the English Channel.

The influence of London's site and situation on its growth and character has altered considerably over the course of time. In its early development, both its regional situation and its site were of considerable importance. Growth was largely restricted to the well-drained terraces, with their abundant drinking water and good soils, but technical development, making adequate drainage and water supply possible on the clays, and the raising, draining and embanking of of the low-lying areas permitted a much wider range of sites. Later the underlying physique affected the growth of London less directly through its effects on communications and through the influence of scenery on residential development. The excavation of the docks in the river alluvium and the construction of the underground railways in the London Clay have both been facilitated by the nature

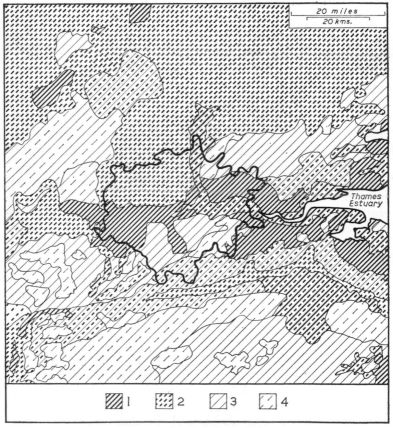

FIG. 4 The physical setting of London: land quality
Key: 1, first class; 2, good; 3, medium; 4, poor.
Areas where different classes of land are intermixed are shown by mixtures of the appropriate shadings. The heavy line marks the limit of the continuous built-up area of London.
Based upon maps of the Land Utilization Survey.

of these materials. In general, the modern growth of London has taken place across good, medium and poor quality land; indeed, the poverty of land has often contributed to its preservation as open space or woodland, while high quality market garden land has been built over (Fig. 4). Beyond the conurbation it is generally the poorest land agriculturally which is the most attractive scenically and where the largest tracts of open land are preserved; both considerations have been important in encouraging residential development. These are the areas where there was much low-density house building before 1939 and where the strongest measures have been taken to prevent further building through acquisition by local authorities and by the National Trust, by their inclusion in the green belt, and by their designation as Areas of Outstanding Natural Beauty, as in the Chilterns and the Surrey Hills.

Early Development of London

Except in so far as it has determined the location of the economic

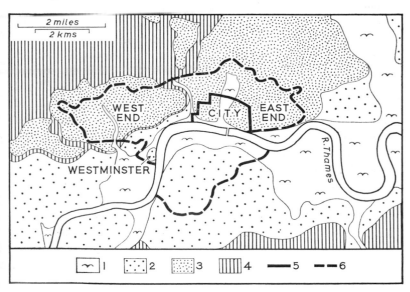

FIG. 5   The physical setting and extent of London c. 1800
Key: 1, alluvium; 2, Flood Plain terrace; 3, Taplow terrace; 4, other formations; 5, London wall; 6, limit of the continuous built-up area c. 1800.
Based on maps by T. Milne, H. Ormsby and the Geological Survey.

heart of the conurbation, the original site of London has little relevance for its present geography. In any case, a relative rise in sea-level of the order of fifteen feet (4·6 m.), the accumulation of the debris of centuries to raise the level of the land surface by an average of ten feet (3 m.), the filling-in of valleys and marshes and the embanking and control of the river have materially altered the physical conditions which the original settlers found.[4] For in detail, London's terrain, like its climate, is in large measure man-made.

The Roman city of Londinium was located on two low hills (now Ludgate Hill and Cornhill) carved out of the Taplow terrace north of the Thames. This site, where the alluvium narrows considerably to make for easier access from the south, was probably the then tidal limit and the lowest possible bridging point; it was also the only point for some distance up- and downstream at which the higher ground north of the Thames reaches the river (Fig. 5). The site had several other advantages. It was fairly easily defensible, for it was surrounded by lower ground—the estuary of the Fleet to the west, the Shoreditch to the east and the tributaries of the Walbrook, which bisected the city, to the north.[5] The river was navigable for large ships and the mouths of the tributary streams provided minor harbours. The wall which enclosed the Roman city followed the limits of the higher ground, while the river, now separated by a 100-yard (91 m.) strip of made ground, then abutted against the edge of the Taplow terrace.[6] The gravel also provided easily-worked land and a ready supply of water and was probably more lightly wooded than the clays to north and south of the river terraces. London also derived considerable advantage from its situation facing the continent at the head of the most important estuary between the Humber and Southampton Water. The radial pattern of Roman roads focusing on London confirmed these advantages, as the railways and trunk roads were to do later.

Another settlement had arisen at Westminster on a small patch of Flood Plain terrace surrounded by marsh. Previously important for its monastery, it became the site of the royal palace under Edward the Confessor and the seat of government, while London developed the interests in commerce and finance, which remain the City's most distinctive features today.[7] Because of restrictions on building, medieval London was not much more extensive than the Roman city, but, following the dissolution of the monasteries, which had previously owned much land around the city, there was expansion east

26

and west along the gravel terraces, particularly after the Great Fire of 1666, which encouraged wealthy merchants to build more spacious houses further west.[8] London and Westminster were gradually joined by buildings along the Strand and, by the end of the seventeenth century, the West End around Piccadilly and St James's had come into being. During the eighteenth and early nineteenth centuries much of the gravel terrace between the City and Hyde Park was covered with houses, many of them laid out in formal estates on the properties of great landowners.[9] East of the City growth was more haphazard, as industrial suburbs arose and as the port, its westward extension restricted by London Bridge, expanded downstream.

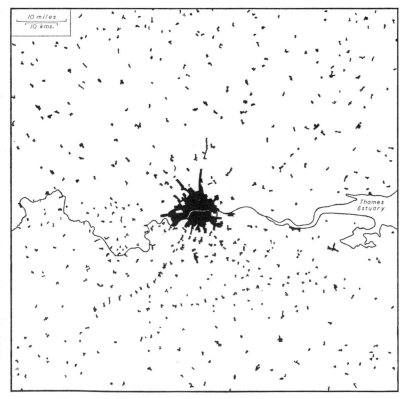

FIG. 6   The built-up area of London at the beginning of the railway age
The representation of the smaller settlements is diagrammatic.
Based upon one-inch maps of the Ordnance Survey.

Problems of water supply and of road and house construction on the London Clay had restricted growth to the gravel ledge north of the Thames, while the marshes south of the river, gradually reclaimed, and the single bridge led to only limited expansion around Southwark. But between 1750 and 1819 five further bridges were constructed, new roads were laid out and the scene set for rapid expansion.

The Growth of Modern London

By the time the first railway was opened in 1836 the built-up area of London covered less than 100 square miles (260 sq. km.) and contained nearly two million people. As Figure 6 shows, its dominance in relation to other settlements within a 30-mile (48 km.) radius was even more marked than it is today. Near London, favoured towns and villages such as Epsom were already used as dormitories by wealthy merchants, but, apart from small market towns like Aylesbury, the country around London was essentially rural. It is true that London's influence on agriculture was then much greater than it is today. Immediately around London on the terraces there were market gardens and orchards, while most of the London Clay outcrop in Middlesex and Hertfordshire was under hay for London's horses and stall-fed cows.[10] But a much wider area was affected and carts came from as far out as 30 miles (48 km.) with agricultural produce.[11] The large number of country houses and landscaped parks was also an indication of London's proximity, but, this apart, the influence of London on settlements was small.

Although the beginning of the railway age may be taken as a convenient starting point for a consideration of the growth of modern London, no dramatic change in the pattern of development took place immediately. Improvements in water supply had permitted expansion on to the London Clay, while the horse-drawn omnibus had already made it possible for people to live further from their place of work. Some of the railway companies were not at first interested in local traffic, but gradually a network of suburban lines arose and the range of possibilities for the rapidly growing population was greatly extended. At first it was chiefly the wealthy who moved and substantial Victorian mansions near many of the stations mark this phase, but, from the 1860s, 'shopkeepers and clerks began to seek villas'.[12] The increase in population and the necessity of rehousing those displaced by road widening, dock construction and rebuilding led, especially after the introduction of cheap workmen's fares, to the considerable growth of working-class suburbs, as at Tottenham. The growth of the docks, too, encouraged eastward expansion. Towns and villages around London were also affected by the opening of railway lines, although their growth was only to a limited extent due to their development as dormitories; the expansion of local industries and the migration of industries from London made an important contribution and, although the remoter rural areas were generally losing population from the middle of the nineteenth century, the towns, particularly those served by railways and near London, grew steadily. The radial pattern of London's expansion along lines of communication became more marked and, although some of the gaps between the fingers of built-up land represent low-lying areas which were avoided, such as the Lea valley, building proceeded with little regard for relief and soil, whose influence on London's growth was now exercised indirectly through the choice of railway routes.

By 1914 the built-up area was contained within a circle eighteen miles (29 km.) across, extending from Edmonton in the north to Croydon in the south, and from Ealing in the west to Woolwich in the east; beyond this lines of settlement stretched out in all directions while villages on the outskirts, like Harrow, were growing fast, in turn to be absorbed into the conurbation. The greatest areal expansion of London took place between 1918 and 1939, when the built-up area approximately doubled, although the population increased by only 17 per cent (Fig. 25). While London expanded in all directions during this period, it was on the London Clay outcrop in Middlesex that the most dramatic change took place; in south-west Essex, north-west Kent and north-east Surrey, too, the built-up area grew rapidly. The underlying cause was the growth of employment in both manufacturing and in offices and service industry. Office employment, increasingly concentrated in central London, tended to promote the growth of purely residential suburbs; but much of the industrial employment was in new or rapidly expanding industrial areas on or near the edge of the conurbation, as in west Middlesex, the Lea valley and Thameside, and resulted in urban development of a much more mixed character, where workplace and residence were much closer. In this period local authorities began to build houses on a considerable scale. The London County Council alone erected nearly 100,000 dwellings, half of them on land outside the county.[13]

29

Improvements in transport played a major part in permitting this great expansion of London. The electrification of suburban railways, particularly those in Surrey, surface extensions of the underground railways, especially in north London, new and improved roads, like the North Circular and Western Avenue, and enlargement of the network of omnibus routes all contributed. Railway electrification, improved bus services and the rise in private car ownership, together with a growing shortage of attractive building sites, also stimulated the development of dormitory settlements beyond the conurbation.

Many of the surrounding towns were also growing rapidly in this period, e.g. the population of Slough rose from 20,285 in 1921 to 52,590 in 1939.[14] This growth was not so much due to the direct effects of employment in the conurbation, as to the attractions of south-east England in general and of proximity to the largest market in the country. Thus, in most of the larger towns it was the growth of local employment rather than of employment in the conurbation which was responsible for their rapid expansion, although those who worked in London gave employment to service industries in the towns in which they resided. The growth of towns beyond the conurbation was most marked in the area north-west of London, in Surrey and in south Essex; many isolated dwellings were also erected in these areas, both as permanent homes for those who had retired or were working elsewhere, or as weekend cottages.

Since the end of the Second World War great outward extension of the built-up area has been prevented by planning control, especially by the creation of the green belt, although land within the conurbation which had been by-passed earlier has since been used for housing. The built-up area is thus more compact than it has been at any time previously in the modern period of expansion. There has also been some change in the pattern of employment, for, while employment in offices has continued to increase, particularly in the Central Area, there has been a fall in industrial employment in Inner London. Most industrial expansion has taken place in areas where industry was already well-established, although a new centre, employing over 25,000 people, has come into being at London Airport, while several smaller estates have arisen around the edge of the conurbation.[15] Infilling and rounding off have also enlarged the settlements within the green belt which now has a population one-quarter larger than that proposed in Abercrombie's Greater London Plan; but the ribbon building and scattered development characteristic of much of the inter-war period is now no longer permitted.[16] Towns beyond the green belt have also expanded rapidly, particularly the eight New Towns; further out, 'second order New Towns', the Expanded Towns like Bletchley, have been receiving London overspill population under the 1952 Town Development Act (Fig. 10).

While the stages of growth of the conurbation are marked by a progressive decline in the density of population from central London to the periphery, new building has not been confined to areas of rapidly increasing population. A whole succession of buildings has occupied sites in the Central Area, while many eighteenth and early

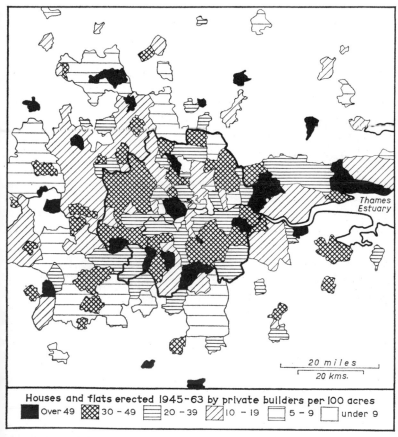

Houses and flats erected 1945–63 by private builders per 100 acres

■ Over 49 ▨ 30 – 49 ☰ 20 – 39 ▧ 10 – 19 ☐ 5 – 9 ☐ under 9

FIG. 7   Private house building in and around London 1945–63
Based on the Housing Return for England and Wales 31st March, 1963.

nineteenth-century buildings have been pulled down, either because they had reached the end of their useful lives or because the land they occupied was required for other more intensive uses, particularly for office buildings. War damage has also contributed; in the Second World War some 80,000 dwellings were destroyed or damaged beyond repair in the county of London alone.[17] Consequently the oldest buildings lie in the zone of nineteenth-century housing around the Central Area. Figure 7 records one aspect of this change, the location of dwellings erected by private builders between 1945 and 1963. Nearly 400,000 have been built in the local authority areas covered in whole or in part by the map; but although the population

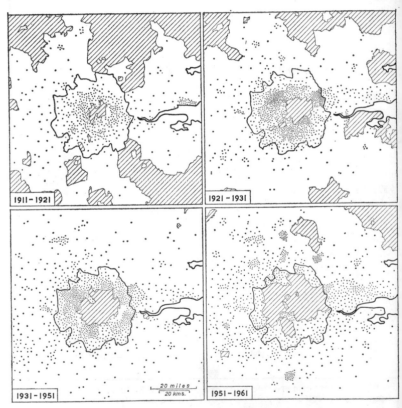

FIG. 8 Population changes in and around London 1911–61
1 dot represents an increase of 100 persons (1931–51, 200 persons).
Shaded areas represent districts losing population. The heavy line encloses
the Greater London conurbation. Based on the decennial censuses.

of the conurbation has ceased to grow, more than a third of these dwellings have been erected within its boundaries, nearly 22,000 of them in the county of London.[18] If a map of local authority housing could be constructed it would show the extent of post-war building and redevelopment in the conurbation even more clearly; for more than twice as many local authority dwellings have been erected in the conurbation, while in the area outside London dwellings erected by private builders are in the majority. The L.C.C. alone has built more than 57,000 dwellings in the county of London, many of them in flats, and probably a large proportion of the 71,000 built by the metropolitan boroughs have also been erected within the county.[19]

Both redevelopment for other uses and the replacement of dwellings involved a reduction in population, the latter in part because of the inadequate provision of land for non-residential uses in the areas of older housing; in Leyton, for example, there were only 4 acres (1·6 ha.) of open space per thousand population, compared with 47 (19 ha.) in Chigwell.[20] Thus, while the outward expansion of the conurbation continued and many new dwellings were erected in areas already built over, population has been falling in the inner areas, although, with the exception of the City of London, they remain the most densely populated parts of the conurbation. The resident population of the City began to decline continuously as early as 1851, when it numbered 127,819, and was only 4,771 in 1961.[21]

Successive censuses show a widening zone of declining population at the centre of the conurbation; from 1901 the county of London began to lose population and since 1939 the population of the conurbation itself has fallen slightly (Fig. 8). Until 1951 the main areas of population growth were within the conurbation, although there has also been a considerable increase in the number of people living outside its boundaries, especially to the west of London and in south Essex. At the same time, areas of rural depopulation which, in the late nineteenth century, included most of the country beyond the present green belt boundary, have diminished in extent, and only the remoter parts, like rural Essex, are still losing population.

Table I records the changing pattern of population growth as given by the decennial censuses. For convenience, Inner London has been equated with the county of London, Outer London with the remainder of the Registrar-General's conurbation, while the population of the rest of Essex, Hertfordshire, Surrey and Kent, together with that of Bedfordshire, Berkshire, Buckinghamshire and Sussex,

TABLE I

Population in and around London 1841–1961

	Inner London	Outer London	Conurbation	Extra Conurbation
	Population 1841–1961			
	'000s	'000s	'000s	'000s
1841	1,949	290	2,239	1,700
1851	2,363	322	2,685	1,833
1861	2,808	419	3,327	1,970
1871	3,261	628	3,890	2,193
1881	3,830	940	4,770	2,394
1891	4,228	1,410	5,638	2,625
1901	**4,536**	2,050	6,586	2,923
1911	4,521	2,734	7,256	3,294
1921	4,485	2,963	7,488	3,590
1931	4,397	3,819	8,216	3,950
1939	4,013	4,715	**8,728**	4,457
1951	3,348	**5,000**	8,348	5,125
1961	3,195	4,977	8,172	**6,253**
	Percentage population change 1841–1961			
	%	%	%	%
1841–51	21	11	20	8
1851–61	19	30	20	7
1861–71	16	50	21	11
1871–81	17	50	23	9
1881–91	10	50	18	10
1891–01	7	45	17	11
1901–11	–	33	10	13
1911–21	–1	8	3	9
1921–31	–2	29	10	10
1931–39	–11	23	6	13
1939–51	–17	6	–4	15
1951–61	–5	–	–2	22

Source: decennial censuses.

has been included as an index of changes in the areas affected by the growth of London, but lying outside its boundaries. The table shows clearly how the area of maximum rate of growth has gradually shifted from Inner London to Outer London and thence to the areas outside the conurbation.

The Character of London and Its Environs

Both the surrounding settlements and the various parts of London differ considerably in character and function, reflecting their development and location. While such differences will be discussed in detail in subsequent chapters, it will be useful to precede these analyses with a more general view, but it must be remembered that they are rarely clear-cut, for in most areas buildings of different ages and functions occur side by side.

The economic heart of the metropolis, the Central Area, accounts for little more than one-hundredth of the built-up area, and, although it consists of those parts of London which were first built over, it also contains many of the newest buildings (Fig. 9). Its resident population is little more than 270,000, but a million and a quarter people enter it daily from homes in other parts of London or beyond the conurbation.[22] Yet it, too, is far from homogeneous. The City, with under 5,000 inhabitants, consists very largely of offices, particularly those concerned with finance, banking, insurance, shipping and commerce.[23] The West End, though containing twice as much office space, characteristically occupied by manufacturing firms, by new enterprises and, in Whitehall, by government departments, is much more diverse; there is considerable small-scale manufacture, a large resident population, and much of the nation's cultural life, including the principal theatres, museums and concert halls and the headquarters of many national societies. Part of the South Bank, where there is much industrial activity along the river, now houses sufficient offices to warrant its inclusion in the Central Area.

Surrounding the Central Area is inner London, comprising those parts of London developed during the nineteenth century at relatively high densities, and hence containing a high proportion of older houses, many of them due for replacement within the next 40 years. Here, too, there are many internal differences. Hampstead, Highgate, parts of Marylebone, Kensington and Chelsea are favoured

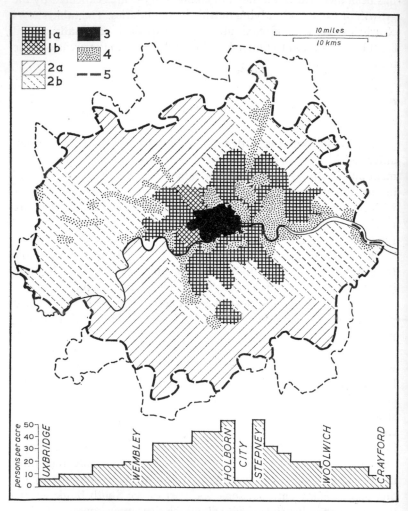

FIG. 9 The Greater London conurbation *c.* 1960
The representation of features on this map is diagrammatic.
Key: 1, mainly residential areas of inner London (*a*, 'better' areas, *b*, other areas); 2, mainly residential areas of outer London (*a*, 'better' areas, *b*, other areas); 3, the Central Area; 4, main industrial concentrations outside the Central Area; 5, limit of the continuous built-up area within the conurbation boundary.
Based on maps made by J. E. Martin and J. Westergaard, and on the decennial censuses.

residential areas and contain much high-value property, both in older houses and in flats; in the 1951 census nearly two-fifths of their residents were in social classes I and II, which cover professional and managerial occupations.[24] While much of the remainder of inner London consists of small terrace houses or large houses in once-fashionable areas, but now deteriorated and in multiple occupation, blocks of flats built by local authorities have been a feature of increasing importance since 1918, replacing cleared slums, houses destroyed during the Second World War, or dwellings in areas for which comprehensive development schemes have been prepared; for example, Somers Town, begun in 1786, is now largely occupied by flats, while more than 9,000 dwellings have been erected in a comprehensive scheme in Stepney and Poplar.[25] Housing, most of it dating from the period when no zoning controls were enforced, is intermixed with industrial establishments, which occur both in local concentrations, as along Thameside, and more widely diffused throughout the area.

Beyond inner London, which accounts for approximately a fifth of the built-up area, the conurbation consists almost entirely of houses erected during the twentieth century, although pockets of older buildings are to be found in the villages which have been engulfed by modern suburban growth. Population densities in these outer parts of London are generally much lower, being everywhere below 40 per acre (100 per ha.), partly because of the greater provision of land for open space and for other non-residential uses, such as recreation grounds and airfields. South of the river, these areas of twentieth-century buildings are mainly dormitories, although there are local concentrations of industry, notably along the Thames, in the Wandle valley and near Croydon. Many of these suburbs, particularly those furthest out, like Banstead and Purley, consist mainly of better-class housing. In the north-east, except in Woodford and along the Epping Forest ridge, a high proportion of the housing belongs to local authorities, and industrial employment in both Thameside and east London is important. The area between the Thames and the Lea is more varied. South of Western Avenue there are several large pockets of industry, many employees live locally and considerable areas are occupied by gravel pits and reservoirs. Further north between Northwood and Southgate there are mainly residential suburbs, from which more than a quarter of the employed population travel to work in the Central Area, and where the average

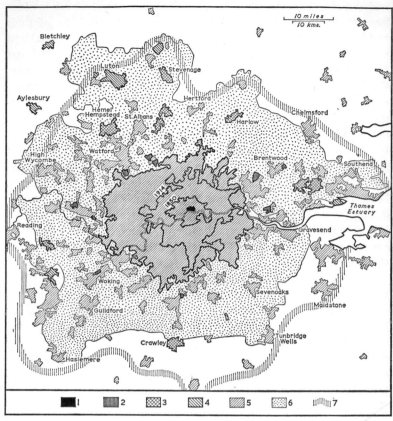

FIG. 10   Features of London and its environs *c.* 1960
Key: 1, City of London; 2, London County Council out-county estates
outside the built-up area of London; 3, New Towns; 4, Expanded
Towns; 5, the remaining built-up area; 6, the green belt; 7, limits
of the main commuter catchment area. The heavy lines mark approxi-
mate limits of the built-up area of London at the dates shown.
Based upon maps of the Ordnance Survey, London County Council,
Ministry of Housing and Local Government and on the 1951 Census.

value of housing is considerably higher than in much of west Middlesex.[26] The Lea valley, like west Middlesex, contains much manufacturing industry and working-class housing, as well as land used
for gravel working and water storage.

The area surrounding London contains both regional and local
contrasts (Fig. 10). The most urbanized sector, the north-west, between the Thames valley and the Hitchin Gap, is crossed by a close

network of trunk roads and main-line railways.[27] It contains a number of towns like Watford with a high proportion of employment in manufacturing industry, but there are also numerous smaller dormitory settlements like Chorleywood and Harpenden and many isolated houses. The urban character of this area has been strengthened by the location there of the two original garden cities of Letchworth (1903) and Welwyn Garden City (1919), which has also been designated a New Town, and of three other New Towns, Hatfield, Hemel Hempstead and Stevenage, while Borehamwood, with two large L.C.C. estates and an employed population of more than 10,000, is also, in effect, a 'new town'. Although urbanized, this part also contains much attractive scenery and most of the land south of the Chiltern scarp is in either proposed or designated green belt or in an Area of Outstanding Natural Beauty which overlaps it.

The north-east, between the Stort valley and the Thames estuary, shows a marked internal contrast in respect of urban development, although with few exceptions none of the area is particularly noteworthy for its scenery. The area north of the London–Ipswich road and railway is largely rural, while south Essex is highly urbanized, with a legacy of much poor, semi-urban development, many dormitory settlements, like Billericay, industrial settlements along lower Thameside and, further down-river, seaside resorts. Its communications are focused on London, so that north–south movement is difficult, while north Essex is generally poorly served by road and rail. One of the two new towns, Basildon, is in south Essex, while the other, Harlow, lies on the western margin of the county.

The south-east is also largely rural, at least south of the North Downs scarp. Along Thameside there are heavy industries and closely spaced towns which are both industrial centres and dormitories. South of the scarp most of the towns are old-established market towns which serve the surrounding countryside and have an admixture of industry and dormitory housing in varying proportions, although nearer London a number of smaller settlements are largely dormitories. The varied relief and the emphasis on horticulture add to the attractions of the area south of the scarp, but, on account of its isolation from the rest of the country and, until recently, its poorer communications, the area has not proved as attractive as the south-west.

The south-west is also a highly urbanized sector because of its close network of electrified railways and because communications are easier with towns north of the Thames. Here, too, there is a contrast between areas north of the scarp and those to the south. Industry is found along Thameside and in many of the larger towns like Farnborough, while west Middlesex is also quite an important centre of employment for people living in Surrey. Large stretches of open space and the use of land by military establishments in the Aldershot region also help to give this area a distinctive character. The country south of the North Downs is much less urbanized, although it contains numerous dormitory towns like Haywards Heath and is popular as a place of retirement; it is also distinguished by its abundance of attractive scenery, much of which enjoys special protection as green belt or as an Area of Outstanding Natural Beauty. The remaining New Towns, Bracknell and Crawley, lie respectively north and south of the North Downs.

As a metropolitan city London's sphere of influence covers the whole country; it is also without rival as the regional capital for south-east England. Its direct influence is limited, for the great majority of those who work in London live in the conurbation, and most of the remainder live within 30 miles (48 km.); but, indirectly, it affects a much wider area. Yet, even if attention is confined to the conurbation itself, it is at once by far the largest urban centre in the country, with a fifth of the urban population; the greatest seaport, with a third of the trade; the largest centre of manufacturing industry, with nearly a fifth of all industrial employment, and by far the most important place for office employment, containing more than two-thirds of all the rateable value of offices in the country. Some of these distinctive characteristics are analysed in the succeeding chapters.

References

The literature on London is vast and, in a general view, it is impossible to document every fact, especially as many are derived from the study of maps. Apart from the Ordnance Survey maps, those accompanying the *Greater London Plan 1944* (H.M.S.O., 1945) and the *Report of the Royal Commission on the Local Government in Greater London* (H.M.S.O., 1960) are particularly useful.

1. D. Defoe, *Tour through the Whole Island of Great Britain* with an introduction by G. D. H. Cole (1927), I, 391.

2. L. D. Stamp, 'Land classification and agriculture' in P. Abercrombie, *Greater London Plan 1944* (H.M.S.O., 1945), 86.

3. See S. W. Wooldridge, 'Some geographical aspects of the Greater

London Regional Plan', *Transactions of the Institute of British Geographers*, 11 (1946), 1–20.

4. H. Ormsby, *London on the Thames* (1924), 28–9.

5. *Ibid*, 42 and 45.

6. C. E. N. Bromehead, 'The influence of its geography on the growth of London', *Geographical Journal*, 60 (1922), 125–35.

7. Ormsby, *op. cit.*, 80–92.

8. O. H. K. Spate, 'The growth of London A.D. 1660–1800' in H. C. Darby (ed.), *An Historical Geography of England before 1800* (1936), 529–31.

9. See especially J. Summerson, *Georgian London* (1945), Chapter 1, an excellent bird's-eye view of the growth of London in the 17th and 18th centuries.

10. See 1st edition Ordnance Survey 6 inch to 1 mile maps and J. C. Clutterbuck, 'The farming of Middlesex', *Journal of the Royal Agricultural Society*, 2nd Series, 5 (1869), 9–18.

11. H. Evershed, 'Agriculture of Hertfordshire', *Journal of the Royal Agricultural Society*, 1st Series, 25 (1864), 283–5.

12. Summerson, *op. cit.*, 45.

13. London County Council, *200,000 Homes* (1962), 13.

14. M. O. Pitt, *New Towns in the London Area*, unpublished Ph.D. thesis (University of Cambridge 1954), Table III.

15. A. G. Powell, 'The recent development of Greater London,' *Advancement of Science*, 17 (1960–1), 77.

16. P. Self, *Town Planning in Greater London*, Greater London Papers, No. 7 (1962), 9.

17. *County of London Development Plan 1951, Analysis* (1951), 29.

18. *Housing Returns for England and Wales 31st March, 1963* (H.M.S.O., 1963), appendix.

19. *Ibid.* and *200,000 Homes, op. cit.*, 13.

20. *Essex Development Plan* (1952), Report of the survey, Part 2, Town Map Areas, Metropolitan Essex, 8.

21. *Census of England and Wales 1861*, 1 (H.M.S.O., 1862), 196, and *Census 1961, England and Wales, Preliminary Report* (H.M.S.O., 1961), 25.

22. J. Westergaard, 'Journeys to work in the London Region', *Town Planning Review*, 28 (1957), 45.

23. W. T. W. Morgan, 'The two office districts of Central London', *Journal of the Town Planning Institute*, 47 (1961), 161–6.

24. *Census 1951, Report on Greater London and five other conurbations* (H.M.S.O., 1956), Table 27.

25. Summerson, *op. cit.*, 266–7 and *County of London Development Plan, First Review* (1960), 174.

26. R. C. Local Government in Greater London, *op. cit.*, Map 7, Travel to work in central London.

27. A full account of the character of each sector will be found in M. O. Pitt, *op. cit.*, Chapters 5–8.

Climate and the Built-up Area

*

T. J. CHANDLER

London's development, the time, area and form of its expansion, has been profoundly influenced by its physical setting, but in its turn the city has become a factor as well as an element of the physical environment; for the masonry, mortar and macadam of London have changed the climate outside as well as inside the walls of its buildings. London has grown in response to mainly economic and social forces, its form has been controlled in large measure by the physiography of the underlying surface and its climate has been changed, accidentally, so that contrasts between the city and the fields and woodland of its rural envelope are reflected in almost as dramatic atmospheric parallels. There is a remarkably close link between the form of the conurbation and the chemistry and physics of its atmosphere.

Contrasts exist on scales ranging from the very local to regional: thus climates differ, in the limit, between two sides of a street or on either side of a garden wall and this complexity, combined with modifications induced by such physical controls as aspect and degree of slope, sometimes make it difficult to quantify the urban influences *per se*. But the imprint of London's growth on the mesoclimates of the conurbation as a whole and of the major units of its urban morphology are clear enough.

Central London

Perhaps the most obvious climatic aberration from natural conditions following the growth of London is the pollution haze which

42

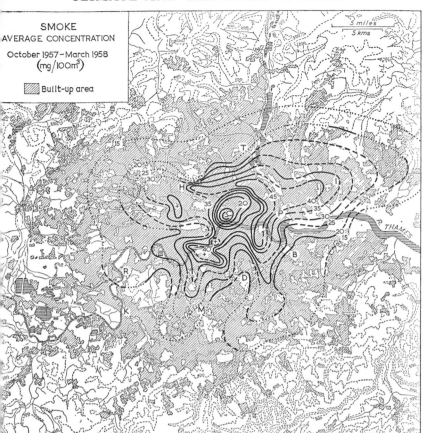

SMOKE
AVERAGE CONCENTRATION

October 1957–March 1958
(mg/100m³)

▨ Built-up area

FIG. 11 Average smoke concentration in London winter 1957–8
Key: B, Blackheath; C, City; D, Dulwich; H, Hampstead; I, Ilford;
K, Kingston; M, Mitcham; P, Poplar; R, Richmond; T, Tottenham.
Based upon statistics of the Department of Scientific and Industrial
Research.

masks all but the taller buildings in a sea of swirling smoke and dust.
The man-made poisons of the city's atmosphere are mainly the
products of combustion in house grates and boilers and by factory
power plants, cars, trains and ships. Domestic sources are responsible for an estimated 84 per cent of the smoke emission in the
county of London,[1] but regional intensities vary from one part of

London to another according to the rate of discharge from the multiplicity of sources, the nature of these sources, and also the efficiency of atmospheric dispersal. These factors change with the time of day and with the seasons, but through the intricacy of spatial and temporal change, a basic pattern emerges of differences between central and suburban London and what we might call the urban-rural fringe. London as a whole stands in marked contrast to its rural setting, as Fig. 11 shows, and in general, smoke concentrations increase towards central districts; but there are important local differences, most of which depend upon the character of the immediate urban development.

In central London, from the West End administrative, shopping and commercial districts, eastwards to the City, modern buildings of steel, concrete and glass rise above the lower but equally massive and closely spaced nineteenth century and older buildings. In the west of this area is a most important group of open spaces bearing upon the local climate: these are St James's Park (93 acres, 38 ha.), the Green Park (53 acres, 21 ha.), Kensington Gardens (275 acres, 111 ha.) and Hyde Park (361 acres, 146 ha.).

The parks help to reduce pollution densities in West End districts such as Westminster and parts of Kensington, which in any case have only a small resident population and are thereby of only limited importance as source regions (Fig. 11). Vegetation in the open spaces helps to filter the passing air and they act in a very true sense as urban lungs to which Londoners escape to breathe something more approaching country air. East of this group of parks, pollution concentrations increase temporarily between the West End and the City of London. The City emerges as an area of remarkably low smoke intensity surrounded by very much more polluted air, a consequence of both its small resident population and the effectiveness of smoke control regulations.

London, is, of course, associated in many people's minds with mists and fogs which Charles Dickens described as 'London particulars', but in central areas it is far more the nature and frequency of fogs, i.e. visibilities less than 1,100 yards (1,000 m.), than their intensity which are most characteristic. Although fogs as a whole are far more common here than in the suburbs (half as many again) or outside London (twice as many), dense fogs, i.e. visibilities less than 44 yards (40 m.) are only a quarter as frequent as at Kew Observatory in the suburbs of west London and their occurrence almost equals that outside the conurbation.[2] Visibility, of course, is controlled by the concentrations and size of both solid particles and droplets suspended in the air, and in this field, pollution plays both a direct and indirect part, for many droplets form around or are mixed with pollutants. The atmospheric conditions (mainly of stability and wind speed) which favour fogs are also those which prevent the efficient dispersal of smoke and gaseous concentrations; hence the fogs or smogs of central areas usually have a rather different chemistry from those outside.

It would seem that the high frequency of fogs in central areas is mainly the consequence of suspended pollution, but really dense droplet fogs in these areas are frequently prevented by the higher temperatures and lower humidities. Fogs also tend to appear rather later in the evening in central areas than in the suburbs for these same reasons, but, trapped between buildings and with their particular chemistry which delays evaporation, they are more persistent in the early morning. Daily commuters are familiar with this cycle whereby they leave their homes in the fresh, clear morning air of the outer suburbs only to find their trains and buses delayed by fogs as they approach central London; in the evening the position is reversed for the conurbation is then enclosed in a swirling annulus of fog.

It is hardly surprising to find sunshine amounts drastically reduced in these central areas so frequently masked by a pollution haze and by fogs and smogs. The atmospheric fuliginosity is most intense, of course, at the time when incoming radiation is weakest—in winter; in December, sunshine hours are cut by more than half at even the most open sites. At the bottom of the numerous man-made concrete chasms there may be no direct sunlight at all. In summer, contrasts between central London and rural areas are very small.

As anyone who has experienced the annoyance of walking through the labyrinth of streets in central London on a windy day well knows, the pattern of airflow in these districts is extremely complex, for the air is very turbulent or gusty. Eddies form across streets orientated across the wind and there is channelling along those aligned in its prevailing direction. Mean annual wind speeds are reduced in central areas but the picture is far from simple. With light winds, under about 9 miles per hour (4 m./sec.) outside London, speeds in the centre are increased by turbulence, though the details vary from month to month. In consequence, night-time values are on the average 0·7 miles per hour (0·3 m./sec.) higher than outside the city. During the day, when regional speeds are usually stronger, central areas have lower values than outside London, averaging 1·7 miles per hour (0·7 m./sec) less.

But of all the modifications induced by the city on its climate, changes in air temperatures are perhaps the most interesting. London is warmer than its rural envelope on all but a few occasions. The mean temperature anomaly changes with the time of day and with the seasons, but at any particular time, cloud amount, wind strength and the lapse rate are the most important determinants.[3] The greatest

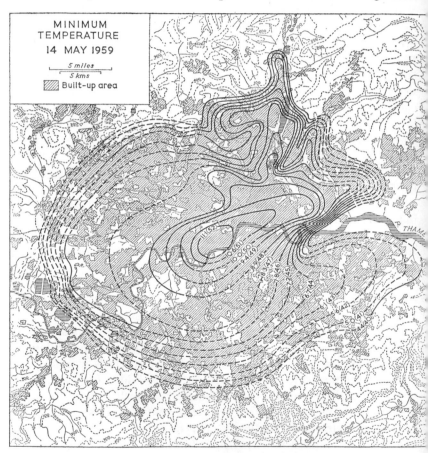

FIG. 12   Minimum temperature in London 14th May 1959
Temperatures are shown in °C (in brackets, °F).
Based on Meteorological Office records and London Climatological Survey.

differences occur by night—most frequently shortly before dawn, and in summer and autumn. Throughout the year the differences in minimum temperatures in central districts and in the country areas around London average 1·9° C. (3·4° F.) by night and 0·6 C. (1·1° F.) by day, but on individual nights the difference may be as much as 9° C. (16° F.). Temperatures are closely related to the character of the immediate environment, being very sensitive to changes in building density and type and to the ratio of open areas and built-over land (Fig. 12). The massive structures of so much of central London conserve in their fabric the sun's heat and that of artificial combustion, releasing it by night and in summer and autumn to maintain high temperatures in the surrounding streets. The pollution haze above the city may also act as a kind of atmospheric blanket reducing the amount of out-going radiation by night. Temperatures are lower in the parks—the difference frequently being of the order of 1–1·7°C. (2–3° F.). Figure 13 shows temperatures recorded along a night-time traverse across London from north-east to south-west (see inset) and passing through the City at the eastern end of the Central Area. It will be seen that temperatures increase in the streets of this district, flanked as they are with tall, massive buildings which both warm the air between them and prevent excessive mixing with the cooler air above.

Figure 14 shows for this same night how the relative humidity varies across the city. The air in central areas is very much drier than in the suburbs or outside the conurbation where there are patches of mist.

Concerning precipitation, the position is more obscure, for in this context it is particularly difficult to isolate any urban influences from others such as topography. There is little doubt that if there is increased rainfall over London, then the total amount is small, but there is some suggestion that there may be changes in the intensity pattern within and beyond the conurbation.

Except where there is some topographic cause, there are unlikely to be any great differences in the frequency of snowfall over London, although the warm air of its heat island may occasionally cause some of the smaller flakes to melt before reaching the ground. Far more significant are differences in the length of the period of snow lying. Owing to the higher temperatures, snow melts more quickly in central parks than in suburban gardens where it disappears earlier than on the fields of the green belt. In central London the number of days

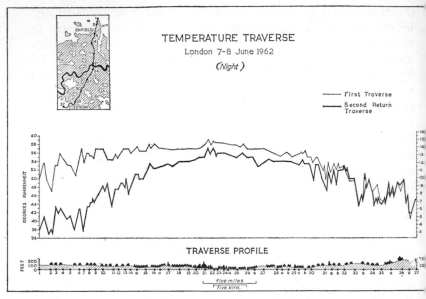

FIG. 13   Temperature traverse across London 7th–8th June 1962
Based on a survey by the author.

of snow lying averages 5·4 days per year, compared with 7·6 at Wisley, south-west of London.

In central London, most of the differences between the conurbation and outside reach their peak, but this is not universally true, as will now be seen.

Suburban London

Surrounding central London is an area from 2 to 5 miles (3·2 to 8·0 km.) deep composed of mainly high-density old residential, industrial and, in the east, dockside areas, nearly all of it developed before 1918. Interspersed within this compact urban sprawl are up-standing areas which raise their heads, frequently capped with parks or commons, above the low-lying, mortar-and-macadam-sealed land which surrounds them. These, like the parks of the centre, form inliers or windows in the prevailing climatic scene.

Forming an outer ring of mainly post-1918 development in Greater London is an area characterized by two-storey, semi-detached and detached houses with gardens along fairly wide roads,

48

by groups of single-storey factories and by frequent open spaces. The lace-like pattern of this urban-rural fringe is best developed in south-west London.

Each of these broadly similar urban regions has its own particular climatic response. Figure 11 shows that pollution concentrations are greatest in the lower Lea valley inner suburban districts of Hackney, Bethnal Green, Poplar, Stepney and Bermondsey, where concentrations during the winter of 1957–8 (which can be taken as fairly typical) averaged more than three times those of the outer suburbs, more particularly those in the north-west, west and south. These north-east districts are characterized by eighteenth- and nineteenth-century factory blocks engulfed by closely spaced ranks of terrace houses, the majority with inefficient coal-burning furnaces and grates. In addition, this low-lying area is inimical to the efficient dispersal of pollutants. Fulham and Battersea to the south-west give a secondary peak in smoke concentrations for similar reasons. There is a notable asymmetry in the pattern of smoke concentration (Fig. 11) and the north-east displacement of zones seems at first sight owing to transport by the prevailing south-westerly winds; but the cause may be as much a response to the nature of the local sources as to any lateral drift from upwind areas, although horizontal displacements are no doubt significant under intense inversions when the upward removal of pollutants is prevented.

Smoke concentrations, in general, decrease outwards from the centre, but distributions are also modified by the topography, the higher parts of the city rising into cleaner air above the heavily polluted atmosphere of the valleys. Thus Hampstead in north London and Wimbledon Common and Dulwich Park south of the Thames are associated with reasonably pure air with obvious health as well as social benefits.

Recent research emphasizes the relative importance of the upward dispersal of pollutants and thereby of the immediate rather than more distant sources. This explains the local character of deposition rates over Greater London, a deposit of carbon, ash and dust which does incalculable damage to health and property. In Poplar the rate reaches the equivalent of 450 tons per square mile (173 m. tons/sq. km.) per year and over most of Greater London values are above 200 tons per square mile (78 m. tons/sq. km.) per year. Around the city, 100 tons per square mile (39 m. tons/sq. km.) per year is fairly typical. [4]

Standing upon some vantage point of the North Downs south of

London, one cannot help but be impressed, on most days, by the contrast of visibilities north over the sprawling mass of suburban London and south over the mainly rural landscape of the Weald. The suburbs are characterized by about 25 per cent more fogs as a whole than outside the city, but dense fogs, i.e., visibilities below 44 yards (40 m.), are between 100 and 300 per cent more frequent. The explanation lies in the contrast of pollution characters and intensities and the form of air movement. As we have already seen, fogs in rural areas are more common in the early evening than in the early morning. Durst's investigation of the winter of 1936–7 showed London's foggiest areas to be the low-lying, heavily settled suburban areas of the Lea valley in the north-east, more particularly Enfield, Edmonton and Tottenham, and with smaller pockets of recurrent fog in the higher parts of north London such as Barnet, Mill Hill and Elstree.[5]

As in the centre, suburban sunshine hours are reduced by the

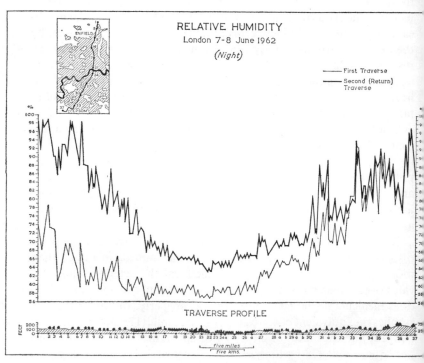

FIG. 14   Relative humidity across London 7th–8th June 1962
Based on a survey by the author.

solid and liquid shroud in which London is commonly enveloped, the cuts being almost insignificant in summer when insolation is strongest and the blanket weak, but amounting to 25 per cent in the outer suburbs and 30 per cent in the inner suburbs in December.

In respect of wind speeds, temperatures and humidities, the suburbs occupy an intermediate position between those in the centre and those of the surrounding rural areas (Figs. 12, 13 and 14), modified locally by the topography. Thus the difference in annual average minimum temperatures in suburban areas and the country around London is 0·7° C. (1·2° F.) and in maximum temperatures 0·2° C. (0·4° F.). As in the centre, the detailed suburban pattern is complex, varying in sympathy with the changing urban scene, but there is an overall climatic form which distinguishes it from the central areas on the one hand and the farmlands beyond London on the other. The latter contrast is the more impressive. Temperature gradients in particular are usually steep near the edge of the built-up area (Fig. 12). On calm, clear nights in summer and autumn, there are sometimes pulsating winds blowing across these thermal gradients towards the warm air of London's heat-island.[6]

Londoners have, for good or evil, changed the climate of their city and most of the modifications follow the major units of its urban form. The alterations have been unconscious, accidental accompaniments of the outward and upward growth, but they are changes worth some consideration in any future planning of the urban area.

References

1. Department of Scientific and Industrial Research, *The Investigation of Atmospheric Pollution*, 31 (H.M.S.O., 1960), 9.
2. T. J. Chandler, 'London's urban climate', *Geographical Journal*, 128 (1962), 284.
3. T. J. Chandler, 'The changing form of London's heat-island', *Geography*, 46 (1961), 295–307.
4. Department of Scientific and Industrial Research, *op. cit.*, 49, 58.
5. C. S. Durst, 'Winter fog and mist investigation in the British Isles', *Meteorological Office Memoir*, 372 (1940).
6. T. J. Chandler, 'Wind as a factor of urban temperatures, a survey in north-east London', *Weather*, 15 (1960), 204–13.

3

The Development of Communications

*

PETER HALL

S uch are the complexities of London's geography of communications, that a whole volume would do the subject scant justice.
Rather than dispense equal injustice to all aspects, this account
concentrates upon two: the morphology of the street pattern; and
the pattern of railways and rail traffic, as affected on the one hand
by London's physical geography and on the other by its rapidly
changing economic geography.

The Street Pattern

'Before the Roman came to Rye or out to Severn strode,
The rolling English drunkard made the rolling English road.'

In provincial England, perhaps; but for London Chesterton was
wrong. His reveller had his day there, between the departure of the
Romans and the end of the Middle Ages; but the road pattern of
London is fundamentally the work of five great sets of planners. The
Romans; the private estate planners, from the seventeenth century to
the present day; the turnpike builders of the late eighteenth and early
nineteenth centuries; the agencies which rebuilt central London so
drastically in the second half of the nineteenth century; and the
arterial road planners of the period since 1918.

Despite the work of later generations, the basic main road pattern
of London is the gift of the Romans, and has a characteristic Roman
simplicity[1] (Fig. 15). Eight main trunk routes radiated from London,
four north and four south of the river. The great western route was

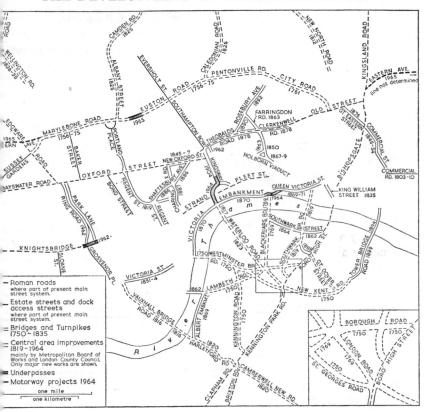

FIG. 15   Some elements in the main-road pattern of inner London

duplicated, two parallel roads running about one mile (1·6 km.) apart for the first nine miles (14 km.) west of London. Seven of these routes stemmed from the Roman city, which is our City too; but the north-western radial, which the Saxons called Watling Street and which we call Edgware Road, started three miles (5 km.) west of the city. The anomaly reflected the changing political geography of Roman Britain. Watling Street was established in 54 B.C., when the object of the Romans was to subdue the Belgic centre at Verulamium (St Albans); its line is the natural continuation of a road from a probable Thames crossing at Westminster. But by A.D. 43 interest had shifted east, to the Belgic centre at Camulodunum (Colchester); this is one reason for the movement of the Thames crossing to the site at London Bridge, and for the development of the City just north of the bridge. A last curiosity is that the Romans found it necessary to by-pass London to the north, so as to connect their Silchester and Colchester Roads directly. Part of this by-pass today bears the significant name Old Street.

Only a little of the Roman network has been permanently lost, mostly along the south-east line to the Channel ports. Some lines disappeared and were later exhumed by Victorian street cutters; for instance the direct line followed by New Oxford Street (1845–7) parallel to the medieval diversion of St Giles's High Street; and the line of the northern by-pass, which was exhumed by the cutting of Clerkenwell Road in 1878.

Of the few unplanned additions to London's street net, the most important are the old medieval field ways, which later became swallowed up by the tide of building. Some, having been pressed into service as main roads, today present serious traffic problems. They include Harrow Road, which branches off from Watling Street and links the Saxon villages of Paddington, Harlesden and Wembley; the line from the Roman Ermine Street through Stoke Newington, Wood Green and Palmer's Green (Green Lanes); and the Fulham Road, connecting Brompton, Walham Green and Fulham. Many of the old field ways, though, were straightened when later estate planners needed bounding lines for their estates.

But what was perhaps the most important medieval contribution to London's street pattern *was* planned. By 1300 the Roman Ermine Street, or 'Old North Road', had been supplemented, and even superseded, by a more westerly line following the lower eastern slopes of the Highgate–Hampstead heights, roughly along the line of today's Hornsey Road; but this line, running as it did through the low ground of Holloway, had become well-nigh impassable. So about this time the people of London cut a new road across the land of their bishop, to make a direct crossing of the eastern spur of the Northern Heights. At the summit the bishop cannily claimed the right to a tollgate; and around it developed the late medieval village of Highgate.[2]

The contribution of the estate planners is not always easy to distinguish, even where it has been relatively well documented, as with the great aristocratic estates of the West End.[3] When the development of these began, after 1630, enclosure had already begun to produce the familiar regular, rectangular fields of lowland England. Around London, tied to the old Roman road lines, their pattern was particularly uniform; and they served as natural guides to the planners of the advancing streets. Within these guides the rectangular grid, relieved by periodic squares, was the logical layout: it was cheap, it permitted easy subletting of individual plots to speculative builders, and it was fully in accord with the advanced ideas of Renaissance town planning, which Inigo Jones introduced from Italy in his Covent Garden scheme of 1631–8. In Soho and Mayfair, Marylebone and Bloomsbury, Bayswater and Belgravia, it became the characteristic mode. Most of these areas took the north–south lines for their chief accents: thus Bond Street, Baker Street, Southampton Row and Sloane Street. To their planners we owe a debt; without them, London's twentieth-century traffic problem would be even worse than it is.

While these planners continued their work in the inner areas, after 1750 the main arteries leading out into the surrounding country came under a new influence. In the late eighteenth century the Home Counties area was the most densely turnpiked in England. Most turnpikes, virtually all before 1750, were improvements of existing roads. But between then and the coming of the first railways to London in 1836–8, the turnpike trusts turned to important pieces of new construction.

There were two places where the need for new roads was most urgent. The first was the south bank. Until 1750, the swelling volume of cross-river traffic had crowded itself on to the narrow, inadequate old London Bridge or on to the Horse Ferry at Lambeth. Then, new bridges followed rapidly: Westminster in 1750, Blackfriars in 1769, Vauxhall in 1816, Waterloo in 1817, Southwark in 1819.[4] They had to be joined to the existing southern radial roads by new links, built through the open land of St George's Fields, the expanse of alluvium inside the great meander of the Thames at this point. Unhampered by buildings, the 'Surrey New Roads'[5] were planned in a series of straight lines and gentle, swinging curves which culminate in the very Parisian *rond-point* of St George's Circus.[6] The Surrey New Roads did not keep their character as rural turnpikes for long; St George's Fields were built over rapidly after 1810, at the same time as the approach to Waterloo Bridge was being incorporated into the system and, further south, new cross-links were built from the new Vauxhall Bridge towards Camberwell.[7]

North of the Thames the main enterprises were all concerned with driving new and more direct links between inner London and the

Great North Road. In the years after 1756 the Marylebone and Islington trusts jointly undertook the New Road between Paddington
and Islington, which was continued eastwards via City Road (1761)
as far as Moorgate, to provide a great by-pass route from the City
to the north-west.[8] Today, this line of roads provides London's
nearest equivalent to the ring boulevard which encircles the central
area of so many European cities. Unhappily, the original stringent
building regulations were evaded as the line of building advanced
northwards across the road in the early nineteenth century;[9] today,
it presents some of the worst problems of traffic congestion in London, although these are being slowly and expensively solved. Then,
north of the New Road line, no less than four new radial turnpikes
were built between 1812 and 1835 to relieve the Great North Road.
The long market street of Islington was by-passed to the east by the
New North Road (1812)[10] and to the west by the Caledonian Road
(1826);[11] the Archway Road (1813) scooped out the eastern slopes of
Highgate Hill, to give a better-graded route avoiding the old village;[12]
most ambitious of all, the Finchley Road (1826–35)[13] provided a
direct, six-mile (9·6 km.) link from the West End to the north road
around the western slopes of London's northern heights, by-passing
all the villages *en route*.

The largest turnpike scheme of all, though, never reached completion. In 1826 the trusts north of the Thames were consolidated by
Act of Parliament. The commissioners of the new system gradually
evolved the idea of a great new outlet from the West End towards
the north-east, which would bridge the Lea valley and eventually
join the main road to Epping. By 1834, they had got the road as
far as Tottenham, along the line Albany Street–Parkway–Camden
Road–Seven Sisters Road; then came the railways, and the ensuing
financial collapse of the turnpikes.[14] So London never got its north-
eastern outlet; and, ironically, road communications in this direction
are still possibly the worst in the whole metropolis.

One major work of the turnpike age was, in fact, no turnpike, and
stands out as an isolated case. It is the line of the Commercial and
East India Dock Roads, built about 1803 by the Indiamen between
the City at Aldgate and Poplar, as an outlet to their new West India
and East India Docks. Essentially this was a local and a private road;
but the opening of a bridge in 1811 across Bow Creek, and its later
improvement, turned it into London's main artery to the north bank
of the lower Thames.[15]

After the railways came, the turnpikes built no more. One of the most urgent priorities of 1836, a by-pass to Brentford High Street west of London, had to await the construction of the Great West Road in 1924.[16] But the very arrival of the railways at the edge of central London brought extra traffic between the stations, and increased congestion within the central area itself. Even before 1850, John Nash had cut Regent Street through the densely-packed area between Mayfair and Soho (1817–23), and the City Corporation had carried through urgently-needed new works like the cutting of King William Street (1835) to the new London Bridge.[17] But really major projects depended upon a more effective local government over the wider metropolitan area, a reform achieved only with the foundation of the Metropolitan Board of Works in 1855. In its short life—it was replaced by the London County Council after 1888—the Board completed a very spectacular programme of new streets, mostly connected with slum clearance schemes, in the very heart of central London.[18] In the 1870s it drove a new line—Clerkenwell Road and Great Eastern Street—between the West End and East End, through the rookeries of Clerkenwell and Shoreditch. In the 1880s it did the same for the slums of St Giles, cutting the north–south artery of Charing Cross Road and the diagonal line of Shaftesbury Avenue; this latter line the L.C.C. continued in the early 1890s along Rosebery Avenue, to give new access between the West End and Islington. The streets of the Metropolitan Board of Works are a very characteristic element of the London landscape. They are invariably lined with commercial premises, of very uniform height, in the flamboyant style of the period, broken only by tenement blocks intended to house the displaced slum dwellers. Compared with Haussmann's reconstruction of Paris during the same period, the Board's planning lacked foresight. Even their major streets were built only 60 feet (18 m.) wide; Haussmann's went up to 130 feet (40 m.).[19]

From 1836 to 1890, then, the main focus of interest was at the centre. Meanwhile, the railways allowed the suburbs to spread; their growth was guided by the existing main roads, whether Roman military way, Saxon field track or eighteenth-century turnpike. Within this framework, the network of minor roads showed progressively less regularity of form. The romantic serpentine line, introduced by John Nash in Park Villages East and West about 1824, was already modifying the traditional rectangular grid patterns, in an area like Thomas Cubitt's Belgravia, shortly after 1825; after 1840 it became *de rigueur* in any estate development with social pretension. The typical developments of the 1860s and 1870s, the villa and garden estates like Ladbroke Grove on the west, Belsize Park on the north-west, and Highbury New Park on the north, all show the new 'free planning' in its purest form, a form taken up and repeated by thousands of speculative builders across the Home Counties after 1918.[20]

The arterial road-builders of the inter-war period were perhaps the most confused and criticized of London's road-planners, and their confusion has bequeathed to a later generation some unnecessary problems. By 1918 built-up London had spread in long fingers along the main radial roads, reducing the utility of the turnpike roads in precisely that zone where there were most of them, between five and fifteen miles (8–25 km.) from central London. Between these old 'high roads'—and, by definition, commonly occupying areas of lower-lying ground—were large tracts of still open land, where poor communications hindered development. The arterial road-builders unwisely tried to solve both problems by the same means. They built the new roads through the open interstices, if possible through their lowest areas where land was cheapest: thus the North Circular Road along the valleys of the Brent and Pymme's Brook, and the Kingston By-Pass along that of the Beverley Brook. They then left private enterprise to exploit the new advantages of access. This would have been less serious had they possessed adequate concepts of traffic engineering or planning control. As it was, the new roads were often too narrow—only 30 feet (9 m.) wide in some cases; no attempt was made to segregate fast-moving from local traffic, by controlling side access; no powers were taken, until the belated act of 1935, to control ribbon development directly along the roads.[21] As a rule the new arterial ways were promptly lined by speculatively-built houses, or even—as in the case of Western Avenue—by local authority estates; in extreme cases, as at Hendon Central or Gant's Hill, whole new shopping centres developed, with attendant traffic congestion at least as serious as along the old High Street. By the early 1960s—only forty years after the construction of the first arterials—new motorways were being planned to by-pass the by-passes, along the Great West Road (M4) and the Watford By-Pass (the M1 extension).

Because they were essentially planned to open up new land, the new arterials in every case stopped short at their inner ends against the built-up edge of 1918 London.[22] Western Avenue and the Great Cambridge Road have no direct link with the old road system at all, and traffic has to filter off into inner London as best it may. Within central London, no major improvement was completed between Kingsway (1900–10) and the Hyde Park Boulevard (1962). There existed a whole series of elaborate plans for completely new roads, from the Royal Commission on London Traffic (1905),[23] through the Bressey–Lutyens Survey (1937)[24] to the Abercrombie Plans (1943–4);[25] but realization foundered on the costs of land acquisition and of construction in heavily built-up areas.

Since 1955 this deficiency has been partly met. One completely new road through the inner Victorian suburbs of west London, the Cromwell Road extension, has been built to connect central London with the Great West Road;[26] its line is continued westwards towards London Airport by the metropolitan section of the South Wales motorway (M4), due for completion in late 1964. By 1970, other major new road links are planned, from north to south across West London from Acton to Chelsea, from west to east across West London from Acton to Paddington, from north to south across East London from Bow Bridge to Kidbrook, from west to east across south-east London from Lewisham to Eltham. The Cromwell Road extension is built, not quite wholeheartedly, on the principles of modern motorway construction: limited side access, and separation of grades at intersections. Its successors will in many cases be true urban motorways. The era of the American freeway has arrived in London; it is still too early to see where it will lead.

The Railway Pattern

London's railway pattern is guided much more closely by its physical geography than is its road pattern. We seldom think of London as having marked relief, but for the early railway builder of the 1830s it presented problems (Fig. 16). Central London rests on a gravel terrace foundation at about 50–100 feet (15–30 m.) above sea-level. North of the river the gravel ends very sharply along an east–west line which is marked almost exactly by what was still, in the early nineteenth century, the New Road (now Euston and Marylebone Roads). This marked approximately the northern limit of building in the early nineteenth century, when the early main-line railways approached central London. North of this line the London

Clay rises quite steeply to the lower slopes of London's Northern Heights, crowned by the Upper Tertiary sands of the Hampstead and Highgate hill mass at 450 feet (135 m.) which falls northwards to the diagonal valley lines of the Brent (flowing SW.) and Pymme's Brook (flowing SE.). Between these streams a spur of high land runs north at about 200–250 feet (60–75 m.) through Finchley towards High Barnet, followed by the medieval High Road to the north. South of the river the land rises much more slowly. There is first the wide expanse of alluvium in the inside of the meander, which has no equivalent on the north bank. Then there are extremely wide expanses of flood-plain terrace at relatively low altitudes (about 50–100 feet or 15–30 m.) before the first marked heights are produced in the 'Southern Heights' of the Wandle–Ravensbourne watershed around the Crystal Palace, which rise to 450 feet (135 m.). The result is that on the whole the northern railways had tunnelling problems and the southern railways embanking problems. The first steam railway in London, the London and Greenwich of 1836, was supported on a viaduct of 878 arches for very nearly its entire length from London Bridge to Greenwich. In contrast, the London and Birmingham, engineered by the Stephensons a year later, made a wide loop round west London through the valley of the Brent before turning abruptly east to tunnel through the lower slopes of the Northern Heights for 1,164 yards (1,065 m.) at Primrose Hill Tunnel, then turning south again down the Camden Bank on a gradient of 1 in 70 (1·4 per cent) to arrive at Euston Station on the border of the terrace gravels.[27] A year after that Brunel brought the Great Western into London without any difficulty, making use of the extensive Taplow terraces of Middlesex and then following the line of the earlier Grand Union Canal through a shallow London Clay cutting.[28] Probably the most difficult route into north London was that of the Great Northern of 1850. By that date the only natural route to the north and north-east, through the Lea valley, had been appropriated by the Eastern Counties Railway. The Great Northern was boldly engineered straight through the Northern Heights, while taking care to avoid their highest point by passing east of it, through the low ground of Holloway; but then it went straight across and through the Finchley–Barnet spur. The result is the most heavily cut and tunnelled main line out of London, with an initial gradient of 1 : 108 (0·9 per cent) to get the line across the Barnsbury spur of the Northern Heights between King's Cross and Holloway and severe ruling gradients of 1 : 200 (0·5 per cent)

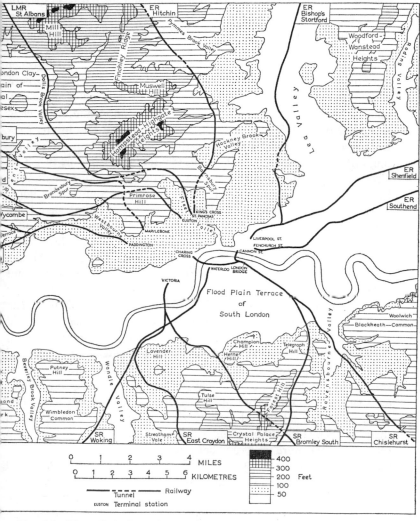

FIG. 16   The relief of London and its effect on the main railway lines
Heights are shown in feet. Metric equivalents are: 400, 120m; 300, 90m;
200, 60m; 100, 30m; 50, 15m.
Based on Ordnance Survey maps.

thereafter.[29] The southern lines, running on their characteristic viaducts across the flood-plain terrace of south London, could in contrast cross the Thames with ease and arrive at termini neatly placed

against the bank of Taplow gravel, like Charing Cross (1864) or Cannon Street (1866). Only the London Chatham and Dover, coming into Victoria in 1860, had difficulty: to meet local opposition in Pimlico it had to bring its line under street level from the Thames bridge, which necessitated a very severe gradient of 1 : 64 (1·6 per cent) out of the terminus.[30] Farther south, the ascent of the Southern Heights was usually made without difficulty. The London and Croydon, branching off from the viaduct of the London and Greenwich at New Cross in 1839, climbed the flanks of Forest Hill by the New Cross Bank, $2\frac{1}{2}$ miles (4 km.) at 1 : 100 (1·0 per cent) through a cutting in London Clay.[31] The London Chatham and Dover, to get its direct line from the south-east into Victoria in 1860, had to bore Sydenham Tunnel for $1\frac{1}{4}$ miles (2·8 km.) under the Southern Heights. On all the southern lines a conspicuous feature is the passage from embankment to cutting, which marks the transition from low floodplain to higher terrace levels, as at Clapham Junction and New Cross.

The other factor controlling railway development was the existing built-up area of London. In the 1830s this had advanced north about as far as the New Road and south of the river only for short distances along the main roads. So the early railways had little difficulty. The London and Birmingham, and the Great Western, were both laid through almost open country. In 1846 the Metropolitan Termini Commission decided that railways should not enter into the central densely built-up area, so that the problem of land acquisition was solved in a particularly drastic way.[32] But when the later main lines approached London, large problems of land acquisition were met. H. J. Dyos has calculated that 76,000 people were displaced from their homes by railway building between 1853 and 1901, of whom no less than 37,000 were uprooted between 1859 and 1867 when some of the major pieces of construction were taking place.[33] The Midland Railway, to get into St Pancras in 1863–8, had to demolish a whole slum—Agar Town—which has quite disappeared from the map of London; the extension of the North London Railway from Dalston Junction to Broad Street in 1865, and that of the Great Eastern from Bishopsgate to Liverpool Street in 1874, both entailed heavy demolition. These lines, projected in the early 1860s, represented an important factor in the decision of the Select Committee of 1863 to extend the 'prohibited area' within which main line railways could not enter central London.[34] It was clear that railways often chose lines through the poorer districts where opposition would be less and where local vestries would be less concerned about losses in rateable values. Parliament was very reluctant to impose on the companies an obligation to re-house, but even when it did so obligations were often evaded: as late as 1898 the Great Central displaced about 1,750 people on the site of its new Marylebone Station before finding other houses for them.[35]

The densely built-up area, though, was apt to deter the railways in one way. The really big space-using activities—goods yards, locomotive sheds, and sidings—would not bear the costs of property demolition; so they were built some distance out, where open land could be cheaply had. Thus the London Tilbury and Southend, which passed through some of the most closely built-up areas of the East End, put its locomotive depot at Plaistow, $4\frac{1}{2}$ miles (7 km.) from its terminus at Fenchurch Street;[36] the Great Western in 1903 had to move its locomotive depot from its original cramped site at Westbourne Park, three miles (4·8 km.) farther down the line to Old Oak Common;[37] as the coal trade developed, all the big coal-carrying lines except the Great Northern found it necessary to build yards outside the built-up area—the London and North Western at Harlesden, the Midland at Brent, the Great Eastern at Temple Mills in the Lea valley, and the Great Western at Southall.[38]

The Development of Commuter Traffic and Suburban Growth to 1914

The London and Greenwich, London's first railway, anticipated fully the most important function of many of its successors: it was an intensive passenger-carrying line with trains at frequent intervals.[39] But the lines which arrived shortly afterwards were remarkably slow in developing their suburban traffic. The London and Birmingham's first station in 1837 was at Harrow, $11\frac{1}{2}$ miles (18·5 km.) from the terminus;[40] a year later, the Great Western's first station down the line was Ealing ($5\frac{3}{4}$ miles, 9·25 km.);[41] the Great Northern's in 1850 was Hornsey (4 miles, 6·4 km.).[42] As late as 1846 Creed, the Secretary of the London and Birmingham, could tell the Metropolitan Termini Commission that the average distance travelled by passengers arriving at Euston was 64 miles (103 km.).[43] But slowly the railways came to realize that large profits were to be made from suburban traffic, and the story of the 1850s and 1860s is one of successive openings of new stations along the existing main lines. The London and Birmingham and its successor the London and North Western[44] opened intermediate stations at Willesden in 1841,[45] Sudbury (now Wembley Central) in 1842,[46] Kilburn High Road in 1852,[47] South Hampstead and Queen's Park in 1879.[48] The Great Northern opened a station at Seven Sisters (now Finsbury Park) in 1861, with two wooden platforms. Rapid suburban development followed and by the late 1860s expensive alterations were being made to the station. 'It is like the weird sisters, or like the daughters of the horse-leech crying, "Give, give!"' complained an indignant Great Northern shareholder.[49]

Not only were new stations opened along the main trunk lines: branches were thrown out to open up the profitable areas between them, like the Great Northern branch from Finsbury Park north-west to Finchley and Edgware, opened in 1867.[50] And whole new lines were built to carry the suburban traffic. The North London had been opened in 1850–2 from the London and North Western main line at Camden Town to the docks at Bow, and was intended as a freight-carrying line which would give direct access from the docks to the north and north-west. But it rapidly became one of the most prosperous of the suburban lines of London; in 1860 a nominally-independent loop line was opened through Kentish Town and Hampstead to Willesden, to skim the rich commuter traffic of the developing Northern Heights; in 1865 the North London finally came into the City, with the construction of the expensive 'Happy After-thought', a two-mile (3 km.) branch south from Dalston Junction to Broad Street.[51] In 1856 the first long-distance commuter line, the London Tilbury and Southend, was opened, with the result that a small colony of City business men established itself in the developing resort at the mouth of the Thames.[52] The Metropolitan extensions of 1868–80 took that railway north-west from Baker Street, above ground and into open country, as far as Harrow, and by 1892 via Rickmansworth all the way to Aylesbury, 40 miles (64 km.) from London.[53] Within twenty years of the opening of the original short line, the Metropolitan had thus turned itself from a strictly 'inner-urban' into a 'suburban' line; a process to be repeated some 40 years later by the tube lines.

The activities of the Metropolitan and the North London show that a rich source of revenue awaited them in the Northern Heights of London; the same was true of the Southern Heights, as the London Brighton and South Coast and the London Chatham and Dover found to their profit. In areas like these the more prosperous commercial classes were escaping, in the 1860s and 1870s, from the thraldom of the morning walk into the City, which had been their usual lot up to 1850.[54] Up to 1880, and beyond, most of this suburban traffic was strictly middle-class traffic. In an inner area like Clerkenwell, in 1884, the middle class was 'seriously diminished' by the flight to the suburbs;[55] its houses had filtered down, in the American phrase,[56] to the working class, which—still heavily dependent on casual labour and lacking the means to pay ordinary railway fares—remained trapped in the congested inner areas. The result, Colin Clark has shown, was a pattern of population distribution with very high densities within walking distance of the centre, falling off quite rapidly outside that radius to rural levels.[57]

By the mid-1880s, though, this pattern was already being modified. In 1861, to get parliamentary approval for the demolitions of working-class homes involved in their Broad Street extension, the North London had to agree to provide special workmen's trains at low fares; in 1864 the Great Eastern, to get into Liverpool Street, had to do the same.[58] By the 1880s the Great Eastern provided workmen's trains from Enfield and Walthamstow at 2d. return, and working-class suburbs were being run up all along their lines, in Tottenham and Edmonton, Leyton and Walthamstow. The result, the manager of the Great Eastern told a Royal Commission in the 1880s, was that:

'Wherever you locate the workmen in large numbers you utterly destroy that neighbourhood for ordinary passenger traffic. Take, for instance, the neighbourhood of Stamford Hill, Tottenham, and Edmonton. That used to be a very nice district indeed, occupied by good families, with houses of from £150 to £250 a year, with coach-houses and stables, and gardens, and a few acres of land. But very soon after this obligation was put upon the Great Eastern Company, and accepted by the Great Eastern Company, of issuing workmen's tickets, speculative builders went down into the neighbourhood, and, as a consequence, each good house was one after another pulled down, and the district is given up entirely I may say now to the working man.'[59]

The Great Eastern, apparently, were willing to face this consequence; they ran more workmen's trains than they were obliged to.[60] Other lines did not, and as late as 1900 would not even grant third-class seasons from many stations in South London.[61] The Royal Commission in 1905 found that a 2d. workmen's fare would take you

2·40 miles (3·86 km.) by the London and North Western, 2·64 miles (4·25 km.) by the Midland, 2·67 miles (4·30 km.) by the London and South Western, 2·72 miles (4·37 km.) by the London Brighton and South Coast, 7·36 miles (11·84 km.) by the South Eastern and Chatham, but no less than 10·74 miles (17·28 km.) by the Great Eastern.[62] It was hardly surprising then that 17·5 per cent of all workmen's-fare passengers into central London termini still came by the Great Eastern,[63] or that contemporary observers noted the great development of the working-class suburbs of the north-east compared with the relatively slow development along the London and North Western line, where workmen's facilities were probably poorest.[64] In the inner areas, after 1900, the railways suffered increasingly from the competition of the electric tramcar, with its greater flexibility of route and its more rapid acceleration;[65] and the stations in the inner working-class districts, which had never been well-patronized, were closed in large numbers. The London and South Western, which had opened relatively few inner London stations, had fewer to close than the others.[66]

The steam age in the London suburbs began its decline in the years 1903–9, when the first electrifications took place on the District, Metropolitan and London Brighton and South Coast lines. But the large-scale electrification had to wait until after the First World War, when, however, it was very rapid. The pattern of the nineteenth-century suburbs revealed very clearly the technical limitations of the steam engine. Because steam gives slow acceleration, stations and suburbs were widely-spaced; because the motor-bus had not arrived to spread the advantages of suburban living far from the stations, suburbs were limited in extent. But within their limits the railways had profound effects as residential pioneers. All over suburban London, the age and style of the buildings tell the same story of growth. First the big railway hotel and shopping range, then the big scattered Victorian villas, in the 1960s often near the end of their useful lives; then the sea of twentieth-century housing that followed the electrification of the line and the arrival of the motor-bus.

The most surprising feature of the evolution of the railways in Victorian London, the 1905 Commission remarked, was the way in which the main-line railway system had come to perform a function —the suburban traffic function—which it was never originally intended to perform, and which it did not perform very efficiently.[67] Ten main lines—seven of them north of the river—approached the

Central Area, carrying both suburban and long-distance traffic with very different characteristics. Within a belt three miles (4·8 km.) wide around the Central Area, there were many other lines built for a variety of purposes, but now virtually all carrying suburban traffic. Almost all of them stopped abruptly at the edge of the Central Area. Farther out the suburbs were served by branches from the main lines, which further increased the pressure on the overloaded approaches to the termini. The obvious answer was to build new suburban lines which ran *through* the centre, without the problems of terminal turn-round. But that had to wait until after 1914.

The pattern of suburban traffic, and of suburban development, by 1900 was extremely irregular. Certain lines had offered good commuter services early, and along these suburbs had developed rapidly: thus the London Brighton and South Coast towards Balham and Croydon, the Metropolitan towards Harrow, the London Tilbury and Southend, the North London. In particular, the aggressive competition south of the river between the South Eastern, the London Chatham and Dover and the London Brighton and South Coast produced a dense, confused network of tracks and a wide suburban spread. In contrast the London and South Western developed its suburban services only after 1870, yet did so very efficiently; but all observers noted the relative slowness of development towards the west and north-west, where the companies had been slower to exploit opportunities—especially for workmen's traffic—and where, importantly, access to the City was often poor. This last fact introduces another, critical, theme. The commuter's road must have a daily end. How was he to reach, easily, his office desk or factory bench? This was one of the most important problems in the economic evolution of Victorian London; and until late in the period, it was not satisfactorily resolved.

Railways and the Central Area

When the 1846 Commission had reported against bringing the railways into central London, they had no real idea of the potentialities of the commuter traffic from the suburbs, which could only build up intolerable pressures on the street system of the Central Area. The Select Committee on Metropolitan Communications, in 1855, had already come to recognize the need for better communication between the main-line stations—communication which was then being provided, *faute de mieux*, by the horse-drawn omnibus.[68] The omnibus was a Parisian invention, imported into London in 1829 by George Shillibeer, a London coachbuilder; the traffic boomed and small companies mushroomed, so that by 1855—the year of the Select Committee—the London General Omnibus Company was being founded in Paris, with the object of taking over London's buses and consolidating the system.[69] This object was largely achieved within a very short time; but meanwhile the problem of communication remained acute, and it was at this time that the Metropolitan Railway, the first underground line to penetrate the Central Area, was sanctioned.

The Metropolitan was opened in 1863 between Paddington and Farringdon Street, via the line of the New Road—following part of the route of Shillibeer's first omnibus. At this date the Select Committee on Metropolitan Railway Communication reported that it should be extended into an inner circle connecting as many of the main-line stations as possible.[70] This ideal was realized only in 1884 when the last link was completed in connection with street improvements between Aldgate and Mansion House. But a system intended to join up main-line stations is not a very good way of carrying commuters. The Inner Circle made a very close circuit of the City but a very loose one around the West End, which was not effectively served by any railway till 1900 (Fig. 33). Apart from the Inner Circle there was an area at the centre, four miles wide and one and a half miles deep (6·4 × 2·4 km.), with no railway service. Except where main line or spur lines approached the City, as at Liverpool Street, Fenchurch Street and Broad Street, interchange to street transport was necessary and facilities were often poor.

The inadequacies of the resulting system had been cogently set out by a Prussian visitor, Gustav Kemmann, in 1892.[71] To Kemmann, accustomed to the gigantic *Hauptbahnhof* and encircling ring railway of the typical German city, London's railway net must have seemed curiously chaotic. Nevertheless, he concluded that it served the needs of the public, with two qualifications. First, rail connections between the main-line stations and the centre of the town were entirely lacking; the traveller was forced to depend on cabs and buses, which partly explained the extremely elaborate arrangements made for cab traffic at the termini. The other was the complete lack of through connections between the south coast (and the continent) and the midlands and north. All suburban traffic had to approach the City either by the underground system of the Metropolitan and District, including the 'widened lines' which brought Great Northern and Midland

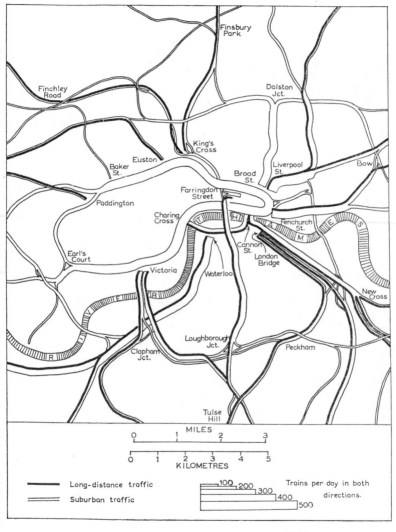

FIG. 17   Rail passenger traffic flows 1888
Based on G. Kemmann.

trains into Moorgate; or by those surface railways which approached the City direct—including the two busiest stations in London, Liverpool Street and Broad Street. The chief need was a connection between the City and West End or within the West End; Kemmann looked forward to the Central London tube, then projected, to remedy this.[72]

These problems could not be met by more railways of the Metropolitan 'cut-and-cover' type; they were too expensive. Some of the later extensions of the Metropolitan had cost over a million pounds a mile.[73] Paris could afford to build underground railways like this after 1900; but she was blessed with Haussmann's boulevards. The tube method of construction, pioneered by the engineer Peter Barlow in 1864, was the answer; in the London gravels and clay, it allowed rapid deep-level tunnelling at lower cost than cut-and-cover. London's first full-scale tube railways, the City and South London in 1890 and the Waterloo and City in 1898, did what early surface lines had also tried to do: connect the City, traditional goal of the commuter, with the south bank. The real shift in London's transport geography came with the Central London, opened in 1900 between the Bank and Shepherd's Bush; for the first time, rail lines penetrated the West End and linked it with the City.[74] In the Edwardian period three more lines completed the revolution: the Baker Street and Waterloo (1906), the Great Northern Piccadilly and Brompton (1906) and the Charing Cross Euston and Hampstead (1907). These lines, all completed by the Underground Electric Railways of London Limited—a creation of the American transport magnate, Charles Tyson Yerkes—were all West End lines, avoiding the City altogether.[75] The Victoria Line (to be completed 1968) only reinforces this trend. The new lines partly met an existing demand, for the commercial core of London was shifting west before the turn of the century; but, more importantly, they themselves created demand, giving the movement westwards an inexorable momentum (Figs. 17 and 18).

This movement has been measurable only since the first census of workplaces in 1921; the City authorities took day censuses of their area throughout the later nineteenth century, recording a net daily in-migration that rose from some 76,000 in 1866 to 344,000 in 1911, but there are no accurate comparative figures for the rest of the Central Area. Between the 1921 and 1951 censuses the shift towards the West End is however very striking.[76]

TABLE II

Net in-movements into the Central Area 1921 and 1951

| | 1921 | | 1951 | |
	number	%	number	%
City	423,012	50·2	334,912	34·0
Holborn	58,513	6·9	88,335	9·0
Finsbury	65,334	7·8	61,747	6·3
St Marylebone	51,500	6·1	102,841	10·5
Westminster	244,406	29·0	396,145	40·3
Central Area	842,765	100·0	983,980	100·0

Source: decennial censuses.

The New Suburban Lines and the New Suburbs 1917–1960

In 1901 the volume of applications to build new tube lines under central London had become so embarrassingly large that a House of Commons committee was appointed to examine and advise upon them. They concluded that undertakings should be encouraged to 'take the rough with the smooth'; that is, the less profitable suburban traffic with the remunerative inner urban traffic.[77] Up to the completion of the original lines of the Edwardian tubes in 1907, no deep-level tube had ventured beyond the safe built-up limits of Victorian London, with the exception of the Charing Cross Euston and Hampstead at Golders Green. Shortly after this, though, the character of the tubes changed spectacularly. The suburban traffic, it was decided, need not be so rough after all; with suitable manipulation, it was worth having, and even encouraging. From inner-urban lines, the tubes became suburban lines also; they threw out long tentacles above ground into open country, ahead of suburban development. The pioneer was the Bakerloo extension over London and North Western electric tracks to Watford, in 1917. In 1922–4 the City and South London and the Charing Cross Euston and Hampstead were welded together into the Northern Line, and extended north to Edgware; two years later the system was extended south, in tube, to Morden; in 1932–3 the Piccadilly was extended greatly at both ends, north from Finsbury Park to Cockfosters, west from Hammersmith to Uxbridge and Hounslow.

71

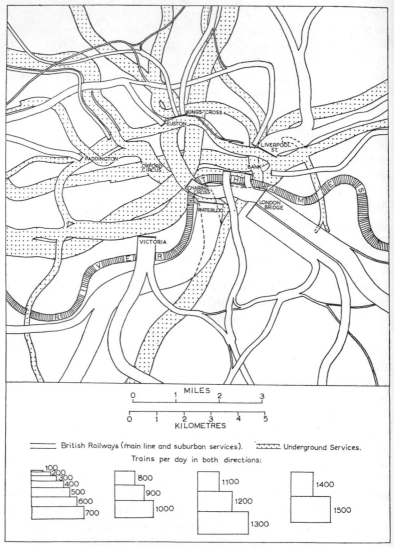

FIG. 18   Rail passenger traffic flows 1962
Based on British Railways and London Transport timetables winter
1961/2.

The extensions were based on a shrewd estimate of the technical
and commercial capacity of tube transport. The tubes were fundamentally inner urban lines; their characteristics—frequent trains,

72

frequent short stops, high passenger capacity including a big peak-load standing capacity—were tolerable to suburban passengers within sharp limits: at the outside, a three-quarter hour journey to or from the centre, which at a speed of under 25 m.p.h. (40 km./hr.) meant a practicable radius of about 10–12 miles (16–19 km.) from the centre. Frank Pick, commercial manager of the Underground group, estimated in 1927 that to break even on such a line, while re-paying over a reasonable period its construction costs, demanded a total of 45 million passenger miles a year, or (assuming an average journey of three miles, 4·8 km.), 15 million passengers a year. But an average line extending 10–12 miles (16–19 km.), with a station every half-mile (800 m.) and an effective direct catchment area of three-quarters of a mile (1·2 km.) each side of the line, and with houses at the typical suburban density, would yield only 45,000 persons. On this basis each of these 45,000, man, woman and child, would have to make an average of 330 journeys a year; which was out of the question.[78] So the line was uneconomic; but it could be made economic, on one condition: that the catchment area must be extended by co-ordinated road transport.

This principle had been perceived right from the first tube railways. The opening of the Central London at Shepherd's Bush terminus in 1900 had been followed in 1901 by the electrification of the London United Tramways line westwards; within a year, suburban development caused rateable values in Acton to rise 14 per cent.[79] But the process became much easier after 1910, when the electric tram was first supplemented and then superseded by the motor-bus; and still more after 1912, when the Underground Electric Railways Company of London acquired control of the London General Omnibus Company, permitting co-ordination of services. By 1919 Frank Pick was already explaining how unremunerative bus services were being developed into open country, in the expectation that suburban development would make them remunerative; and how the fares on buses from the Golders Green tube terminus were manipulated so as to encourage traffic within four miles (6·4 km.) of the station.[80] Sometimes, in the years after 1919, the process got out of hand; Pick ruefully confessed in 1936 that the 1926 extension to Morden, and the linking bus services, had caused such rapid expansion out towards Ewell and Sutton that the inner section of the line was already seriously overloaded.[81]

But within the critical ten-to-twelve mile (16 to 19 km.) limit, the tubes continued to exploit their opportunities to the utmost. The final crop of extensions, the £40 million 'New Works' Programme of 1935–40, planned to take the Northern line well into Hertfordshire, the Central into rural Essex and Buckinghamshire. Before it could be completed, war and the establishment of the post-war planning system intervened; after 1945, the existence of the green belt caused some of the outermost sections to be abandoned, and today the preliminary works stand derelict, strangely, among the fields that have been sterilized to the developers. The Victoria Line (1968) marks a return to the urban tube of Edwardian days; its chief function is to act as a central feeder for the traffic from the main-line termini.

Between the wars, the rapid expansion of suburban services was accomplished by a gentleman's agreement to divide territory. Save for the Morden extension, the tubes did not expand south of the river; here the Southern Railway were left to electrify their existing surface lines. The first south-bank electrification, from London Bridge to Victoria via Peckham Rye, had been in 1909; but the main period of rapid suburban conversion was between 1925 and 1935.[82] Electrification, plus track and signalling improvements, allowed extraordinary accelerations of the old steam services to take place; savings in journey times ranged from 18 to 33 per cent.[83] The former surface stations had been more widely-spaced, for steam operation, than the new tube stations were; and this if anything allowed suburbia to expand farther south of the river.

But the Southern, most enterprising and successful of the inter-war main line railway companies, were not content to stop at the practicable limits of the suburban service. In 1933 they electrified their line to Brighton (51 miles; 82 km.) and introduced regular-interval express services that made the London journey in an hour. This was merely the start of a system of wholesale long-distance electrification which, at its completion in 1962, encompassed the whole sector of south-east England between Portsmouth and the north Kent coast (cf. Fig. 75). The commuter country could now extend indefinitely, limited only by the economic factor of the season ticket price and by the technical factor of the track capacity at the London end.

Here the Southern showed great foresight. By 1936 built-up London had almost reached the 10–12 mile (16–19 km.) limit, and 10,000 people a day were commuting from Brighton.[84] The need now was for a new type of fast service, with few stops, lower

THE DEVELOPMENT OF COMMUNICATIONS

frequency and greater seating capacity, to serve a limited number of centres between 15 and 50 miles (24–80 km.) from central London. By a curious accident, the post-war planning system has fortified the trend: the establishment of the green belt, the continued growth of population in the London Region, the planners' determination to stop the old sprawl and canalize the growth into a limited number of towns, these factors together are establishing a new pattern of commuting, which marks a return to the Victorian pattern. Then, sporadic suburbs around the widely-spaced steam railway stations; between the wars, universal sprawl around the closely-spaced electric railway stations; since 1945, even more sporadic growth around widely-spaced stations offering express electric or diesel services. This process began to develop on a large scale only in the 1950s: comparison between the workplace figures in the 1921 and 1951 censuses shows that in the intervening period the main trend was the growth of commuting from the suburban ring of the Greater London Conurbation (Outer London), six to fifteen miles (10–24 km.) from central London.[85] The traffic from further afield did not substantially increase, and was still in 1951 a small part of the whole. But between 1951 and 1962 there was an increase of 97,000 in average daily arrivals during the morning peak period (7–10) at London main-line stations, and a large proportion of these must have been commuters from outside the fifteen-mile (24 km.) ring.

TABLE III

Total movements to work into the Central Area 1921 and 1951

	1921		1951	
	Numbers	%	*Numbers*	%
From L.C.C. Area	544,312	59·5	467,591	45·0
From Suburban Ring	284,944	31·1	457,908	44·0
From outside Conurbation	86,429	9·4	114,298	11·0
Total	915,685	100·0	1,039,797	100·0

Source: decennial censuses.

The new pattern of traffic threatens to bring about a recurrence of the transport problem of Victorian London: the congestion of the approaches to the main-line termini. By 1960 it was already predicted that the newly-electrified Kent coast lines would not be able to cope with the expected increases of population in Kent by 1970, without expensive duplication of the approaches to central London.[86] One way out of this impasse may be the construction of new tube lines direct from surface stations in the suburban ring of the conurbation to central London, to relieve some of the overload on the most congested inner parts of the main lines. The Victoria Line, which will connect at Finsbury Park with the main line to King's Cross and at Seven Sisters with the electrified line from Bishop's Stortford to Liverpool Street, will perform this function. But other projects of similar character, urgently recommended by a Working Party in 1949, have been shelved: they include the extension of the Victoria Line southwards to East Croydon, and a new tube from Hackney Downs through the City to Victoria.[87] There seems no doubt that if the present growth of commuting continues, its pressure will force some of these projects off the shelf.

Acknowledgement

The author wishes to express his special thanks to Mr. G. Ottley for reading and making comments and corrections on a draft of this chapter.

References

1. This account is based on I. D. Margary, *Roman Roads in Britain*, 1 (1955), Chapter 2.

2. See the account in J. Norden, *Speculum Britanniæ* (1593, edition of 1723), *Middlesex*, 15.

3. e.g. J. Summerson, *Georgian London* (1962), Chapters 12 and 14. For a detailed study of street development (including the influence of fieldways) cf. C. L. Kingsford, *The Early History of Piccadilly, Leicester Square, Soho & their Neighbourhood* (1925), passim.

4. G. A. Sekon, *Locomotion in Victorian London* (1938), 22–3; P. M. Carson, *The Provision and Administration of Bridges over the Lower Thames 1701–1801, with special reference to Westminster and Blackfriars*, unpublished M.A. thesis (University of London, 1954), passim.

5. *County Reports of the Secretary of State on Turnpike Trusts*, No. 2 Surrey, 4. P.P. 1852, XLIV.

6. T. Fairman Ordish, 'History of metropolitan roads', *London Topographic Record*, 8 (1912–13), 38–46; H. J. Dyos, *The Suburban Development of Greater London, south of the Thames*, unpublished Ph.D. thesis (University of London, 1952), 41–3, 46, 53.

7. Ordish, *op. cit.*, 78–9.

8. *Ibid.*, 16–17.

9. C. A. A. Clarke, *The Turnpike Trusts of Islington & Marylebone from 1700 to 1825*, unpublished M.A. thesis (University of London, 1955), 231.

10. Ordish, *op. cit.*, 88.

11. *Ibid.*, 58.

12. *Ibid.*, 26–8.

13. *Ibid.*, 66–7.

14. *Ibid.*, 89–90; *Sixth Report of the Commissioners of Metropolis Turnpike Roads*, Appendix 10, P.P. 1831–2, XXIII; and *Seventh Report*, 10, P.P. 1834, XL. The road had been built as far as Holloway when they took it over.

15. Ordish, *op. cit.*, 29, 90.

16. *Eleventh Report of the Commissioners of Metropolis Turnpike Roads*, Appendix 3, P.P. 1837, XXXIII.

17. John Summerson, *John Nash* (1949), 130–6; Sekon, *op. cit.*, 10.

18. P. J. Edwards, *History of London Street Improvements, 1855–1897* (1898).

19. Sir John W. Barry, Address on 'The streets of London', *Journal of the Royal Society of Arts*, 47 (1898–9), 13–14.

20. For the planning of the Estate at Ladbroke Grove see H.-R. Hitchcock, *Early Victorian Architecture in Britain*, 1 (1954), 442–5.

21. *Restriction of Ribbon Development Act*, 1935 (25 & 26 Geo. V. Ch. 47).

22. See the map in W. A. Robson, *The Government and Misgovernment of London* (1948), 196.

23. *Report, Royal Commission on London Traffic*, para. 69, P.P. 1905, XXX. They also recommended the comprehensive improvement of Marylebone and Euston Roads, which has yet to be carried out (1964).

24. Sir C. Bressey and Sir E. Lutyens, *Highway Development Survey 1937* (*Greater London*), (H.M.S.O. for Ministry of Transport, 1938).

25. P. Abercrombie and J. H. Forshaw, *County of London Plan* (1943); P. Abercrombie, *Greater London Plan 1944* (H.M.S.O., 1945).

26. This road was first officially advocated in 1910. *Report of the London Traffic Branch of the Board of Trade 1910*, 18, P.P. 1911, XXXIV.

27. E. Course, *London Railways* (1962), 155.

28. *Ibid.*, 171; E. T. MacDermot, *History of the Great Western Railway* (1927), I, 46.

29. C. H. Grinling, *The History of the Great Northern Railway* (1898), 28.

30. Course (1962), *op. cit.*, 96.

31. E. Course, *The Evolution of the Railway Network of South East England*, unpublished Ph.D. thesis (University of London, 1958), I, 86.

32. *Report Royal Commission Metropolitan Railway Termini*, 21, P.P. 1846, XVII.

33. H. J. Dyos, 'Railways and housing in Victorian London', *Journal of Transport History*, 2 (1955–6), 14.

34. *Third Report of the Select Committee on Metropolitan Railway Communication*, para. 1, P.P. 1863, VIII.

35. Dyos (1955–6), *op. cit.*, 19.

36. Course (1962), *op. cit.*, 123.

37. *Ibid.*, 187.

38. G. Kemmann, *Der Verkehr Londons mit besonderer Berücksichtigung der Eisenbahnen* (Berlin 1892), 180.

39. Course (1962), *op. cit.*, 28.

40. M. Rees, *The Economic and Social Development of Extra-Metropolitan Middlesex during the Nineteenth Century (1800–1914)*, unpublished M.Sc. thesis (University of London, 1955), 50.

41. *Ibid.*, 56; Ealing was opened shortly after the line was, so for a short time the first station was at West Drayton and Yiewsley.

42. *Ibid.*, 70.

43. *Royal Commission Metropolitan Railway Termini, Minutes of Evidence*, Evidence of Creed, Q. 1730, P.P. 1846, XVII.

44. From 1846.

45. Course (1962) *op. cit.*, 167.

46. Rees, *op. cit.*, 50.

47. Course (1962), *op. cit.*, 165; Rees, *op. cit.*, 51, has 'between 1848 and 1851'.

48. Course (1962), *op. cit.*, 165; Rees, *op. cit.*, 51.

49. Grinling, *op. cit.*, 257.

50. M. Robbins, *Middlesex* (1954), 80.

51. M. Robbins, *The North London Railway* (1953), 2–5; W. L. Steel, *The History of the London and North Western Railway* (1914), 251.

52. H. D. Welch, *The London, Tilbury and Southend Railway* (1951), 25.

53. C. Baker, *The Metropolitan Railway* (1951), 17–20.

54. Sekon, *op. cit.*, 1, 8–9.

55. *Royal Commission on the Housing of the Working Classes, Minutes of Evidence:* Evidence of Boodle, Q. 1132, P.P. 1884–5, XXX.

56. R. U. Ratcliff, *Urban Land Economics* (New York 1949), 321–3.

57. C. Clark, 'Transport—maker and breaker of cities', *Town Planning Review*, 28 (1957–8), 237–250; 'Urban Population Densities', *Bulletin de l'Institut International de Statistique*, 36.4 (1958), 60–8.

58. C. E. Lee, *Passenger Class Distinctions* (1946), 53, 54–5; R. C. Housing Working Classes, *op. cit.*, Evidence of Calcraft, Q. 9961. Workmen's fares were first introduced by the Metropolitan in 1864, without obligation; Lee, *op. cit.*, 51.

59. R.C. Housing Working Classes, *op. cit.*, Evidence of Birt, Q. 10217.

60. *Ibid.*, Evidence of Calcraft, Q. 9965.

61. Dyos, (1952) *op. cit.*, 322. These cost more per mile than the workmen's fares.

62. *Royal Commission on London Traffic*, Appendix 6, Table 42, P.P. 1906, XLI.

63. *Ibid.*, Table 43.

64. *Report Royal Commission London Traffic*, para. 135, P.P. 1905, XXX, referring to suburban traffic generally; F. McDermott, *The Railway System of London* (1891), 3–4.

For evidence from the 1880s, cf. R.C. Housing Working Classes, *op. cit.*, Evidence of Calcraft, Q. 9981–3.

65. Dyos (1952), *op. cit.*, 262–8.

66. Course (1962), *op. cit.*, 89, 144, 228–30.

67. Report R.C. London Traffic, *op. cit.*, paras. 34, 117–131.

68. *Report of the Select Committee on Metropolitan Communications*, iv, P.P. 1854–5, X.

69. T. C. Barker and M. Robbins, *A History of London Transport*, I, *The Nineteenth Century* (1963), 20, 74–81.

70. Third Report S.C. Met. Railway Communication, *op. cit.*, paras. 9, 12.

71. Kemmann, *op. cit.*

72. *Ibid.*, 25–31.

73. *Royal Commission on London Traffic*, Vol. VII, *Report by Advisory Board of Engineers*, 108, P.P. 1906, XLV; C. A. Luzzetti, *The Construction of the London Underground Railways*, unpublished B.Litt. thesis (Oxford, 1937), 59, 65.

74. B. G. Wilson & V. S. Haram, *The Central London Railway* (1950).

75. For an account of Yerkes' work cf. A. A. Jackson and D. F. Croome, *Rails through the Clay* (1962), Chapters 4 and 5 passim.

76. *Census 1921, Workplaces; Census 1951, Usual Workplace & Residence.*

77. *Report of the Joint Select Committee on London Underground Railways*, ix, P.P. 1901, VI.

78. F. Pick, 'Growth and form in modern cities', *Journal of the Institute of Transport*, 8 (1926–7), 165.

79. Rees, *op. cit.*, 116, quoting R.C. London Traffic, Minutes of Evidence, Q. 5065; P.P. 1906, XL. For the L.U.T. see Charles E. Lee, 'Some Notes on the History of the London United Tramways', Supplement to *The Omnibus Magazine* (August 1932).

80. *Proceedings of Select Committee on Transport (Metropolitan Area)*, Q. 3437, 3454–5, P.P. 1919, VII.

81. F. Pick, 'The organisation of transport with special reference to the London Passenger Transport Board', *Journal of Royal Society of Arts*, 84 (1935–6), 216.

82. H. W. A. Linecar, *British Electric Trains* (1949), Chapter 6.

83. P. Burtt, *Railway Electrification & Traffic Problems* (1929), 55.

84. Pick (1936), *op. cit.*, 215.

85. Censuses 1921 and 1951, *op. cit.*

86. P. A. White, 'The problem of the Peak', *Journal of the Institute of Transport*, 28 (1958–60), 270–2.

87. British Transport Commission, *London Plan Working Party*, Report to Minister of Transport (H.M.S.O. 1949), para. 50.

North-west London 1814–1863

*

HUGH C. PRINCE

Almost all the metropolis has been built or rebuilt since the end of the seventeenth century, the vast majority of it since 1814. The earlier phases of development are portrayed in Sir John Summerson's *Georgian London* and the nineteenth-century growth of Camberwell is studied in H. J. Dyos's *Victorian Suburb*. The present account owes much to their methods of approach. It attempts to describe historically the spread of building from the edge of Georgian London through the Victorian suburbs to the boundary of the county between 1814 and 1914, pausing to survey the scene in 1814, again in 1864, and finally in 1914.

North-west London, covering Marylebone, St Pancras and Hampstead, is a particularly interesting area to study. It contains three contrasting physical divisions: in the south, the flat, well-drained Taplow terrace; in the centre, the uneven surface of the London Clay; in the north, the high ridge of the Northern Heights, capped with Bagshot Sands and Pebble Gravels. At the end of the Napoleonic Wars only the Taplow terrace was extensively built on, the remaining seven-eighths of north-west London lying in meadow, pasture, heath and woodland. At the beginning of the First World War four-fifths of the area was built over, the remaining open spaces jealously preserved for public recreation. The vast areas covered with buildings in the nineteenth century were almost entirely residential. Until the late nineteenth century very little of north-west London was occupied by industrial and commercial premises, much the largest non-residential occupiers within the built-up area being the railways.

80

The building of the north-west is loosely related to the phenomenal increase of London's population during the nineteenth century. In 1811 just over one million people, or one in every ten Englishmen, lived in what is now the county of London, but most of the population lived in rural areas. A century later the nation was predominantly urban, and four and a half million people, or one in every eight, lived in the county of London. The increase in population was by no means steady: spurts of rapid growth from 1811 to 1831 and from 1861 to 1881 were followed by intervals of relatively sluggish growth. Nor was the increase evenly distributed: while Hampstead increased from a village of 5,000 inhabitants to a borough of 85,000, the population of the City of London decreased from 120,000 to 20,000. In 1881 the declining City and expanding Hampstead contained about equal numbers. Between these opposite trends may be traced the rise and fall of Marylebone and St Pancras. Marylebone recorded its highest population in 1861, then declined; St Pancras, after seventy years of prodigious growth, reached a peak in 1881 (Table IV). Population changes were only partly caused by natural increase or decrease, by an excess of births over deaths or of deaths over births. The greatest changes were the result of people moving from neighbouring districts and from areas outside London. Throughout the nineteenth century more people moved out of the City than into it, while the suburbs received people not only from the City but from other parts of Britain and from overseas. At the end of the century more people moved away from the crowded inner suburbs of Marylebone and St Pancras than into them; movement set in the direction of Hampstead and more distant areas.

Building activity responded crudely and insensitively to population changes; at times it satisfied or exceeded the demand for houses, at others it lagged behind. Its progress was intermittent and irregular. Building booms erupted in 1816-26, 1868-80 and 1900-09; they were punctuated by spells of depression and inactivity during the Napoleonic Wars, again before the opening of the Victorian era, and briefly in the depression of 1891. The Regency boom displays a rich variety of architectural styles: it presents John Nash's spectacular terraces and intellectual compositions by Sir John Soane, weighty civic monuments such as the British Museum by Sir Robert Smirke or lighter ones such as University College by William Wilkins. The Church Building Commissioners bestowed upon a not deeply-religious quarter of the town Grecian temples by William Inwood,

TABLE IV

Population of north-west London,
City of London and county of London, 1811–1911

	Hampstead	St Pancras	St Marylebone	City of London	County of London
1811	5,483	46,333	75,624	120,343	1,139,355
1821	7,263	71,838	96,040	124,137	1,379,543
1831	8,588	103,548	122,206	122,491	1,655,582
1841	10,093	129,763	138,164	123,563	1,949,277
1851	11,986	166,956	157,696	127,819	2,363,341
1861	19,106	198,788	161,680	112,013	2,808,494
1871	32,281	221,465	159,254	74,844	3,261,396
1881	45,452	236,363	154,910	50,569	3,830,297
1891	68,126	235,345	143,487	37,702	4,227,954
1901	81,942	235,317	133,301	26,923	4,536,267
1911	85,495	218,387	118,160	19,657	4,521,685

Source: Census of England and Wales. The figures of population from 1811 to 1881 relate to parishes; from 1891 to 1911 to metropolitan boroughs as constituted under London Government Act, 1899.

the designer of St Pancras new church, and Thomas Hardwick, who designed St Marylebone new church. Private wealth financed bold schemes by Thomas Telford, who engineered Archway Road, and Thomas Cubitt, who built the streets around Gordon Square and Tavistock Square. The Victorian boom soars to a hundred steeples, towers and chimneys: the skyline is pricked by the spires and pinnacles of Sir George Gilbert Scott's St Pancras station, by the baronial fortresses of the Prudential building and University College Hospital designed by Alfred Waterhouse, by the lofty Dutch gables and masses of glass in Richard Norman Shaw's houses in Fitzjohn's Avenue, Hampstead, and, above all, by the Gothic revival churches of William Butterfield, S. S. Teulon, J. L. Pearson and G. E. Street. The Edwardian boom is manifest in the high-roofed cottages by C. F. A. Voysey, the Garden Suburb at Golders Green planned by Raymond Unwin and Barry Parker with some solid brickwork by Sir Edwin Lutyens, a zealous church by Sir Ninian Comper at Clarence Gate and some early essays in modernism by Charles Holden. Such buildings provide the suburbs with architectural landmarks; they may or may not help us to understand the character of different areas.

Different localities acquired their own special character, not only because they were built at different periods by different architects, but because of differences in the nature of the ground, of the means of travelling to work, of the decisions of landowners, and of the class of residents.

The built-up area in north-west London is by no means flat and uniform. The southern slopes of Hampstead and Highgate present serious obstacles to horse-drawn traffic and are too steep to be climbed by surface railways. Land near King's Cross was liable to flooding by the Fleet River until the late nineteenth century, while districts such as Highgate and Primrose Hill lack dependable sources of water. Sites on river terraces yield gravel and brickearth for building materials; on the London Clay special precautions may have to be taken in laying foundations, in draining and in paving.

The journey to work is not simply a matter of distance, but of the means of conveyance. As long as the journey was made on foot the town marched radially inward and outward, covering the shortest distance between City workplace and suburban home. The Blooms-bury suburbs built for pedestrians were compact, intersected by many narrow pathways, passages, courts and alleys through which a walker could take short cuts to reach his destination. Large wheeled carriages, unlike pedestrians, had to keep to paved roads, so the building of houses for carriage folk followed main roads such as Edgware Road, Finchley Road and Highgate Road in long ribbons, or entered spacious precincts furnished with paved circuses, broad crescents, squares and mews. Bus and tram passengers lived close to bus routes along main roads, while railway travellers clustered around their suburban stations, forming new pedestrian quarters, like villages, at South Hampstead or Golders Green.

Ultimately the decision to build rests with a landowner, subject to controls imposed by the state and by local authorities. Innumerable local differences in the direction, width and density of streets, in the style of houses, in the provision of amenities mark unmistakably the differences between adjoining estates. Large estates such as those of Edward Berkeley Portman and the Duke of Portland were laid out in the grand manner, their lessees bound by severe restrictions as to the manner of using the land. The Duke of Bedford and the Crown set aside large open spaces to enhance the value of surrounding building plots, but small or impoverished proprietors often built densely and meanly. At least one landowner, Sir Thomas

Maryon Wilson, the possessor of an entailed estate, found it impossible to induce a builder to develop his land on short-term leases, with the result that some 400 acres (160 ha.) in central Hampstead remained vacant until his death in 1869.

Landowners decide what type of buildings are put up, but the character of a suburb is determined by the people who inhabit it. During the nineteenth century in north-west London the segregation of different social classes was sharply defined. Between the terraces of the aristocratic Portman estate and the villas of St John's Wood a brick wall was built, and John Nash contrived a more formidable barrier between his Regent's Park terraces and Camden Town. When they were first occupied, neighbourhoods were broadly differentiated by their type of houses, gardens, churches, chapels, clubs, schools and shops, but towards the end of the nineteenth century social distinctions were more finely drawn. An enormous gulf separated the inhabitants of Somers Town and St John's Wood, and important differences existed between the residents of Bedford Square, Fitzroy Square and Gordon Square, or between those of Maitland Park, Belsize Park and Frognal. The history of the suburbs suggests how some of these differences arose.

The North-west in 1814: The Taplow Terrace

During the Napoleonic Wars building activity was nearly at a standstill. In 1803 J. P. Malcolm reported, 'The present war has been a great check to the enterprising spirit of builders; consequently the improvements have been nearly confined to the Northern side of the metropolis, and have chiefly been in the hands of one eminent builder, Mr. Burton.'[1] While London's frontier was temporarily held in check, it was possible, even at close quarters, amid the confusion of builders' yards and brick kilns, to trace the edge of building along a continuous line (Fig. 19).

A compact, well-ordered, well-defined built-up area lay to the south of the New Road. The New Road was England's first by-pass road, a broad carriageway to divert heavy wagons and coach traffic from Watling Street across open country from Paddington to Clerkenwell and thence to the City, skirting the fashionable streets and squares of the great estates. The New Road, now Marylebone, Euston and Pentonville Roads, was begun in 1756. In 1761 it was continued from the Angel Islington to Moorgate by the City Road.

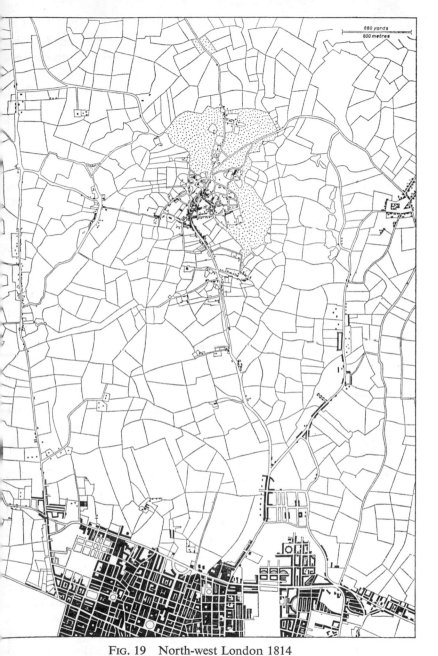

Fig. 19   North-west London 1814
The stippled areas are open spaces.

Based on R. Horwood, Plan of the Cities of London and Westminster and
parts adjoining, Third Edition, augmented by William Faden, 1813;
J. & W. Newton, Hampstead, 1814; Thomas Milne, Plan of the Cities of
London and Westminster, circumjacent Towns and Parishes, 1795–99.

The line of the by-pass road lay close to the northern edge of the Taplow terrace, the gravel ledge on which much of eighteenth-century London was built. In 1815 John White remarked:

'It is not a little singular, that with very few exceptions as to small spots, the whole gravel district will be built upon, when that space of the Crown estate which lies within a few hundred feet of the New Road is covered with buildings. The gravel strata there approach their terminations, as if to say to builders, "Thus far shall the town extend, but no farther. Here is the limit of local springs of fresh water, and here health and comfort require you to stop." '[2]

The well-lit, paved streets and elegant places of the Portland estate, with houses designed by Robert Adam and John Johnson for judges, generals, and Irish bishops, reached the New Road in Marylebone in 1775.[3] On the Fitzroy estate, Charlotte Street, a wide and admirable street of excellent and uniform houses, was erected about 1791. The south and east sides of Fitzroy Square fronted with Portland stone from designs by Robert Adam, begun in 1790, housed a colony of artists, but in 1807 it was reported that 'the remainder has been a dreary chasm at least fifteen years.'[4] On the Bedford estate, Bedford Square and Gower Street, begun in 1776, had settled down as respectable quarters for lawyers and other professional practitioners. In 1800, after a lapse of nearly a quarter of a century, James Burton was commissioned to begin work on a parallel axis to the east, leading from Great Russell Street to Russell Square, the first London square to be landscaped from plans submitted by Humphry Repton. In 1792 James Burton also applied for building leases on the neighbouring Foundling estate, and by 1802 he had built 600 houses in Bloomsbury. In 1807 he obtained another lease to build over the whole of the land belonging to the Skinners' Company, adjoining both the Bedford and Foundling estates. Tavistock House, Burton Street and Burton Crescent (now Cartwright Gardens) thrust a salient of neat but shoddily built houses towards the New Road in St Pancras. Some of the pernicious effects arising from 'such an unnatural and forced enlargement of the town' during this closed season were apparent in the poor buildings, 'preserving an attractive exterior, which Parker's stucco, coloured bricks, and balconies, accomplish; and a fashionable arrangement of rooms on the principal floors, embellished by the paper hanger, and a few flimsey marble chimney pieces are the attractions of the interior . . . and to this finery every thing out of sight is sacrificed.'[5]

By 1814 the lines of future development south of the New Road were clearly drawn. To the west of Marylebone the building of the aristocratic Portman estate was advancing triumphantly northwards from Great Cumberland Place (1789), through Bryanston Square (1811) and Wyndham Place to the New Road. 'This neighbourhood is of very recent date,' wrote J. P. Malcolm in 1807, 'and distinguished beyond all London for regularity, the breadth of the streets and the respectability of the inhabitants, the majority of whom are titled persons, and those of the most ancient families.'[6] The northward march of the Bedford estate was anticipated by Euston Square, an unpretentious but charming range of stuccoed houses, which sprang up in 1811 astride the New Road.

Between the newly built-up areas lay stretches of open land and vestiges of old settlements. The village of St Marylebone was enveloped and almost obliterated by the formal precincts of the Portman and Portland estates, numbering among its vestrymen in 1811, the Marquis of Hertford, Earl Manvers, Viscount Wentworth, the Bishops of Durham, Chichester and Exeter, Admiral Lord Radstock, Admiral Lord Hotham, and eighty other gentlemen.[7] Tottenham Court survived as a straggling hamlet with half a dozen taverns and a toll gate standing at the entry to the Hampstead Road. Timber merchants, shopkeepers, artisans and craftsmen occupied premises south and west of the New Road, and at the southern end of the hamlet, on the site of a filled-in pond, stood the Tabernacle. Founded in 1756 by the evangelist George Whitefield, who preached here until his death in 1770, it drew large congregations from rows of cottages and back alleys, yet unpaved, undrained, unlit and unpoliced. It was a disorderly district, the occasion of its annual fair marked by scenes of wild debauchery. Drunken, brawling crowds came to watch cock fighting, bull and bear baiting. In an attempt to reform the manners of the populace and to avert the threat of serious rioting, the fair was suppressed in 1808, but other spectacles succeeded it.

Lamb's Conduit Fields, Long Fields and other parcels of open land between Tottenham Court and the Fleet River had long ceased to be farmed. Acts of vandalism, thieving and damage by dogs greatly reduced the profits of farming. In 1807 John Middleton remarked: 'The fields are never free from men strolling about in pilfering pursuits by day, and committing greater crimes by night. The depredations every Sunday are astonishingly great.'[8] Not only was farming decayed, but the land itself was badly damaged. Lamb's Conduit, which originally supplied clean water to the Foundling Hospital estate, was now diverted to a cold bath for ladies and gentlemen, opened in 1785. A patch of derelict land adjoining it, known as the Field of the Forty Paces, was frequented as a duelling ground. Near the New Road was a frightful wasteland of pits, ponds, dust heaps and rubbish dumps. At night a zone of brick kilns was described by the Rev. Henry Hunter as forming 'a ring of fire' and pungent smoke around the city. 'The face of the land,' he wrote in 1811, 'is deformed by the multitude of clay pits from which is dug the brickearth used in the kilns which smoke all round London.'[9] Not only brickearth but also dust, cinders and roadsweepings were pounded into bricks, so great was the demand for cheap building materials. To the south of King's Cross, the 'considerable hill' known as Smith's Dust Heap, which had accumulated for over a century, was cleared at the end of the Napoleonic Wars. It is reported by William Hone to have been sold to the Tsar of Russia to make bricks for the rebuilding of Moscow.[10] Another heap is described by Charles Dickens, adjoining Boffin's Bower, home of the Golden Dustman, in *Our Mutual Friend*. Yet others were levelled to make way for later buildings, including University College.

The North-west in 1814: the London Clay

Beyond the New Road, London Clay emerges from beneath a cover of Taplow terrace gravels. The clayland stretches a distance of two miles (3·2 km.) north from St Marylebone new church to Haverstock Hill, or three miles (4·8 km.) measured from St Pancras new church to Highgate Hill. Close to the New Road was an incongruous medley of derelict land, cattle pastures and meadows. In a small area between Hampstead Road and Pancras Road, John Tompson's map of the parish of St Pancras, 1804, marks scores of ponds and kilns, eight brick fields, seven cow liers, five meads and meadows, five burying grounds, and, adjoining the pleasure grounds of St Chad's Wells, a smallpox hospital. The stiff clays 'would have been little or no value in a state of aration,' wrote Middleton, but they supported 'extraordinary good pastures and meadows, with all conveniences proper for a cowman.'[11] In 1811, 'The old brick-grounds converted into pasture, together with a quantity of unbroken pasture land, form a green open tract around London, especially on the north of it, which is almost solely in the possession of the cow-keepers, who supply the metropolis with milk.' By applying heavy dressings of manure, the fields, although mown at least once a year and heavily grazed, were 'preserved in almost perpetual verdure, and soon recruit themselves after being fed down.'[12] Middleton noted that some farmers in Paddington, Marylebone and St Pancras occasionally mowed their grassland twice in one summer, 'but such persons always ought to have, and most of them actually have, previously provided rotten dung sufficient to cover the ground soon after the second mowing.'[13] To supplement their grazing, cattle were also fed turnips and hay with judicious additions of molasses and distillers' wash. The land was divided into small fields, enclosed by neat hawthorn hedges. Farms were widely scattered and mostly less than 100 acres (40 ha.) in extent. The two largest farms in the district were Mr Willan's 500-acre (200 ha.) farm in Marylebone Park and Thomas Rhodes's 450-acre (180 ha.) farm at Camden Town.

The ancient hamlets of St Pancras, Kentish Town and Kilburn were situated on the banks of the Fleet and Tyburn streams. Along-side many old houses, farms and dairies, were a number of smithies and substantial inns catering for coaches, wagoners and drovers making their way north up Watling Street or across the hills of Hampstead and Highgate to the Great North Road. By 1811 these hamlets were no longer rural. Kentish Town was described as a long street 'consisting chiefly of boxes and lodging houses for the accommodation of the inhabitants of London, with boarding schools, public houses, etc.'[14] New rows of houses had almost linked the original settlement with Green Street in Highgate Road to produce an unbroken ribbon of buildings from the Black Horse in Royal College Street to the Bull and Last at the foot of West Hill. Kilburn had acquired a similar ribbon of residences and hostelries along Watling Street.

A number of springs which fed the Fleet and Tyburn had developed seedy resorts, thronged by the populace of London on Sundays and holidays. Kentish Town had an Assembly House which survived until 1853. St Pancras had a spa and tea gardens adjoining the burial ground of old St Pancras church. Near King's Cross was St Chad's Well, whose spacious tea gardens were overlooked by a smoking tile kiln and a smallpox hospital. The gardens remained open until 1840, the pump room surviving until 1860. Bagnigge Wells, at the southern end of King's Cross Road, was the most popular resort on the Fleet.

It, too, was surrounded by kilns and dust heaps, but its proximity to the City and its well laid-out pleasure ground attracted large numbers of visitors. The last entertainment was presented in 1841; shortly afterwards the gardens were closed and the house demolished. Kilburn, in the Tyburn valley, had a spring of chalybeate water, but being situated a good morning's walk across the fields from Marylebone was less frequented than the resorts on the Fleet. In the early nineteenth century the Fleet was still marked on maps as the River of the Wells, but the state of its water belied the description. It was a filthy ditch laden with sewage and refuse from some of the most crowded districts in London. Before the end of the eighteenth century it was covered in as far as Holborn Bridge, but the upper course remained open and occasionally overflowed. In 1809 cattle and horses were drowned in its flood waters and in 1818 a great flood at King's Cross swamped two spas, forced its way through the streets and destroyed thousands of bricks standing in the brickfields. Flooding continued until 1872, when the Metropolitan Board of Works built a new sewer.[15]

Two entirely new settlements were also described as hamlets in 1811. Somers Town, founded in 1786, was growing rapidly. On the east, Judds Place was backed by a few mean streets of low houses; on the west, a grid of formal streets surrounded Clarendon Square. In the middle of the square was the Polygon, composed of detached blocks of houses facing outwards, their courts of gardens tapering towards the centre. One of the first public buildings erected in Somers Town was a Baptist chapel called Bethel. Building ceased between 1797 and 1803, but the population was increased by the arrival of a thousand French *émigrés*. Malcolm noted that 'they decline every attempt towards sociability with the English, and will not learn our language, though we are so fond of theirs.'[16] Their separateness was emphasized by the building of a Roman Catholic church in 1808.

Camden Town, projected in 1791, was described twenty years later as 'another still newer hamlet' forming a line of houses along the east side of the Hampstead Road, south of the Old Mother Red Cap. On the west side, on Lord Southampton's property, Arlington Street and Southampton Street were built, and in 1807 when the inmates were removed from the old workhouse to a new building in King's Road (now St Pancras Way), Camden Town began to expand along Kentish Town Road. The most imposing building in the district was the Royal Veterinary College, erected in 1791 along the broad axis of Great (now Royal) College Street.

Remarkable architectural novelties such as the Polygon, and a variety of chapels for Wesleyans, Anabaptists, Independents and the first Roman Catholic church built in England since the Reformation set a 'beyond the fringe tone' for the new localities. What the streets lacked in social prestige, and such amenities as good paving, street lighting, and night-watchmen they made up in radical and independent attitudes. It was a district congenial to pamphleteers, journalists, cartoonists, and radical politicians who mixed with the ranks of carpenters, retired publicans, leatherworkers, haymakers and brickmakers.

The North-west in 1814: The Northern Heights

The surface of the clayland rises steeply north of the new streets in Camden and Kentish Towns to the face of the Northern Heights, a ridge capped with Bagshot Sands and pebble gravel, whose crest rises above 400 feet (120 m.) in places. From Cricklewood and Kilburn in the west the Northern Heights stretch for five miles (8 km.) in a north-easterly direction across Hampstead Heath, Highgate, Muswell Hill and Alexandra Palace to the low ground at Wood Green and Holloway. To the residents of Bloomsbury and Marylebone the distant hills presented a cheering prospect, inviting them to explore its picturesque scenery.

'The most perfect and delightful landscape,' declared Malcolm, 'is that from Hampstead Heath, when the wind blows strong from the east. Then it is that the clear bright sand of the foreground, broken into a thousand grotesque shapes, gives lustre to the projecting front of Highgate, topped with verdure, and serving as a first distance, from which in gradual undulations the fields retire, till lost in a blue horizon.'[17]

The steep southern slopes presented a formidable obstacle to communications. Roman Watling Street and Ermine Street kept to low ground on the western and eastern flanks, but the Great North Road struck boldly uphill from Kentish Town to Highgate, confronting wagoners with one of the most arduous and dangerous climbs out of London. The daily exertions of wagon teams labouring up the hill, drawing loads of coal and beer, were familiar to the inhabitants of Highgate. They frequently witnessed 'men flogging, shouting and swearing at the overtasked horses for three and six hours together.'[18] 'Highgate and Hampstead hills', observed Middleton in 1807, 'are a tax of one horse in every team, on the farmers of Finchley and Hendon, who are obliged to drag every load up either one or other of them.'[19] Accidents might befall vehicles not fitted with rollers or safety brakes. In 1781 a writer in the *Gentleman's Magazine* complained of Highgate Hill: 'Not a day passes, nor has probably ever passed, but some accident has happened on this hill; and I will venture to say that the injuries sustained upon it, could they be ascertained, are enormous, not to mention the delay it occasions to the traveller, and the labour to the horses, at which every humane heart must bleed.'[20] In 1837 Queen Victoria herself was saved only by the prompt action of the innkeeper of the Fox and Crown when the carriage in which she was travelling rushed down West Hill out of control.

Owing to the distance from the City and the difficulty of access the Heights remained largely rural in character. They lay beyond the zones of brick kilns, dairies, graziers, nurseries and market gardens. They possessed no arable land, and almost all their permanent grass was devoted to hay production, yielding one crop a year, manured every three years. The occupiers of small farms of less than 100 acres (40 ha.) managed to make a living from the proceeds of their hay sales; but J. J. Park observed in 1813, 'The village of Hampstead has been peculiarly attractive to commercial and professional men; and the operation of wealth is strongly perceivable in the condition of its landed property. To those who have acquired opulence in this way, the possession of a country villa is incomplete without the addition of something which may be called *a farm*.'[21] The remaining open land lying in unimproved heath was of no value to farmers. The right to graze cattle and horses on the commons without stint was more of a liability than an asset. Even the soil itself was not protected from the depredations of the commoners. Not until 1806 was the right to cut turf and remove gravel abolished, and the Lord of the Manor reserved the right to make grants of land from the commons to copyholders. The heaths were a grievous threat to the life and property of farmers and residents alike, harbouring gipsies and vagrants, providing cover for highwaymen, thieves and cut-throats who plundered the traffic going to and from London.

Small hamlets, country houses, isolated farms and rustic cottages were the only settlements in this pastoral setting. Small groups of houses ranged around a green with a well or a pond, and a church, were the basic units. Highgate clustering round Pond Square is a characteristic hamlet, although its open space was not a square, and its pond was filled in 1864. Hampstead contained no less than six such hamlets at North End, West End, South End, Church End, New End and Fortune Green. Elsewhere in the pastoral districts of south and east Middlesex are scores of hamlets of similar form, bearing names such as 'end' or 'green'. Neighbouring Hornsey has Crouch End, Fortis Green, Stroud Green; Tottenham, West Green, Wood Green, Page Green, Bounds Green; Finchley, East End, North End and Church End; Hendon, Golders Green; Willcsden, Church End, Kensal Green, Sherrick Green, Willesden Green, to name but a few.[22] In 1814 every one of these ends and greens was identifiable as a separate settlement, but no longer as an exclusively rural settlement.

Dr Johnson, more at home in town than in country, took lodgings in Hampstead to concentrate on his writings and refresh himself in the country air, and many others followed his example, to retire from the distractions of city life or to find a quiet spot in which to spend their old age. Among the residents of Hampstead and Highgate in 1814 were actors, painters, engravers, architects, publishers, playwrights, essayists, poets, retired London tradesmen, East India merchants, Hudson Bay Company officials, churchmen, army and naval officers and at least one retired female pickpocket. Some, such as the painter Romney, built new houses; others, such as Richard Steele, restored old cottages. Dozens of large residences, mansions of five bays and three storeys, were built in Highgate and Hampstead at the end of the seventeenth and beginning of the eighteenth century. Many were set in spacious grounds, but others were arranged in urban groupings. Hampstead had some minute picturesque squares, some dignified terrace houses and the spacious Church Row built in 1720. Highgate possessed England's first street of semi-detached houses, The Grove, built in 1688, by William Blake, an educational reformer.

As a watering place Hampstead enjoyed a brief spell of glory at the beginning of the eighteenth century. Well Walk boasted a pump room and assembly rooms, the physician of the spa built a substantial mansion, Burgh House, the Kit Cat Club met at the Upper Flask Inn and a number of other clubs and places of entertainment were established. Some amusing pieces of Batty Langley Gothick appeared in the Vale of Health and East Heath Road, cottages assuming rustic guises with fanciful names like Woodbine Cottage and Holly Cottage. Hampstead's reputation as a fashionable resort was tarnished by the proliferation of disreputable clubs and gambling dens. Throngs of Londoners were drawn by races on the Heath and by the fair; but two of the most disorderly establishments were not in Hampstead village. Belsize House and the Chalk Farm Tavern were frequented by violent as well as dissolute persons.

The character of the country between the hamlets was transformed by the creation of a number of large parks. The most magnificent of these was Kenwood, a landscape garden of 200 acres (80 ha.), with lawns sweeping down from the front of Adam's house to an ornamental lake. The water reflected the sham façade of a palladian bridge and the encircling belt plantation of beeches. Further east was Lord Southampton's residence at Fitzroy Farm, whose grounds were laid out by Humphry Repton, and in Hampstead, Rosslyn House and Belsize House possessed fine parks.

The locality was acquiring some of the attributes of a suburb. Street lighting and a patrol of watchmen were introduced in 1774, but the distance of five miles (8 km.) separating it from the City, the long steep climb from Camden Town and Kentish Town placed it beyond the reach of most daily travellers. A further discouragement to building on Highgate Hill was the difficulty of obtaining water. In 1811 Highgate was still described as a 'somewhat romantic' rural retreat, 'in the shade of its hanging groves.' Its seclusion was emphasized by the lull in building. Neither Hampstead nor Highgate had, according to Rev. Henry Hunter, received much 'accession of building latterly, and its population does not appear to have increased for many years past.'[23]

The Great Wen and Regent's Park 1814 to 1837

In 1814 building activity had been at a standstill for nearly fifteen years and few Londoners could have remembered the turmoil and confusion that had accompanied the previous building boom in the 1770s and 1780s. Nor could they have shared the apprehensions of Joseph Tucker, viewing the scene at the height of the boom in 1773. Appalled by the prospect of the Wen growing unchecked, he had written: 'If therefore the Increase of Building, begun at such an early

Period, was looked upon to be no better than a Wen, or Excrescence, in the Body Politic, what must we think of those numberless streets and squares which have been added since?'[24] By 1814 that fear had been forgotten. Old men, such as Thomas Pennant, had lived to see great benefits arising from that period of expansion. He recalled with satisfaction that Oxford Street had been transformed from 'a deep hollow road and full of sloughs; with here and there a ragged house, the lurking place of cut-throats,' into as handsome a street as any in Europe.[25] The immediate call was for more houses to accommodate the growing population; but no sooner had building begun than the old cry was taken up again. A redoubtable champion of English countrymen, William Cobbett, was roused to furies of indignation wherever he saw the Great Wen swelling. 'What,' he asked, 'is to be the fate of the great wen of all? The monster, called by the silly coxcombs of the press, "the metropolis of the empire"?'[26] Whether or not his readers agreed with his proposal to disperse the Wen by removing half a million of its inhabitants, many were alarmed that London might lose its identity as a city if expansion continued, and some shared the view that it ought to be stopped.

The frontier of Georgian London, along the New Road and the edge of the Taplow terrace, was decisively breached by two streams of bricks and mortar surging over Camden Town and Marylebone. In 1809 Lord Southampton granted building leases for the erection of 500 third-rate houses on 50 acres (20 ha.) lying to the west of Hampstead Road, between St James's Chapel and Britannia Lane. The development of the adjoining Camden estate began in earnest with the building of Bayham Street in 1812. In Marylebone, at the same time, E. B. Portman let the greater part of his land north of the New Road to David Porter, a local chimney sweeper, 'without any restriction in the mode of covering it.'[27] Within a few years Allsop's Farm, Lord's Cricket Ground and an adjoining nursery disappeared; Baker Street was projected across the New Road; Dorset Square was laid out and houses were pushed to the boundary of the estate (Fig. 20).

The new streets were thrown up hurriedly in the cheapest possible manner. In 1814 John White described the buildings on Lord Southampton's estate as 'miserable modern erections,' and 'inferior houses.'[28] Nor was the character of neighbouring estates much better. In 1810 John Nash lamented that 'houses of such a mean sort as have been built at Somers Town, and are now building on Lord

95

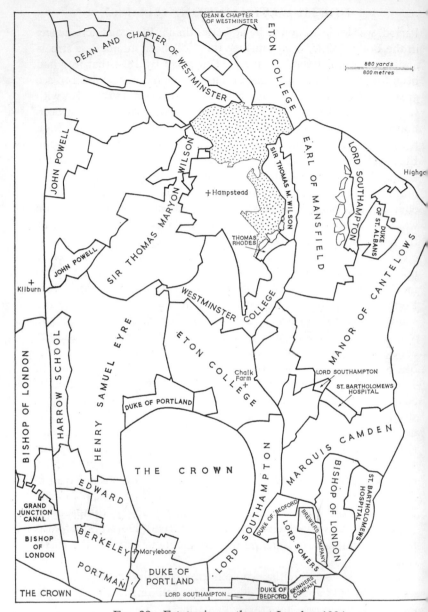

FIG. 20 Estates in north-west London 1834
Based on B. R. Davies, Topographical Survey of the Borough of Saint
Mary-le-Bone, 1834; Tithe Survey, Hampstead, 1839; F. Howkins, The
Story of Golders Green, 1923.

Southampton's ground, should disgrace this apex of the Metropolis, particularly as there is sufficient space on the lower grounds for any increase of buildings required for the lower classes; and it is demonstrable that Lord Southampton, Mr Portman, Mr Eyre and the Duke of Portland are not advancing their best interests in permitting their grounds to be covered with such buildings.'[29]

What was lost in Camden Town was not simply a few acres of ground covered with 'miserable fourth-rate building', but a unique opportunity to embark on a grand design for a spacious, elegant and commodious quarter of the metropolis, worthy of the capital of a nation soon to triumph over Napoleon and lead the world in industry and commerce. Appealing for a bold and generous plan, John White urged that: 'Some monument of the arts, capable of impressing posterity with a sense of the dignity, opulence and happiness of this nation, seem to be required to mark the epoch.'[30] That the occasion was not irrevocably lost was due almost entirely to the foresight of the architect, John Nash, and the tenacity of his patron the Prince Regent.

Between 1803 and 1811 leases on the Crown estate at Marylebone Park expired and an outline programme for the development of the property was drafted by John Fordyce, Surveyor-General to the Office of Land Revenues. Two detailed plans were prepared. The scheme devised by Thomas Leverton and Thomas Chawner was almost entirely devoid of originality. It recommended that the estate should be used 'chiefly as Building Ground' and that two-thirds of it should be reserved for villas.[31] It also recommended that a gridiron pattern of streets and squares should be extended in straight lines from the Portland estate to the northern boundary of Marylebone Park. This pedestrian proposal was rejected in favour of a bold and highly imaginative scheme submitted by John Nash, a scheme that was open to criticism in points of detail and objectionable on account of its cost. The whole project might well have been drowned in a flood of personal recriminations had the Prince not supported it with determination.

The genius of Nash's scheme was that it created urban scenery within the setting of a landscape garden. It captured for the first time the vision of a park city, a garden townscape, furnished in stucco with Park Crescent, Park Square, nine splendid terraces, two secluded Park Villages and a grand approach through Regent Street. The treatment of the park was inspired by the work of Humphry Repton,

G

with whom Nash collaborated some years earlier; but the felicitous disposition of urban façades in such a setting was solely the product of Nash's lofty imagination. Nash saw that its success would depend on the application of three principles: first, that noblemen's and gentlemen's houses should enjoy extensive prospects over open parkland; secondly, that a broad approach, drive or carriageway should lead directly from the seat of government at Carlton House, Whitehall, the Houses of Parliament and the Law Courts; thirdly, that fashionable residences should be firmly segregated from inferior dwellings. None of these principles, except perhaps the last, was entirely new in town planning, but the resulting composition was highly original.

The focus of attention was Regent's Park. Nash firmly discarded John White's idea that it should provide a pleasure ground for the health and comfort of the general public; he did not wish to add, in Wyndham's phrase, to the 'lungs of the metropolis'. His intention was simply to create spacious vistas for the residences fronting the park, and to build a number of villas in the shelter of secluded groves in the middle of the park. The park was designed solely for the benefit of the residents, 'that the attraction of open space, free air, and the scenery of nature, with the means and invitation of exercise on horseback, on foot, and in carriages, shall be preserved or created in Mary-le-bone Park, as allurements and motives for the wealthy part of the public to establish themselves there.'[32] The water of the Tyburn was ponded into a lake equal in size to the Serpentine, some of the material dug out being used for brickmaking, some for grading a 50-foot (15 m.) wide carriage-way to follow the perimeter of the park, the Outer Circle, 'to be separated from the scenery only by a sunk fence.' In 1811 trees were planted on various parts of the estate, but in the following spring those planted opposite Portland Place were removed, the subsoil dug out, and the building of Park Crescent commenced. It was originally intended to extend the Crescent to form a complete circus, but some years later the lessee went bankrupt and the plan was abandoned. In its place Park Square was built in 1823–5. It was a happy improvisation, creating a most appropriate foyer to the spacious park beyond. While it was being built the great terraces began to rise around the park. They were sketchily designed compositions, like wedding cakes, richly decorated outside, but plain within. The execution of the work was entrusted to James Burton, who was responsible for York, Cornwall and Clarence Terraces begun in 1820. In 1822 work began on Sussex Place, and in 1823 on Hanover Terrace. As building progressed Nash's façades soared to new heights of fantasy. Cambridge and Chester Terraces, 1825, were followed in 1826 by Cumberland Terrace, the whole range rising to a skyline dancing with urns and statuary by Bubb, their fronts dressed with screens of columns supporting paper-thin carved pediments. It is magnificent theatrical scenery.

The interior of Regent's Park was not finished in the manner Nash intended. It lacked splendid eyecatchers, a fanciful pleasance for the Prince Regent, fountains and a long basin in front of Cumberland Terrace. Only a handful of villas were built, and the park remained open, more like a prairie than the well-wooded enclosure of St James's Park. Its vistas, which should have been heavily framed by trees, were frittered and diffuse. Architecturally scenery was diversified by the building of the Zoological Gardens, opened in 1827, the Gothic court of St Katherine's Hospital, and the Colosseum, a sixteen-sided rotunda with a portico and cupola, opened in 1829.

The boldest stroke of Nash's scheme was to thrust a new street through the built-up area from Regent's Park to Charing Cross to give the residents of the principal houses direct access to the offices of government in Westminster. The line of the road was drawn to bring Regent's Park closer to Westminster than four out of five of the principal streets and squares in the West End. It was to be a thoroughfare of magnificent dimensions suitable for fast-moving carriage traffic. Portland Place, the widest and most elegant street in London, was to be the model for the new street, a grand leading avenue of uniform splendour, curved to bring its great edifices progressively into view, on a rising plane with a fine object at its termination. The line of Portland Place was continued southward through the grounds of Foley House into a completely new street, Langham Place. The difficulty of crossing Oxford Street was overcome by creating a circus, and 'the two divisions of the town insensibly united in the best possible manner.' Between Oxford Street and Piccadilly rows of poor houses were pulled down and numbers of narrow streets, lanes and passages closed to form Regent Street. The street was to be a great shopping centre with shops selling articles of taste and fashion beneath a lofty colonnade surmounted by a balustrade. The covered way would enable shoppers and 'those who have nothing to do but walk about and amuse themselves' to saunter at leisure every day of the week, 'instead of being frequently confined to their houses by rain.'[33] The street was longer and twice as wide as Bond Street, affording room for all the fashionable shops in London, its fifteen feet (4·6 m.) wide pavement being broad enough for all the fashionable shoppers. At its lower end Regent Street swept majestically round a quadrant to the third major crossing spanned by Piccadilly Circus. From there it entered Lower Regent Street and Waterloo Place. The demolition of the royal mews and the laying out of Trafalgar Square, completing the scheme, were carried out after Nash's retirement.

The third guiding principle formulated by Nash was the principle of class segregation. Early Georgian schemes, with few exceptions, were designed to house more or less self-contained communities, representative of all classes from noblemen, churchmen, doctors, tradesmen to servants. By 1811 the social structure of different parts of London no longer corresponded with that ideal. Bloomsbury was overwhelmingly professional, legal and mercantile; Tottenham Court was artisan and artistic; the Portland estate was occupied by servants of the Church and State; the Portman estate was aristocratic; Camden Town and Somers Town were predominantly lower-class. Nash was not the first to recognize these divisions, but he was the first to make them an object of planning, to design methods of effectively separating one class of residents from another.

In 1811 the Crown estate was already enclosed on three sides by buildings, only the north lying open to the heights of Hampstead and Highgate. Nash considered 'the period must be very remote when this shall be built over.' On the east and west neighbouring landowners had begun to enclose their property with fences, walls and iron railings. Leverton and Chawner proposed to 'do away with these intended barriers,' but Nash preferred to strengthen them. He planned to use the Regent's Canal as a ha-ha on the north, and to deploy his terraces as bulwarks to seal off and protect 'that best-built part of the town from the annoyance and disgrace which threaten it on either side.'[34] 'There will be no other access,' he declared, but Portland Place and Baker Street. On the east he planned Albany Street so 'that neither the commercial canal, nor its wharfs, nor the elongation of Portland Street, as a near way to Hampstead and Highgate, nor the markets, nor the streets between the canal and Portland Street, incommode or interfere with the privacy and rural scenery of the proposed parks or circular roads, the street continued from Portland Road cutting off all communication between them.'[35]

Within the estate there were few passages connecting the mews and servants' quarters with the main terraces, while tradesmen's quarters were firmly separated from both. The distinctions between the different precincts were heavily emphasized by different styles of architecture. The villas for the nobility were palatial, the terraces were decked out in triumphal Roman orders, the markets were fronted with low houses of good proportions in plain brick, the barracks were massive and severe. The most original creations were the semi-detached residences built in the Park Villages for a small community of doctors, guardsmen's ladies, a successful journalist and Alexander Maconochie, professor of geography in the newly founded London University. All the houses were deep-eaved, roofed with Welsh slates, faced with stucco and embellished with screens of trellis work. They appeared in a variety of romantic styles, as rustic Gothic cottages, Swiss chalets, Lombard villas with fingers of round-headed windows, false lights, pediments and lunettes to disguise the partition. Their gardens were picturesquely landscaped down to the banks of the canal, to compose a model of rusticity and seclusion that was to be imitated in many garden suburbs.

In choosing a line for the great approach road leading to Regent's Park, Nash sought to strengthen 'the line of separation between the habitations of the first class of society and those of inferior classes.' North of Oxford Street he observed that 'the principal streets and squares are situated west of Portland Place,' continuing southward from Oxford Street to Piccadilly; he proposed to follow the line of Swallow Street between Oxford Street and Piccadilly because it 'would make the like separation of the houses of the different classes of society.' 'It will also be seen, by the plan,' he asserted, 'that the whole communication from Charing Cross to Oxford Street will be a boundary and complete separation between the streets and squares occupied by the nobility and gentry, and the narrow streets and meaner houses occupied by mechanics and the trading part of the community.'[36] To prevent cross movement all but four side streets were closed, forcing carts and drays to conduct their traffic 'by means of the back streets without interfering with the principal street.'

Nash's scheme was justly criticized for its many practical defects. Gravel pits and brick kilns were opened in unsightly positions near the New Road and behind Allsop's Farm. Insufficient thought was given to the problems of water supply and drainage. A reservoir at the top of Primrose Hill managed by the New River Company and iron pipes of the Chelsea Company feeding the west averted a serious water shortage, but Nash's proposal for a new sewer was unsatisfactory. It was, however, an improvement on the naïve suggestion by Leverton and Chawner that the existing sewers might 'be rendered effectual, if care be taken not to sink the basement storeys of the Houses too deep.'[37] Nash recognized the absolute necessity of digging a new drain to serve 1,000 acres (400 ha.) of land and to provide an outlet for excess water from the new canal. His assessment of the magnitude of the problem was correct, but in detail his calculations differed widely from those of the Commissioners of Sewers for Westminster and from those of J. Rennie. The cutting of the Regent's Canal introduced further complications to the drainage problem, but Nash made use of it not only as a fosse to enclose the northern boundary of the park but also, by forming a basin and wharves on the east side of the property, to supply corn, straw, hay, coal, timber, building materials and vegetables to three markets on the east.

In addition to hotels and other public buildings, Nash envisaged new churches, 'placed so as to terminate the vistas of streets, or embellish the squares and circuses, and to enliven the scenery.'[38] For some observers the provision of churches was a more serious matter. In 1813 the West End was described as 'wearing the appearance of a quarter appropriated to persons under sentence of excommunication,' and, on behalf of the residents of the Portland estate, John White urged 'the necessity of doing something in aid of the accommodation demanded by the services of the established religion.'[39] In 1818 the state began to repair the obvious weakness in the armour of its establishment, by making one million pounds available through the Church Building Commissioners. Their zeal was such that, if church building were an index of piety, the whole north-west of London might be said to have undergone a rapid regeneration, if not conversion, during the Regency period. Excluding Thomas Hardwick's new Marylebone church, built in 1813–17, no less than eleven Commissioners' churches were built in St Pancras and Marylebone and one was built in Hampstead. The Inwoods designed new St Pancras church, 1819–22, All Saints Camden Town, 1822, St Peter's Regent Square, 1822–24, and St Mary Eversholt Street, 1824–27; Nash himself produced drawings for All Souls Langham Place, 1822–24; Sir Robert Smirke was engaged on St Mary's

Wyndham Place, 1823; Sir John Soane designed Holy Trinity Mary-lebone Road, 1828; L. Vulliamy drew St Michael's Highgate, 1830. While the leading architects of the generation were commissioned by the established church, Roman Catholics built St Aloysius Somers Town, 1808–16, St Mary's Holly Place Hampstead, 1816, Our Lady Lisson Grove, 1836, and a dozen new chapels were raised by various non-conformist sects.

Nash's great design profoundly altered the social geography of north-west London. It spared Regent's Park from the kind of mediocre development which ruined Camden Town; it secured the exclusiveness of the West End in Marylebone and Westminster; it set the tone for future developments in Hampstead. Narrowly viewed, the architecture was much less impressive than the town planning. The façades of Regent Street, wrote Leigh Hunt, 'are great improvements as far as they concern what has been done away; but we cannot so much admire them in themselves.' Their effect, on a minor scale, was that of a street in Turin: 'But there is a flimsiness and want of art in the details . . . it has the misery of a trick.' [40] After Nash few other schemes attempted to attain similar heights of elegance. One of the last essays in the grand manner was Thomas Cubitt's completion of the Bedford estate in a style and quality of building superior to anything which had been built previously for the speculative market. Lacking the theatrical flair of Nash, Cubitt relied on sound construction and faultless proportions. The work of build-ing was protracted. Tavistock Square, Woburn Place, Woburn Square, Torrington Place and part of Gordon Square were com-pleted between 1820 and 1829, but Gordon Street, Endsleigh Street and Endsleigh Place remained unfinished in 1858. In 1830 the fashionable demand for town residences in sedate squares and ter-races was declining; by 1860 even well-built, conveniently-situated houses such as those on the Bedford estate were attractive to few but the academic staffs of the British Museum and University College.

The models for nineteenth-century suburban building were not the imposing façades of Regent's Park, but the informal groups of semi-detached villas discreetly hidden in the park villages. Their design may have been inspired by plans for the development of the Eyre estate at St John's Wood, an estate that Nash examined when pre-paring his survey of Regent's Park. The earliest scheme for the Eyre estate was drawn in 1794 by Spurrier and Phipps, City auctioneers. [41]

The layout observed the conventional formalities, by including a church, market, straight streets, square and crescent. Somewhat less orthodox was its British Circus, a mile in circumference, and it is significant that Nash placed a similar circle in the centre of his design for Regent's Park. But what was entirely novel in the Spurrier and Phipps project was that pairs of semi-detached villas, each occupying over an acre (0·4 ha.) of ground, were to cover the whole area. A version of the plan, slightly modified by the 26-year-old architect John Shaw, was exhibited at the Royal Academy in 1803. The proposal for a British Circus was abandoned in 1807, when the first building plots were leased. Two years later Alpha Road appeared in the Marylebone rate books, and by 1810, when a further plan was presented, much of the land was already taken but not yet built upon. Little remained of the original proposals, but the intention to build an estate of semi-detached houses, or double villas, was carried out before Nash built his park villages. The first house in Alpha Road was built and occupied by the architect, Charles Heathcote Tatham, a widely travelled connoisseur, author of several books of designs, who went bankrupt in 1834. All the early houses were more urban than rustic in appearance, faced with stucco, roofed with Welsh slates, arranged like terrace houses for vertical living on three floors above a basement. Their style was by no means revolutionary or brazenly exotic, but the conservative Portman estate regarded them as dangerous neighbours. It showed its hostility by building a brick wall along the boundary, closing the roads, and forbidding communication between the estates. On the east the Crown lands were shut off by the Regent's Canal. Ostracized by indignant neighbours, the district offered sanctuary to Bohemians such as T. H. Huxley, George Eliot and Mr Cross, the notorious Earl of Kinsale and a surgeon accoucheur. It retained until late Victorian times an air of 'faint impropriety'.[42]

On the west, the Eyre estate was bordered by land belonging to Harrow School. In 1809 a line of substantial villas stood fronting Watling Street when John Shaw was invited to design a parallel axis to be fronted with semi-detached villas. North of Hamilton Place the scheme lapsed into chaos through bad management.

North and east of Primrose Hill, beyond Park Village and St John's Wood, lay 230 acres (93 ha.) of land belonging to Eton College.[43] In 1824 the estate was surveyed and it was reported that it would be most suitable for villa development. An Act of Parliament was passed authorizing the College to grant building leases and in 1829 a fifteen-acre (6 ha.) site adjoining Haverstock Hill was offered to builders in half-acre (0·2 ha.) plots for terms of 99 years. John Shaw, son and pupil of John Shaw, the planner of the Eyre and Harrow properties, was appointed surveyor. He produced no master plan and seems to have taken little interest in the layout of the estate, although he designed individual houses in Adelaide Road, Provost Road and Eton Rise in debased Regency and collegiate Tudor styles. The greater part of the development was carried out by Samuel Cumming, a carpenter from Great Titchfield Street, who first applied for leases in Adelaide Road in 1843. Cumming had no qualifications as an architect; he was a building contractor, practising Thomas Cubitt's methods, employing and directing a full-time staff of craftsmen, obtaining loans through lawyers. Between 1843 and 1849 he put up 200 houses along Adelaide Road, Provost Road and Eton Road. The houses were deep-eaved, slate roofed, stucco finished, in nondescript Italianate styles incorporating details copied from Grecian, Egyptian, Venetian and Gothic examples. They were inoffensive, deliberately undistinguished houses, only remotely classical yet no more than vaguely romantic. They were built to please respectable but undiscerning clients. In 1851 the largest single group of residents were prosperous shopkeepers and small manufacturers. People of independent means, pensioners, lawyers, doctors, writers, artists and professors occupied most other houses. They were mostly regular churchgoers, and a site in Eton Road was reserved for St Saviour's Church, built in 1856 at a cost of £9,000.

North and west of the Eton estate lay open country, a countryside of small fields enclosed by heavily timbered hedges. Along Watling Street, beyond the last villa in Kilburn, Cobbett wrote on 19th June, 1822,

'through Edgware, Stanmore and Watford, the crop is almost entirely hay, from fields of permanent grass, manured by dung and other matter brought from the Wen. Near the Wen, where they have had the first haul of the Irish and other perambulating labourers, the hay is all in rick. Some miles further down it is nearly all in. Towards Stanmore and Watford, a third, perhaps, of the grass remains to be cut. It is curious to see how the thing regulates itself. We saw, all the way down, squads of labourers, of different departments, migrating from tract to tract; leaving the cleared fields behind them and proceeding on towards the work yet to be performed.'[44]

Fast on the heels of the haymakers came the surveyors and speculative builders, now approaching the slope of Haverstock Hill. As
they came they were met by builders advancing downhill from
Hampstead village. At the end of the Napoleonic wars building
activity boomed in Hampstead. Groups of cottages were built in
Holly Place and Benham's Place; in Belsize Lane, Hunter's Lodge,
a turreted Gothic cottage ornée with ogee windows was built; and
modest stuccoed houses and terraces spread down the hill to Downshire Hill and Keats Grove. The scene was changing fast when
Leigh Hunt wrote:

> *'Dear Hampstead, is thy southern face serene,*
> *Green hills and dells, trees overhead now seen,*
> *Now down below, with smoking roofs between,*
> *A village revelling in varieties.'*[45]

In 1818, when the lines were written, the poet was living at one of the
new houses in Downshire Hill which had come to disrupt the serenity
of Hampstead's southern slopes. In the same year, his friend, John
Keats, moved into another new house nearby. In 1810 S. T. Coleridge
settled at the Grove at Highgate and in 1827 John Constable came to
Well Walk in Hampstead. They found peace in villages inhabited
largely by retired officers and colonial officials. London was still
remote.

Improved engineering methods enabled better roads to be built
and brought fresh traffic. In 1813 Thomas Telford succeeded in laying a solidly paved arterial road up Highgate Hill, building a majestic
archway 36 feet (11 m.) above the road in place of an arch that
collapsed in the previous spring. Shortly after the opening of the
new road, Gregory Bateman, a solicitor, was forced to sell his 40-
acre (16 ha.) estate on Highgate Hill. The cost of rebuilding of Kentish Town House on the model of Wanstead House had thrown him
into debt and earned the house the name of Bateman's Folly. The
house and part of the estate were bought by a wealthy barrister who
made many picturesque improvements, introduced deer into the
park, built new lodges and altered the carriage entrance. Further
down the hill smaller parcels were acquired by a German sugar
merchant, a druggist and two actors. On the western slopes of Hampstead, a group of villas were built along Finchley Road, a new turnpike road from Marylebone to Finchley completed in 1835. Some
large establishments with stables and coach-houses were built near

the crossroads at Swiss Cottage, and Kidderpore Hall with four adjoining mansions was situated in the hayfields near Fortune Green.

In 1829 George Shillibeer ran London's first omnibus service along the New Road from Paddington Green to the Bank of England. Within four years 600 omnibuses were operating in London, conveying thousands of passengers daily from the West End to the City. By 1834 competition had grown so fierce that Shillibeer was driven out of business and the streets of north-west London were jammed with horse buses. The solitude of Kentish Town, Paddington and Kilburn was disappearing.

From the Opening of the London and Birmingham Railway to the Metropolitan 1837–1863

The advance of middle-class residences beyond Regent's Park into the peaceful countryside of St John's Wood, Portland Town and Chalk Farm was beginning to slacken, when the London and Birmingham Railway cut and tunnelled towards its London terminus, permanently fixing a social barrier between west and east. Nowhere in London is the contrast between two sides of the tracks more sharply drawn than between the terraces of Regent's Park and the opposing terraces of Camden Town (Fig. 21).

The London and Birmingham Railway was a completely alien intruder in London. It was promoted specifically to afford Birmingham manufacturers a main line of communication with the port of London, to relieve the congested and unreliable canals of their traffic. The construction of 112 miles (180 km.) of line to be worked by primitive locomotives was a costly feat of engineering. It was designed conservatively, maintaining a ruling gradient of 1 in 330 and curves of not less than 600 yards (550 m.) radius. The overriding consideration was to provide swift and direct means of conveying goods between the two terminal depots in Birmingham and London. At the London end, the line terminated at Camden Town where freight was to be transferred to the Regent's Canal for shipment to the docks at Blackwall. Passenger services received scant attention. The Camden Town depot lay on the edge of the built-up area, inconveniently located for those wishing to transact business in the City. The possibility of attracting local passenger traffic seems not to have been considered, the nearest station to London being Harrow, 11½ miles (18·5 km.) distant.

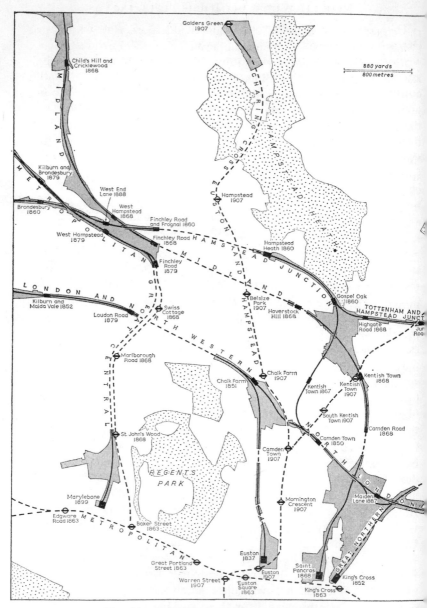

FIG. 21   Railways in north-west London 1914
The stippled areas are open spaces, the shaded areas railway land.
Based on London County Council, Municipal Map of London, 1914;
E. A. Course, London Railways, 1962; T. C. Barker and R. M. Robbins,
A History of London Transport, Vol. I, 1963.

The coming of the railway wrought a fivefold change in the character of residential districts in north-west London. First, the work of excavating cuttings, digging tunnels, raising embankments altered the form of the ground on a greater scale than any previous construction. Secondly, the entry of the railway into the built-up area necessitated the demolition of houses, the blocking of streets, the diversion of drains and watercourses. Thirdly, the railway introduced industrial activities to residential districts: it brought an invasion of northern engineers and Irish navvies; it charged the atmosphere with fire and smoke; it made the streets resound with the clang of iron and the hiss of steam. Fourthly, new estates were built to house not only hundreds of workers employed by the railway but also carters, coal merchants and other tradesmen. Finally, large houses in the district were vacated by their former occupants, some being converted into shops, offices and boarding houses, others falling into disrepair.

Powerful landowners sought parliamentary protection for their property. The London and Birmingham Railway Act of 1833 contained several clauses safeguarding the interests of Eton College, stipulating that the railway was to be buried in a tunnel under the estate, that air shafts were to be sited conveniently, that bridges, fences, drains were to be made good, that material dug from the cuttings was to be removed, and that tunnel entrances were to be furnished with 'substantial and ornamental facings to the satisfaction of the Provost and Fellows.'[46] Buddon's castellated arches erected to these requirements were fitting monuments both to the College and to the railway company, but the digging of the three-quarter mile (1·1 km.) tunnel through London Clay cost many lives, 'scarcely a day passing without one or more of those poor fellows being borne from the Chalk Farm Tunnel for an inquest and speedy interment.'[47] By 1836 the contractors had charged £34,151 in excess of their estimate to provide additional support to strengthen the two tunnels.

In 1835, in order to build a passenger station close to the New Road at Euston, the railway obtained powers to extend its line south of the Camden Town depot, vaulting across the Regent's Canal and down a steep incline cut through newly-built streets. The scene of work in 1836 is faithfully described by Charles Dickens in his account of Stagg's Garden in *Dombey and Son*:
'The first shock of a great earthquake had, just at that period, rent

the whole neighbourhood to its centre. Traces of its course were visible on every side. Houses were knocked down; streets broken through and stopped; deep pits and trenches dug in the ground; enormous heaps of earth and clay thrown up; buildings that were undermined and shaking, propped by great beams of wood. Here, a chaos of carts, overthrown and jumbled together, lay topsy-turvy at the bottom of a steep unnatural hill; there, confused treasures of iron soaked and rusted in something that had accidentally become a pond. Everywhere were bridges that led nowhere; thoroughfares that were wholly impassable; Babel towers of chimneys, wanting half their height; temporary wooden houses and enclosures, in the most unlikely situations; carcases of ragged tenements, and fragments of unfinished walls and arches, and piles of scaffolding, and wildernesses of bricks, and giant forms of cranes and tripods straddling above nothing.'[48]

Dickens observes in detail the first changes taking place in a neighbourhood 'as yet too shy to own the Railroad':

'One or two bold speculators had projected streets; and one had built a little, but had stopped among the mud and ashes to consider farther of it. A brand-new Tavern, redolent of fresh mortar and size, and fronting nothing at all, had taken for its sign The Railway Arms; but that might be rash enterprise—and then it hoped to sell drink to the workmen. So, the Excavators' House of Call had sprung up from a beer-shop; and the old-established Ham and Beef Shop had become the Railway Eating House, with a roast leg of pork daily, through interested motives of a similar immediate and popular description. Lodging-house keepers were favourable in like manner; and for the like reasons were not to be trusted. The general belief was very slow. There were frowzy fields, and cow houses, and dunghills, and dustheaps, and ditches, and gardens, and summerhouses, and carpet-beating grounds, at the very door of the Railway. Little tumuli of oyster shells in the oyster season, and of lobster shells in the lobster season, and of broken crockery and faded cabbage leaves in all seasons, encroached upon its high places. Posts, and rails, and old cautions to trespassers, and backs of mean houses, and patches of wretched vegetation, stared it out of countenance. Nothing was better for it, or thought of being so.'

Some strove to make the best of their new situation. A tavern which had formerly enjoyed uninterrupted views towards Primrose Hill, now offered its customers an unrivalled view of the giant chimneys of the engine house and of the cable drawing trains up the Camden bank.

The changes in Camden Town, great as they were, were followed in the 1840s by yet more sweeping changes. When the excavators had finished 'there was no such place as Stagg's Gardens. It had vanished from the earth. Where the old rotten summerhouses once had stood, palaces now reared their heads, and granite columns of gigantic girth opened a vista to the railway world beyond. The miserable waste ground, where the refuse-matter had been heaped of yore, was swallowed up and gone; and in its frowzy stead were tiers of warehouses, crammed with rich goods and costly merchandise.' And behind the warehouses stood new factories: a soap factory on the site of the old workhouse in Camden Town, a steam gun factory in Albany Street and a cotton mill to the west of Hampstead Road. Along the banks of the Regent's Canal between acres of timber yards and coal wharves rose the works of the Imperial Gas Company.

Between the canal and the railway new streets and new houses struck out into the country at steam's own speed. The Duke of Bedford leased the ground for the building of two squares which were to form the centres of Bedford New Town, north of Euston station, and vacant plots in Camden Town were eagerly snapped up for the building of offices, boarding houses, and new public houses. At the same time, on the Brewers' estate, Goldington Crescent was laid out and neighbouring streets built by a local builder. Adjoining the Regent's Canal a small estate leased by the Church Commissioners to a shrewd lawyer, William Agar, was ripe for development. Agar had built for himself a small residence, Elm Lodge, and planted mulberry trees in his park on the northern side of the property, the rest being farmed by dairymen and market gardeners. In 1841 the greater part of the estate was parcelled into building plots and let for terms of 21 years. Hovels and tenements were run up by journeymen bricklayers and carpenters working on Sundays and in other spare time. No provision was made for drainage or water supply and many of the houses were occupied before they were finished. In 1851 Dickens described Agar Town as an English Suburban Connemara:

'Along the canal side the huts of the settlers, of many shapes and sizes, were closely ranged, every tenant having his own lease of the ground. There were the dog-kennel, the cow shed, the shanty, and the elongated match-box styles of architecture. To another, the ingenious residence of Robinson Crusoe seemed to have given his idea.

Through an opening was to be seen another layer of dwellings at the back: one looking like a dismantled windmill, and another perched upon a wall, like a guard's lookout on the top of a railway carriage. Every garden had its nuisance—so far the inhabitants were agreed—but every nuisance was of a distinct and peculiar character. In the one was a dung-heap, in the next a cinder-heap, in a third which belonged to the cottage of a costermonger, was a pile of whelk and periwinkle shells, some rotten cabbages, and a donkey; and the garden of another exhibiting a board inscribed with the words "Ladies' School", had become a pond of thick green water.'[49]

Not only Agar Town but parts of Somers Town were slums from the day they were first occupied. In *Nicholas Nickleby* Dickens takes Squeers and the captive Smirke on a cab journey to lodgings in Somers Town, through 'several mean streets, which the appearance of the houses and the bad state of the road denoted to have been recently built.'[50]

From the new hovels the scourge of dirt and dinginess spread to older buildings in the district. The Polygon in Clarendon Square fell into disrepair, rents remained unpaid, garbage was thrown in the streets, area railings were pulled down, and water butts broken. As the old inhabitants left, washerwomen, dustmen and Bow Street runners moved in. By 1850 Dickens noted that 'whole families of sweeps were regularly born of sweeps in the rural districts of Somers Town and Camden Town.'[51] A street near the Veterinary College 'all built on one monotonous pattern, like the early copies of a blundering boy who was learning to make houses' was 'principally tenanted by gentlemen students who bought live donkeys and made experiments on them in their apartments.' In this street Tommy Traddles had lodgings in a house bearing 'an indescribable character of faded gentility.'[52] But the majority of houses in Camden Town and Somers Town were occupied by the early clerk population who might be seen any morning 'pouring into the City, or directing their steps towards Chancery Lane and the Inns of Court. Middle-aged men, whose salaries have by no means increased in the same proportion as their families, plod steadily along, apparently with no object in view but the counting house.'[53] Among that throng of clerks, Bob Cratchit might have been seen hurrying to reach Scrooge's office before nine o'clock.

The coming of the London and Birmingham Railway had far-reaching consequences for north-west London, but largely failed to achieve the objectives set by its promoters. While receipts from passenger traffic were greater than had been expected, income from goods traffic was much below expectation. Manufacturers complained that Camden Town was too remote and inaccessible to serve as a terminal depot: 'the Port of London is scarcely available to them owing to the difficulty and expense of transit to and from the railway station.'[54] In 1846 a new line was proposed to link Camden Town with the quays and warehouses of the East and West India Docks. This would have the effect of reducing transfer costs on freight traffic by at least 50 per cent, and would increase the volume of passenger traffic by enabling 'parties from a distance to proceed direct to the place of embarkation for foreign steamers.' The proposed line was drawn through Islington, Hackney and Bow to 'avoid all expensive house property' and to minimize engineering difficulties. In 1846, after long and costly parliamentary proceedings, an Act was passed authorizing the construction of the East and West India Docks and Birmingham Junction Railway. In 1847 work had hardly begun when it was interrupted by a financial crisis, and again in 1848 it was delayed by 'numerous difficulties attending the purchase of property.'[55] In 1849 the engineers decided to review the plans 'to entrench as little as possible on the more valuable property,' and 'to reduce the portion taken to the smallest quantity consistent with the proper construction of the works.' A total sum of over £569,000 was paid for land and compensation and over 100 rights of way crossed by the line had to be restored or purchased. In November 1849, when three-quarters of the track was laid, seven arches of a great viaduct spanning the Fleet valley at Camden Town collapsed 'owing to the peculiar character of the London Clay.' The viaduct was quickly rebuilt, but in 1850 work in Camden Town was halted again because of 'the difficulty of obtaining some house property lying in the centre of the line.' In August it was reported that 'this obstacle having now been nearly removed, the works will be resumed.' The final link with the main line at Chalk Farm was made on 9th June, 1851 and the line was opened for traffic. The *Illustrated London News* described the journey through the green fields of Bow into the meadowlands of Hackney with extensive views over the marshes towards the well-wooded heights of Epping. 'Passing onwards through the verdant fields we came to the retired village of Homerton,' finally, 'after passing several beautiful villas, we arrived at Camden Town, where the railway is constructed on a brick viaduct of good proportions.'[56]

The first two years of operating disappointed the hopes of those who had promoted the line. The cost of land had been grossly underestimated and engineering difficulties had been greater than anticipated. When the line was opened earnings from goods traffic proved derisorily small, from coal traffic negligible until 1852, when a contract worth £5,000 was signed, but receipts from passenger traffic were encouraging. Week by week the number of passengers increased, and passenger fares soon amounted to ten times the revenue from goods traffic. In August 1852 the directors reported: 'Adjoining the railway in every district land is rapidly being covered with houses, affording proof that the facilities offered by the railway attract population to its neighbourhood and that the large amount to which the passenger traffic has risen, at the stations already opened, will yet be considerably increased.'[57] But building at this time was fitful and haphazard, carried out by small businesses on small parcels of land. North of the Regent's Canal compact blocks of narrow streets of mean houses crowded as far as Prince of Wales Road; north-east of Camden Road station Camden New Town was laid out in cramped squares and gaunt terraces; yet further north Ebenezer Maitland built a new orphanage in 1847, and by 1855 Maitland Park had grown to a small community of villas, schools and humble Tudor almshouses.

In 1853 the directors of the E. & W. I. D. & B. J. R. sent a circular letter to shareholders announcing their intention to adopt the name of the North London Railway, and vigorously to expand passenger services. To explain the change of policy it was stated: 'When the railway was first projected it was not expected that the passenger traffic would form so important a portion of the company's business, consequently no provision was made in the original capital for the purchase of the plant required for this description of traffic.'[58] Under its new, more appropriate name, the company entered into arrangements with the parent main line company, now called the London and North Western Railway, and with the newly opened North and South Western Junction Railway to extend passenger services from Fenchurch Street to Bow, Camden Town, West London Junction at Willesden and on to Kew Junction to connect with the Windsor line. From August 1853 the North London ran the first suburban passenger service in north-west London, proudly declaring: 'There can be little doubt that much new traffic will result from this communication as it will afford easy access from the City and all northern suburbs of London to Kew Gardens and other points of attraction.'[59] The introduction of the new service caused severe congestion on the main line between Chalk Farm and Willesden, and before the end of 1853 a fresh application was made for a relief line, the Hampstead Junction Railway, to carry suburban traffic by way of Kentish Town, Gospel Oak, Hampstead Heath, Finchley Road, Edgware Road, Harlesden and on to Old Oak Common. In 1860, when this link was completed, more than half the Outer Circle had been formed. Around the new stations fresh clusters of buildings arose. In 1858, on a few acres of meadows and watercress beds, the foundations of Lismore Circus and the short streets radiating to Gospel Oak Village were laid. In 1856, on meadows adjoining Picketts Farm, the first Italianate villas of South Hill Park were built; and in South End new rows of shops were opened. With the infilling of St John's Park between Haverstock Hill and South End, Hampstead lost its separate identity as a village surrounded by open country. It was tenuously joined to London.

Meanwhile yet deeper gashes were being struck at the vicinity of Maiden Lane. In 1844 the Great Northern Railway issued its prodigious prospectus to lay 328 miles (525 km.) of track between York and London on a ruling gradient of 1 in 200, to dig eight tunnels on the southern section of the line, including one through the Northern Heights and another burrowing under the Regent's Canal, and to build a terminus on the New Road at King's Cross. The proposal raised a storm of protest from rival companies and from property owners who fought it tenaciously for two parliamentary sessions. The battle cost the company £423,620 in legal fees, but the opposition comforted themselves with a forecast that the project would 'stick fast in the treacherous London Clay.' In fact, the work was carried through with commendable speed by Thomas Brassey and an army of 5,000 or 6,000 men. By August 1849 three-quarters of the line was constructed and excavators were emerging from the Copenhagen Tunnel, when the North London viaduct collapsed in their path. In 1850 the first train left London from a temporary depot in Maiden Lane, and during the next two years the engineers pushed southward under the Regent's Canal to a 45-acre (18 ha.) site from which the old smallpox hospital and hundreds of houses had been removed. The building of the station with stables for 300 horses and vast coal stores was completed at a cost of £123,000. In October 1852 King's Cross was opened for public traffic, but the Great Northern appeared to have learned nothing from the experience of the London and North Western. The directors saw no reason why they should provide regular services for a district occupied only by the 'mansions, villas and gardens of the aristocracy and merchant princes.'[60] Their trains served only four stations within fifteen miles (24 km.) of the terminus, at Hornsey, Southgate, Barnet and Potters Bar.

A prospect of suburban traffic was offered to the Great Northern from an entirely different quarter. It followed lengthy discussions on possible means of reducing the burden of horse-drawn traffic in the New Road, now a crowded city thoroughfare. The construction of a new surface railway in a densely built-up area was impracticable. The cost of land and compensation would have been prohibitive. It was suggested it might be cheaper to build a railway above the house tops, on the model of the London and Greenwich Railway, or, alternatively, to drain the Regent's Canal and lay a track on its bed. The most imaginative idea, put forward by Charles Pearson, the City Solicitor, was to construct an underground railway beneath the New Road. The scheme could not hope to succeed without making connections with and drawing traffic from main-line railway companies, and Pearson sought the backing of the Great Northern and Great Western Railway companies. In 1853 the Great Western Railway promised £175,000 and the Corporation of the City of London offered £200,000 on harsh terms. The City also made available a site for the terminus on an open space vacated by the old city cattle market. With an assurance of financial support the Metropolitan Railway Company began the difficult task of cutting open the New Road to lay London's first underground railway. Costs of construction, excavating, building retaining walls and arches to bear the weight of a roadway overhead were nowhere less than £39 and on difficult sections as much as £108 per linear yard.[61] In 1862 the line was nearly complete when the Fleet Sewer burst and flooded the tunnel to a depth of ten feet (3 m.). From the safe distance of Riceyman Steps Arnold Bennett recalls the scene of horror:

'The earth quaked. The terrific scaffolding and beams were flung like firewood into the air and fell with awful crashes. The populace screamed at the thought of workmen entombed and massacred. A silence! Then the great brick piers, fifty feet in height, moved bodily. The whole bottom of the excavation moved in one mass. A dark and fetid liquid appeared, oozing, rolling, surging, smashing everything in its restless track, and rushed into the mouth of the new tunnel.

The crown of the arch of the mighty Fleet Sewer had broken. Men wept at the enormity and completeness of the disaster.'[62] But the damage was repaired and in January 1863 the opening of the line was celebrated with joyful festivities. By August relations with the Great Western were strained to breaking point, the partnership was hastily dissolved and the company faced the threat of running the railway with no trains of its own. The Great Northern generously provided locomotives and rolling stock, while the Metropolitan ordered stock designed specially for continuous working in tunnels. At the end of the year the tunnels were encrusted with soot and protests against the smoke reached alarming proportions. Recognizing the danger of exposing clean-shaven skins to the sulphurous atmosphere, the company granted permission to its staff to grow beards and moustaches. But traffic multiplied and the line prospered.

References

1. J. P. Malcolm, *Londinium Redivivum*, 1 (1803), 5.
2. John White, *Some Account of the Proposed Improvement of the Western Part of London* (1815), 98.
3. John Summerson, *Georgian London*, revised (1962), 164.
4. Malcolm, *op. cit.*, 4 (1807), 350.
5. John Nash, 'Report of Mr. John Nash, architect in the Department of Woods; with plans for the improvement of Mary-le-Bone Park,' White, *op. cit.*, Appendix III, xxvii.
6. Malcolm, *op. cit.*, Vol. 4, 352.
7. Luke Heslop, 'Resolution of the Vestry of the parish of St Mary-le-bone, 26th March 1811', White, *op. cit.*, Appendix V, lxxvi.
8. John Middleton, *View of the Agriculture of Middlesex* (1807), 612.
9. Henry Hunter, *The History of London and its Environs*, 2 (1811), 2, cited in G. B. G. Bull, 'Thomas Milne's land utilization map of the London area in 1800', *Geographical Journal*, 122 (1956), 25–30.
10. William Hone, *Year Book* (1826); Frederick Miller, *Saint Pancras Past and Present* (1874), 52.
11. Middleton, *op. cit.*, 287.
12. Hunter, *op. cit.*, Vol. 2, 3.
13. Middleton, *op. cit.*, 287; also 580, 668.
14. Hunter, *op. cit.*, Vol. 2, 75.
15. Walter E. Brown, *The St. Pancras Book of Dates* (1908), 10, 12; Miller, *op. cit.*, 63–4.
16. Malcolm, *op. cit.*, Vol. 1, 8.
17. *Ibid.*, 12.
18. William Howitt, *The Northern Heights of London* (1869), 412.

19. Middleton, *op. cit.*, 521.
20. See Howitt, *op. cit.*, 411.
21. J. J. Park, *The Topography and Natural History of Hampstead*, with additions and corrections (1818), 135.
22. J. E. B. Gover, Allen Mawer, F. M. Stenton, S. J. Madge, *The Place-Names of Middlesex*, English Place-Name Society, 18 (1942).
23. Hunter, *op. cit.*, Vol. 2, 85, 86.
24. Josiah Tucker, *Four Letters on Important National Subjects* (1773), 45, cited in H. J. Dyos, *Victorian Suburb* (1961), 49.
25. Thomas Pennant, *Some Account of London*, 5th edition (1813), 170, 243.
26. William Cobbett, *Rural Rides*, 1 (1912), 43.
27. Nash, *loc. cit.*, xiii.
28. White, *op. cit.*, 24.
29. Nash, *loc. cit.*, xxvi–xxvii.
30. White, *op. cit.*, 2.
31. T. Leverton and T. Chawner, 'Report of Messrs Leverton and Chawner, architects in the Department of Land Revenue; with plans for the improvement of Mary-le-Bone Park, 4th July 1811', White, *op. cit.*, Appendix II, v.
32. Nash, *loc. cit.*, xxxi.
33. *Ibid.*, xlix.
34. *Ibid.*, xxvii.
35. *Ibid.*, xxxvi–xxxvii.
36. *Ibid.*, xlviii.
37. Leverton and Chawner, *loc. cit.*, vii.
38. Nash, *loc. cit.*, xxxvii.
39. White, *op. cit.*, 80.
40. Leigh Hunt, *A Saunter through the West End* (1861), 75.
41. Summerson, *op. cit.*, 175–6.
42. Elizabeth Bowen, cited in Nikolaus Pevsner, *The Buildings of England: London except the Cities of London and Westminster* (1952), 354.
43. John Summerson, 'The growth of an early Victorian London Suburb,' Lectures delivered at London School of Economics, 20th–27th February 1958.
44. Cobbett, *op. cit.*, Vol. 1, 84.
45. Leigh Hunt, *Description of Hampstead*, (1818).
46. 3 William IV, Cap. 36, Sections 103–11.
47. Miller, *op. cit.*, ix.
48. Charles Dickens, *Dombey and Son*, Chapter 6.
49. Idem, *Household Words* (1851).
50. Idem, *Nicholas Nickleby*, Chapter 38.
51. Idem, *Sketches by Boz*, scene 20.
52. Idem, *David Copperfield*, Chapter 27.
53. Idem, *Sketches by Boz*, scene 1.
54. East and West India Docks and Birmingham Junction Railway, *Prospectus* (1846), 1.
55. Idem, *Directors' Report* (24th August 1848), 3.

56. *Illustrated London News* (15th November 1851), cited in R. M. Robbins, *The North London Railway* (1938), 11.

57. East and West India Docks and Birmingham Junction Railway, *Directors' Report* (27th August 1852), 12.

58. Idem, *Circular Letter from the Directors* (17th June 1853), 1.

59. North London Railway, *Directors' Report* (5th August 1853).

60. Charles H. Grinling, *The History of the Great Northern Railway 1845–1895* (1898), 126.

61. C. Baker, *The Metropolitan Railway* (1951), 1–2.

62. Arnold Bennett, *Riceyman Steps* (1923), Chapter 3, 12.

5

North-west London 1864–1914

*

HUGH C. PRINCE

During the fifty years from 1814 to 1864 great changes took place in north-west London. Had the writer of 1815, who observed the limit of building at the edge of the Taplow terrace and declared, 'Thus far shall the town extend, but no farther,' returned in 1864, he would have seen not only the whole of the gravel terrace but much of the London Clay tract occupied by buildings. The new houses and the land adjoining them were a little cleaner and tidier than those of 1814. London's rubbish was no longer tipped on empty spaces at the end of the last street and the old dumping grounds between King's Cross and Tottenham Court had been cleared for building. 'They drive us out,' complained a refuse collector in 1844, '. . . they say they do not like our men, and they do not like our carts; we are not very pleasant sort of people.'[1] Household rubbish was now taken long distances by cart and by barge, while valuable stable manure was carried to distant market gardens by rail. New houses in St John's Wood and Gospel Oak were less crowded than those in Somers Town or Tottenham Court. Their cesspools and privies, set in moderate-sized gardens, were less offensive than those in confined courts and alleys in older districts, but occupants of some old houses in Marylebone had benefited from the provision of indoor piped water and new drains. Another improvement was that building sites on the London Clay were not scarred with pits and kilns, the subsoil yielding neither gravel nor brickearth. Roofs were now covered with Penrhyn slates. Peterhead granite, Italian marble, Birmingham brassware, iron railings, iron

120

beams, deal planks and joists were imported by canal and by railway. The distinctive character of the new suburbs, François Guizot observed: 'the extreme neatness of the houses, the wide footpaths, the effect of the large panes of glass, of the iron balustrades, and of the knockers on the door, impart to the city an air of careful attention and an attractive appearance, which almost counterbalance the absence of good taste'.[2]

The sharp frontier of the built-up area had disappeared. Strings of villas, stables and inns lined both sides of the Edgware Road as far as Kilburn and straggled loosely towards Cricklewood. A ribbon of building followed the line of Archway Road to Highgate, and small groups of houses, set in spacious grounds, were dotted along Finchley Road. St John's Wood and Portland Town formed a continuous built-up salient as far as Boundary Road. It was flanked by the open space of Primrose Hill, beyond which buildings occupied outlying patches in Adelaide Road, Maitland Park, St John's Wood Park, South End and Gospel Oak. Camden Town was densely built as far as the Regent's Canal, but between there and Kentish Town the streets were punctuated with vacant sites. Since the coming of the railway no large-scale development had taken place. Building had been carried out on small estates or on small portions of large estates. Rows of houses, shops and Railway Taverns clustered at the approaches to railway stations, and shoddy models of park villages were erected within easy walking distance. Viewed on a map, the built-up area of north-west London was blotchy and formless (Fig. 22).

The most striking contrast between north-west London in 1814 and 1864 was not the blurring of the distinction between built-up areas and open country but the deepening social gulf between affluent residential areas in Marylebone and poor districts in St Pancras. The divisions of 1814 were turned on their sides. The former boundary between built-up terrace gravels and London Clay meadowlands followed an east–west line along the New Road. The new social divide followed a north–south line along the railway line from Chalk Farm to Euston, continuing south of the New Road along the boundary between the Portland and Southampton estates.

In Marylebone fashionable squares and places echoed to the rattle of hundreds of private carriages, main streets were furnished with elegant shops, great houses kept armies of domestic servants and its

880 yards
800 metres

FIG. 22   North-west London 1864
The stippled areas are open spaces.
Based on Post Office Directory, London, 1864; E. Stanford, Library Map
of London and its Suburbs, 1862.

spacious park was a playground for well-dressed children in the care of governesses. The noise and grime of its only railway, the Metropolitan, were trapped under the ground. Its ragged quarters were hidden in a maze of close streets behind Lisson Grove, where colonies of thieves, prostitutes, costermongers, threepenny lodging houses for Irish labourers, dingy brokers' shops and a turkish bath huddled alongside common mews let out to cabmen.[3] In Huntsworth Mews, north of Dorset Square, two rows of neglected livery stables harboured over a hundred families in dismal obscurity. South of the New Road little had changed since 1814, while north and west of Regent's Park, the gardens of St John's Wood were now shaded with tall trees and shrubs. Hedges, lawns and the ivy on the walls of its well-kept villas were neatly trimmed. It was a quiet and pleasant neighbourhood.

In St Pancras a whole generation had been born and grown to adulthood amid the sights and sounds of railway construction. Since 1835 no year had passed without some street being demolished, some tunnel excavated, some viaduct built, some fresh invasion of navvies. The raw brickwork of new cuttings and the abiding scars of poverty were too deep and too numerous to be concealed. The new railway stations were fronted by London's earliest and most glittering gin palaces. Camden High Street was a busy shopping centre, crowded with omnibuses and wagons, enlivened by the bustle of its street vendors, refurnished with large public houses and the Bedford Music Hall opened in 1861. Behind the High Street stretched miles of drab houses, each accommodating two or more families, or a family with lodgers. The most respected personalities in the district were devoted ministers, such as David Laing, who preached in temporary iron chapels. Two other native celebrities were Tom Sayer, the boxer, and Dan Leno, the champion clog dancer and comedian, who was born in 1861 in a frightful slum in Eve Court. In Somers Town a number of marine store dealers, china shops, secondhand clothiers, and cheap haberdashers traded precariously on the credit they could obtain from a community of hard-working railwaymen, mechanics, coal heavers and sailors' wives. In Agar Town was to be found 'the lowest effort of building skill in or near London,' 'a collection of the very lowest order of labourers' cottages,' whose condition was still deteriorating.[4] The worst hovels on the bank of the Regent's Canal offered shelter to a derelict population of aged and infirm. The larger premises were occupied by dustmen, woodcutters, costermongers and street hawkers. The whole district was overrun by rats, dogs, donkeys and chickens. In 1849 it was stricken with cholera.

Efforts were made to improve the sanitation of the area. In 1847 the first public baths and washhouses in St Pancras were opened at Tolmers Square and during the first year over 113,000 bathers availed themselves of the facilities.[5] At the same time in Pancras Road the first hideous stronghold erected by the Improved Industrial Dwellings Company provided flats for 110 working-class families. The venture succeeded in yielding a small profit and the death rate among its tenants was lower than among the population in neighbouring streets, but it did nothing to alleviate the distress in Somers Town and Agar Town. The rents were beyond the means of any but industrious artisans. By 1864 the blight of Somers Town had spread to the south of Euston Road. James Burton's terraces in Cartwright Gardens had been converted into cheap lodging houses for students, clerks and warehousemen, the mews behind providing stables for cabmen. To the north, the coming of the railway had begun to disfigure Kentish Town. The stucco fronts of Regency houses were cracked and peeling, and on Saturday nights the High Street resounded with the voices of Irishmen and Northerners as the public houses disgorged their customers.

Of the regions identified in 1814, the Northern Heights alone preserved their distinctiveness fifty years later, to be described in 1869 in William Howitt's *The Northern Heights of London*. Hampstead owed its special character to 'rows of trees, either lime or elm trees, planted along the broad footpaths in boulevard style . . . and its old narrow roads winding under tall trees are continually conducting to fresh and secluded places, that seem hidden from the world, and would lead you to suppose yourselves far away from London.'[6] Highgate also remained 'beautiful for its situation, and fragrant with its memories of the past.'[7] Artists still found peace in its secluded groves. Sir George Gilbert Scott, the architect, Clarkson Stanfield, the painter, John Drinkwater, the playwright and Coventry Patmore, poet and critic, lived here. But the Heights had ceased to be a refuge from the City. 'Its easy approach at all times from the city,' wrote Howitt, 'made it at once the resort and the abode of a great number and a great variety of those who lived and worked there.'[8] The influx of bankers, merchants and other 'affluent frequenters of the metropolis' was increasing, and from the lower slopes of the heights stations at Kentish Town, Gospel Oak, Hampstead

Heath, Finchley Road and Edgware Road were attracting increasing numbers of clerks and shop assistants. Buses of the newly formed London General Omnibus Company also served South Hampstead, Swiss Cottage and Kilburn.[9] Open spaces on the outskirts of the metropolis were increasingly sought by orphanages, schools, almshouses and cemeteries. In the 1840s the Northern Heights suffered their first serious outbreaks of metropolitan epidemics of scarlet fever, cholera and smallpox. In 1850 the Smallpox and Vaccination Hospital, removed from the site of King's Cross Station, occupied a large building on Highgate Hill and in 1869 the North-Western Fever Hospital came to Lawn Road Hampstead. In 1857 Hampstead began to reform its sanitation by clearing cesspools, closing private wells and laying new sewers and drains. By 1864 the standard of hygiene and public services compared favourably with those of any district in the metropolis. The district had piped water, a fire brigade, a police force and paved streets illuminated by over 2,000 gas lights. But large tracts of land remained in farms in addition to the heaths and woodlands crowning the Heights.

A Railway Network and Late Victorian Suburbs 1864-1913

The changes that took place in north-west London at the end of the nineteenth century are intimately connected with the development of its suburban railway network. During the first half of Queen Victoria's reign railways entering the area were, for the most part, alien and unwelcome intruders, fiercely competing among themselves to convey Birmingham wares and Yorkshire coal to London's docks and gasworks. They were reluctant to provide services for suburban passengers, nor were they adequately equipped to do so. The first line to reach the City, the East and West India Docks and Birmingham Junction Railway, was not designed to carry local passengers. It was hardly expected that the circuitous journey from Chalk Farm to the City by way of Hackney and Bow would be quicker and more pleasant than by bus. Several years elapsed before the company decided to change its name and devote its main energies to attracting the type of traffic that paid it best. By 1853 the North London was making determined efforts to forge a coherent system out of the scattered lines of hostile companies. The completion of a network stimulated the expansion of building between Kentish Town and Hampstead. At the end of the century the completion of the Inner

Circle and the extension of the Metropolitan Railway towards the Chilterns coincided with a similar expansion between Swiss Cottage and Kilburn. Beyond Hampstead the arrival of the tube in 1907 was followed by the rapid development of Golders Green. In the half century before the First World War the spread of building in north-west London is closely associated with the formation of a network of suburban passenger railways providing regular services to the City. It was almost entirely unrelated to the opening of new main lines terminating in St Pancras and Marylebone.

Each new railway thrust into the sprawling built-up area was inevitably more difficult and more costly to construct than its pre-decessors. On the other hand, a large railway company could not afford to be without a London terminus. It could not for long with-stand the competition of its better-situated rivals, nor could it find allies to forward its London traffic without delay. In 1862 the Mid-land Railway's valuable coal traffic was brought to a standstill for weeks at a time by the London and North Western at Rugby and by the Great Northern at Hitchin; the survival of the company, operat-ing 500 miles (800 km.) of track in the coalmining areas of the Mid-lands, was dependent on securing an extension from Bedford to London. The scheme was certain to cause a great upheaval not only in St Pancras but also in Hampstead.

The Act of 1863 contained 87 clauses protecting the interests of Hampstead and St Pancras property owners, those relating to the Belsize estate being particularly onerous, requiring the company not to deviate more than ten yards (9 m.) from the line on the deposited plan, nor to encroach upon Belsize Avenue, nor, in constructing the Belsize Tunnel, to sink any shaft, to erect any workshop, to use any engine or machine, to dig or deposit any bricks, ballast or other materials within a distance of 100 yards (91 m.) from Belsize House. Other clauses provided for the diversion and alteration of Kentish Town Road, Camden Road, Old St Pancras Road, for the raising of Finchley Road eight feet (2·4 m.) above its former level at the western entrance to Belsize Tunnel, for the building of a dozen new bridges, for the reconstruction of scores of sewers, water mains and gas pipes, for the removal, under the supervision of the Bishop of London, of bodies from the burial ground of old St Pancras church, for the rebuilding of St Luke's church in St Pancras, for the preserva-tion of the houses and gardens in Camden Square, where the railway was to be enclosed in a tunnel without ventilation shafts and the plantations restored within six months.[10] These were harsh restrictions but the company faced more serious difficulties.

Before work could begin thousands of houses and hundreds of acres of land had to be purchased. In 1864 the line was staked out, much of Agar Town was acquired and the work of demolition commenced.

'The Midland came; and when it came wrought a mighty revolution. For its passenger station alone it swept away seven streets of three thousand houses and a church; old St. Pancras churchyard was invaded; and Agar Town was almost demolished. Yet those who knew the district at that time have no regret at the change. Time was when here the wealthy owner of a large estate lived in his mansion; but after his departure the place became a very "abomination of desolation." In its centre was what was named La Belle Isle, a dreary and unsavoury locality, abandoned to mountains of refuse from the metropolitan dustbins, strewn with decaying vegetables and foul-smelling fragments of what had once been fish, or occupied by knackers' yards and manure making, bone boiling and soap manufacturing works, and smoke belching potteries and brick kilns. At the broken windows and doors of mutilated houses canaries still sang and dogs still lay sleeping in the sun to remind one of the vast colonies of bird and dog fanciers who formerly made Agar Town their abode; and from these dwellings wretched creatures came, in rags and dirt, and searched amid the far-extending refuse for the filthy treasure by the aid of which they eked out a miserable livelihood; while over the neighbourhood the gasworks poured their mephitic vapours and the canal gave forth its rheumatic dampness, extracting in return some of the more poisonous ingredients from the atmosphere, and spreading them upon the surface of the water in a thick scum of various and ominous hues. Such was Agar Town before the Midland came.'[11]

The railway paid dearly for the satisfaction of demolishing it. In 1867 the shareholders were told that the original estimates had been greatly exceeded and that an additional £2,150,000 would be called for. 'It has, in fact, been found that the value of property required and the amount of compensations have been enormously in excess of what was anticipated, and it would seem that the cost of carrying the works of a railway into London is such as to defy all previous calculation.'[12] By 1869 the company had added further to its burdens, by laying four lines instead of three and by purchasing 470 acres (190 ha.) of land instead of 209 acres (85 ha.) originally proposed.

The construction of the line within areas already built-up presented special difficulties for the engineers. Sites had to be found to receive thousands of tons of subsoil excavated from cuttings and tunnels. The brickearth was used for making millions of bricks, but London Clay was too hard for this purpose. Some of the unwanted spoil was carted across London to pile on the Thames embankment, some was dumped on the site of the goods depot between Kentish Town Road and the Hampstead Junction Railway, and some was removed to the Brent valley. Workshops extended from Gospel Oak Fields to Bartram Park on the slopes of Haverstock Hill. Ritson, the contractor for the approach to St Pancras, excavated over 200,000 cubic yards (150,000 cu. m.) of earth, relaid the Fleet Sewer, sank concrete caissons 50 feet (15 m.) into the clay and built the massive arches to carry St Pancras station 17 feet (5·2 m.) above the level of Euston Road. In 1866, following a public outcry, work was stopped until Parliament was satisfied that the bones from St Pancras churchyard were properly removed and reburied. Firbank's contract to build Belsize Tunnel was also the subject of complaints but work was not halted. Two Hampstead clergymen raised subscriptions to put up a temporary church and school room for the navvies and their families. Through Gospel Oak Firbank dug a deep cutting, encased with thick retaining walls, buttressed overhead with iron girders to hold 'the inordinate pressure of the London Clay.'[13] The contractors' yard at Gospel Oak was described by Frederick Williams as 'quite a little town in itself, with offices, dwellings, workshops, stables, etc. About 150 men are employed in or near the yard, and it is the home of above 100 horses. Mr. Firbank has about 1,300 men employed upon his length and many portions of the work are prosecuted night and day without intermission. The tunnel is about a mile and a quarter (2 km.) in length and in many parts above 100 feet (30 m.) deep.'[14] The tunnel was lined with eight layers of brickwork using 30,000,000 bricks and another 60,000,000 bricks were laid in St Pancras station. The line was opened in 1868 and orders were then given that 'the hotel should be carried to the necessary height and finished in a permanent manner, and that those portions that were originally intended for the company's offices be added to the hotel.'[15]

A warehouse was provided for Bass's Burton Ale and 3¼ acres (1·3 ha.) of land were laid out as coal yards. Beneath the station spacious cellars were made ready to receive fish, potatoes and milk, and 50 shops were built into the frontage on Euston Road. Above the station rose London's largest railway hotel, culminating in the great clocktower and the spires and pinnacles of Sir George Gilbert Scott's design.

Some of the families displaced by the railway crowded into the already congested houses in Somers Town. Some moved into new five-storey industrial dwellings, some moved to Kentish Town and Tufnell Park, and a few went further afield. Near the summit of the Northern Heights Baroness Burdett-Coutts founded Holly Village in 1865. It provided accommodation for her workpeople in Gothic cottages situated around a village green.

The Midland Railway added to the volume of noise and dirt in St Pancras but, apart from the rumble of coal trains to be heard on a still night, it hardly disturbed the peace of Hampstead. It disappeared from sight in the Belsize Tunnel and made a small contribution to the daily movement of passengers from Haverstock Hill and Finchley Road. It had a share in the great expansion of Hampstead between 1861 and 1901, but that expansion was much more closely associated with the improvement of suburban services by the North London Railway and, in particular, with the opening of its City terminus in 1865 (Fig. 33).

The new line from Dalston to Broad Street Station greatly reduced the length of the journey from north-west London to the City, the destination of most Victorian commuters. It also changed the character of the North London Railway from a small conservative business catering only for first- and second-class passengers into a vigorous enterprise carrying a large proportion of the City's daily traffic. Not only had the company to pay over one and a half million pounds for its two miles (3·2 km.) of new line, but under the terms of the Act it was obliged to run parliamentary trains to Dalston, providing early morning services with third-class carriages and workmen's fares. In an attempt to increase its efficiency it collected data on train speeds and stopping times, on the effectiveness of brakes; it tested new methods of working under conditions of fog and frost, installed the first reliable system of interlocking points and introduced gas lights in passenger carriages.[16] A new suburban line from Tottenham to Hampstead, opened in 1868, was not a success, but other joint services operated by the North London with neighbouring companies enabled Hampstead travellers to reach most stations in the London area.[17] During the morning rush hour frequent trains from Mansion House, Richmond, Kew, Kensington and Willesden Low Level stopped at Hampstead on their way to Broad Street. Hundreds of agreements were drafted to regulate running powers, working expenses, tolls, freight charges, the maintenance of stations, points, signals, accident liability, to license hackney cabs plying for hire at stations, to control advertising, to provide special facilities at docks and sidings, to speed the conveyance of milk, livestock and parcels as well as passengers. The North London also provided special trains for a great variety of holiday excursions and public occasions. In the Directors' Memorandum Book, notes on special trains refer, for example, under the letter B, to band concerts, Baldwin's balloon ascents at Alexandra Palace, Barnum's circus at Olympia, Beatrice, Princess, visit to Hatfield, Belgian volunteers, Brass band to Southend, Bursey's concert, Buffalo Bill's first public performance at the American extension.[18] Hampstead Heath received more than 100,000 passengers every Easter Monday, Whit Monday and August Bank Holiday. In 1870 an excursion platform was added to accommodate the bank Holiday crowds.[19]

Between 1870 and 1890 the normal weekday traffic of Hampstead Heath grew faster than its Bank Holiday traffic. In 1870 most of the area between Adelaide Road and Hampstead village lay in green fields, its winding lanes bordered by hedgerows of hawthorn, wild rose and elder. Beyond the Eton College estate little building had taken place since 1850. As early as 1841, Henry Wright, a City banker, sold the 244-acre (99 ha.) Belsize Park estate for development but, apart from the making of a block of roads south of Belsize Avenue, little else was accomplished. Not until 1877 was the first handsome house built in Hampstead Hill Gardens on the opposite side of Rosslyn Hill. The resumption of building on the southern slopes of Hampstead coincided with the mid-Victorian building boom, but there were other reasons why the development of the area was postponed for so long. On the largest estate in Hampstead, the 416 acres (168 ha.) belonging to the Lord of the Manor, no building took place during the lifetime of Sir Thomas Maryon Wilson. He had no money to build on his own account and, because his estate was entailed, he could only grant leases for 21 years or for his own life. As he was also a bachelor there was no heir-apparent to agree to the breaking of the entail, and Parliament refused to make any concession to him because of the opposition of the inhabitants.[20]

In 1869 Sir Thomas died and the estate passed to his brother, Sir John Maryon Wilson. Work now began in earnest. In 1878 Fitzjohn's Avenue was laid out as 'one of the most beautiful avenues in the suburbs of the metropolis'. Towering red brick mansions rose behind the newly planted plane trees and looked out on the spreading suburb through wide bay windows. Between Hampstead Towers in Ellerdale Road, which the architect Norman Shaw built for himself in 1875, and the bottom of Fitzjohn's Avenue ranged the Dutch and 'Jacobethan' residences of City bankers, Lloyds' underwriters, ship-owners, auctioneers, a silk manufacturer, a wine merchant, a public house broker, a chairman of the Brighton line, a director of Hull docks, an Australia merchant, a Master of the Clothworkers Company, an Arctic explorer and an Islamic scholar. At the same time the district became cosmopolitan. A great many Germans, including some wealthy merchants 'of good standing in the City,' settled here, and in 1890 it was reported that 'it is now nothing unusual to hear occasionally, by chance, almost as much if not sometimes more German spoken than English.'[21] Frognal, a well-wooded district, 'somewhat apart from the busy haunts of men,' was shorn of its timber in the 1880s when new large houses were built there. In 1890 F. E. Baines described Arkwright and Prince Arthur Roads, Belsize Park, Canfield, Daleham, Maresfield and Netherhall Gardens as 'the creation of yesterday.'[22] In 1889, excluding a draper's shop and a hotel in Kilburn High Road, 36 houses in Hampstead had rateable values assessed at more than £400. The majority were mansions built after 1870, no less than seventeen were situated in or adjacent to Fitzjohn's Avenue and Frognal, and all except six stood in the Town Ward.

While the North London Railway brought the southern slopes of Hampstead within easy reach of the City, the Great Northern pioneered its Northern Heights branch, the Edgware Highgate and London Railway.[23] Highgate station was opened in 1867 and in 1868 trains were run to Ludgate Hill and in 1869 to Moorgate. The railway attempted to provide a frequent service to the City at peak hours, but its performance was far from perfect. The gradients between Finsbury Park and Highgate were very steep, and congestion on the main line caused many local trains to be delayed. Nevertheless, building spread from Highgate to Muswell Hill in the 1870s.

In 1870 the open heaths and commons lying between Hampstead and Highgate were not yet built on; neither were they preserved as public open spaces. Sir Thomas Maryon Wilson, as Lord of the Manor, claimed the liberty of building on Hampstead Heath and shortly before his death laid the foundations of a house on the summit. His successor, not wishing to contest the claim in the lawcourts, agreed to sell his manorial rights over the heath to the Metropolitan Board of Works for £55,045. In 1871 the Hampstead Heath Act made 240 acres (97 ha.) a public open space. In 1889, 267 acres (108 ha.) of Parliament Hill Fields were sold to the London County Council for £302,000. With the acquisition of the 36-acre (14·5 ha.) Golders Hill Park and the 80-acre (32 ha.) Hampstead Heath Extension at the beginning of the present century, the area of open space was enlarged to 624 acres (252 ha.). In 1889 another generous addition was made to the public open space of the Northern Heights when Sir Sidney Waterlow presented Lauderdale House and 26 acres (10·5 ha.) of parkland to the London County Council.[24]

On the western side of Hampstead the Metropolitan Railway thrust its main line north-west from Baker Street towards the Chilterns. In 1868 St John's Wood Road, Marlborough Road and Swiss Cottage were opened. Swiss Cottage station then stood at the edge of open country and at the opening ceremony 'the whole company spent a few minutes admiring the beautiful country.'[25] In 1879, when the line was extended to Finchley Road, Kilburn and Willesden Green, hundreds of drab houses had begun to cover the area between Finchley Road and Edgware Road. The railway advanced, confident that population would follow. It was a bold pioneering venture.

The Metropolitan offered swift, cheap and direct services to the City and connections with other main-line termini. As the main line pushed north-westward the Inner Circle was completed. Baker Street became a very important junction and took on the functions of a terminus. Blocks of flats, shops and offices sprang up in a district which previously had been occupied only by large private residences. On a site adjoining the station, in fashionable Marylebone Road, Madame Tussaud's Waxworks Exhibition was housed in 1884. In 1911 the railway company moved its head office to the station and built a vast apartment block containing over 1,000 rooms. The main line carried ever-increasing numbers of workers to the City and West End, and in 1905 greatly increased its efficiency and standard of comfort by electrifying the line.[26]

West Hampstead was already filled with houses and shops when the Great Central Railway sought powers to construct a trunk line to a London terminus in Marylebone. This was the last and most costly project of its kind to be completed in London, a fragment of Sir Edward Watkin's grandiose plan to connect Manchester and Paris by means of a direct line running across London and under a Channel tunnel. Although Sir Edward held the chairmanship of the Great Central, the Metropolitan, the South Eastern and sat on the boards of the Great Eastern, the Great Western and the Cheshire Lines, his plan was not completed.[27] A House of Commons Committee appointed to examine the first application for a London extension was embarrassed by the intended site for the terminus and favourably impressed by the weight of argument presented by opposing property owners.[28] In 1893 a fresh proposal received approval on the harshest terms. The Hampstead Vestry were authorized to ensure the restoration of drains, sewers, gas mains, rights of way, to prevent the company depositing subsoil or materials anywhere within the parish, to have the railway built in a tunnel at sufficient depth to enable buildings to be erected 'of a class at least equal' to those removed, or, where the crown of the tunnel was too close to the surface to permit rebuilding, the ground was to be levelled, covered with turf, and not to be used for exhibiting advertisements. A separate clause dealt with the protection of Hampstead's Baths and Washhouses in Finchley Road, providing for the maintenance of water supplies and laundry services during the eight months allowed for demolition and rebuilding. Marylebone was much more extensively disturbed than Hampstead. No less than 30 streets were stopped up and ceased to be public thoroughfares, two entirely new roads had to be built and hundreds of mains services re-laid. Taking the line over the London and North Western's main line and over a busy section of the Regent's Canal presented the engineers with some difficult problems, but none more curious than the task set by the Marylebone Cricket Club who required them to demolish buildings, clear the land, excavate a tunnel, build a covered way to the Metropolitan station at St John's Wood, restore the surface, and 'relay the same with best turf on soil spread to a depth of eighteen inches (0.45 m.) in a manner fit for and adapted to the purposes of the club to the reasonable satisfaction of the engineer of the club.' A penalty of £5 a day was imposed should the company fail to complete the work between September and April. The front of all buildings overlooking the Portman estate had to be 'of a reasonably ornamental character' and the company's coal yard had to be roofed in. The trustees of H. S. Eyre not only obtained £300,000 for land and compensation but also required the company to lay the line in a tunnel under the estate, limit the discharge of smoke and steam, build an eight feet high wall (2·4 m.) beyond the tunnel entrance and 'not to erect any dwellings for the rehousing of persons of the labouring classes upon any part of the St John's Wood estate.'[29] For the families displaced by the demolition of their homes the railway company undertook to build new dwellings and to run workmen's trains as far as Neasden.

The contractors made every effort to complete their tasks as speedily as possible. In July 1895, 7,345 men, 73 locomotives, 32 steam navvies and 100 horses were at work on the two and a quarter miles (3·6 km.) from Finchley Road to Marylebone. In the spring of 1897 the tunnel under Lord's Cricket Ground was finished punctually and in March 1899 the line was opened. At the beginning of the new century, when the finishing touches were put on Marylebone station, the total cost of the work amounted to £6,200,000.[30] The railway made great changes in the landscape of Marylebone, but hardly disturbed the tranquillity of St John's Wood. In Marylebone several hundred families, turned out of their homes, crowded into the congested neighbourhood of Lisson Grove. When new housing was offered to them, the rents were too high to attract any but well-paid clerks and tradesmen. The slum dwellers were displaced, not rehoused.[31] The new railway yards crossed the barrier between the stately Portman estate and the villadom of St John's Wood, but the elaborate precautions written into the Act saved their properties from any appreciable loss of amenity. The labouring classes were effectively prevented from entering St John's Wood and the residents of sedate villas in Acacia Road slept peacefully, remote from the sounds of trains muffled in the tunnel.

In 1899 the crests of the Northern Heights lay on the edge of open country. They afforded fine viewpoints, recommended to American visitors by Charles Alvin Gillig's *London Guide*.

'There are no prettier suburbs in the environs of London,' he wrote, 'than those found along the range of hills encircling it on the north, from whose summits on a clear day, two prospects may be had, so widely differing in character that the presence of one would seem to preclude the propinquity of the other. Looking to the north, one sees a panorama of pastoral landscape, with here and there bits of forest and clustering villages, so exquisitely beautiful, so serene and complete, so full of repose, that he would scarcely suspect that, at the opposite point of the compass, lay the homes, the shops, the factories, the vast paraphernalia of commerce, the magnificent architecture of Church and State, the luxury of wealth, the squalor of poverty, the highest and lowest conditions of life—all the concomitants of a city of nearly six million people.'[32]

There was no question of a surface railway reaching the summit of Hampstead Heath. The gradients were too steep and the property too valuable. The proposal for a Charing Cross Euston and Hampstead Railway was for a tube railway to be cut with a Greathead Shield and Price's rotary excavator. The station at Hampstead was to be the deepest tube station in London, almost 200 feet (60 m.) below street level.[33] The scheme received parliamentary approval in 1893, but ten years passed before any action was taken. Then the company was taken over by Charles Tyson Yerkes, a Chicago millionaire, who made the far-sighted decision to extend the line beneath the summit of the heath and down the hill to a cross-roads in the middle of pasture land at Golders Green. On that open site the terminus was built, and the fields around it became at once the most valuable prize to fall into the hands of speculators since the Metropolitan Railway reached Swiss Cottage. The district was unspoiled by industry, with no village to stand in the way of new streets, its lowest hollow, near Child's Hill, filled with surplus earth from the tunnel. Between 1904 and 1907 land values multiplied six fold. In June 1907, on the occasion of the opening of the line, the editor of the *Tramway and Railway World* predicted that 'the progress of time is certain to lead to great building operations in the northern suburbs served by the railway, and their development as residential districts for people employed in the west central area of London is likely to be very great.'[34]

The anticipated development was not long delayed. Indeed, the first new house was built at the corner of Finchley Road and Hoop Lane as early as 1905 on land acquired by the Finchley Road and Golders Green Syndicate.[35] That estate and the neighbouring Woodstock estate were hurriedly laid out with new streets and closely packed with buildings. But the two largest territories, one containing more than 300 acres (120 ha.) belonging to the Church Commissioners, the other, 326 acres (132 ha.) belonging to Eton College, were treated in a very different manner. The Church land was spaciously planned and building proceeded slowly. Spaces for three parks and recreation grounds were set aside and taken over by

135

Hendon Council. From the Eton College property 80 acres (32 ha.) were acquired for the Hampstead Heath Extension, and in May 1907 deeds were signed by Henrietta Barnett for the purchase of 243 acres (98 ha.) by the Hampstead Garden Suburb Trust. Barry Parker and Raymond Unwin, who designed Letchworth Garden City, were commissioned to prepare plans for the new garden suburb in consultation with Sir Edwin Lutyens. The guiding principles of the scheme were that no more than eight houses should be built on each acre, that the height of buildings and alignment of streets should conform with the shape of the ground, that streets should offer a variety of distinct and attractive vistas, that hedges, walks and fences between neighbouring houses should be avoided. The attempt to establish a civic centre without cafés, cinemas, shops or other commercial enterprises was a mistake. Nor were the planners successful in their aim to create a community in which different classes lived together. The Garden Suburb, like the rest of Golders Green, became a dormitory for London's commuters.

Between 1907 and 1914 Golders Green was covered with 3,611 new houses; its population rose from 9,710 to 23,790; and in 1914 more than ten million passengers passed through the tube station. It was a fully-grown suburb with a complicated pattern of streets and tramways, a new sewage works, cemeteries and public parks.

North-west London in 1914

The outbreak of the First World War interrupted the spread of building. For a short period Hampstead Garden Suburb looked across green fields and hedges towards the meadows of the Brent valley. London paused to survey the last corner of open country it possessed before throwing miles of red brick and concrete over rural Middlesex (Fig. 23).

All but a small area of the Northern Heights, preserved as public open space, had been built over since 1864. Among the first buildings were a number of hospitals, schools, orphanages, almshouses and other charitable institutions, many of which had been removed from sites in the City and crowded inner districts of London to spacious surroundings on the outskirts. One of the earliest was the Orphan Working School, moved from Hoxton to Maitland Park in 1847, and one of the latest was University College School, moved from Gower Street to Frognal in 1907. The rest of Hampstead was almost

FIG. 23   North-west London 1914
The stippled areas are open spaces.
Based on London County Council, Municipal Map of London, 1914.

entirely residential. The great majority of buildings were private houses with shops, schools and churches to serve their needs. In 1914 none of the large houses had been converted into flats and there were no departmental stores on the Heights.

The outward appearance of Marylebone changed little between 1864 and 1914. The most imposing new buildings were shops fronting Edgware Road, Oxford Street, Wigmore Street, Baker Street, Marylebone Road and Great Portland Street, thoroughfares now daily jammed with cabs and buses. The resident population declined continuously after 1861, although new blocks of flats provided accommodation for more families than the houses they replaced. On the other hand, the conversion of private houses into doctors' consulting rooms in Harley Street, Wimpole Street, Welbeck Street, the clearing of sites for hospitals, schools, offices, storerooms, displaced thousands of families, and many large households moved to quieter districts in Kensington and Hampstead.

In 1914 St Pancras looked very different from 50 years previously, but its population had changed little. More new houses had been built in Kentish Town and near Highgate than had been destroyed by the railway. It was only after 1871, when commercial establishments encroached upon the area south of Euston Road, that the number of inhabited houses in St Pancras decreased. In Tottenham Court Road and Hampstead Road, piano makers and furniture shops suffered repeated fires, added new storehouses and depositories, enlarged and rebuilt their premises. Other sites were taken by booksellers, stationers, printers, binders, tailors' cutters and dressmakers. Tottenham Court Road, wider and better paved than in 1864, the first thoroughfare in St Pancras to be illuminated with electricity, was now a great shopping street. On the north of the Bedford estate, near the main-line termini, stood the Russell, the Imperial and other large hotels, catering for an increasing number of travellers visiting London. Great post offices, telephone exchanges, banks, headquarters of trades unions and charitable institutions took the place of private houses. North of Euston Road railways now occupied several hundred acres of land and much of the adjoining area was taken by warehouses, private sidings, the Railway Clearing House, parcels sorting offices, overnight lodging houses for train crews, and endless rows of stables. The worst of the slums were pulled down by railway companies, by private benefactors and by municipal authorities. Tall Industrial Dwellings and two Rowton

Houses overshadowed the low streets of Camden Town, Somers Town and Grays Inn Road. In 1902 the Borough Council built its first Working-Class Dwellings in Pancras Road, and in 1906 the Working Men's College was opened in Crowndale Road. Between 1873 and 1893 a dozen giant Board Schools, new fire stations and police stations were built, busy streets were widened, baths, wash-houses and public lavatories were opened, and a number of old burial grounds were made into public gardens.[36] The area remained grimy and congested but its standards of hygiene were greatly improved. In 1914 the infant mortality rate compared favourably with those of western districts of Marylebone, Paddington, Kensington, Fulham and Hammersmith.

Since 1914 the gaslights, the music halls, the tramways, the work-men's trains, the thousands of horses, carts and hansom cabs have disappeared from north-west London. Stables and coach-houses have been demolished or converted into garages, many horse troughs and drinking fountains have been removed, a dozen stations have been closed, a dozen churches stand empty, scores of public houses have been pulled down or stripped of their cut glass and brass fittings, hundreds of private houses have become offices or lodgings and thousands more have been destroyed or cleared away in improvement schemes. But what remains in the landscape is an impressive legacy from the nineteenth century: four-fifths of the area has been built over or covered by railway tracks. The nineteenth century has also contributed three distinctive features to the present landscape of the suburbs: the slate-roofed semi-detached house, the suburban railway station, and the Victorian church.

References

1. Report of Royal Commission on Health of Towns (1844), cited in J. L. and Barbara Hammond, *The Bleak Age*, revised (1947), 59.
2. François P. G. Guizot, *Embassy at the Court of St. James 1840* (1862), 3, cited in R. J. Mitchell and M. D. R. Leys, *A History of London Life* (1963), 293.
3. John Hollingshead, *Ragged London in 1861* (1861), 143–61.
4. *Ibid.*, 131, 129–42.
5. Walter E. Brown, *St. Pancras Book of Dates* (1908), 24.
6. William Howitt, *The Northern Heights of London or Historical Associations of Hampstead, Highgate, Muswell Hill, Hornsey and Islington* (1869), 55.

7. Frederick Miller, *Saint Pancras Past and Present* (1874), 325.

8. Howitt, *op. cit.*, v.

9. London Transport, *London General* (1956), 16.

10. 26 & 27 Victoria, Cap. 74, 22nd June 1863.

11. Frederick S. Williams, *The Midland Railway: Its Rise and Progress: A Narrative of Modern Enterprise* (1875), 332.

12. Midland Railway, *Circular to Shareholders* (17th Dec. 1867), cited in Williams, *op. cit.*, 240.

13. Williams, *op. cit.*, 353.

14. *Ibid.*, 355.

15. *Ibid.*, 258; Midland Railway, *Minutes of Bedford to London Extension Committee*, British Transport Commission (B.T.C.) Records, MID 1/279.

16. G. A. Sekon, *Locomotion in Victorian London* (1938), 152–4; R. M. Robbins, *The North London Railway* (1938), 16–28.

17. G. H. Lake, *The Railways of Tottenham* (1945); 26 & 27 Victoria, Cap. 205, 28th July 1863; Tottenham and Hampstead Railway, *An Inventory of Acts and Agreements*, B.T.C. Records GEN. 4/3 121; Charles E. Lee, 'Some forgotten London services', *Railway Magazine*, 89 (1943), 86–91, and 'More forgotten London services; *ibid.*, 90 (1944), 8–12.

18. North London Railway, *A Reference Index and Memorandum Book*, B.T.C. Records LIB. 4/83.

19. *Ibid.*, 51–2; Board of Trade, *Returns of Accidents and Casualties 1892* (H.M.S.O., 1893), 99–115.

20. Henry Sharpe, 'The acquisition of the Heath for public enjoyment in perpetuity', in F. E. Baines (ed.), *Records of the Manor, Parish and Borough of Hampstead* (1890), 146.

21. Karl Blind, 'A German retrospect,' *ibid.*, 510.

22. Henry Wash, 'Topographical changes,' *ibid.*, 34.

23. H. L. Hopwood, 'The Edgware, Highgate and London Railway,' *Railway Magazine*, 45 (1919), 1–7; D. S. Barrie, 'Northern Heights branches of the L.N.E.R.', *ibid.*, 85 (1939), 109–18; G. F. A. Wilmot, *The Railway in Finchley* (1962), 7, 16, 19, 22.

24. Brown, *op. cit.*, 52.

25. Sekon, *op. cit.*, 162.

26. C. Baker, *The Metropolitan Railway* (1951), 16–39.

27. *Dictionary of National Biography. Supplement 1901–1911*, 3 (1920), 601–3; Harold Pollins, 'The last main railway line to London', *Journal of Transport History*, 4 (1959–60), 85–95.

28. House of Commons Select Committee, *Manchester, Sheffield and Lincolnshire Railway Extension to London Bill, Minutes of Evidence*, 1 (1891), B.T.C. Records PYB, 1/1556.

29. 56 Victoria, Cap. 1, 1893, Sections 1–115.

30. Great Central Railway, *Half Yearly Reports 1889–1905*, B.T.C. Records RAC. 1/141.

31. H. J. Dyos, 'Railways and housing in Victorian London,' *Journal of Transport History*, 2 (1955–6), 19, 90–100 and 'Some social costs of railway building in London,' *ibid.*, 3 (1957–8), 25, 29.

32. Charles Alvin Gillig, *London Guide*, 13th edition (1899), 58.

33. E. Course, *London Railways* (1962), 217; A. A. Jackson and D. F. Croome, *Rails through the Clay* (1962), 34–6, 64–9, 87–98.
34. Editorial, *Tramway and Railway World* (4th July 1907), 4; also J. P. Thomas, *Handling London's Underground Traffic* (1928), 216–23.
35. F. Howkins, *The Story of Golders Green and its Remarkable Development* (1923), 19, map facing 20.
36. Brown, *op. cit.*, 41–57.

The Suburban Expansion of Housing in London 1918–1939

*

JAMES H. JOHNSON

etween the two world wars about one-third of the total increase in population of England and Wales was found in Greater London.[1] This considerable rise was the ultimate cause of the growth of inter-war suburbs òn all sides of London, although the creation of an effective demand for new houses and its supply by speculative builders was conditioned by a whole series of social and economic factors. Nor was every residential suburb identical, since the suburban ring around London contains internal variations, which reflect such complexities as the pre-existing pattern of urban development, variations in the nature of transport and the degree to which employment was provided locally for suburban dwellers.

Pre-existing Residential Building

Most of the suburban expansion between the wars lay outside the administrative county of London, which, with the exception of a relatively small area in the south-east, was largely built-up before the First World War. Indeed before 1918 certain parts of London had already spread beyond the area administered by the London County Council; and this pre-existing building modified the form of the later inter-war suburbs (Fig. 24).

In the Lea valley, for example, working-class houses spread into Tottenham and Enfield between 1871 and 1900. The form of this growth was largely a result of the building of the Great Eastern Railway into Liverpool Street, since this company was compelled to provide cheap workmen's services as a compensation for dwellings

142

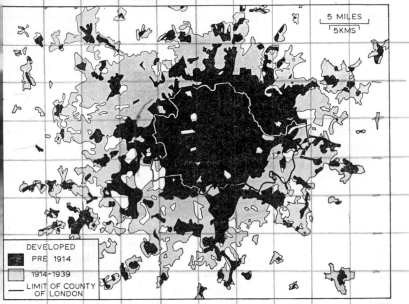

FIG. 21   Date of development of outer London
Based on the Report of the Royal Commission on Local Government in
Greater London.

demolished during the construction of the line into London.[2] Pre-
1918 building in East and West Ham also had an emphasis on working-class housing: West Ham had considerable industrial developments linked with the railways and the nearby docks, while East
Ham was given its character through being a dormitory suburb for
the adjoining borough.

Willesden, too, exhibited early residential growth outside the
county of London; but here it was more commonly the houses of the
quite well-to-do which fingered out along the railway lines between
1870 and the end of the nineteenth century.[3] In spite of the mesh of
lines passing through this district, workmen's services were poor,
since, although all the railway companies were obliged to offer cheap
fares after 1883, the precise impact of this legislation depended on
the enthusiasm with which it was implemented by the various lines.[4]
Similarly Acton began its modern growth in 1860; and an indication
of its early character is given by its famous upper middle-class suburb
of Bedford Park, which was founded in 1875.[5] Both Acton and
Willesden formed part of the continuous built-up area of London

by the end of the nineteenth century. By this time, too, their character was beginning to change as both received the impact of suburban industry and as the late nineteenth-century housing lost its first youth.[6] South of the Thames Wimbledon also represented an extension of later Victorian London, with large mansions grouped around the common, which has served to maintain the social desirability of the area.

All these districts were contiguous with the built-up area of London, but the railways also brought residential building in detached communities, often grafted on to some pre-existing rural centre. Harrow, for example, contained substantial residential development before the First World War. Residential building clustered around Harrow Hill, especially after the district was tapped by the Metropolitan Railway in 1880.[7] The London and North Western Railway also passed nearby; but although a station had been in existence on this line since 1837, little suburban growth took place here until the company started to seek suburban traffic in the 1850s.[8] By the First World War the clusters around these two stations had grown together to form a considerable settlement.

Pinner provides a similar example in the same area, although on a smaller scale. Here a rural village, already modified by the nearby presence of London, was linked more firmly to it in 1886 by the Metropolitan Railway.[9] Almost immediately substantial houses were built, either singly or in small groups, close to the old village High Street, which was somewhat self-consciously preserved (Plate 14). Centres like Mill Hill and Barnet provide further examples of the same kind of process.

In north-west Middlesex, however, these detached portions of London were relatively widely spaced and they were mostly small. They were widely spaced because the pre-existing villages, around which late nineteenth-century building clustered, were located only where hills of better drained deposits stand out above the great clay expanse of northern Middlesex, as at Harrow, where Bagshot beds lie on top of the London Clay and are capped by pebble gravels; or as at Pinner, where the lighter Reading Beds appear in the centre of a small anticline. The London Clay itself was avoided, partly because it posed more difficult problems for builders before main drainage had been completed, but also because other areas about London were more profitable for house construction as a result of the nature of transport. Even after the railway companies operating to the north-west of London had become more interested in attracting commuter traffic, they found it difficult to compete with other lines because their termini were not close to 'The City', where the jobs of most daily travellers were located at that time.[10]

As a result, these detached clusters of late nineteenth-century building compared neither in size nor in number with those found south of the Thames. Croydon, for example, was a large and long-established borough, flanked both to the north and south by several miles of late nineteenth-century building. Kingston also had a separate existence of its own, but added considerable late nineteenth-century growth after it became more firmly linked to London. Other pre-existing clusters of suburban development were found in places such as Sutton, Cheam and Beckenham (Fig. 24). Partly this was because the various railway lines south of the Thames were more dependent on local passenger traffic and were keen to provide commuter services; and at the end of the nineteenth century their termini were more accessible to central London offices. In addition, the physical landscape some miles south of London was certainly more diverse and possibly agriculturally richer than to the north. As a result there were more villages and country towns in this area, around which late Victorian suburban development took place.

In summary, then, the general pattern of pre-existing building was one in which working-class London had extended beyond the administrative county to the north and the east, along railway lines and docks. To the south late nineteenth-century development had clustered around small pre-existing settlements. To the west and north-west the houses of the well-to-do had spread out to Willesden and Acton, but were losing their middle-class appeal; and better houses were also found in rather small detached groups, clustered around a few villages.

Inter-war Growth: a General Statement

Figure 25 represents the residential growth of outer London between 1918 and 1939. Within the administrative county only some areas in Woolwich, Greenwich and Lewisham had not been largely occupied by the end of the First World War.[11] Some of the new inter-war houses were fitted between developments which already existed. In Willesden, for example, relatively small groups of inter-war houses were built between the late nineteenth-century housing.

In other parts of London the previous outward growth of the city had covered areas outside the administrative county more completely. Thus in East and West Ham most twentieth-century building took place around the outer fringes of the already built-up area, rather than interdigitated with it. Islands of earlier suburban housing south of London were soon linked with the conurbation by the outward extension of its continuous built-up area. To the north-west the amount of inter-war residential building was greatest; and here it was less broken by earlier developments.

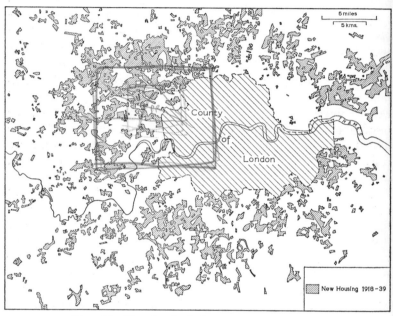

Fig. 25   Housing built between 1918 and 1939
Based on the Greater London Plan 1944.

Many writers have noted the monotonous similarity of these new suburban houses, although perhaps the idea of their dull anonymity can be pressed too far. Even when viewed on a broad scale there are some variations among the outer suburbs and Figures 26 and 27 show one aspect of these, by distinguishing between houses of different value.[12]

Homes which cost less than £1,000 between the wars formed an uneven ring around the administrative county. Notable patches of

146

relatively cheap houses were found to the south-east in Bexley and in Crayford Urban District. In the south-west they were found in boroughs like Sutton and Cheam, Merton and Morden, and Malden and Coombe. Between these two groups smaller areas lay close to Croydon and Beckenham. North-east of London most inter-war housing fell into this class: here it lay in a belt between Hornchurch and Chingford. But the greatest single block of housing sold at less than £1,000 for each house was in Middlesex, where it occupied a broad zone between Wembley and Feltham.

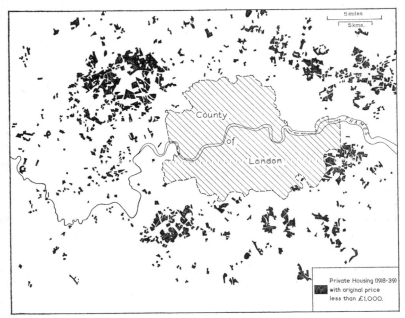

FIG. 26   Lower value private enterprise housing 1918–39
Based on the Greater London Plan 1944.

Although more expensive houses were built at a lower density, they covered a smaller total area of land and were located in less tightly grouped patches. Housing which cost more than £1,000 was notably absent from west Middlesex and from Essex. To the south it generally avoided the area adjacent to the southern boundary of the administrative county, but tended to be found to the south-west of the conurbation, in a belt stretching east–west across districts like Coulsdon and Purley, Banstead, and Epsom and Ewell. North of London the more expensive houses were found in Finchley and Hendon, in smaller patches in Harrow and Wembley, and along the northern fringes of the built-up area.

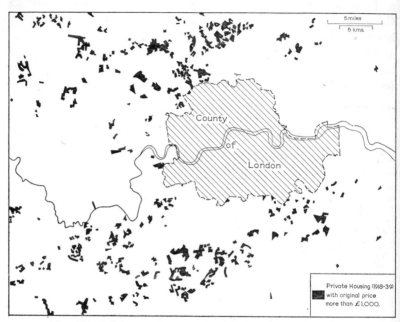

FIG. 27   Higher value private enterprise housing 1918–39
Based on the Greater London Plan 1944

The impression produced by this simple method is not completely satisfactory. It does not give, for example, a clear indication of the distribution of working-class and middle-class suburbs, since many people, who would look upon themselves as middle class, owned houses costing less than £1,000. The general picture it provides, however, has been elaborated and confirmed by J. Westergaard's more detailed analysis of the socio-economic zones of the conurbation, as revealed by the 1951 population census.[13] Westergaard found it possible to divide the middle and outer zones of the conurbation into those areas with a relatively low social status and those where it was relatively high (Fig. 28). Residential areas around the inner parts of London with a relatively low status have been extended to the northeast (a sector centred on the Lea valley), to the east (on both sides of the Thames), and to the west (along arterial roads across Middlesex).

SUBURBAN EXPANSION OF HOUSING IN LONDON

These segments of lower middle-class and upper working-class housing contained industrial employment either within or adjoining them. The main middle-class areas lie between these industrial sectors and are more purely residential in function.[14] The character of these different suburbs thus rests partly on the distribution of industrial employment; but it has also been influenced by the nature of housing closer to the centre of London. Those areas which are less socially desirable tend to have grown as an extension of similar areas around the fringes of Victorian London.

As the suburbs expanded new shopping centres were built to serve

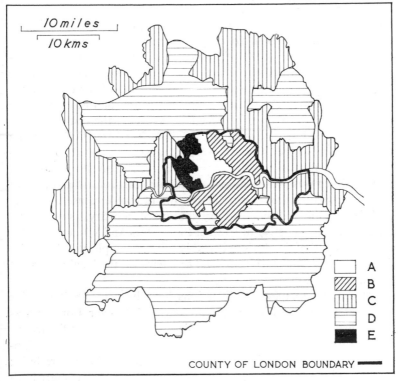

FIG. 28   Socio-economic zones of the London conurbation

Key: *A*, central London zone; *B*, inner working-class zones; *C*, middle and outer zones of relatively low social status; *D*, middle and outer zones of relatively high social status; *E*, West End and Hampstead zones.

Based on a map by J. Westergaard.

149

their inhabitants. Unlike suburban manufacturing, the general distribution of these shopping centres is relatively even and reflects the distribution of population and its buying power. In detail, however, it is less logical, since some of these centres were produced by an expansion of the facilities of small towns and villages, while others were completely new and characteristically are to be found around a suburban railway station, in many ways the most important single feature in these communities.[15]

The Improvement in Transport

It is difficult, however, to establish the precise relationship between inter-war suburban growth and the provision of more efficient transport. In various parts of London the building of new railways preceded the development of suburbs, the classic examples in the inter-war period being provided by the extension of the tube lines.[16] But it is also possible to find places where suburban building came earlier than the provision of effective links with the centre, as, for example at the L.C.C. out-county estate at Becontree.[17] Even along railway lines where services were expressly designed for commuters, the outward growth of suburbs depended on the demand for houses, which was greatly influenced by such factors as the supply of credit to potential house purchasers, the rate of increase of family units in London and the local distribution of industry, as well as by the existence of effective links with the centre. And when particular examples are examined, the picture is further complicated by variations in the enterprise of individual builders and the local pattern of land-ownership.[18]

Yet even when these qualifications have been made, it remains true that the general suburban growth of inter-war London was closely associated with the improvement and extension of the means of travelling to work. In the newer suburbs there were three developments of particular importance: some new railway lines were built; services on existing lines were improved; and motor transport both by car and bus was more firmly added to the range of urban transport facilities.

Most notable perhaps was the extensive electrification of the Southern Railway in the 1920s, thus improving the efficiency of the close mesh of lines, already providing commuter services south of the Thames. Developments north of the river were mostly associated with the electrification of much of the Metropolitan Railway and with the extension of the Underground. This extension was achieved both by building new tracks and by means of links with pre-existing surface railways.[19]

The opening of new lines between the wars had its greatest impact on northern Middlesex, where commuter services had been relatively poor and earlier suburban building somewhat restricted. The Northern Line, for example, was extended on the surface from Golders Green to Edgware in 1924. In 1917 the Bakerloo line was linked with the tracks of the former London and North Western Railway to provide a service to Watford; and in 1932 a new line was laid to Stanmore. By 1933, too, the Piccadilly line had been extended to Cockfosters.

Those and other improvements meant that the scatter of railway stations in outer London was thickened and train services were improved. In addition, the railways were more effectively linked with the areas around them as a result of motor bus services. In this development the creation of the London Passenger Transport Board in 1933 was an important event, since it meant some measure of unified control over passenger traffic in the London area. During this period, too, the immediate pull of the railway for suburban development was lessened by the diffusion of private motor-cars among an increasing proportion of suburban dwellers.

Road travel was particularly important in the north-western suburbs of London, since it allowed journeys to work in other directions than straight into the centre of the conurbation. In this section of London, in particular, many people were beginning to travel around the fringes of the built-up area, drawn by the new suburban location of industry. Here it is relevant to recall the improvement of suburban main roads, which had some effect on suburban house-building, but more upon the location of manufacturing. Most famous of these inter-war developments, perhaps, are Western Avenue, passing through one of the major industrial areas of Great Britain, and the North Circular Road, both constructed in the early 1920s. New roads were most important to the west and north-west of London, since it was here that the heaviest road transport was generated by twentieth-century industry.

The journey to work which was made upon these transport routes is sometimes looked upon as being a simple movement into central

London. Certainly the daily journey into the Central Area provides the clearest index of the interdependence of the various parts of the conurbation, but the importance of this movement for residents in all the twentieth-century suburbs should not be exaggerated.

In that part of the conurbation which lies outside the administrative county as many as 61 per cent of the journeys made to work in 1951 could be classified as 'short' (i.e. they were made to a destination no further than an adjoining local authority area).[20] Nearly all these short journeys were to a destination which was also within the out-county ring of the conurbation. Thirty-nine per cent of the journeys made could be classified as 'long' (i.e. further than an adjoining local authority area), but only about half of them (or 20 per cent of the total journeys to work) were to the centre of London. Only seven per cent of the people who lived in the out-county ring of the conurbation had long daily journeys to other areas within that ring (Table V).[21]

TABLE V

Journeys to work from the out-county ring of Greater London 1951

	Number	%
'Short' Journeys to		
The Central Area	3,000	0
Rest of London Administrative County	75,000	3
Out-County Ring of Conurbation	1,381,000	57
Outside Conurbation	22,000	1
Total 'Short' Journeys	1,481,000	61
'Long' Journeys to		
The Central Area	493,000	20
Rest of London Administrative County	236,000	10
Out-County Ring of Conurbation	174,000	7
Outside Conurbation	29,000	1
Total 'Long' Journeys	932,000	39

Source: Simplified from calculations by J. Westergaard in *London Evidence, op. cit.*, vol. 5, 657, table IVa.

There were, of course, considerable local variations, partly due to distance from the centre, but more commonly the result of the local provision of jobs. The more exclusive a residential area, the less

likelihood there was of much local employment. Thus the more con-
sistently middle-class areas of outer London depended on the
central area for the employment of more than a quarter of their
night-time population. The working-class suburbs of Essex were
more self-contained. Even so, considerable numbers travelled daily
from here into the City and the East End. The outer suburbs of
west Middlesex, on the other hand, stood out most clearly from
the rest of the suburban ring, because they had only tenuous daily
links with central London, as a result of the large number of local
jobs and their greater number of non-professional inhabitants.[22]

The Changing Distribution of Population

If improved transport services and a changing location of industry
allowed the outward spread of London, in the last resort a basic
cause of its growth was the increasing population of the conurbation.
Although a detailed examination of these rising numbers lies outside the scope of this study, it is perhaps sufficient to indicate the
attraction of the conurbation for the service industries as well as for
market orientated manufacturing, which grew disproportionately
rapidly in the London area. Ultimately it was this increased number
of jobs that supported the growing population of Greater London,
which rose from 7·5 million in 1921 to 8·2 million in 1931, and
reached 8·7 million in 1939.[23]

In reality the actual population movements hidden behind these
figures were much more complex than a simple flow into the new
suburbs from elsewhere in the British Isles. For one thing, much of
the increase was the result of an excess of births over deaths in the
conurbation itself: between 1921 and 1931, for example, natural increase was responsible for over 60 per cent of the total rise in the
population of Greater London.[24] A further complication was produced by an outward movement of people from inner London, caused
partly by the relief of congestion in the older residential quarters and
partly by replacement of older housing by other forms of urban land
use, especially around the Central Area. As a result, the total population of the administrative county of London fell by over 446,000
between 1921 and 1939 which, when natural increase is allowed for,
probably represents a net outward movement of about 638,000.[25]
Most of these people must have moved to new extensions of the
continuous built-up area of London or to new housing around

pre-existing towns, which increasingly became satellites of the conurbation.

Other demographic complications tend to go unrecorded in census returns. Many of the people born outside the Home Counties, who eventually ended up in the new suburban houses being built between the wars, did not move there directly. It is a reasonable speculation that families moving into London often took temporary accommodation in the inner residential areas before buying new houses. Certainly, an analysis of the records of one south London building firm suggests that almost all the purchasers of the new houses, which it was building around the fringes of the built-up area in 1931 and 1932, moved from older houses elsewhere in London.[26] For that matter, it is likely that immigrants into inner London were more often than not young unmarried adults. Sub-divided houses in areas such as parts of Hampstead and Paddington provided their first accommodation—the precise area depended on their income and social pretensions—and then later, when they married, they sought an individual dwelling unit elsewhere in the conurbation.

Since most of the building around London was constructed by private speculative builders, the majority of those people who eventually came to live in outer London were selected by their ability to put down a deposit and meet regular mortgage payments; but they also passed through a demographic filter. For many people the desire for a semi-detached house with a garden cannot have manifested itself until their family included a young child. As a result of both these factors, the typical family moving into a new suburban estate was a lower middle-class couple in their late twenties or early thirties, with one or two children. The quality of suburban living was largely conditioned by the resultant structure of population and society.

The increasing population of outer London had its impact strengthened by the lower densities of building which were becoming fashionable. But while the architectural origins of inter-war suburbia may be traced back in a devious line to Hampstead Garden Suburb, Letchworth Garden City and beyond, a demographic factor also contributed to the design of the new houses. The idea of having a small family, which was achieving acceptance among the upper middle classes before the First World War, was more widely diffused through the British population after 1918. Between 1921 and 1931, for example, class differences in fertility were considerably reduced and the average number of children per marriage was reduced to about two.[27] Hence there was a general demand, at least among those people who could afford to live in suburbia, for small houses, typically with three bedrooms. When these houses were provided with gardens of a socially acceptable size, the housing developments which resulted frequently had a density of about twelve houses to the acre (30 per hectare).

Some early official recognition of this empirically derived density is perhaps shown in the town planning scheme prepared for 6,500 acres (2,600 ha.) of Middlesex by the Ruislip and Northwood Urban District Council and King's College, Cambridge, the largest local landowner. This scheme, one of the few stimulated by the 1909 Housing Act, was approved in 1914; about half of the area which it covered was scheduled for development at twelve buildings to the acre, and the rest at a somewhat lower density.[28] In fact, massive suburban expansion did not take place here until the 1930s, but when it came the main lines of the scheme were adhered to, in particular the suggested housing densities.

The Provision of Houses

In calculating the demand for houses the number of family units is probably a more critical index than mere population totals. When assessed in these terms, the housing requirements of the Home Counties between 1921 and 1931 were 33 per cent greater than the total number of dwelling units which were already standing in 1921.[29] To meet this demand over half a million houses were built in this area between 1921 and 1931, which was many more than in any other part of Britain. Even so, by 1931 the deficiency in most of the Home Counties was still over 20 per cent of requirements and the ultimate result of this demand was the building of over 780,000 new houses in this area between 1931 and 1939.[30] Admittedly not all of these were in the immediate vicinity of the conurbation, but the figures serve to indicate the general position in south-eastern England.

In fact the demand for houses within the conurbation was even more severe than these figures indicate. Miss Bowley has calculated that if the administrative county of London is taken together with Middlesex, Essex, Kent and Surrey, the deficiency of houses in 1931 was over 27 per cent of the requirements.[31] If Middlesex and the

L.C.C. area are singled out, the result is even more striking, since in 1931 the deficiency of houses in relation to requirements here was over 43 per cent. Indeed, in Middlesex, where the new light industries were particularly concentrated, the shortage of houses was actually greater in 1931 than it had been in 1921.[32]

The potential demand remained relatively constant, but the number of houses built in various years between the two world wars bore a complex relationship to the general state of the economy, the income of the people to be housed and the system of government subsidy that was operating at any particular period. These factors also influenced the relative number of new houses constructed by private enterprise or local authorities. Here it is perhaps sufficient to record that a higher than average number of houses was built in the London area and that most of them were erected by private enterprise for owner-occupiers.[33]

Since very few of the private houses built around the fringes of London in the decade immediately following the First World War qualified for a subsidy, they were clearly designed for occupation by better-off purchasers. Certainly money for house-purchase could be raised more easily than in the past, as a result of the continued expansion of the building society movement.[34] But although a considerable expansion in private building was encouraged by credit being made more generally available, the purchaser still needed some capital of his own. At least 25 per cent of the purchase price of a house was required for a deposit, together with the other expenses implicit in moving home. Hence in the immediate post-war years it was a middle-class group which could afford to abandon older, less easily managed houses within London, or could purchase a new house immediately on moving into the conurbation. This may also explain the impression, which is difficult to illustrate quantitatively, that a greater proportion of the suburban houses built at this period were detached, rather more substantial structures, in comparison with those to be built later.

In the 1930s, however, owner-occupation became possible for an even greater range of people. Paradoxically enough in a period of grave national economic difficulties, the mid-1930s were marked by a boom in house-building, which was particularly noticeable in the London area. Of the 1,810,000 houses built by private enterprise in England and Wales between 1931 and 1939, approximately 754,000 were in the Home Counties.[35] A basic explanation of this situation was the concentration of demand in the London area and the fact that this region was relatively prosperous during the Great Depression; but more general factors were also operating.

During the period of economic uncertainty building societies proved to be a popular outlet for investment, and as a result they, in their turn, were anxious to lend money. After 1932 the interest rates which they charged to borrowers dropped to between 5 and 5½ per cent, thus making house purchase cheaper.[36] At the same time the actual costs of building construction had been declining noticeably after 1928; but between 1932 and 1935 they reached the lowest level recorded during the inter-war period.[37]

The problem of finance was even further alleviated by the greater possibility of buying a house with a smaller capital outlay. In particular this development was a result of the 'Builders' Pool' arrangement, under which a builder would pay a sum of money to a building society as collateral security and the society in return would advance up to 95 per cent of the purchase price of a new house. Arrangements of this type had been accepted earlier by some societies, but during the 1930s they became more important, so that by 1938 possibly half the business of some large societies was transacted on this basis.[38]

The builders' pool arrangement favoured the larger firms, which because of their superior credit-worthiness could negotiate better terms. One large London company, for example, was able to offer a house costing £800 for as small a deposit as £25, with legal expenses being paid by the builder.[39] The larger builder was also favoured in the competition for business by his ability to construct a greater number of houses at one time. It has been estimated, for instance, that on a site where 40 houses are being built, there is an average saving of 350–450 man-hours per house, compared with one where four houses are being constructed.[40] In addition there were also savings through the bulk purchase of materials and the use of standardized parts. As a result it is almost true to say that by the 1930s the suburban speculative builder was either relatively large or defunct.

These developments had an effect on the nature of suburban building in the 1930s. After the impediment of finding a large deposit had been reduced, the range of people who were able to move into a new privately-owned house was broadened. Perhaps reflecting the lower income of the purchasers, the average house of this period tended to be smaller.[41] The typical house, too, probably formed part of a large estate, a form of development which reflected the growth of larger building companies and the need to streamline production for a highly competitive market. One large builder in south London, for example, produced 2,000 houses per annum during the peak years of the 1930s. Frequently this company would complete as many as 12 houses per week on a single estate; and, working on this scale, it was possible to maintain a constant labour force.[42]

The physical expression of this period of suburban house-building is most clearly seen in Middlesex, where suburban industrial expansion ran parallel to the building of houses. Here smaller, cheaper houses were required, just at the period when the larger builder was coming to dominate the scene. It has been suggested that the success of the larger builders in north-west Middlesex was the result of the sub-soil conditions found on London Clay, but in the twentieth century at least this deterministic theory can largely be discounted. Perhaps the more fastidious builder took somewhat more care in laying foundations, but as L. D. Stamp has pointed out: 'London no longer depends on shallow wells in gravel; tar macadam and concrete have banished the terrors of muddy roads, and efficient drainage copes with surface run-off.'[43] Probably more important was the fact that there were considerable stretches of land, convenient to transport routes, on which there was relatively little previous building. As a result, large estates could be laid out and considerable stretches of country were covered by large areas of small three-bedroom, semi-detached houses, typical of the suburban development of the period.

In all cases where a number of houses is being built the pre-existing pattern of land ownership is likely to be important, especially in controlling the precise limits of a particular piece of building. As estates grew in size this factor became more important to developers, since frequently these large-scale building operations had to be preceded by the purchase and amalgamation of a number of pieces of land. One estate in north-west Middlesex, on which about 400 houses were built and rather more were planned, will serve as an example. Before construction began, the purchase of six separate parcels of land had to be negotiated in order to form a compact estate, which would be efficiently orientated towards main roads and be convenient to existing railway stations.[44] It is interesting to note that this site, although it is largely situated on the London Clay, was chosen in preference to a location on a different sub-soil in south London.

SUBURBAN EXPANSION OF HOUSING IN LONDON

Towards the end of the 1930s, however, convenient sites close to railway stations were becoming more difficult to obtain. The difficulty here was not so much one of price, since in these pre-war developments the cost of land was less critical than it has now become. In fact, the cost of providing roads and services was a more important charge, so that, although land suitable for building suburban houses might range in price from £500 to £1,000 per acre, the site costs of a typical house would only vary between £140 and £180.[45] A more important factor was the limited extent of convenient sites, with the result that in the late 1930s large builders were forced to erect estates of only, say, 40–50 houses on these more desirable locations. Indeed, at least one large building company reacted to what seemed, in the context of the pre-war situation, to be a growing shortage of sites by buying up older properties in inner London with a view to redevelopment.[46]

Local Authority Housing

In the growth of the suburban ring around London, local authority housing played a relatively small part (Fig. 29). Taking the inter-

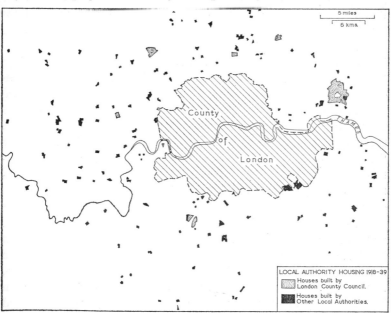

FIG. 29 Local authority housing 1918–39
Based on the Greater London Plan 1944.

159

war period as a whole, most local authorities around the fringes of the conurbation were not faced with a massive housing problem, and it was only within the L.C.C. area that there were a large number of people to be rehoused who were unable to purchase their own homes somewhere in the conurbation. Not only were there considerable areas of early nineteenth-century houses within the administrative county which needed to be replaced, but also the inner residential areas of London were particularly attractive to in-migrants seeking cheap, if unsatisfactory, accommodation.

Within London both the L.C.C. and the Metropolitan Boroughs provided housing, although in this work the contribution of the L.C.C. was dominant. Of the total of 119,879 dwellings provided by the London housing authorities between 1919 and 1945, 89,031 were built by the L.C.C.[47] These new dwellings were provided either in flats—an expensive solution and one that was not totally suitable for large families—or in the so-called 'cottage estates'. These latter consisted of two-storey houses, usually semi-detached or arranged in short terraces. They varied in size from the 218 houses erected on the Norbury estate to the huge estate of over 25,000 dwellings built at Becontree. During the interval between 1919 and 1942, when building operations almost completely ceased during the war, the L.C.C. built 59,591 cottages, a figure which may be compared with the 29,276 flats erected during the same period.[48]

Even in 1919 there was little land left within the administrative county suitable for the large, low-density cottage estates, which were normally built around the fringes of the continuous built-up area of the conurbation. As a result the L.C.C. had to obtain land outside the county of London; and it was in these outer London areas that the largest of the cottage estates were located and made their contribution to suburban expansion. The Downham estate, which extended over the southern limit of the L.C.C. area into Bromley, was opened in 1925 and reached a population of over 32,000. The St Helier estate near Carshalton, where building commenced in 1930, housed over 40,000 people. The Watling estate in Hendon, opened in 1927, eventually provided homes for over 18,000. Large as these developments were, they did not compare with the Becontree estate, to which over 112,000 people were exported from inner London into the three local government areas of Ilford, Dagenham and Barking.[49]

Between 1919 and 1931 over 90 per cent of new dwellings were provided by the L.C.C. in cottage estates as opposed to flats. After this date, however, the proportion decreased, falling to an average of less than 40 per cent between 1935 and 1940.[50] This changing emphasis was produced by alterations in the housing subsidies provided by the central government: in 1930 government help was concentrated on accommodation which was directly designed to relieve over-crowding, and in 1935 a further change meant that subsidies were given towards blocks of flats built on relatively expensive land.[51] As a result of these two changes the most important cottage estates, which were commenced between 1920 and 1927, were completed by 1932; and local authority building was notably absent from the great expansion of suburban houses in outer London during the mid-1930s.

The two main qualifications of successful applicants for houses on these estates were a need for subsidized housing and residence in London. As a result the people who moved to L.C.C. suburbs were in a lower income group than the inhabitants of the privately-built houses. Becontree will serve as an example of the type of people who were housed. Nearly all the male working population of this estate could be classified as 'employees' in 1931, with an average family income generally under £4 a week.[52] But they were not the very poorest workers. In 1931, of the 12,000 men working in 'manufacturing',* nearly 8,000 were classified as 'skilled' and an additional 500 were foremen, managers or superintending staff of some kind.[53] This occupational structure must have applied to most out-county estates, as the lowest-paid workers could neither have afforded the rents nor the travelling expenses involved in living in them.

Although a different social class was being catered for in the local authority houses, the population structure of the new estates bore a close similarity to that found on private developments. During its early years, for example, the Becontree estate housed a higher than normal proportion of children and of men and women aged 30–40.[54] As among the middle-class purchasers of private suburban housing, the provision of better living conditions for their young families must have been an important motive among those who undertook the higher rents of the out-county estates. In the first years at Becontree they also undertook what was probably a more difficult journey

* 'Manufacturing' was the only occupational group to which a classification into 'skilled' and 'unskilled' could be reasonably applied.

to work; and, perhaps in lesser measure, this was also true of other suburban cottage estates.

Post-war Developments

Looked at broadly, the extension of the continuous built-up area ceased at the end of 1939, since the implementation of the green belt policy has restricted London's further outward growth after the Second World War. One partial exception to this was provided during the immediate post-war decade by the extension of existing L.C.C. out-county estates and the foundation of new ones.

Some of these local authority houses can be looked upon as the outward extension of working-class London in directions which had already been pioneered by private builders between the wars. The Hainault estate in Essex, where over 2,800 dwellings were erected after 1945, may be taken as an example of this. Other L.C.C. developments represent an extension of working-class houses into sectors of the conurbation where it had previously been uncommon. Thus at Headstone Lane over 1,100 houses were grafted on to a middle-class section of northern Middlesex, developed in the 1930s; or on the Merstham estate over 1,500 houses were introduced into the Surrey stockbroker belt.[55] Even so, it probably remains true that since the war more important developments have taken place actually within the continuous built-up area of suburban London than as a result of its outward extension; and, in conclusion, it is relevant to examine these recent changes briefly.

When inter-war residential building was halted in 1939, a considerable number of unused frontages remained within the suburban ring. Sometimes the roads for an estate had been laid out, but not all the houses planned had been erected; there were small gaps in the built-up area, which were too small for profitable development under pre-war conditions; and some country roads, swallowed up in the expansion of London, had not been completely lined with houses. For these and other reasons land still remained for building: the Greater London Plan estimated that there was land for about 23,000 houses within the built-up area of the conurbation.[56] Almost all these spaces have now been occupied.

Further changes are related to the post-war increase of land values in outer London, which must owe much to the restriction of building in the green belt. This has made it worthwhile to use some pre-

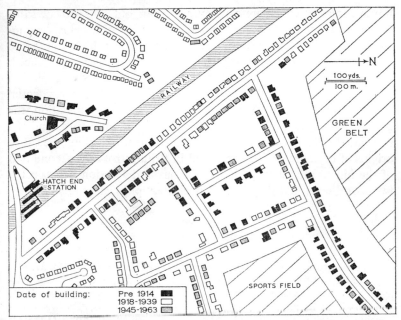

FIG. 30   Date of house building near an outer London railway station

Before the First World War a limited number of houses were built close to Hatch End station, their inhabitants being served by steam trains to Euston. In 1922 the line to Euston was electrified and in 1917 the station was also served by London underground trains, with the result that much of the surrounding area was built-up between the wars. Since the Second World War new housing has been erected in the large gardens associated with pre-1914 development and in the gaps left when house-building was halted in 1939.

Based on a survey by the author.

viously developed land more intensively. The areas affected by this trend are the patches of low-density housing built at the end of the nineteenth century, which pioneered suburban development in outer London. (Fig. 30). This intensification has taken place in a number of ways. The large gardens of the older properties, particularly if they have street frontages, have been used to provide sites for individual houses. In addition, some of the older houses have been sub-divided into flats. Some, indeed, have been completely demolished to provide land for new dwellings, usually in the form of maisonettes or, if there is enough space to allow a large development, in flats.

Yet the inter-war houses which were built around the older properties remain unchanged. In spite of a reputation for shoddiness, these houses, some of which are now over 40 years old, still provide satisfactory accommodation. Often architecturally disastrous and inefficiently laid-out, they nevertheless represented a higher standard of comfort than most of their purchasers had previously experienced. To the geographer they provide a visible indication of the revolution in living which accompanied the provision of lower residential densities for a substantial proportion of the urban population, the growth of employment in new suburban light industries, and the associated adjustments in the means of transport within cities. The origins of these trends can be traced in Britain from the second half of the nineteenth century; but it was around London between the two world wars that they had their clearest physical expression.

References

1. P. Abercrombie, *Greater London Plan 1944* (H.M.S.O., 1945), 27.

2. The idea of mitigating the consequences of displacement by an insistence on working-men's trains being provided can be traced from 1861, and this later became general practice, see H. J. Dyos, 'Railways and housing in Victorian London', *Journal of Transport History* 2 (1955–6), 11–21 and 90–100, ref. on 93; also Chapter 3 above.

3. J. C. Morris, *The Willesden Survey 1949* (Corporation of Willesden, 1950), 9.

4. M. Robbins, *Middlesex* (1953), 81.

5. N. Pevsner, *The Buildings of England: Middlesex* (1951), 21.

6. Morris, *op. cit.*, 10; Robbins, *op. cit.*, 219.

7. E. Course, *London Railways* (1962), 199.

8. Robbins, *op. cit.*, 80.

9. *Ibid.*, 320.

10. *Report Royal Commission on London Traffic* (H.M.S.O., 1905), I, 66–7 and table on 64–5.

11. *Administrative County of London Development Plan, 1951: Analysis* (1951), Fig. 5, 26.

12. Based on Abercrombie, *op. cit.*, folding map no. 3, between 30 and 31.

13. J. Westergaard, 'The growth and structure of Greater London' in *Royal Commission on Local Government in Greater London, Written Evidence* (H.M.S.O., 1962) (hereafter referred to as *London Evidence*), vol. V, 668–99, espec. 675–80; see also J. Westergaard, 'The structure of Greater London' in Centre for Urban Studies, *London, Aspects of Change* (1964), 91–144, espec. 101.

14. *Ibid.*, 677.

15. There have been two recent studies of these shopping centres: A. E. Smailes and G. Hartley, 'Shopping centres in the Greater London area', *Transactions and Papers Institute of British Geographers*, 29 (1961),

201–213; and W. I. Carruthers, 'Service centres in Greater London', *Town Planning Review*, 33 (1962–63), 5–31.

16. For a series of photographs showing development around Edgware tube station, see *County of Middlesex, Development Plan, 1951: Report of the Survey* (n.d.), photos 3, 4, and 5, facing p. 19.

17. T. Young, *Becontree and Dagenham: a report made for the Pilgrim Trust* (Becontree Social Survey Committee, 1934), 60–1.

18. For a number of detailed examples, but mostly drawn from the late nineteenth century, see Course, *op. cit.*, Chapter 10, 197–219.

19. For a more detailed treatment of this topic see Chapter 3, pp. 73–6.

20. This discussion is based on J. H. Westergaard, 'Journeys to work in the London Region', *Town Planning Review*, 28 (1957–58), 37–62; see also Westergaard's contribution in *London Evidence, op. cit.* V, 681–5.

21. Table simplified from information in Table IVa in 'Evidence submitted by the Centre for Urban Studies at University College London', *London Evidence, op. cit.*, V, 657.

22. *London Evidence* (Westergaard), *op. cit.*, V, 683–4.

23. *Census of England and Wales 1951, County Report: London* (H.M.S.O., 1953), Table A, xiii.

24. *Census of England and Wales 1931, County of London* (H.M.S.O., 1932), 2, Table 2.

25. Abercrombie, *op. cit.*, 27.

26. Wates (Streatham, 1928) Ltd., Sales Ledger.

27. Eva M. Hubback, *The Population of Britain* (1947), 27–31 and 35.

28. Department of Civic Design, University of Liverpool, *Land Use in an Urban Environment* (Liverpool, 1961), 157, Fig. 5 and 204, Fig. 14.

29. Marian Bowley, *Housing and the State, 1919–1944* (1945), 282, Appendix 2, Table 9b.

30. *Ibid.*, 66, Table VII; *ibid.*, 281, Appendix 2, Table 9a and 271, Table 2. The 'Home Counties' are here Bedfordshire, Berkshire, Buckinghamshire, Essex, Hertfordshire, Kent, London, Middlesex, Surrey and Sussex.

31. *Ibid.*, 66, Table VII.

32. *Ibid.*, 71.

33. *Ibid.*, 281, *Appendix* 2, Table 9a; Sir H. Bellman, 'The Building Trades' in British Association, *Britain in Recovery* (1938), 395–438, ref. on 406.

34. Sir H. Bellman, 'Building Societies—some economic aspects', *Economic Journal*, 43 (1933), 1–39.

35. Calculated from Bowley, *op. cit.*, 281, Appendix 2, Table 9a.

36. *Britain in Recovery, op. cit.*, 426.

37. Ministry of Health, *The Cost of House-Building: First report of the committee of enquiry appointed by the Minister of Health* (H.M.S.O., 1948), 60, graph A.

38. Bowley, *op. cit.*, 175; Bellman (1933), *op. cit.*, 6.

39. I am grateful to Mr. R. W. Wells, of the Artizans' and General Properties Co., Ltd. for discussing these matters with me.

40. Ministry of Health, *The Cost of House-Building: Second report of the committee of enquiry appointed by the Minister of Health* (H.M.S.O., 1950), 16.

41. *Cost of House-Building: First Report*, *op*, *cit*., 61, graph B.
42. Personal conversation, Mr. N. Wates.
43. L. D. Stamp, 'Land classification and agriculture' in Abercrombie, *op. cit*., 86–96, ref. on 89.
44. I am grateful to Mr. R. W. Wells of the Artizans' and General Properties Co. Ltd. for drawing my attention to this example.
45. This calculation assumes 12 houses to the acre (30 per hectare) and the cost of providing roads and services to be £100 per house.
46. I am grateful to Mr. N. Wates for discussing with me the matters mentioned in this paragraph.
47. London County Council, *London Housing Statistics, 1952–53* (1953), 19, Table 4.
48. *Ibid.*, 30, Table 12a.
49. *Ibid.*, 34–40, Table 13.
50. *Ibid.*, 30, Table 12a.
51. 'Financial provisions of post-1918 Housing Acts', *ibid.*, 11–13.
52. Young, *op. cit.*, 385–8, Appendix 10c.
53. *Ibid.*, 332, Appendix 7c.
54. *Ibid.*, 322–3, Appendices 6a and 6b.
55. London County Council, *Housing: a survey of the post-war housing work of the London County Council, 1945–1949* (1949), 13; L.C.C., *London Statistics*, 5 (1963), 99, Table 98.
56. Abercrombie, *op. cit.*, 195–6, Appendix 10.

The Central Area

*

D. F. STEVENS

There are many 'Londons' and unfortunately for the statistician or town planner even more concepts of Central London. For the purposes of this chapter, however, I have followed the Central Area adopted for the 1961 Census of Population.[1] Although long-term trends will have to be examined on some other basis from time to time this definition has the merit both of encompassing almost all the activities normally found in a conurbation centre and of having won most general recent acceptance.

Thus defined the Central Area of London embraces an area of 11·15 square miles (2,876 ha.). Concentrated in these few square miles are the functions of the Crown and Government, Church, Law, Press, Finance, Banking and Insurance, the major commodity and wholesale markets, most of the institutions of the University of London, the teaching hospitals, the headquarters of the majority of Britain's leading business enterprises, nationalized industries and corporations, and the professional organizations and trade unions. Central London is also the nation's main cultural, entertainment, shopping and tourist centre and the focus of communication by road, rail, cable and wireless. In many other countries government and commercial functions are carried on in different cities and the capital is often not the main cultural centre. The pre-eminent part which London plays in almost every aspect of national life is a justified source of pride: it is also the key to London's principal problems today.

D. F. STEVENS

The Historical Development of Central London

It seems unlikely that what is now Central London was ever continuously occupied before Roman times. The Romans, however, found that the site had many natural advantages (Chapter 1) and London soon became the economic centre of gravity of Roman Britain and the focal point of the Roman military highway system, although it was never the capital. In the second century A.D. the Romans improved the natural defences of the site by building a wall enclosing an area of some 330 acres (133 ha.).[2] It is doubtful if the area within the wall was ever fully developed in the Roman period and, after the Romans withdrew from Britain in A.D. 410, the city was soon sacked by Saxon invaders and possibly destroyed. A Saxon settlement grew up in the seventh century, to be destroyed in turn by marauding Danes and re-established by the Saxon King Alfred in A.D. 882. Under Alfred's direction the walls were repaired, trade re-established and re-population encouraged. The growth of London has been continuous since this time.

Minor Roman settlements were established at the southern end of the Bridge in Southwark and little more than a mile (1·6 km.) to the west at Westminster. There is much doubt about the subsequent history of Westminster, but it seems probable that a Saxon church was established here in the seventh or eighth century and that a royal palace existed nearby.[3] Both were rebuilt in the reign of Edward the Confessor (A.D. 1042–1066) and the development of Westminster by the Crown as a rival community to the City may be said to date from this time. In 1352 Westminster was selected as a port for the Wool Staple, but geography and the restrictions imposed by London Bridge were against its development as a port (see Chapter 8). The Crown had more success in matters under its direct control. King Edward established London (Westminster) as the capital of England in 1042, Henry II (1154–1189) removed the Treasury from Winchester (the old capital) to Westminster and Henry III (1216–1272) fixed the Law Courts at Westminster where they remained until moved to the Strand in 1882. Until his reign parliament had been summoned to wherever the king might be on his travels about the kingdom. Thereafter Westminster became the home of the royal family, the seat of Court, a permanent meeting place for parliament and the centre of administration and justice. Meanwhile the City grew prosperous in trade and commerce particularly with the

Hanseatic merchants who were granted land for a trading centre on the site of the present Cannon Street station. As the population of the City expanded it outgrew the originally lavish space within the Roman walls. Never seriously threatened after the time of the Norman Conquest and strongly protected by the Tower of London to the east and the now-vanished Baynards Castle to the west, the City no longer needed a wall and when the river section collapsed in the twelfth century it was not rebuilt. By this time Southwark had grown into a thriving suburb and the City had spread westwards across the Fleet, largely, it is thought, owing to the sale of Westminster Abbey lands in the second half of the tenth century. As a result the administrative boundary of the City today is at Temple Bar nearly half a mile (0·8 km.) to the west and the administrative area of the City today is not the 330 acres (133 ha.) within the Roman wall but 677 acres (247 ha.).

In this western suburb of the City the religious order of the Knights Templars established themselves in the twelfth century, and built the round Norman church which still survives. The order was later suppressed and part of its property was leased to a body of lawyers; from this beginning a legal precinct has developed, located midway between the commercial and political capitals of the country and occupying 'a geographical position that helped the English lawyer to discover his true political function as mediator between Crown and people' (G. M. Trevelyan).

The main highway between the two centres was the line of Fleet Street and the Strand. South of the Strand in the sixteenth and early seventeenth centuries several riverside palaces were erected, many of which, such as Somerset House and Northumberland House, have left their names on the map of London. These buildings and the cottages that extended up the lanes north of the Strand loosely linked Westminster with the City, although both St Martin's and St Giles could still claim to be 'in the Fields' at this time. During the seventeenth century the link was completed. Inigo Jones developed the Covent Garden estate in 1631 as a high-class residential area for merchants who wished to escape the overcrowded and pestilent conditions in the City, Lincoln's Inn Fields were developed by mid-century and building reached as far as Red Lion Square in the 1680s.

In Westminster further development was taking place. Henry VIII confiscated Wolsey's palace in Whitehall and abandoned the decaying palace of Westminster adjoining the Abbey to the needs of administration and justice; but the Whitehall palace was itself burned down in 1698. Nearby, St James's Square and the adjoining area north of the royal park of St James were built up in the 1660s and building continued northward into Soho. Soho Square and surrounding streets were added in the 1680s, Seven Dials in the 1690s.[4]

Meanwhile two events of immense significance had occurred. In 1660 the City of London was still medieval, insanitary and over-crowded. Honeycombed with narrow lanes, lacking sanitation or piped water, the whole area presented an appalling health and fire risk. By this time the population within the walls was about 100–150,000 and the total population of London about 500,000. The plague of the summer of 1665 reduced this figure by 90–100,000 and the Great Fire of 1666, consuming an area of about 437 acres (177 ha.), rendered over 80,000 homeless.[5] These twin blows might well have ended the City's existence as a commercial centre, but the vitality of its institutions and the lack of any suitable alternative brought about a speedy rebuilding. Unfortunately the ambitious plans prepared by Wren, Evelyn and others were not carried out. The homeless needed homes and the merchants and shopkeepers premises from which they could re-establish their livelihoods. Re-building was thus piecemeal and confused. Few new streets were created although certain requirements were laid down as to street widths, building heights and materials.[6] Plague, fire and City taxes also led to an exodus from the City.

The former mansions along the Strand had become embedded in new small houses and shops by the end of the seventeenth century and were mostly demolished and replaced by mean streets erected by speculators. A new aristocratic quarter grew up in Mayfair north of St James's. By 1708 Berkeley Square had been planned and some houses built as far west as Bolton Street and as far north as Bruton Street. The Hanover Square area was laid out about 1715 and Gros-venor Square a little later. On the south side of St James's Park development began in Queen Anne's Gate about 1704 and in Smith Square after 1721. Little else was built in this district until Thomas Cubitt developed Belgravia (1825–50) and Pimlico (1835–1850).

The westward and southward growth of London led to the end of the City's monopoly of a bridge across the river when Westminster Bridge was opened in 1750. A third bridge at Blackfriars was opened in 1769. Better cross-river communications and the improvement of the road system south of the Thames encouraged the speedy development on north Lambeth and Southwark. In the early eighteenth century continuous building in Lambeth was restricted to the river frontage, while in Southwark it was limited to Bankside, with some ribbon development to the south. By 1800 north Lambeth had coalesced with the former villages of Kennington and Vauxhall and building stretched along the Thames as far east as Rotherhithe. The construction of Vauxhall (1816), Waterloo (1817) and Southwark (1819) Bridges consolidated this growth. Apart from the main road pattern which was bold, even dramatic, building was unplanned and soon degenerated into a confusion of industrial, commercial and slum dwellings made worse by the later construction of railway viaducts to termini in the City and West End.

North of the Thames, beyond Oxford Street, lay the village of St Mary-le-bourne in open farmland, through which the New Road was constructed in 1756 as an east–west link to by-pass the chaotic road system to the south. As the eighteenth century progressed St Marylebone, too, became a fashionable residential area and a number of fine squares and streets were laid out, Cavendish Square in 1717, Portman Square in 1764 and Portland Place in the 1770s. East of Portland Place development was also proceeding, but with more modest buildings, a fact which has had interesting implications for the subsequent history of the area. Further east again, beyond the old lane to Tottenham Court, Bedford Square and Gower Street were begun in 1776, Russell Square about 1800 and the Torrington, Woburn, Tavistock and Gordon Square areas as far north as the New Road between 1820 and 1850. The future character of this area, now the London University precinct, was foreshadowed by the building of the British Museum (Great Russell Street), begun in 1823, and of University College (Gower Street), begun in 1827. East of this area building also proceeded from south to north. The Foundling Hospital was outside London when building commenced in 1742. Mecklenburgh and Brunswick Squares date from the 1790s and most of the development to the north is early nineteenth century, culminating in the Regent Square and Argyle Square areas of about 1820. The same pattern is repeated further east again in Finsbury where urban development, which began in Clerkenwell after the Fire, was completed in the north of the borough in the 1830s in the Bloomsbury style.

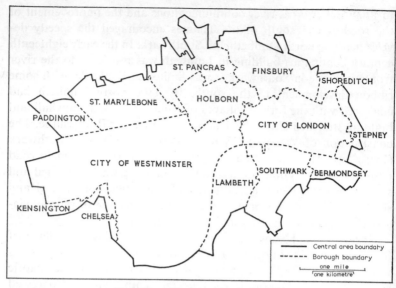

FIG. 31   The Central Area 1961
Based on 1961 Census.

Transport and the Central Area

The continuously built-up area of London of about 1830 corresponds closely with our present definition of the Central Area, but the coming of the railways led to the rapid growth of the belt of mid-Victorian suburbs in places such as Bayswater, Islington, Camberwell and Battersea. In addition to encouraging the decentralization of population, the development of railways in London also permitted a much greater concentration and specialization of activities at the centre; indeed, it was the importance of the City as a commercial centre which called the railway network into being. Once established, however, the railways gave great impetus to both the already existing trends of residential decline and employment growth. The population of the City changed little between 1801 and 1851 when it numbered about 128,000. By 1861 it declined to 112,000. In the next decade four new railway termini within the City boundary joined Fenchurch Street Station, and the Metropolitan and District Railways also entered the City. At the same time the main-line railways became interested in the development of suburban traffic (see Chapter 3). The result was a decline in the population of the City by

nearly 40,000 between 1861 and 1871 (Fig. 32). By 1891 it had fallen
to a third of the 1861 figure and today stands at under 5,000. The
same pattern was repeated elsewhere in the Central Area, although on
a less dramatic scale. The borough of Holborn also declined in
population after 1851 and the other central boroughs of Finsbury, St
Marylebone and Westminster after 1861. By 1921 the combined population of the five central boroughs was little more than half what it
had been in 1861 and by 1961 less than a third (Table VI). The situation since 1939 is shown in Figure 32.

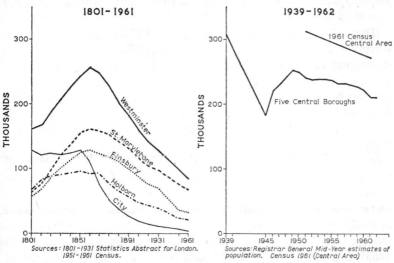

FIG. 32   Population change in the Central Area 1801–1962
Based on the decennial censuses and on the Registrar-General's mid-year
estimates of population.

TABLE VI

Population in the Central London Boroughs 1801–1961

Borough	1801	1861	1891	1921	1961
City of London	128,129	112,013	37,702	13,709	4,767
Finsbury	67,103	129,031	109,981	75,995	32,887
Holborn	55,515	94,074	66,781	43,192	22,008
St Marylebone	63,982	161,680	143,487	104,173	69,045
Westminster	160,759	257,232	201,969	141,578	85,735
Total	475,488	754,030	559,920	378,647	214,442

The existence of the twin nuclei within the Central Area was reflected in the early nineteenth-century road pattern. North and south of London the main approach roads divided to West End or City destinations; to the north at Finchley (Tally Ho) and Tottenham (Seven Sisters) with secondary foci at the Archway and Camden Town; to the south, much closer in because of the relatively smaller extent of the built-up area, at New Cross and Kennington, also with secondary foci at the Elephant and Castle and St George's Circus. To east and west the main roads were drawn together at Hammersmith, Shepherd's Bush and Aldgate, to continue as single highways into the Central Area.

The railways now repeated this pattern (Fig. 33). Whatever the direction of its approach to the metropolis each company endeavoured to obtain a foothold in the City, so great was its importance as a source of revenue and traffic. As a result, many railway systems became double-headed, with both a West End and a City terminal.[7] South of the river, for example, the competing South Eastern, London Chatham and Dover, and London Brighton and South Coast companies established their West End termini at Charing Cross and Victoria (the last two sharing) and their City termini at Cannon Street, Blackfriars and London Bridge respectively. Any railway company that could not serve the City directly made strenuous efforts to serve it indirectly. Thus, the Great Western, marooned at Paddington by the growth of London in the west, assisted in promoting the Metropolitan, the world's first underground railway, in 1863[8] and the London and South Western, likewise isolated at Waterloo, promoted its own tube railway, the Waterloo and City, in 1898.

The result of this competition was to give the City a very complete system of rail communication, without which its subsequent commercial growth could not have taken place. By 1891, when the residential population of the City had fallen below 38,000, the day population was over 310,000, showing a net daily inward movement of over a quarter of a million people.

The situation was very different in the West End. Here there was less intense competition for land and more modern and more spacious residential quarters. The 1846 Royal Commission on Metropolitan Railway Termini had opposed the building of railway termini south of Euston Road or east of a line along Edgware Road, Park Lane and Vauxhall Bridge Road and even the Metropolitan

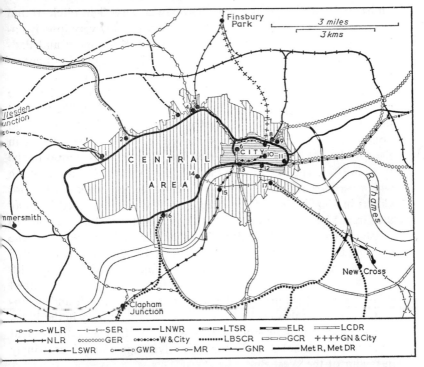

FIG. 33   Railways and the Central Area

Key: WLR, West London Railway; SER, South Eastern Railway; LNWR, London and North Western Railway; LTSR, London Tilbury and Southend Railway; ELR, East London Railway; LCDR, London Chatham and Dover Railway; NLR, North London Railway; GER, Great Eastern Railway; W & City, Waterloo and City; LBSCR, London Brighton and South Coast Railway; GCR, Great Central Railway; GN & City, Great Northern and City; LSWR, London and South Western Railway; GWR, Great Western Railway; MR, Midland Railway; GNR, Great Northern Railway; Met R, Met DR, Metropolitan and District Railways. The WLR and ELR were managed jointly by the main-line companies which they linked. The NLR was a satellite of the LNWR which it provided with dock and city connections. Note the connection from St Pancras and King's Cross to Moorgate ('the widened lines'); a similar connection with Euston was begun but never completed.

Stations: 1, Paddington; 2, St Marylebone; 3, Euston; 4, St Pancras; 5, King's Cross; 6, Holborn Viaduct; 7, Moorgate; 8, Broad Street; 9, Liverpool Street; 10, Bank; 11, Fenchurch Street; 12, Cannon Street; 13, Blackfriars; 14, Charing Cross; 15, Waterloo; 16, Victoria; 17, London Bridge.

175

and District Railways, though they drew a very tight circle round the City just over half a mile (0·8 km.) across, only very loosely encircled the residential areas of the West End, Kensington and Paddington where the circle was one and a half miles (2·3 km.) across (Fig. 33).

These comparatively poor facilities were vastly improved by the coming of the tube railways after 1890. The first tubes, like the first underground railways, were constructed as City links, the City and South London Railway from Stockwell to King William Street in the City in 1890[9] and the Waterloo and City from Waterloo to the Bank in 1898. The first tube in the West End was the Central London which was opened from Shepherd's Bush to the Bank via Oxford Circus in 1900.[10] The Baker Street and Waterloo followed in 1906, the Great Northern Piccadilly and Brompton from Hammersmith to Finsbury Park via Piccadilly Circus at the end of 1906 and the Charing Cross Euston and Hampstead in 1907. It should be noted that, with the exception of the Central which linked the City with West End, all these lines were exclusive to the West End and linked it with growing suburbs to the west, north-west, north and north-east. When the tubes pushed out into the open country in the 1920s and 1930s, as the main-line Metropolitan and District railways had done before, the balance of economic advantage swung increasingly in favour of the West End.

This is shown most vividly by a comparison of the rail services from a suburb like Finchley before and after the arrival of the tube.[11] In 1940 the former Great Northern branch to Barnet was added to the Northern Line of the London Passenger Transport Board tube system, and, whereas the winter morning peak service (7.30 a.m. to 9.45 a.m.) in 1902/3 comprised two trains to the West (King's Cross) and twelve to the City (five to Moorgate and seven to Broad Street), the service available in 1962/3 comprised 38 trains to the West End (Charing Cross) and 20 to the City (Bank). (See also Figs. 17 and 18.)

As a result the West End has been transformed in the last 60 years from a superior residential area to a prosperous shopping, entertainment and, more recently, business district. It is unlikely, with the decline of the population to the north and south of Oxford Street which they grew up to serve, together with the outward growth of London, that the Regent Street and Oxford Street stores could have remained in business, far less expanded, without the increased accessibility provided by the tube.

A number of other aspects of the development of the tubes remain to be mentioned. First, there is the manner in which the Northern Line after 1926 re-emphasized the duality of central London with its West End and City branches, the only line to divide in central London. Secondly, the relative paucity of tube railways in the south, particularly the south-east, has had an important effect on the development of major suburban shopping centres in this area,

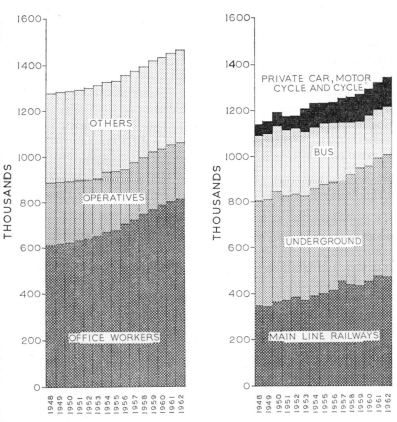

FIG. 34 Employment and journeys to work in the Central Area 1948–62

Employment: estimates based on unpublished data for the 1951 Census, supplemented by National Insurance returns, Factory Inspectors' records and L.C.C. surveys.

Journeys to work: figures for public transport based on London Transport Board censuses, those for private transport on author's estimates (1948–50), L.T.B. estimates (1951–56) and L.T.B. censuses.

which are much nearer the Central Area than in the north, where the influence of central London is clearly very much stronger.[12] Thirdly, there is the effect on central London of the transformation of the tubes after the First World War from an urban to a suburban system of transport. As successive belts of suburbs were built and cars and buses used as feeders to the tubes, a situation developed in the morning peak periods in which trains from an outer suburb such as Edgware are full by the time they arrive at intermediate points like Hampstead and are then subjected to an additional load of transfer passengers from more distant points on arrival at the main line termini at the edge of the Central Area. This situation has in turn encouraged the growth of car commuting from the inner suburbs in recent years.[13] Yet, road improvements, however necessary on other grounds, are no solution to the commuting problem (Fig. 34). London urgently needs further tubes, to improve both access to the Central Area and movement within it. One entirely urban line, the Victoria Line, is under construction and several other proposals are now receiving attention.

The Major Economic Activities of the Central Area: Land Use

Competition for a scarce natural resource is the keynote to the distribution of land uses in the Central Area. A high degree of accessibility has produced high land values which in turn dictate the intensive use of land; less intensive or space-using activities thus tend to be squeezed out. This tendency, together with the desire for more spacious living conditions and the increased mobility provided by modern transport, is the principal reason for the decline of the resident population at the centre. Low-density industrial plants and storage activities have also declined, while social and cultural facilities come under constant pressure from business and commercial uses. The high cost of central locations and the degree of cohesion in certain activities also lead to the growth of specialized centres where the importance of accessibility or social cachet may outweigh cost.[14]

Localization within the Central Area is true of manufacturing, office and service activities. Some of these areas are very well known, such as Fleet Street (newspapers), Harley Street (medicine) and Savile Row (tailoring); but there are many others, such as optical instrument manufacture in Clerkenwell, cinema film processing in

TABLE VII

Floor space of principal building uses
City of London, 1939–1962

Use category	1939 million square feet	%	1949 million square feet	%	1962 million square feet	%
Offices	37·6	44·5	31·5	55·6	43·7	60·2
Industry	9·9	11·8	4·8	8·5	5·3	7·3
Warehouses	22·3	26·4	10·3	18·2	10·4	14·3
Residential	1·0	1·2	0·7	1·2	0·8	1·1
Other uses	13·6	16·1	9·3	16·5	12·4	17·1
Total floor area	84·4 (7·8 m.sq.m.)	100·0	56·6 (5·2 m.sq.m.)	100·0	72·6 (6·7 m.sq.m.)	100·0

Source: City Corporation.

the Wardour Street area, fur storage in Upper Thames Street, music publishers in Denmark Street and travel offices in the Cockspur Street–Lower Regent Street area.

Unfortunately it is impossible to trace changes in land and building uses over a period for the Central Area as a whole, but data are available for the City of London since 1939 (Table VII).[15]

This period of comparison is interesting, since the extent of bomb damage in the City during the Second World War, when nearly a third of all floor space was destroyed, countered the inertia existing among owners of valuable freehold premises and hastened redevelopment on lines most in accord with the economic needs of the times. It will be seen that whereas the office area has increased by 12·2 million square feet (1·1 million sq. m.) since the war, there has been very little industrial building (and this mainly in the newspaper industry) and virtually no net gain in warehouse or residential use. However, the Barbican scheme to the north of the new commercial area along London Wall, which is to house some 7,000 persons, will substantially add to the residential area when completed.

Table VIII shows the distribution of land and building uses in central London in 1957 for an area somewhat smaller than that defined at the beginning of this chapter, excluding certain parts of Paddington, Knightsbridge and Pimlico. In such a densely built-up

TABLE VIII

Land use and floor space in the Central Area, January 1957

Use Category	Site area	Per cent of total land area	Floor space	Per cent of total floor area	Floor space/ site area ratio
	millions of square feet	%	millions of square feet	%	
Employment uses					
Offices	25·0	11	139·4*	35 ⎫	5·5:1
Industry	12·9	6	41·6	10·5 ⎬ 58	3·2:1
Warehouses	15·8	7	50·5	12·5 ⎭	3·2:1
Service uses					
Entertainment and Public Buildings	16·2	7	30·1	7·5 ⎫	1·8:1
Shops	9·2	4	31·3	8 ⎬ 18	3·4:1
Education	4·3	2	10·5	2·5 ⎭	2·3:1
Residential uses					
Hotels, boarding houses, etc.	30·2 ⎫	14	22·8	6 ⎫	2·5:1
Private dwellings ⎭			54·8	13·5 ⎬ 19·5	
Other uses	17·7	8	11·6	3	—
Total built-up area	131·3	59	392·6	98·5	—
Open space	12·9	6	—	—	—
Public utilities	21·6	10	5·6	1·5	—
Roads	56·4	25	—	—	—
Total land area	222·2	100	398·2 (37·0 m.sq.m.)	100	—
River	17·7	—	—	—	—
Total Central Area	239·9 (22·2 m.sq.m.)	—	—	—	—

Source: L.C.C.

* Includes ancillary floor space in office buildings, e.g. car parking space, boiler rooms, etc. The actual office floor area in January 1957 was 96·5 million square feet.

area as central London it is surprising to find that buildings cover only three-fifths of the land area (plus a proportion of the area devoted to utilities), and that a quarter of the total area is devoted to roads. Nearly a quarter of the built-up area supports residential uses, including hotels, but the area devoted to offices alone is not far short of this (and by 1964 will certainly be very much closer), while industry and warehousing each claim more than a tenth of the total building space. The balance is even more uneven when one considers relative floor areas. Offices account for more than a third of all floor space in central London and the addition of industrial and warehouse space gives a total floor space for the major employment uses of over 230 million square feet, or 58 per cent. All residential uses combined account for less than a fifth of the total floor space in spite of the large residential areas of north Finsbury, St Pancras, north Lambeth and Southwark included in this definition of central London.

Offices

The growth of administration is a feature of the employment patterns of all advanced economies and reflects a decreasing dependence upon manufacturing activities, increasing complexity and specialization of economic activity and growth in the size of the business unit.

In Britain the growth of the major trading companies in the seventeenth and eighteenth centuries necessitated a parallel expansion in banking and insurance facilities. In the nineteenth century finance and insurance facilities developed to support Britain's role as the world's major exporter of manufactured goods, while at home banking was put on a surer footing and commerce facilitated by the extension of limited liability.

London obtained a disproportionate share of the growth of office employment in the nineteenth century because of her very real natural advantages. Among these was her location at the hub of the road and, later, the rail network of the country, the proximity of parliament, the large residential population, the growth of the port and the already well-developed financial and commercial mechanism of the City. The establishment of the major national price-fixing markets was particularly characteristic of the mid-nineteenth century. As business expanded specialized centres grew up, such as the Coal Exchange (1849), Stock Exchange (1854) and the Wool

Exchange (1874), to replace the unsatisfactory arrangements of the Royal Exchange or the former haphazard dealings in City coffee houses.

The growing functions of government, deriving in part from the demands of two world wars and in part from increased national concern with social welfare, also brought about an increase in government employment in offices. Since the outbreak of the First World War in particular several completely new departments have been established, for example, the Ministries of Labour (1916), Pensions (1917), Transport (1919) and National Insurance (1945). Quasi-governmental bodies have also proliferated, such as the British Broadcasting Corporation (1926), British Overseas Airways Corporation (1939), the National Coal Board (1948) and the United Kingdom Atomic Energy Authority (1954). New research bodies grew up, for example, the Department of Scientific and Industrial Research (1916) and the Medical Research Council (1920). All these organizations had to be staffed and their staffs accommodated: all selected central London for their administrative headquarters.

The early trading companies needed no head offices. The East India Company, for example, founded in 1600, was carried on from the home of its first Governor and it was not until 1726 that a head office was erected in Leadenhall Street. The Bank of England followed in Threadneedle Street in 1732. In Whitehall, government offices were erected for the Admiralty in 1726 and for the Treasury in 1736. In 1789 Somerset House was erected on the site of one of the former Strand mansions to house a complex of government departments, the Royal Academy and the Royal Society. As the size of business grew in the early nineteenth century many firms moved out of their former premises over shops and the like into purpose-built buildings and the City began to develop as we know it today. But office building was not limited to Whitehall and the City even at this time. The County Fire Office was one of the most important buildings in Nash's Regent Street scheme and several insurance company head offices were located in the Fleet Street–Strand area in the 1830s.[16] The constantly expanding need for further offices is also seen in the predominance of commercial premises along the principal new roads constructed by the Metropolitan Board of Works and City Corporation, such as Victoria Street (1852–71), Shaftesbury Avenue (1877–86) and Queen Victoria Street (1867–71). When the London County Council's Kingsway–Aldwych scheme was completed in 1905 the main frontages were almost exclusively devoted to offices.

The inter-war period, particularly the 1930s, saw a further rapid expansion. In the City the Bank of England was extended and most of the principal banks moved into new headquarters. Other major projects of this period were the Unilever Building (Blackfriars), the *Daily Telegraph* and *Daily Express* buildings (Fleet Street) and Britannia House (Moorgate). Outside the City, office building was particularly extensive in three main areas, the Strand where the principal buildings were Brettenham House, Shell Mex, the Adelphi and South Africa House, the eastern area of Mayfair (Berkeley Square House, Lansdowne House and Curzon House) and Millbank (Thames House, Imperial Chemical Industries, Millbank, Great Westminster House). Yet, south of the Thames, the L.C.C.'s own headquarters at County Hall and the London Fire Brigade were joined by only one government building, Lambeth Bridge House and

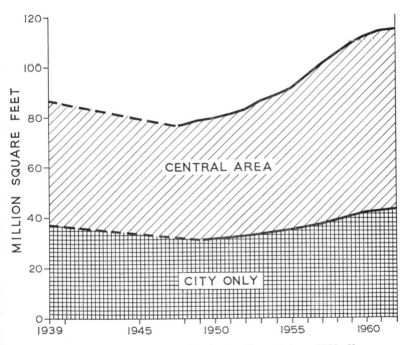

Fig. 35   Office accommodation in the Central Area 1939–62
Based on L.C.C. and City Corporation records.

one commercial office for W. H. Smith and Son on the Albert Embankment. During the Second World War there was further dispersal as many firms moved into former residential buildings, particularly in Mayfair and Belgravia, when their City premises were damaged or destroyed.

For some years after the war there was little office building owing to the system of building licensing control. When these controls were removed in 1954 there were fifteen years of stagnation in office building to be made good, nearly ten million square feet of bombed office floor space to be replaced and a much expanded demand to be met. Building proceeded very rapidly at first, mainly on bombed sites (Fig. 35). More recently the annual net addition to London's stock of offices has slowed owing to a slackening of demand, the necessity of first demolishing existing premises and the limitations imposed by town planning controls. In the City war damage was made good by 1957 and a new office area has been established along the new road of London Wall. In Whitehall the pre-war Whitehall Gardens project has been completed. Nearby, virtually the whole of Victoria Street has been, or is to be, rebuilt. Other major office concentrations have been established along Theobald's Road and New Oxford Street where bomb damage was heavy, Euston and Marylebone Roads and south of the river along the Albert Embankment, around Waterloo Station and in Southwark.

Although the majority of offices are still concentrated in the City and Westminster, recent construction has led to much wider dispersal within the Central Area (Fig. 36). The proportion of post-war offices is particularly high in Paddington, Southwark and Marylebone, but very little building has taken place east of the City.

The growth of offices and new office areas in London provides an interesting case history of the inter-relation of economic forces and town planning. The effect of such strong localizing factors as the major commodity exchanges, the Stock Exchange and the Baltic Exchange in attracting firms engaged in related activities while repelling others has already been noted. Parliament, the Law Courts and the Press have the same effect elsewhere in the Central Area. Expanding demand has therefore led to the development of other areas for general head-office purposes.[17] The location of the new Prudential and Pearl Insurance Company head offices in High Holborn outside the financial area of the City after 1880 is indicative of this type of movement, which was continued by Unilevers, Shell

Mex and Imperial Chemical Industries between the wars. Since the Second World War land use has become a matter of public control under the Town and Country Planning Acts, but it is unlikely that the more remote areas zoned for offices would have succeeded had it not been for expanding demand and limitation elsewhere. Pressure of demand abruptly ended the former prejudice against a head office south of the river and a number of major companies have located here, for example, the Shell Oil Company, Richard Costain Ltd., the Decca Group of Companies and the United Africa Company. The high cost of accommodation in the West End has also forced government offices across the river. In the inter-war years the expansion of government offices was deflected southwards along Millbank, with only one office across the Thames. Now, as the leases of expensive West End accommodation expire, Ministries less concerned with the day-to-day business of government (Transport, Health, Works and Housing and Local Government) are being located south of the river.

Where town planning measures have opposed economic trends they have been less successful. The decentralization of population and employment from congested inner areas was one of the basic principles of the Greater London Plan of 1944[18] and of the L.C.C. Development Plan of 1951.[19] Nevertheless, it has been calculated that total office floor space in the Central Area, which was reduced from 87 to 77·5 million square feet (8·1 to 7·2 million sq. m.) during the war, had grown to 114·8 million (10·7 million sq. m.) by mid-1962, an increase of nearly a third, while office employment has grown from 615,000 in 1948 to about 815,000 by mid-1962 and is continuing to increase at over 15,000 a year.

Growth on this scale has caused alarm in many quarters. Not only does the expansion of offices threaten other uses at the centre, particularly housing, and increase congestion, but any increase of employment at the centre means a corresponding demand for housing elsewhere in the London Region within daily commuting distance, pressure upon the green belt and the overloading and uneconomic use of transport facilities. Progressively tighter measures of control have been introduced at the centre and the decentralization of inessential activities is being strongly pressed, but it is unlikely that these measures will do more than slow the rate of growth.[20]

Industry

Industry is much less important than offices in the Central Area, in terms both of land use and employment, and is tending to decline. In addition planning action to reduce industrial employment in the Central Area is reinforced by the much greater space demands of modern industry to accommodate larger manufacturing units, single-storey workshops and continuous flow production methods. Decline has probably been continuous since the First World War, but it can be measured only since 1938 (Table IX).

It will be seen that in the areas where bomb damage was heavy in the Second World War (City and Finsbury) industrial employment was almost halved. In the case of the City this decrease can also be compared with the loss of industrial floor space (Table VII). In all central boroughs except the City, where the making good of war damage has led to a small increase in industrial employment and floor area, the number of factory operatives has continued to decline; in the five central boroughs it is now only just over half the 1938 figure, while the number of factories has declined by more than

TABLE IX

Factory employment (operatives only) in the Central Boroughs 1938–1962

Borough	1938	1947	1954	1957	1962
City of London	35,094	20,803	19,772	19,331	22,081
Holborn	14,750	10,864	10,717	12,061	10,828
Finsbury	66,556	36,229	32,478	30,395	29,660
St. Marylebone	29,783	21,015	17,851	17,030	13,566
Westminster	46,528	39,584	38,342	32,110	27,690
Total employed	192,711	128,495	119,160	110,927	103,825
Number of Factories	12,650	7,523	6,821	6,918	5,772
Average number of operatives per factory	15·2	17·1	17·5	16·3	18·0

Source: Ministry of Labour Factory Inspectorate.

half. There is thus a surprising, though slight increase in the average number of operatives per factory compared with 1938, although Central Area workshops are still very small—smaller in fact than this average would seem to indicate, owing to the inclusion in the total of the large printing establishments of the major national daily newspapers.

The relative importance of various industries in the Central Area in 1957 is shown in Table X. The clothing trades are the largest employers of labour, followed closely by printing, with instruments and jewellery, engineering, food, drink and tobacco and woodworking relatively much less important, although highly characteristic of the area. Yet the broad categories of the Standard Industrial Classification are not sufficiently precise for the purpose of identifying particular Central Area trades. The branches of the clothing industry located at the centre are those most concerned with fashion, women's outerwear, tailoring, and associated finishing trades. Mass produced goods such as underwear and hosiery are located where space is more abundant and speed of execution much less important. Printing can be divided into two: newspaper printing, largely in the Fleet Street area, and job printing centred upon Clerkenwell. Book printing is no longer a central activity although magazine printing, where again time is important, is found in the Central Area, in particular in the secondary printing district of Stamford Street south of the river. Limited space requirements and linkage with the West End showrooms are clearly important factors in maintaining the jewellery trades in the Central Area and the teaching hospitals represent an important locational tie for surgical instrument makers. Engineering is mainly small scale, but food and drink manufacturing covers a wide range, from small bakeries and confectioners to large breweries employing several hundred people. Woodworking also consists of two main branches: furniture manufacture and shopfitting. Bulk, the risk of damage in transit and a wealthy local clientele were once important to the former; but the furniture-making area west of Tottenham Court Road has now almost completely disappeared, while the Shoreditch (Curtain Road) district, only partly in the Central Area, has grown. Improved communications, increased standardization and the space requirements of the furniture industry are likely to bring about further decentralization.

Since the subject of London industry is dealt with more fully in Chapters 9 and 10, only a few generalizations about industry in the

TABLE X

Manufacturing industry in the Central Boroughs 1957

	Industrial Group	Number of Factories	Number of Operatives	Rank
III	Bricks, glass, etc.	54	601	
IV	Chemicals	78	1,559	
V	Metal manufacture	18	123	
VI	Engineering	457	6,582	4
VII	Vehicles	191	2,095	
VIII	Other metal goods	224	2,550	
IX	Instruments and Jewellery	613	7,726	3
X	Textiles	119	1,343	
XI	Leather	467	4,070	
XII	Clothing	2,596	33,885	1
XIII	Food, Drink and Tobacco	234	5,685	5
XIV	Woodworking	356	4,269	6
XV	Paper and Printing	823	32,820	2
	Other industries	688	7,619	
	Totals	6,918	110,927	

Industrial Groups I and II are not represented in the Central Boroughs.
Source: Ministry of Labour Factory Inspectorate.
1948 Standard Industrial Classification.

Central Area are necessary. Central Area industries tend on the whole to be small-scale and to need little floor space per worker. Specially designed buildings are generally not required; in fact, several Central Area trades, such as clothing, printing and furniture making, often operate for limited periods prior to redevelopment in premises which they could not normally afford. A central location is often imperative where speed of execution is necessary. This applies both to the fashion trades and to job printing, but most especially to the newspaper industry. Attention has previously been drawn to the establishment of a legal precinct half way between the government and commercial centres of the capital. A similar location has been selected by the Press. News sources are near at hand—Parliament, the Law Courts, the City financial and commercial organizations and the entertainment centre of the West End and, although the newspaper industry requires much space, nearness to sources of information and location at the hub of international radio and telephone communications and of the national rail network for distribution purposes are the paramount location factors. Outliers of the Fleet Street press area are found in Covent Garden, Grays Inn Road and Stamford Street. News is the most perishable of all commodities, but similar considerations also apply to the location of the food and drink industries, among which bakeries, ice cream manufacture, meat products and bottling are important. The location of brewing, on the other hand, is less a question of the perishability of the final product than the result of heavy investment in fixed plant.

The existence of a large labour pool is also important. In the past immigrant labour has played a major part in the development of the East End clothing industry. Today the large labour pool on which industry in central London can draw is important for industries with seasonal fluctuations in labour requirements, e.g. clothing, and for those which need highly trained and qualified staff, such as the instrument and jewellery trades. Generally speaking, the more expensive the product the less site costs matter. Bespoke furniture making and tailoring thus developed in the West End while the poorer quality products of both industries were diverted to less costly localities such as Shoreditch and Stepney. Newer industries producing high-quality products, such as pharmaceutical, photographic and electrical goods, were unable or unwilling to find central sites and thus tend to be located in the inter-war suburban belt of London.

Little is known at present about the importance of industrial linkages to the manufacturing activities of the Central Area and the localization of industries which results.[21] What is quite clear is that the confusion of activities in the Central Area is much more apparent than real and that the existing distribution must be respected by town planners if the economic framework of London is not to be disrupted. Certainly there is a very wide field here which would repay much greater study by urban geographers, with results which could well have important implications for the future guidance of planning policy towards industry in Central London.

Shops

Central Area shops have to provide for the local resident population, a day population more than five times as great, visitors and holidaymakers from the rest of Britain and tourists from abroad,

There is, therefore, a wide variety of shops and shopping districts in central London.

Some shopping streets still maintain their local character and mainly serve a local population, for example, Marchmont Street and Marylebone High Street. Others, though providing for local shopping needs, are more dependent upon a very much larger day population for their continued existence, such as Brewer Street, Soho, and Strutton Ground, off Victoria Street. Street markets and stalls provide a useful means of temporarily expanding more permanent facilities to cope with the heavy lunch-hour demand. Good examples, often in the less salubrious side streets, may be found in Lower Marsh, Lambeth, Leather Lane, High Holborn, and Whitecross Street, Finsbury. Middlesex Street (Petticoat Lane), on the City/Stepney border is now, of course, a tourist attraction in its own right.

The character of shopping streets where the resident population is small is very different. Victoria Street and Kingsway, with their assortment of office equipment suppliers, tobacconists/confectioners, restaurants and coffee bars, are representative of this type in the West End, and Cheapside in the City. The type of shop also reflects the composition of the working population: thus men's outfitters predominate in Cheapside, but both men's and women's clothing shops are found in Victoria Street, reflecting the fact that there are many more women in West End offices than in the City.

As with so many other uses, shops have migrated westwards. In the early nineteenth century the fashionable shops were grouped around St Paul's Churchyard and Ludgate Hill and developed westwards along Holborn and St Giles. As fashionable new residential areas developed in the West End, shops followed. Thus the genesis of the Oxford Street–Bond Street–Regent Street area as London's principal shopping district lies in the growth of a wealthy local clientele in the eighteenth century. Many of the major stores date from the early 1800s.[22] Regent Street (1817–25) was designed as a shopping street and Bond Street seems to have developed as such by 1850. In 1900 the Oxford Street shopping area did not extend further west than Marylebone Lane and Selfridge was considered very unwise to erect his store so far west in 1909.

There has been little subsequent movement. Unlike many other cities, e.g. New York which grew northwards along Manhattan, London has grown outwards in all directions and the tubes and, later, the motor-buses gave easy access from most districts. It is also fortunate that the surrounding area has not decayed, as has happened in many American city centres. Only Shoolbreds in Tottenham Court Road, which closed in 1930, and Whiteleys in Bayswater, which recently reduced its sales area, have been affected in this way. There seems little danger of further contraction. Several stores damaged or destroyed in the war have been rebuilt and others extended, while the rebuilding of several more is either in hand or proposed on their present sites. It is significant that Thomas Wallis and Company's store at Holborn Circus between the City and West End, demolished by bombing in 1941, has not been rebuilt, but now functions on a smaller scale at the western end of Oxford Street. Only one major store is located east of a line Southampton Row–Kingsway and most of them are concentrated in Oxford Street and Regent Street. Other important stores are to be found elsewhere and three outlying areas of Knightsbridge, Kensington High Street and Queensway have developed in high-class residential areas (Fig. 38).

As with offices, local specialization has developed within the West End shopping area. Bond Street is the home of the small, often exclusive speciality shop. Regent Street has at least twice as many independent shops as branches of multiple stores, although the number of independents is tending to be reduced, particularly by the entry of the booking offices of major airline companies which have overflowed into Regent Street from the banking–insurance–travel area of Lower Regent Street to the south. Oxford Street is the least exclusive of the three and the one with the most multiples.

It is a matter of some surprise that such very different types of shops are found in the same area. Very broadly, the West End shopping district seems to have a dual function. First, it is a centre for the sale of the rare, exclusive and unstandardized product, for example, *haute couture* and antiques. Such goods have a limited, widely-dispersed clientele. Maximum sales are therefore achieved at the point of maximum accessibility. Secondly, it serves as a centre for comparative shopping purposes. Only here can the widest range of any particular product be seen and a purchase made on the fullest consideration of relative designs, colours, materials, and costs. The wider profit margins on a limited number of sales in the first category offset the smaller profits from a very much larger number of sales in the second. Both types of shop can therefore survive in a highly competitive environment.

191

D. F. STEVENS

Hotels

London's hotel accommodation has always compared badly with that of other leading European cities. A few high-class hotels were included in Nash's improvements in the Lower Regent Street–Haymarket area in the 1820s, but it was not until the 1850s and 1860s that the Westminster Palace, the Langham and, later, the railway hotels began to meet the increased demand.[23] Prior to this, the successors of the old coaching inns in the City had provided accommodation for visitors, but, with the growth of offices and the decline of the resident population and entertainment facilities, they were no longer well sited. Many City hotels closed during the nineteenth century: now only two remain. (Fig. 37.)

The area for hotel building has also moved westwards. In the 1880s and 1890s the Strand and Trafalgar Square were particularly favoured and the Cecil, Savoy, Grand, Metropole, Victoria and Carlton hotels were erected. All, except the Savoy, have now been replaced by, or converted into, offices not, it would seem, because they were inconvenient or badly sited, but simply because offices gave a higher return. Meanwhile the hotel district moved further west and the Park Lane (1927), Mayfair (1927), Dorchester (1929) and the Cumberland hotels (1933) were opened. Since the Second World War the erection of the Westbury, Hertford, Hilton and the Carlton Tower hotels indicates that the westward trend continues.

Figure 37 shows how few hotels lie east of a line Woburn Place–Southampton Row–Kingsway, although widely distributed west of this line. Four main hotel areas may be distinguished: the Bloomsbury group, which is very varied in size and character, and depends on the northern main-line termini; the Mayfair–Strand group, the principal hotel area in London and the location of the most expensive hotels; the Bayswater group, which comprises mainly small and comparatively inexpensive hotels outside the Central Area; and a Gloucester Road–Earl's Court group, also outside the Central Area which is increasing in importance because of proximity to London Airport and the Air Terminal; there is also a minor centre in Pimlico based on Victoria.

A complex of reasons would seem to be responsible for this grouping, among which are the type of property for conversion, estates' policies, proximity to road, rail and air communications, proximity to entertainment facilities and, now, ease of parking. The value of agglomeration of hotels in more or less the same price range might, however, be the principal factor in the development of distinct hotel districts.

London received over a million and a half overseas visitors in 1960 and probably more than two million visitors from the rest of Britain spent part at least of their holidays in London. The number of hotel beds available for visitors is probably in excess of 50,000, about half of which are in good class hotels. The question is often asked whether London's hotels can cope with the anticipated growth of tourism. The answer would seem to be that, although more than 4,500 hotel bedrooms have been added since 1948 and planning permission has been granted for a further 8,000, the hotel industry will regulate itself to a condition of semi-scarcity in order to maintain a sufficiently high occupancy rate to cover overheads and rising labour costs.

Entertainment: Theatres, Cinemas and Concert Halls

The home of the theatre in Shakespearian times was in Southwark where the gathering of mobs was less to be feared than in the City itself. Thereafter and until the mid-nineteenth century there were only two theatres in London licensed for the performances of legitimate drama, the Theatre Royal, Drury Lane, and the Royal Opera House, Covent Garden, although lighter entertainment was to be found in many other places including the famous 'theatres' of the Vauxhall and Ranelagh Gardens.[24] Following the easing of the licensing system, it was natural that new theatres should be erected in the more populous and wealthy West End, but they were excluded from the better residential areas such as Mayfair and Belgravia and from Crown land.

The most active period of theatre building in London came between 1890 and 1914, immediately after the completion of Shaftesbury Avenue and Charing Cross Road and contemporary with the completion of the Kingsway–Aldwych scheme. These new streets provided excellent sites of high publicity value and even today 12 of 41 theatres in the Central Area are located here (Fig. 39). The second wave of theatre building in the late 1920s was not related to any major road programme and was thus more sporadic.

There has been some tendency to areal concentration since 1945. Four theatres have been lost in the Kingsway area. The Kingsway Theatre and Holborn Empire were destroyed during the war, the

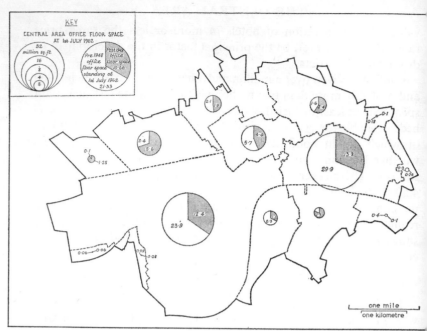

Fig. 36   Office floor space in the Central Area
Based on L.C.C. surveys.

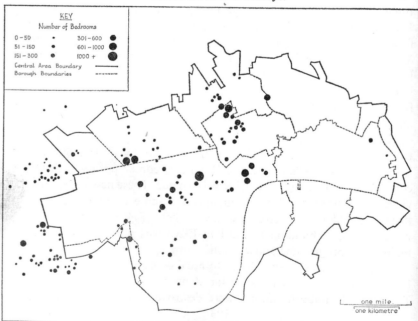

Fig. 37   Hotels in the Central Area
Information supplied by the British Travel and Holidays Association.

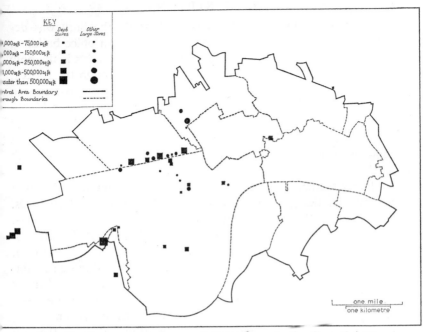

FIG. 38   Department stores and large shops in the Central Area
Based on L.C.C. surveys.

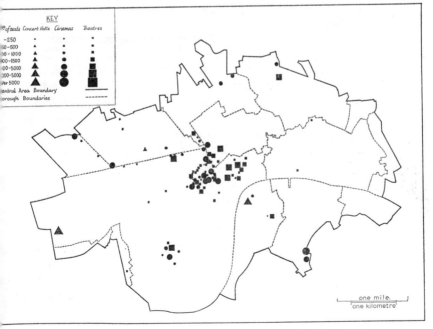

FIG. 39   Theatres, cinemas and concert halls in the Central Area
Based on L.C.C. surveys.

Gaiety was damaged and not reopened, while the Stoll was demolished and rebuilt as a smaller theatre within an office building, but has recently been used as a cinema. The St James's is the only outright loss of a theatre in use since the war although the L.C.C., as the local planning authority, has had to resist strong pressure to demolish most of the remainder and replace them with offices. Meanwhile, the Royal Court and Queen's theatres have been reopened and a new theatre, the Mermaid, has been opened in the City. The proposed National Theatre will adjoin County Hall on the South Bank.

The first cinema in London was the Biograph near Victoria Station and the great period of cinema building the late 1920s. Several former theatres and music halls were also adapted as cinemas. Like shops, some cinemas in the more heavily populated parts provide a local service, e.g. at King's Cross and Paddington, but most of the cinemas in the Central Area are part of the West End's entertainment district. The major cinemas are more localized than the theatres and are found principally along Coventry Street and around Leicester Square. Bearing in mind that cinema audiences are generally less wealthy than theatre audiences, it is noteworthy that this is the area of central London best served by the tube railways which had already pushed well out into the suburbs before the cinema became a popular form of entertainment.

As with shops and theatres, some contraction and concentration has taken place as a result of changes in public taste and of the impact of television. The Marble Arch Pavilion and the Tivoli in the Strand have been converted into shops, the Odeon, Tottenham Court Road (on Shoolbred's site), and the Connaught have been closed, and the Gaumont, Haymarket, reduced in size. At the same time the new Columbia cinema in Shaftesbury Avenue has been opened and the Casino and Royalty (on the Stoll site) have been added to the number of cinemas.

Figure 39 shows only three concert halls, none of which is centrally located. The Royal Albert Hall, scene of the annual promenade concerts, rallies and political meetings, was erected in 1871, and can hold nearly 7,000. The Royal Festival Hall on the South Bank was erected by the L.C.C. in 1951 as part of the Festival of Britain celebrations and has accommodation for nearly 3,400. There is also the smaller Wigmore Hall. The Royal Festival Hall also incorporates a smaller recital room and work is now in progress to add a second concert hall. An exhibition gallery is also proposed nearby which, together with the National Film Theatre at Waterloo Bridge and the National Theatre, should firmly establish the South Bank area as an important cultural centre.

The Future of the Central Area

The future of central London can be assessed only against the background of the likely future pattern of growth of south-east England as a whole (Chapter 15). There seems little reason to doubt that the same major trends will be operating in the next twenty years as in the recent past and that public policy, though it may modify, is unlikely to reverse them. The three main characteristics are the growth of London within south-east England, the decline of population in the inner area and the increase in employment within the conurbation, in particular in the Central Area itself.

Population decline has been continuous in the Central Area since 1861 and, broadly speaking, continues in an ever-widening belt around the centre. Planning action has been successful in recent years in preventing the replacement of dwellings by offices and several important current schemes include a large residential element. Nevertheless, the resident population of the Central Area is likely to continue to decline and, in due course, this might have serious implications for the manning of such essential services as the railway, Post Office and the wholesale markets which have unusual hours, as well as for those who work in hotels, restaurants and entertainment. On the other hand, the building of luxury flats may once again become an attractive proposition now that further restrictions have been put on office building.

Projection of the future pattern of employment in the Central Area is bedevilled by the lack of satisfactory current data except at Census intervals, when they are generally given only for whole boroughs. Figure 34, which is compiled from a number of official sources, is an attempt to make good these deficiencies for the present Central Area since 1948, but, as no direct correlations are possible, it must be emphasized that the figures given cannot be better than informed estimates. This shows that employment in offices has increased by 200,000 since 1948 while the decrease of 30,000 in the number of factory operatives has more than offset the relatively small increase in the number of other workers (17,000) (Table XI).

TABLE XI

Estimated employment changes in the Central Area, 1948–1981

Year	Office Workers '000s	Operatives '000s	Others '000s	Total '000s
1948	615	275	388	1,278
1951	630	270	390	1,290
1962	815	245	405	1,465
1971	906	241	428	1,575
1981	929	244	458	1,631

Source: Estimates based on unpublished data from 1951 Census of Population Occupation Tables (by workplace not residence), National Insurance Statistics and L.C.C. Surveys.

Both the government and the L.C.C. have recently imposed additional restrictions on office building, but, with the continued need for more accommodation and with outstanding approvals for over fourteen million square feet (1·3 m. sq.m.), it is clear that there will be no immediate halt to further expansion, although some slowing of the rate of growth is apparent. At July 1962 there were 114·8 million square feet (10·7 m. sq.m.) of office accommodation in the Central Area: if demand stays buoyant, it is estimated that the total will reach 136 million (12·6 m. sq.m.) by 1971 and 144 million (13·4 m. sq.m.) by 1981, equivalent to office populations of about 906,000 and 929,000 respectively.

Industrial employment, on the other hand, is likely to continue to decline as a result of rising land values and the replacement of the obsolete property which provides a temporary refuge for the more mobile types of industry, e.g. the clothing industry of Soho and the Great Portland Street area. In the long run, however, a rising standard of living may lead to more manufacturing activity of a specialized luxury character which may well be located in central London for reasons of speed of execution and contact with customers. A small rise after 1971 has, therefore, been anticipated in Table XI.

Prior to 1957 there was little interest in hotel building in central London, but activity has recently quickened and several large new hotels have been completed and others are in course of erection. So far the main interest has been in the provision of de luxe accommodation in the Mayfair and Knightsbridge areas, but this market has become saturated and there is a need for less ambitious though good quality hotels for the less wealthy tourist now reaching Britain in increasing numbers.

Although the future of the West End shopping district seems assured, some disturbing trends must be faced.[25] Together with increasing car ownership and use goes the increasing difficulty of moving about central London by private car. At the same time the car equalizes distances. A housewife previously tied to central London for her 'leisure' shopping by public transport may find a major suburban centre like Watford or Bromley even more accessible by car. The further dispersal of population and the increasing number of married women at work, who are therefore obliged to limit their major shopping visits to week-ends, are other important factors favouring suburban Saturday family shopping rather than West End weekday shopping by the housewife alone. Any tendency to further standardization of products would reinforce this trend. The provision of car parking space for shoppers by the West End stores is only a partial solution and it remains to be seen whether they can adapt themselves to economic changes as successfully in the second half of the twentieth century as they did in the nineteenth.

The theatre in London is probably as healthy today as it has ever been, but it is under pressure from the demands of commerce. Town planning measures have been successful in preventing the replacement of theatres by offices, but cannot compel the use of a theatre as such or prevent its use for some other form of entertainment. In the long run the future of the West End theatre will depend on the extent of its public support, but some further geographical concentration seems likely. Further concentration and some contraction of the West End cinemas is also probable.

The westward movement of a number of the principal functions of the Central Area, already noted in this chapter, will continue. To the north the growth of the Central Area is constrained by Regent's Park, by a large housing area and by extensive areas of railway land adjoining the main-line termini. An industrial belt running through north Finsbury, Shoreditch and Stepney, the commercial and dock area east of the Tower and the riverside wharves and railway land at London Bridge and Bricklayers Arms limit expansion in these directions. To the south the embanked railway lines out of Waterloo provide an effective barrier and in the south-west there is the large area of industry and tangle of railway lines around Nine Elms. There are no similar barriers in the west and north-west and it is

D. F. STEVENS

therefore in these directions that future growth is to be expected. Indeed, it has already begun. South of the river office development along the Albert Embankment is virtually complete and other centres have become established at the Elephant and Castle and in Westminster Bridge Road. Other offices have spilled over from the City along the main roads radiating from St George's Circus. In the west Knightsbridge has become an attractive location for offices and hotels and the distribution maps of hotels and shops (Figs. 37 and 38) show how well represented these uses already are in Kensington and Bayswater. There is strong pressure for additional offices in this sector of London and applications for new hotels also show a further westward trend. Improved communications in this area, such as the Western Avenue Extension and West Cross Route, will further enhance its attractiveness.

References

1. As defined in the *Census of England and Wales 1961, County of London* (H.M.S.O., 1963). See map facing p. xxii.
2. *The City of London. A Record of Destruction and Survival.* (Corporation of London, 1951). Part II is devoted to the historical development of the City and is well illustrated.
3. Nikolaus Pevsner, *The Buildings of England: The Cities of London and Westminster* (1962), on whom I have principally relied for dates in the remainder of this section, thinks the tenth century more likely.
4. The personalities and their motives involved in these schemes are well described in J. Summerson, *Georgian London* (1945) and in S. E. Rasmussen, *London: the Unique City* (1937).
5. W. G. Bell, *The Great Fire of London in 1666* (1920). The devastated area is compared to that of the Second World War in *The City of London. A Record of Destruction and Survival, op. cit.*, (map facing page 149).
6. T. F. Reddaway, *The Rebuilding of London after the Great Fire* (1940).
7. E. Course, *London Railways* (1962). For South London lines see also H. P. White, *Southern England*, Vol. II of a Regional History of the Railways of Great Britain (1961).
8. C. Baker, *The Metropolitan Railway* (1951).
9. T. S. Lascelles, *The City and South London Railway* (1955).
10. The best account is to be found in Alan A. Jackson and Desmond F. Croome, *Rails through the Clay* (1962).
11. G. F. A. Wilmot, *The Railway in Finchley* (1962), 36.
12. W. I. Carruthers, 'Service centres in Greater London', *Town Planning Review* 33 (1962), 5–31.
13. A. Bull, 'Problems of commuter traffic in conurbations', *Proceedings of the Institution of Mechanical Engineers*, 176 (1962), 961.

14. The subject of urban economic analysis has received remarkably little attention. Principal studies in this field are A. Weber, *Theory of Location of Industries*, trans. C. Friedrich (1929); A. Lösch, *The Economics of Location* (New Haven, 1954); and W. Isard, *Methods of Regional Analysis: an introduction to Regional Science* (1960).

15. The spatial arrangement of the principal trades and activities in the City in 1938 is shown in *The City of London. A Record of Destruction and Survival*, *op. cit.*, map facing p. 32.

16. Pevsner, *op. cit.*, 93.

17. W. T. W. Morgan, 'Office regions in the West End of London', *Town and Country Planning*, 29 (1961), 257.

18. P. Abercrombie, *Greater London Plan 1944* (H.M.S.O., 1945), Chapter 3.

19. London County Council, *Administrative County of London Development Plan 1951*, *Analysis*, Chapter 11.

20. *Ibid.*, paras. 1278–97; L.C.C., *A Plan to Combat Congestion in Central London*, (1957); L.C.C., *Administrative County of London Development Plan, First Review 1960*, County Planning Report, paras. 555–567; Town and Country Planning Association, *The Paper Metropolis* (1962); L.C.C., *Town Planning Committee Report on Office Development in London*, London County Council, 19th March 1963; *London. Employment: Housing: Land*, Cmd. 1952 (H.M.S.O., 1963); Town and Country Planning Act, 1963.

21. See however J. E. Martin, 'Industry in Inner London', *Town and Country Planning*, 25 (1957), 125–8; and P. G. Hall, *The Industries of London since 1861* (1962) Chapters 4–7.

22. J. W. Ferry, *A History of the Department Store* (1960), Chapter 6, is mainly historical.

23. S. Medlik, *The British Hotel and Catering Industry* (1961) contains several useful references, but is not particularly concerned with central London hotels.

24. Raymond Mander and Joe Mitchenson, *The Theatres of London* (1961) is again mainly historical, but useful.

25. George Sternlieb, 'The future of retailing in the Downtown Core', *Journal of the American Institute of Planners*, 29 (May 1963), 102–112, gives a good account of current United States' problems which have not yet arisen in London.

The Growth of the Port of London

*

JAMES BIRD

'Write an account of the advantages possessed by London as a capital.' This was one of the questions asked of candidates at a recent elementary public examination in geography. Of the acceptable statements in the answering essays, the two most frequent were: 'London is the lowest bridging-point on the Thames' and 'The Thames made London a great port'. Today there are in fact nine regular crossings downstream of London Bridge, and Professor Rodwell Jones once came to the conclusion that

'the local environmental factors which made the site of the city favourable for early bridging were certainly more in evidence in early times than they are today.'[1]

But he was careful to point out that even this conclusion was only made possible by a comparative study of early city sites near other estuary heads and also by the negative evidence provided by the once unfavourable nature of other nearby sites along the Thames.[2] If we grant that the first consideration in the foundation of Londinium was its role as a bridge-head on the northern bank of the Thames, nevertheless very soon the river itself became a routeway connecting the infant settlement with the mainland of Europe. Ever since London has relied on its river approaches, with the single interruption of the early Saxon episode of 'every vill for itself' when two-way trading links with Europe were broken, the city has made continual demands upon the Thames and its riparian lands. All these demands have been met, since in dealing with the growth of the port of London

202

we are dealing with a success story. Current returns show that London receives just over one-fifth of all shipping entering United Kingdom ports and deals with a little over one-third of the nation's foreign seaborne trade. London has always been the largest British port.

The theme of growth may be studied in two aspects: the physical enlargement of the lay-out of the port and the chief reasons behind such development; and, secondly, the increase in the trade handled by the port. During the early stages up to this century it is perhaps sufficient here to take as given the statement, 'London's trade increased year by year', and to concentrate upon the physical enlargement of the port at the bridge-head. This 'bridge-port' developed into the modern organization embracing seventy miles (113 km.) of a tidal waterway, and the illustrations have been chosen to bring out some of the contrasts along the Thames water highway. There will also be room to discuss briefly the growth of the port's trade in this century.

The Port at the Bridge-head

From the early thirteenth century the river was spanned by old London Bridge (1209–1832). Its wide piers and narrow arches acted as a weir, causing a separation of river traffic upstream from the sea-going vessels moored immediately downstream in a reach of the river that became known as the Pool of London. As early as the fourteenth century many ships were too large to ground upon the layer of mud immediately beneath the quaysides. They anchored in the Pool, and their cargoes were transhipped by wherries, plying between the floating warehouses and those city quays that had the site advantage of being downstream of the blockading bridge. This advantage was overtly confirmed as a result of *An Acte lymiting the tymes for layeng on Lande Marchandise from beyonde the Seas, and touching Customes for Sweete Wynes*, 1 Elizabeth, c.11, 1558.

'. . . That yt shall not bee lawfull to . . . lade or putt . . . of or from any Wharfe Keye or other Place on the Lande, into any shippe . . ., any Goodes Wares or Marchaundises . . ., but onely in the daye light . . . upon sume suche open Place Keye or Wharfe . . . as yor Highnes . . . assigne and appointe, by vertue of y^r Highnes commission . . .'

The following year the Commission appointed under the Act

chose the 'sume suche open Keyes' in London; they were all sited between the bridge and the Tower on the northern side of the river. These wharves became known as the Legal Quays where all dutiable—and hence the most valuable—cargo had to be landed and shipped (Fig. 40). The site of the port thus became clearly established, even constricted, since the Legal Quays were not extended for 244 years, despite an enormous increase in traffic. It is true that under an Act of 14 Charles II, c.11, 1662, H.M. Customs were permitted to give special 'sufferance' for the landing of cargoes elsewhere.

'It is enacted and ordained . . . That the Kings Majesty may from time to time by his Highnes Commission or Commissions appoint all such further places Ports Members or Creeks.'
But as late as 1761 we find the Customs Board reporting that:
'they had always been very tender in the use of their authority to permit unloading at a sufferance quay, except in cases of single Ships and of absolute necessity . . .'[3]
However, by the end of the eighteenth century some 3,700 feet (1,130 m.) of sufferance wharves nearly trebled the mere 1,400 feet (430 m.) of legal quay frontage. This extended the port downstream and over on to the south bank. But consideration of the disadvantages of the sufferance wharves shows how little real physical expansion was achieved, and how difficult it was for the port to spread even to the opposite bank of the Pool.

The sufferance to land cargo was temporary. Wharfingers were therefore not likely to sink great capital into the quayside installations. A further great disadvantage of the sufferance wharves was their distance from established city markets, being 'remote from the seat of business.'[4]

'Some of them were situated at a great distance from the legal quays; to several there was no access save through the dwelling-houses of the proprietors; others excluded all goods but those belonging to the proprietor; extra fees had to be paid to customs officers for goods landed at those places.'[5]
Chaos resulted from the failure to expand the port. Every kind of eighteenth-century criminal sought a share of plunder from floating cargoes waiting weeks to be unloaded.

William Vaughan (1752–1850) was the leader in the movement to expand the port by means of commercial wet docks. In many pamphlets and in evidence before Select Committees he cogently argued that the port must expand away from the open tideway within the

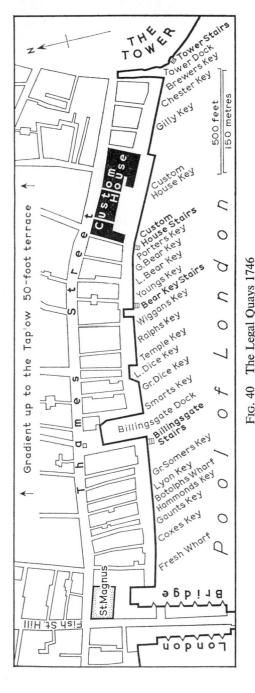

FIG. 40   The Legal Quays 1746

This has been redrawn from John Rocque's Map of London and shows the entire extent of the then Legal Quays of the port, deriving authority from a Royal Commission, August 28th, 1559 (appointed under an Act 1 Eliz., c. 11, 1558) and amended by an Act 13 & 14 Chas. II, c.11, 1662).

protection of massive walls surrounding wet docks. These would give security by lessening the risks to merchants and leaving the river free for those trades that were the most bulky and least valuable and accompanied by the fewest risks and temptations. The need for impounded docks did not at first arise from any inadequacy in the river's depth. As Vaughan put it:

'It is the opinion of professional men and those best informed about the River Thames from knowledge or experience, or daily occupation that the difficulty does not proceed from nature or want of water, but from the great crowd of shipping that are always pressing into the Pool for accommodation.'[6]

Docks and the Example of the Tilbury Dock System

The result of the successful agitation to expand the port was the opening of the first commercial docks in 1802, equipped with legal quays, although they were two miles (3·2 km.) downstream of the city limits. They were excavated in the northern flood-plain of the river. Until this happened the Corporation of the City of London had blocked all movement for the port's reform because it realized that expansion could only take place downstream of the Corporation's jurisdiction bounded by the Tower of London. Even with the opening of the early docks by private companies, the City Corporation still remained as conservator of the river. But the Port and Navigation Committee of the Corporation was not required by statute to improve the river. When a particularly bad shoal occurred the Committee merely came to an *ad hoc* arrangement with the ballast men for its removal. No regularization of the river bed was begun until 1857. The jurisdiction of the City's conservancy was held to extend from Yantlet Creek in Sea Reach (Fig. 41) to Staines, some 30 miles (48 km.) upstream of London Bridge, under the first of six charters dated 1197, though a crucial Act appears to have been 4 Henry VII c.15, 1489.[7] The interest of this lies in the fact that within the history of the conservancy of the Thames resides the first appreciation of the Thames waterway as a whole. The present conservator of the river is the Port of London Authority (hereafter called the P.L.A.), with conservancy authority over the whole of the tidal Thames.[8]

The nucleus of each of the five dock systems of the port (located on Fig. 41) was established by 1886 when the first part of the Tilbury Docks was opened, while the very earliest sections of London's

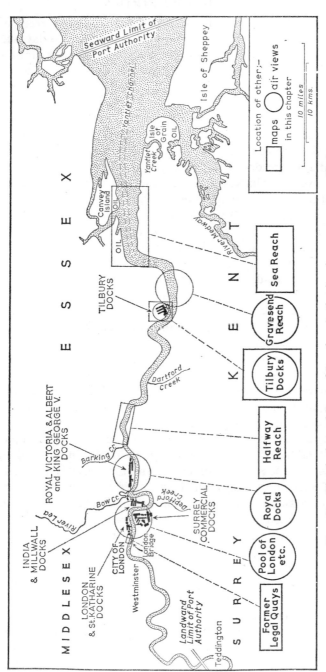

FIG. 41   The docks and Port of London Authority river conservancy limits

present dock systems were designed in the closing years of the eighteenth century. The last major alteration to the lay-out was opened in 1944 when the new north quay of the Royal Victoria Dock came into use. Within that long period of dock design lasting 150 years two basically different types of lay-out may be discerned: *dock elaboration* and *simple lineal quayage*. These are labels to denote the results of two fundamentally different aims of dock engineers in the era of the sailing ship on the one hand and then in the era of the 'long' ships of the twentieth century. It must also be remembered that at first the docks skimmed off all the most valuable traffic; today riverside wharves play an important role complementary to that of the dockside quays (Fig. 43, right). The *elaborate* dock perimeter was designed by dock engineers to obtain as much quay length as possible for a given water area, giving, it was claimed at the time, '. . . the greatest facilities for the trade that can be desired.'[9] The early docks were also equipped with a tidal basin so that small sailing vessels could be crowded in near high tide and then be hauled one at a time into the dock. Another advantage of a tidal basin near an entrance lock was thought to be its provision of slack water making an easier approach to the entrance offset from the tidal streams of the river.

In 1914 a far-sighted port engineer F. [later Sir Frederick] Palmer wrote:

'The value of long straight quays, or of quays susceptible of development in straight lines would be apparent from a brief study of the enormous growth in the size of steamers.'[10]

The increasing length of ships rendered obsolete the original purpose of the tidal basins and outstripped the short runs of quays alongside the older branch docks, or at the short peninsulas within larger docks. Such short quays could no longer berth the largest class of deep-sea passenger/cargo liner. The length of quayage now required for most efficient berthing of such vessels is at least 1,500 feet (458 m.) in one line, with an entrance lock at least 750 feet (229 m.) long, with up to 30 feet (9·2 m.) minimum of depth in the approach.

Figure 42 summarizes these changes by concentrating upon one of the five dock systems—at Tilbury. This system was begun in 1882 by the East and West India Dock Company at a site 26 miles (42 km.) downstream of London Bridge. It was also as much as sixteen miles (26 km.) downstream of the Royal Docks operated by the rival London and St Katharine Docks Company. The reason for a site so

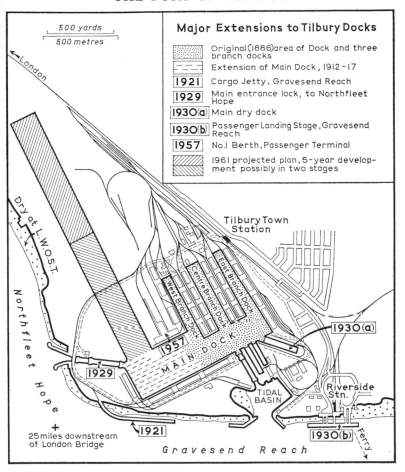

Major Extensions to Tilbury Docks

▓	Original (1886) area of Dock and three branch docks
⌐ ─ ─ ⌐	Extension of Main Dock, 1912–17
1921	Cargo Jetty, Gravesend Reach
1929	Main entrance lock, to Northfleet Hope
1930(a)	Main dry dock
1930(b)	Passenger Landing Stage, Gravesend Reach
1957	No.1 Berth, Passenger Terminal
▨	1961 projected plan, 5-year development possibly in two stages

Fig. 42   Tilbury Docks
Original elaborate dock perimeter and later additions of simple lineal quayage

far downstream may be sought in the poor navigability of the Thames in the last quarter of the nineteenth century. Indeed, the East and West India Dock Company would have preferred to expand their East India Docks at a site only seven miles (11 km.) from London Bridge:

'but it was decided not to proceed with the proposed extension on the ground that the principal difficulty lay not so much in accommodating the ships in the docks as in the River Thames itself, which is sinuous and shallow for about 20 miles [32 km.] below London Bridge, navigation being impossible for large steamships except at or near the time of high-water.' [Written in 1895][11]

The port was beginning to pay the price for neglecting to apply steam dredging to the river channel. Indeed a comprehensive programme of dredging the river was not embarked upon until after the P.L.A. was set up in 1909.[12]

The site selected for Tilbury Docks in 1882 was far enough downstream so that the steamships of that time could be sure of getting into the docks on one tide. The 600 acres (242 ha.) of marshland purchased by the dock company formed a triangular site, lying within the angle made by Gravesend Reach and Northfleet Hope to the south and west and bounded on the north-east by the London Tilbury and Southend Railway which reached the north riverside in 1850 to serve the ferry to Gravesend. This railway was to provide the 25-mile (40 km.) link from the docks to London. The surface of the marshland was six feet (1·8 m.) below high water of ordinary spring tides and protected by a river embankment which was used as a convenient coffer-dam during the excavation of the docks. The Buried Channel stratum of Thames gravel (known as Thames Ballast) was found at an average depth of 40 feet (12·3 m.) below very soft mud and clay with layers of peat. Beneath the gravel the Chalk was found. Indeed, trending west–east across the site of the present Main Dock a valley was discovered cut in this Chalk from which the gravel had been removed—indicating a former alignment of the Thames a little to the north of its present course. The north-west to south-east alignment of the branch docks was made necessary by the shape of the site. To gain the 695-foot (212 m.) long entrance lock, vessels approached from the river via the slacker water of the Tidal Basin. This artificial embayment opening out from Gravesend Reach has proved very prone to silting, as forecast by witnesses at a Select Committee hearing even before the docks were built.[13] Today no less than one-eighth of the total material dredged from the whole of the River Thames has to be scooped out of the mud trap of the Tilbury Tidal Basin. Besides the three berths in this basin used by small vessels, the docks proper provided 28 berths for ships up to 400 feet (122 m.) long. The south-western part of the Main Dock was not quayed 'at which point any future extension would be made.'[14]

This extension was begun in 1912 and finished in 1917, providing extra berthing-space for the war effort.[15] A riverside cargo jetty was opened in 1921, equipped with warehouse accommodation built like a hold within a ship. In 1929 an entrance lock was opened from the Main Dock Extension giving access to Northfleet Hope. It was 1,000 feet (305 m.) long, the largest in the port, and without a tidal basin. Although the ebb-tide runs across this entrance at a speed of up to $3\frac{1}{2}$ knots ($7\frac{1}{2}$ km. per hour), there is slack water with only slight eddies downstream during the flood.[16] A north–south alignment would have been better for navigational purposes, and the lock would then have been in line with the ebb-tide. But in the 1920s the P.L.A. was not prepared to authorize construction of a large dock, only now envisaged, to which the north–south entrance lock would have had to lead. In 1930 a new dry dock was opened in the south-east corner of the docks and in the same year an ocean passenger terminal was provided with the opening of the Floating Passenger Landing Stage, built on the same principle as the Princes Landing Stage, Liverpool. The Tilbury Stage provides one liner berth in Gravesend Reach and a berth at the eastern end for the Tilbury–Gravesend ferry service. Until 1957 this stage provided the only berth exclusively serving a passenger terminal in the whole port.

In the six years after 1948 the P. & O. and Orient Lines added six new ships of about 29,000 tons gross to their fleets with a maximum length over 700 feet (214 m.) long. The Main Dock is 600 feet (183 m.) wide, and it was realized in 1954 that if a new dock were to be constructed from the north-west corner of the Main Dock, the vessels then entering the lock might be as long as 800 feet (244 m.). Accordingly it was decided to widen the Main Dock to a bottom width of 900 feet (274 m.) so that even these very long vessels could be turned after entering the Main Dock and then be towed stern first into any projected new dock.[17] On the tongue of land 900 feet (274 m.) wide between this site for a future dock and the Western Branch Dock, No. 1 Berth Passenger Terminal was constructed, 842 feet (257 m.) long. Cutting back this tongue of land also allows a vessel up to 700 feet (214 m.) long to turn into the east quay of the West Branch Dock. These details show how an old dock system can be progressively remodelled and extended, although there may be no dramatic headline of 'A New Dock Constructed!'. In fact a completely new system has been added to the original Tilbury Docks. The present lay-out shows the two contrasting designs: the branch docks and tidal basin of the original dock elaboration pattern; and the western entrance and long quays for the longest vessels in the

Main Dock. The proposed additional dock is not a branch dock at all since its quays will be longer than those of the Main Dock, and it has nothing in common with the older branch docks. It would be a splendid gesture if it were to become known as the Palmer Dock, since the Main Dock Extension, the 1,000-foot (305 m.) western entrance, and the dock yet to be built were all included among the improvement works planned by that far-sighted engineer, Sir Frederick Palmer, as long ago as 1910.

The role of Tilbury in the Port of London is to berth the very largest ships using the port. All cargoes are in transit, and if imports are destined for warehousing, they can be taken by road, rail or barge to 'up-town' warehouses. P. & O. and Orient liners use three berths at the splendid Main Dock South Quay for the Australia passenger/cargo mail service. Imports from the West Africa Conference Lines are discharged at the Main Dock West Quay. In the Branch Docks liners trading to West Africa, India, and Burma are regularly berthed, while continental traffic is found in the Tidal Basin, East Quay, and near the head of the West Branch Dock. This latter berth consists of a ramp for 'roll-on–roll-off' vessels trading to Antwerp and Rotterdam. These ships are a development of wartime tank-landing craft and can carry up to 100 lorries, trailers, and containers across the North Sea. They might be looked upon as the road vehicle counterpart of a train ferry and offer similar advantages: speed of transhipment, avoidance of expensive packaging for awkward loads, and reduction of pilferage and breakage.

Before passing on to outline the growth of the trade of the port during this century, it may perhaps be useful to review the chief characteristics of all the dock systems (Table XII).

The Growth of the Port's Trade

A few of the many available statistical facts illustrating the growth of the port's trade are presented in the three composite graphs of Figure 43. The graph on the top left shows firstly the growth in the total net registered tonnage of shipping arriving and departing, recorded at quinquennial intervals (line A, discontinuous because of the world wars). This line may be compared to one based on a 20 per cent increase every ten years, *compounded* at the end of each decade, with the war years assumed to have no increase (line A[1]). The remarkable increase during this century can scarcely go on at

212

THE PORT OF LONDON

TABLE XII

Chief characteristics of the five London dock systems

(Figures in brackets represent mileage from London Bridge downstream to a point opposite the principal entrance lock)

[Metric equivalents are given within square brackets]

London and St Katharine Docks (2 miles) [3·2 km.]
Principal entrance lock: 350 × 60 × 28 (depth*) in feet [106·5 × 18·3 × 8·2 metres].
Total length of quays, 4 miles [6·4 km.]; total water area, 45 acres [18½ ha.].
These are the principal warehousing docks of the port, with no trans-ocean traffic, since liners up to 2,300 gross tons are trading to the continent of Europe.

Surrey Commercial Docks (3½) [5·6]
Principal entrance lock: 550 × 80 × 35¼* (feet); [175 × 24·2 × 10·75 m.].
Total length of quays, 8¾ miles [14 km.]; total water area, 136 acres [55 ha.].
Dominated by the discharge of softwood timber, these docks also deal with cargo liners of up to the 10,000 gross tonnage class from North America, India, and north-west Europe.

India and Millwall Docks (6¼) [10]
Principal entrance lock: 584 × 80 × 35* (feet); [178 × 24·2 × 10·7 m.].
Total length of quays, 8 miles [12·8 km.]; total water area, 155 acres [63 ha.].
This dock system combines features of docks upstream (extensive warehousing) and downstream (deep-sea trading), but vessels are of medium-size with connections to all continents except Australasia.

Royal Docks (10½) [16·9]
Principal entrance lock: 800 × 100 × 45* (feet); [242 × 30·5 × 13·7 m.].
Total length of quays, 10 miles [16 km.]; total water area, 230 acres [93½ ha.].
Simple lineal quayage for long passenger/cargo liners is a dominating feature, since each of three docks has quays of three-quarters of a mile (1·2 km.) in one interrupted line for vessels up to 25,000 gross tons class regularly trading to all continents, with warehouses only for meat and tobacco, but there are dockside grain mills.

Tilbury Docks (24½) [38·6]
Principal entrance lock: 1,000 × 110 × 45½* (feet); [305 × 33·5 × 13·8 m.].
Total length of quays, 4 miles [6·4 km.]; total water area, 105 acres [42½ ha.].
These docks are the base for the largest ships (P. & O.—Orient) regularly using the port, up to the 30,000 gross ton class, with all cargoes in transit (no warehouses).

* Depths of entrance locks below Trinity High Water, a Port of London datum, approximately 11·4 feet (3·47 m.) above Ordnance Datum.

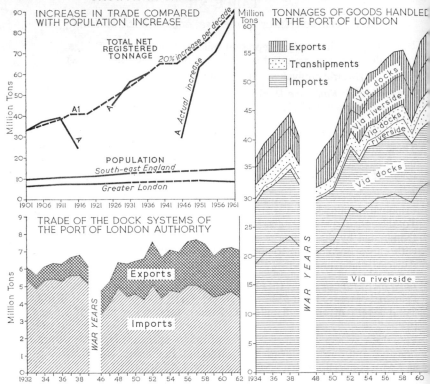

FIG. 43 Growth in trade of the Port of London

Top left: Rate of increase in the trade of the port compared with rates of increase in population.

Line A: Total net registered tonnage of vessels that arrived and departed with cargoes and in ballast from overseas and coastwise at five-yearly intervals; *Line A[1]:* Line showing increase of 20 per cent every ten years, compounded at the end of each decade (war years assumed to have no increase); Increase in population of south-east England (south-east of Solent–Wash line) and Registrar-General's Greater London conurbation at decennial intervals.

Right: Tonnages of goods handled in the Port of London

The line within each category separates tonnages handled within the docks, above the line, from tonnages handled within the river, below the line. The actual weight of cargo transhipped is counted twice, once as imported, once as exported. (Years ended 31st March.)

Bottom left: Trade of the dock systems of the Port of London Authority

The figures represented are confined to the tonnages of goods which passed over the quays of the docks. (Years ended 31st March.)

this compounded rate, but it is a vivid illustration of growth when compared with the growth of the population of south-east England and of the population of the Greater London conurbation. Since the Second World War there have been various forces at work controlling the increase in the population of the conurbation (see below and reference there cited), but it is perhaps surprising that the port's trade in this century should be at a rate greater than the growth of population in south-east England with its absolute increase of $4\frac{1}{2}$ million people between 1901 and 1961. This is an increase of nearly 50 per cent. However, the tonnage of shipping using British ports per head of population increased by 53 per cent between 1901 and 1961 and London's share of the national trade remained the same at 19 per cent.[18] From this we can deduce that London's increased trade in this century is a reflection of the growth of the nation's seaborne trade as a whole.

Less dynamic has been the rate of growth of the population of the Greater London conurbation. In the *Report of the Royal Commission on Local Government in Greater London 1957–60*[19] an interesting commentary was made upon developments within Greater London since Sir Patrick Abercrombie's *Greater London Plan 1944* was published. One of 'five assumptions' of this latter plan was 'that the Port of London will continue to be one of the world's great ports.' In 1944 Sir Patrick laid down the fundamental principle that the population of the Greater London Plan region should not grow above the 1938 figure. In fact it did so in 1952. The Herbert Commission (*vide supra*) listed ten factors which, in its opinion, were at work in the region and had caused this result. From the statement of these ten factors the following précis may be devised: in the years after the Second World War the number of jobs available in central London increased at a rate faster than the rest of the country, and this employment expanded more rapidly than population. The Herbert Commission pointed out that one of the reasons for the continued growth of employment in the London region was that the machinery for controlling the creation of jobs had been more successful as regards industry than as regards commerce. Indeed, it would have been unwise to attempt to curtail the trade of the Port of London at a time when it was essential that the import and export trades should be efficient arteries of the national economy. The desire to restrict the growth of industry and population in the conurbation has been coupled with a scarcely compatible realization that it would not be in the national interest to restrict the growth of the port's trade.

Figure 43, right, shows a breakdown of the tonnage of cargoes, and the increase of exports since the Second World War is almost as impressive as the growth of the total trade. Fifty-five per cent of the tonnage imported via the docks never touches the quays but is delivered as 'overside' cargo into part of the 6,300-strong barge fleet, then to be towed to the ultimate landing-place along the river or in a warehousing dock. The percentage of dock export cargo moved alongside the ship by barge is less—just over 40 per cent. Thus we gradually work through the statistics to reach a real growing point of cargo movement—the export tonnage actually moved across the dock quays. The post-war increase of this movement is clearly shown on Figure 43, bottom left. Before the Second World War such dock quay exports were about 1 million tons per annum; now they exceed $2\frac{1}{2}$ million tons and over 80 per cent is brought by road vehicles. The dock quays and the dock road approaches were never designed for such a volume of road traffic, and this problem has been referred to as the 'ingrowing toenails' of the port. [20] The number of road vehicle movements is staggering.

Table XIII gives for the first time a statistical glimpse of the amount of road traffic borne on the road system of the docks and their approaches. If we discount the 'other vehicle' category of cars, bicycles, *etc.*, which nevertheless makes up over half the traffic numbers and adds considerably to the load, there remains the fundamental transport by 10,000 lorries and vans entering and leaving the docks every day. It is difficult to grasp the size of these vast alternating currents. If all the goods vehicles wanted to use the same port approach road at the same time, there would then be a traffic jam some 40 miles (64 km.) long. The above figures, striking as they are, do not include Tilbury Docks, nor do they include the road traffic to and from many of the 600 riverside wharves. These myriad traffic streams all combine, throb, and disperse as best they may in quite impromptu fashion. Under such free-lance conditions there can be little forecasting of the precise time of arrival of road vehicles, or even of the order in which they will pass through the dock gates.

Rail delivery of exports at ports has the merit of being properly programmed, avoiding congestion at quayside transit sheds. British Railways Export Express Service began in November 1956, assuring next-day arrival at specified ports for traffic in full wagon-load quan-

TABLE XIII

*Average daily road traffic entering and
leaving four of London's five dock systems*

(The count* was made on four weekdays from June 24–27, 1962)

Dock System	Inbound			Outbound			Total of Vehicles in both Directions
	Heavy Goods†	Light Goods†	Other Vehicles	Heavy Goods†	Light Goods†	Other Vehicles	
	numbers	numbers	numbers	numbers	numbers	numbers	numbers
London	897	223	963	916	240	968	4,207
Surrey Commercial	982	437	1,848	940	378	1,786	6,371
India and Millwall	1,907	616	2,476	2,019	522	2,467	10,007
Royal	4,136	1,732	8,400	4,248	1,654	8,629	28,799
Total	7,922	3,008	13,687	8,123	2,794	13,850	49,384

* This was made as part of the London Traffic Survey, and the London County Council kindly made the figures available so that they could be included here.

† In this classification 'heavy goods' refers to vehicles with two rear axles, or with dual tyres; vehicles with a rigid body and three or more axles; and articulated vehicles or vehicles with trailers: 'light goods' refers to vans; or vehicles with two axles, single tyre.

tities. The service was subsequently extended to ten large ports and 330 railway stations. Inland depots have been established where exports that do not make up a full wagon load can be combined or 'concentrated' into suitable consignments. The service runs to the Port of London from 146 railway stations, the most distant being Newcastle, Lancaster, and Bristol.

The transit sheds alongside dock quays are used for extensive sorting of goods to Bills of Lading, and in recent years import consignments have been broken down to 'individual packages for labelling and dispatch in ones and twos to hundreds of consignees.'[21] Such extensive sorting might well be done at reception depots well away from the port area. If seaborne cargoes are to be carried extensively in standardized containers, as seems very likely, these inland depots might also become container filling centres concentrating 'less-than-container' loads. On the quayside the transit operation would be simplified, containers moving on conveyor belts through the side-ports of the ship. Little manhandling of individually-shaped packages would then be necessary.

The Port in the River

The river itself is a great port dealing with two-thirds of the total tonnage of cargoes (Fig. 43, right), with 140 miles (225 km.) of tide-water frontage. Not all this is available, however, for port development. There are the areas of the riverside already built over for other uses in central and west London; but only one-eighth of the frontagers with water access make no use of the river whatever. On the inner convex shoulders of down-stream meanders it is harder to maintain a deep-water approach to a berth fairly close to the shore than is the case where the tidal currents hug the outer concave bends. There are, of course, further contrasts due to the distance of the riverfront site from the centre of London. It is quite possible to divide the tidal Thames into sections wherein the functions of the riverside contrast strongly with neighbouring reaches. These changes are plainly visible to the river passenger with an alert eye, and three of the contrasts are shown in the accompanying illustrations.[22]

Plate 21, top, shows a view of the Pool of London, with its river-side multi-storey warehouses adjacent to the general wharves of public wharfingers who mostly deal with imported foodstuffs for wholesaler consignees. Navigation by high-decked ocean-going vessels is impossible upstream of London Bridge where wharves receive cargoes towed upstream in barges, which have been loaded overside from ships in the docks. Here is the other terminus of the most common barge route in the port leading from the docks to riverside wharves. An example is the importation of New Zealand butter and cheese into the Royal Albert Dock, its delivery overside into barge, and its final reception into the cold and cool stores of the proprietors of Hay's Wharf Ltd. who now control all the wharves, except one, on the southern side of the Upper Pool, immediately upstream of Tower Bridge.[23]

This riverside scene may be compared with the more extensive lay-outs adjoining Halfway Reach fourteen miles (22 km.) down-stream of the Upper Pool (Fig. 44). Dagenham Dock Estate is an early example of an industrial estate on the Thames where marsh-land of the former flood-plain was consolidated and berthing facilities

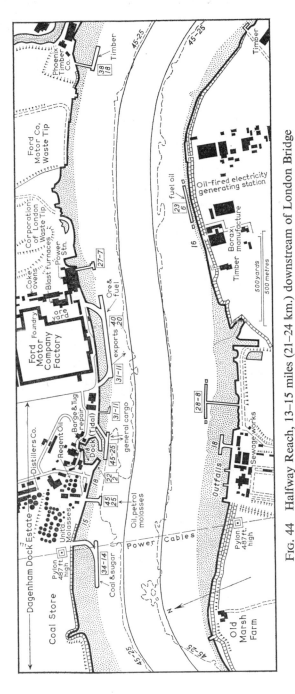

Fig. 44 Halfway Reach, 13–15 miles (21–24 km.) downstream of London Bridge

Figures represent depths in feet at high and low water springs respectively (spring tidal range of 20 feet, 6·7 m.); single figures represent depth at high water springs; areas drying out at low water springs are represented by stipple. The sailing channel, represented by continuous lines, is 600 feet wide by 27 feet L.W.O.S.T. (183 × 8·25 m.). Railways are omitted. The riverside frontage should be compared with the Pool immediately downstream of London and Tower Bridges, and with Gravesend Reach (Plates 21 and 22 respectively).

provided for 'public' use by various industries as tenants of the estate company.[24] The Ford Motor Company's factory is on a site originally made available by the industrial estate development at Dagenham Dock. The Ford Wharf, 1,800 feet (548 m.) long, is the largest private wharf on the Thames. It is possible to see an ore carrier unloading at the eastern end while a general cargo vessel loads road vehicles and tractors at the western end. The tips for waste and household refuse east of the car factory show that there are undeveloped areas upon lower Thameside. But the dominant contrast with the Pool is that the individual wharves and jetties penetrate into deeper water and serve premises laid out on a much larger scale on the marshes of a former flood-plain. There is for example, the gigantic No. 3 site coal store in the Dagenham Dock estate.

The characteristic of extensive lay-outs becomes even more plain to see 33 miles (53 km.) downstream of the Upper Pool alongside Sea Reach (Fig. 45). The most valuable single commodity handled in the river is oil, and the present pattern of refinery distribution on the Thames is bound up with the history of the Mucking Light as an

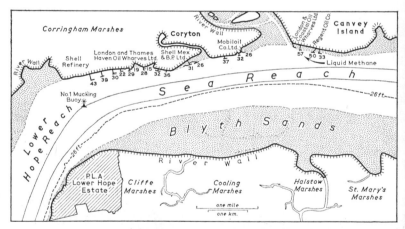

FIG. 45　River and riverside contrasts north, south, east, and west of No. 1 Mucking Buoy, 32½ miles (52·5 km.) downstream of London Bridge

Figures at north bank oil jetties represent minimum depths in feet. The sailing channel, represented by continuous lines, is 1,000 feet wide by 30 feet L.W.O.S.T. (305 × 9·15 m.). The stippled area dries at L.W.O.S.T.; the position of the 26-foot (7·9 m.) minimum depth contour is shown only to the south of the sailing channel to indicate the extent of the shoal lying off and over the Blyth Sands. The spring tidal range in Sea Reach is about 18 feet (5·5 m.).

importing limit for sea-going tankers from 1872–1938.[25] This limit was close to the present No. 1 Mucking Buoy and it resulted in all the major oil installations being sited east of the Light; since the Second World War sites upstream have become less attractive for refineries because of the increasing dimensions of sea-going tankers. The marshes south of Sea Reach have not so far been used for industrial purposes because the deep-water channel lies closer to the northern shore as it sweeps into the Reach from the Lower Hope.

Dickens set the opening pages of *Great Expectations* on the Cooling Marshes, south of Sea Reach.

'Ours was the marsh country, down by the river, within, as the river wound, twenty miles of the sea . . . this bleak place overgrown with nettles was the churchyard; . . . and . . . the dark flat wilderness beyond the churchyard intersected with dykes and mounds and gates, with scattered cattle feeding on it, was the marshes; and the low leaden line beyond was the river.'

This description is still exact. The P.L.A. will, however, be consolidating its Lower Hope [marshland] Estate within a decade, using river dredgings pumped ashore. The significance of this site is that it lies close to the deep-water channel in Lower Hope Reach. The estate was acquired in 1930 and 1931 by the P.L.A. with the intention of using the site for petroleum imports, but parallel developments on the north shore by various oil companies caused this scheme to be put in abeyance. From the direction of the Lower Hope the whole of the extensive flat land on the Cliffe and Cooling Marshes, hitherto blocked off from deep water by the Blyth Sands to the north, could be made available for very large industrial lay-outs dependent on tidewater access. Island jetties could certainly be established north of Blyth Sands for more direct importation of liquid cargoes pumped ashore. As recently as 1952 the marshes east of Tilbury–Gravesend (Plate 22, bottom) could be called isolated from London, although that very isolation made the northern marshes favourable to the establishment of oil depots. But the Dartford–Purfleet Tunnel, the Kent motorways, the Channel Tunnel, and Britain's general position with regard to continental Europe have converted this isolation into one of the most favourably-placed large and empty potential industrial sites in the whole of Britain.

From the original bridge-head the port has grown to embrace the whole tidal waterway. But within that distance the process of filling up the empty areas has still a long way to go. In the inter-war years the shape of the conurbation could have been compared to a circle and the port to its east–west diameter extending just outside the circle, like London's Underground sign, ; but the diameter is now ready for fuller development eastwards for fifty miles (80 km.), pointing to the Rhine and the heart of a united Europe, with or without Britain. A logical description of the immediate influence of Greater London must now take the reader down to the shores of the North Sea. The time-lag between writing this chapter and going to press will no doubt offer a tantalizing glimpse of the continuation of this growth process (see *Addendum*).

The growth of the port—its physical extension and the increase of its trade—from the past into the future forms a continuum. London still makes demands on the Thames, and there is still plenty of room for their further fulfilment. Such great opportunities: such great expectations.

Addendum: post-1962 Developments

The story continues. In June, 1963 the first stage of the Tilbury Docks Extension was begun. By 1965 this will have provided another two deep-water berths and also two berths for 'roll-on–roll-off' vessels where road vehicles can be driven directly on or off ships. A seaward extension to the port occurred in 1964 when the P.L.A. received statutory powers to extend its downstream limit to a line approximately twenty-two miles east of that shown on Figure 41 (*Port of London* (*Extension of Seaward Limit*) *Act*). In 1962–63 the net registered tonnage of shipping entering the port was a record at 94,131,935; and a 250 per cent increase in this figure since the beginning of the century (cf. Figure 43, top left) is almost wholly due to an increase in the average size of vessel and not to an increase in vessel numbers. Hence the desire of the P.L.A. to have powers to regulate more closely the navigation of these larger ships in an area of the estuary where shipping lanes from the North Sea and English Channel combine; where tidal information must be accurate, and where future dredging may be a possibility.

The Report of the Rochdale Committee (H.M.S.O., Cmnd. 1824, 1962) was largely accepted by the Government in 1963. This Committee surveyed all British ports and one of its principal recommendations was that two ports should receive the highest priority for major development—London and Southampton. There is no reason to believe that the National Ports Council set up in 1964 with Lord Rochdale as Chairman will advise reversing this basic policy of major growth for the port.

References

1. L. R. Jones, *The Geography of London River* (1931), 18. Other accounts of the port are Sir Joseph Broodbank, *History of the Port of London*, 2 vols. (1921); J. Bird, *The Geography of the Port of London* (1957); and idem, *The Major Seaports of the United Kingdom* (1963), Chapters 14–17, 328–410.

2. Jones, *op. cit.*, 14.

3. P.R.O. Treasury Papers, Bdl. 408, No. 88, Cust. Comrs. to Lords of Treas., 1761, Aug. 12, quoted by E. E. Hoon, 'The organization of the port of London', *The Organization of the English Customs System 1696–1786* (New York, 1938), Chapter IV, 122–66. This work contains much useful information regarding the role of H.M. Customs in the pre-dock era.

4. *Report from the Committee Appointed to Enquire into the Best Mode of Providing Sufficient Accommodation for the Increased Trade and Shipping of the Port of London*, May 13, 1796, xvi.

5. Hoon, *op. cit.*, 127.

6. W. Vaughan, *Observations and Facts Drawn Up for the Committee of Merchants that were Appointed the [?] of March 1794 to Examine into the State of Legal Quays . . .* , MS. in Vaughan Papers, Vol. 3, No. 6, 3. [Held at Port of London Authority library.]

7. A. Pulling, *A Practical Treatise on the Laws, Customs, and Regulations of the City and Port of London* (1844), 320–2, *et seq.* Yantlet Creek is still the eastern limit of the area within which the bed and soil of the river is vested in the P.L.A.

8. The limits of the jurisdiction of the P.L.A. are marked on Figure 41.

9. A. Giles in discussion upon the original projecting jetties of the north quay of the Royal Victoria Dock (see Plate 19), W. J. Kingsbury, 'Description . . . of the Victoria (London) Docks, etc.', *Minutes of the Proceedings of the Institution of Civil Engineers*, 18 (1858–9), 445–89, 470.

10. In discussion on F. E. Wentworth-Shields, 'The construction of the White Star Dock and adjoining quays at Southampton', *Proceedings of the Institution of Civil Engineers*, 195 (1913–14), 34.

11. J. F. Scott, 'The construction and equipment of the Tilbury Docks', *Minutes of the Proceedings of the Institution of Civil Engineers*, 126 (1895), 276–88, 276.

12. This neglect of the river is treated as the 'Second Crisis' in the port's development in J. Bird, *The Major Seaports of the United Kingdom, op. cit.*, 354–6.

13. R. Capper, J. Abernethy, and A. Giles, witnesses quoted in *Minutes of Proceedings before the House of Commons Select Committee on Private Bills* 1882.

14. Scott, *loc. cit.*, 278.

15. F. M. G. Du Plat Taylor, 'Extensions at Tilbury Docks 1912–17', *Minutes of the Proceedings of the Institution of Civil Engineers*, 215 (1923), 165–200.

16. F. W. Davies and W. Mackenzie, 'Major improvement works of the Port of London Authority 1925–30', *Minutes of Proceedings of the Institution of Civil Engineers*, 240 (1934–5), 258–340, 259.

17. C. Peel, A. J. Carmichael, and R. F. J. Smeardon, 'No. 1 Berth, Tilbury Dock, *Proceedings of the Institution of Civil Engineers*, 8 (1957), 331–62, 333.

18. It is perhaps rather dangerous to use one criterion alone when analysing a port's trade. Tonnage figures are not available for the early years of this century. In 1901 London's share of the national foreign seaborne trade by value was 30·1 per cent; from 1958–60 the average share was 36·3 per cent. This increase was due to the greater share in London's trade taken up by manufactured exports (see below in text).

19. H.M.S.O., 1961, Cmd. 1164, 83–90, paras. 327–49.

20. See also the author's complaint in *The Geography of the Port of London*, *op. cit.*, 185–6.

21. S. Turner, 'The Port of London—planning for the future', *The Dock and Harbour Authority*, 52 (1962), 42–45, 44.

22. A more complete survey is given in *The Major Seaports of the United Kingdom*, *op. cit.*

23. A. Ellis, *Three Hundred Years on London River: the Hay's Wharf Story* (1952) is the company history.

24. Samuel Williams & Son Ltd., *A Company's Story in Its Setting* (1955) is the company history.

25. The limit is now Crayford Ness, 18 miles (29 km.) downstream of London Bridge. For historical details see B. E. Cracknell, 'The petroleum industry of the Lower Thames and Medway', *Geography*, 37 (1952), 79–88.

1. The City of London

A view of the City looking south-west from Whitechapel to Bankside beyond the River Thames. From the Tower of London on the east to the Temple on the west, the river, with its frontage of wharves and warehouses, forms the southern boundary of the City. The mouths of two tributary streams, the Wallbrook and the Fleet, are now covered by Cannon Street and Blackfriars Stations. On the eastern and northern borders of the City railway termini at Fenchurch Street, Liverpool Street, Broad Street and Moorgate also occupy low-lying ground. The Roman Wall, following the line of London Wall and Moorfields, right foreground in the view, encloses two low hills. On the east, at the centre of the photograph, on a site now occupied by Leadenhall Market, lie the foundations of a Roman basilica. From there Cornhill leads down to the intersection of seven streets around the Royal Exchange, the Bank of England and the Mansion House in the valley of the Wallbrook. To the west, Cheapside rises to a hill crowned by St Paul's Cathedral. From the steps of St Paul's Ludgate Hill descends steeply to the Fleet valley.

2. St Paul's Cathedral

The western part of the City from Queen Victoria Street, in the foreground, to Barbican on its northern boundary, background left in the picture, was extensively damaged in the Second World War. On the bombed sites to the north and east of St Paul's, between Aldersgate Street and Moorgate, tall office blocks are being built.

3. SOUTHWARK

Downstream from Blackfriars Bridge, in the foreground, the Thames passes under Blackfriars Railway Bridge, Southwark Bridge, Cannon Street Railway Bridge, London Bridge, Tower Bridge to the Pool of London. On the right bank lies Southwark, which has grown from a Roman settlement at the southern end of London Bridge. Near the bridge-head stands Southwark Cathedral, hemmed in by wharves and a railway viaduct. A number of old inns flank Borough High Street, and Chaucer's Tabard stood at the beginning of the Old Kent Road. Few traces remain of the Elizabethan theatres and places of entertainment established in Southwark outside the jurisdiction of the City of London. They have been swept away to make room for bridges, roads, railways, warehouses, breweries, printing works in Stamford Street, in the bottom right-hand corner of the picture, Bankside power station and a number of new office blocks.

4. WESTMINSTER

A mile to the west of the City lie the seats of government and administration. The Abbey and the royal palace of Westminster were built on the dry ground of Thorney Island a few feet above areas once subject to flooding by two arms of the Tyburn stream. The Palace of Westminster is now incorporated in the Houses of Parliament and the yards of Westminster School now adjoin the cloisters of Westminster Abbey. The former marshy lands have been drained and embanked and now carry the offices of government departments in Whitehall. Westminster Bridge links Westminster with the south bank. The Royal Festival Hall, County Hall—the headquarters of the London County Council—and St Thomas's Hospital occupy sites fronting the river. A little way back stands the tower of the new Shell building, looking across the river to the dumpy white block of Shell Mex House, and behind York Road spread the roofs of Waterloo Station, London's largest and most modern terminus.

5. BLOOMSBURY

A view looking east across the rectilinear pattern of spacious streets and squares on the Bedford estate. Building began in 1776 in Bedford Square, in the south-west, the right foreground in the photograph. In 1800 Russell Square on the east was laid out and building advanced northward along this axis to Woburn Square and Tavistock Square, on the extreme left of the view. In 1823, when the building of the British Museum began, the estate lost its exclusively residential character. In the neighbourhood of the main-line railway stations, hotels opened, of which the most ornate, the Russell and Imperial Hotels, were built in 1898 on the far side of Russell Square. The development of a university precinct, foreshadowed by the founding of University College in 1826, entered a new stage in 1932, when Sir Charles Holden designed the Senate House, and planned buildings to house the institutes and schools of the university. It received an important accession in 1952 when Birkbeck College moved to its new building in Malet Street.

6. REGENT'S PARK

A view looking east from Marylebone to Camden Town sides of Regent's Park. On the west, in the foreground, stretches a serpentine lake fringed by trees and villas, now occupied by Bedford College. In the background are the façades of Cumberland and Chester Terraces, designed by John Nash in 1825 and 1827, enjoying spacious prospects across the landscaped park.

7. RAILWAY WORKS IN OLD ST PANCRAS CHURCHYARD 1865

A contemporary engraving in *The Illustrated London News*, August 1865, showing the construction of the Midland railway. The removal of bodies from the churchyard of old St Pancras church was the subject of a public inquiry, following local protests. The church and some trees remain, in a small public garden, but the early nineteenth-century terraces have been replaced by blocks of municipal housing.

8. St Pancras and King's Cross

Looking north from Euston Road towards Camden New Town, showing an area largely occupied by railway tracks, stations, goods depots and coal yards. Beyond the gas-works in the centre of the photograph can be seen the locks and basins of the Regent's Canal, crossed by the main-line tracks of the Midland Railway. Sir George Gilbert Scott's St Pancras station hotel front, 1868–74, in the words of Walford, 'Stands without rival for palatial beauty, comfort and convenience.' Adjoining it on the left are the goods depot, milk depot and Bass's ale store. On the right is the Great Northern Railway's terminus at King's Cross, built by Lewis Cubitt in 1851–2, depending, as *The Builder* observed, 'on the largeness of some of the features, the fitness of the structure for its purpose, and a characteristic expression of that purpose.'

9. De Beauvoir Town, Shoreditch

An extremely rigid geometrical plan for a speculative estate laid out about 1840. The houses are mainly semi-detached villas—an innovation at this period, when most London houses were still being built in terraces. The main north–south road on the right margin of the picture, Kingsland Road, follows the line of the Roman Ermine Street.

10. Canonbury Park

A layout typical of the 'free planning' of the 1860s, with semi-detached villas standing in large, well-wooded gardens. The area was opened up for suburban development by the North London Railway, shown in the north-west corner of the picture. Passengers gained direct access to the City by the extension of the North London Railway to its Broad Street terminus in 1865.

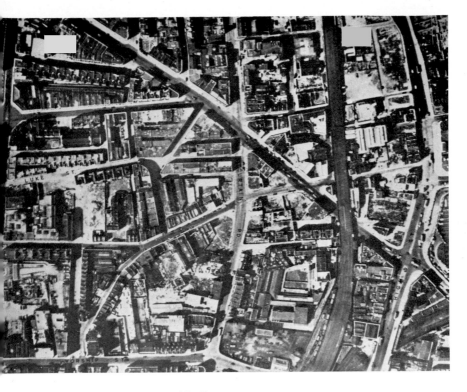

11. Shoreditch

The curving street on the eastern edge of the picture, Shoreditch High Street, follows the line of the Roman Ermine Street, the main road to York. The area west of it was developed from Tudor times; Curtain Road commemorates the Curtain Theatre, one of the earliest theatres in Elizabethan London. Towards the western edge of the picture there is evidence of geometrical planning, but the chaotic disorder in the south centre is more characteristic of the unplanned development in this district. The area had degenerated into a slum quarter by the 1860s; it was transformed by the construction of the North London Railway spur into Broad Street in 1861–5, running north–south in the eastern half of the picture, and by the cutting of Great Eastern Street diagonally across the area in the 1870s as part of a new direct highway between the Docks and the West End. The slums were replaced by tenement blocks, multi-storey warehouses and workshop blocks, evident in the north-west corner of the picture.

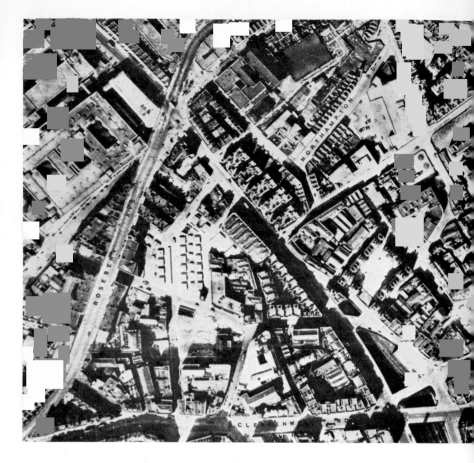

12. CLERKENWELL

An area of extensive comprehensive redevelopment in mid-Victorian
times, *circa* 1860–90. The area was built over in the early nineteenth
century by speculative builders: on the higher ground in the north-east the
layout was geometrical, but in the centre and south a labyrinth of slum
property grew up in the valley of the Fleet River. In the 1860s a new road,
Farringdon Road, was cut diagonally from north-west to south-east
across the area in conjunction with the Metropolitan Railway, which
emerges from a tunnel in the south-east corner at the approach to its
original terminus at Farringdon Street Station. The slums were replaced by
densely built tenements, whose height is indicated by the long shadows
cast across Farringdon Road. In the late 1870s another main road,
Clerkenwell Road, was cut from east to west across the southern part of
the area, and in the 1880s Rosebery Avenue was cut from south-west to
north-east as part of a new artery connecting the West End and Islington;
both were accompanied by new tenement blocks. Rosebery Avenue crosses
the lines of the old streets at very acute angles, and had to be carried over
the Fleet valley on a viaduct, passing above the level of the old streets. In
the north-west corner of the picture is the Post Office sorting office at
Mount Pleasant, built on the site of the old Coldbath Fields Prison.

13. FINCHLEY ROAD

Built in 1826–35 as a turnpike road, Finchley Road provided a direct link between the West End and the Great North Road at Finchley. It ran through open country on the western flank of the hill on which the old village of Hampstead stood. In 1868 the main line of the Midland Railway was tunnelled under the hill and a station built at the tunnel mouth on Finchley Road. In 1879 a station on the Metropolitan line pushing north from Baker Street to Harrow and the Chilterns was opened under Finchley Road. Residential development followed rapidly. To the south-west of the Metropolitan station and on the slopes rising above Finchley Road to the east, it took the form, typical for the date, of free-standing villas set in large gardens. The land between the two railways was, however, occupied by railway yards, factories and warehouses. In 1963 plans were announced for the comprehensive redevelopment of this district west of Finchley Road.

14. Pinner, Middlesex

Running across the centre of the photograph is the main street of the old village with its medieval church and some surviving seventeenth-century buildings. In 1886, when the Metropolitan Railway, seen at the bottom of the picture, reached the village, suburban development began, at first near the station. More rapid development followed the electrification of the line in 1905, and during the present century new shops have been opened and expanded. The old village street now forms a service centre for the growing suburb.

15. WEMBLEY, MIDDLESEX

A typical private enterprise housing estate of the 1930s. This picture, taken in 1939, shows an estate located south-west of South Kenton station, just visible at the top of the photograph. The unimaginative, drawing board layout of roads and crescents, uniform in width and curvature, serves to emphasize the monotonous repetition of semi-detached dwelling units, standardized in their design and specifications.

16. Harold Hill, near Romford, Essex

This view, taken in 1951, shows a recent 'out-county' estate, built by the
London County Council in the years immediately following the Second
World War. The buildings in the foreground are temporary houses, which
give a monotonous impression, but the permanent dwellings in the centre
show the effect of mixing flats among semi-detached houses and short
terraces typical of pre-war 'cottage' estates. The result of attempts to preserve existing woods and spinneys between blocks of permanent houses
can be seen at the top of the picture. Open spaces have also been used to
divide the estate into two neighbourhoods.

17. Nineteenth-century offices in the City of London

Albert Buildings, Queen Victoria Street, brilliantly contrived in 1871 by F. J. Ward to fit into the acute angle formed by Queen Victoria Street, a new City thoroughfare, opened out in 1867–71, and narrow older back streets. Unlike many City buildings of this period, it makes the most of its new-found space, ranging up to the full permitted height of four storeys, with an ingeniously devised attic storey above. Its arcaded, Lombardic Gothic exterior adds an entirely felicitous and slightly fanciful touch to a utilitarian structure. By comparison with offices of an earlier date, its rooms are high and well lighted, but it offers much less floor space for letting than a modern building of the same size.

18. Twentieth-century office block in Marylebone Road

Castrol House, Marylebone Road, designed in 1957 by Collins, Melvin, Ward and Partners, to face Marylebone Road, a section of the inner ring road around the West End, a new location for offices nearly three miles west of Queen Victoria Street. Space is conserved by building a fifteen-storey tower block, which rises sheer above a low, two-storeyed platform. The effect of height is lightened by glazed curtain walls and a delicate mesh of framework traced on the outer surface. By comparison with Albert Buildings, Castrol House makes no concessions to romanticism, but offers 142,000 square feet of floor space for offices, and enjoys more light and comfort than earlier offices in the City.

19. THE ROYAL DOCKS LOOKING EAST

This photograph taken in 1934 shows the original right-angle jetties that gave an elaborate outline to the north quay of the Royal Victoria Dock. The white lines show the present perimeter obliterating the site of the former Tidal Basin, indicated by the letter 'T'. This dock now receives vessels via the Royal Albert Dock, beyond, since the original entrance lock, in the foreground, was spanned by the Silvertown Way Viaduct in 1934 as part of a road improvement programme, and only barges enter from the west.

20. Tilbury Docks

Looking south, with a 28,000-ton class P. & O.-Orient liner at the Main Dock south quay and a sister ship in dry dock. Note the smaller ships in branch docks and the cluster of dumb barges.

21. THE POOL OF LONDON

Looking south-eastwards downstream, with, on the left bank, the Tower of
London, St Katherine Docks, London Docks, and, in the distance part
of the India Docks. Multi-storey warehouses, with long-jibbed riverside
cranes, operated by public wharfingers line the riverside. The Surrey
Commercial Docks are prominent on the right bank, background, within
a river meander.

22. GRAVESEND REACH LOOKING SOUTH-EAST

With the Tilbury Floating Passenger Landing Stage in the foreground, this view twenty-six miles downstream of London Bridge shows the beginning of the extensive empty marshes on the south, or far, side of the river east of Gravesend.

23. Radlett 1932

This view from the south shows Radlett in 1932. The village is grouped around the railway station, on the main line to St Pancras, and building is in progress to the north and west of the village, left centre in the photograph. The lack of trees in front of the newly-erected houses contrasts with the well-wooded aspect of the district in 1959, on the right-hand margin of Plate 24. To the west of the railway line, on the right of the photograph, are the clumps and belt plantation of Newberries Park as they appeared before building took place.

24 RADLETT 1959

This view from the north shows the southern part of Radlett in 1959. There is a marked contrast between the now maturely wooded gardens of houses built in the inter-war years to the west of the railway, on the right-hand side of the picture, and the post-war development in Newberries Park to the south-east, on the left of the railway. The gardens of the new houses lack trees, apart from some surviving parkland timber. The background shows the character of the green belt and the short distance separating Radlett from Borehamwood, of which a few houses are to be seen at the top edge of the photograph.

25. WENTWORTH, SURREY, AND CANVEY ISLAND, ESSEX

These two photographs give a close view of the differences in density and character of dispersed houses beyond London. On the left are large houses, built in the style of Tudor farmhouses, surrounded not by farmland but the fairways of a Surrey golf course, their spacious gardens well cared for and heavily timbered. On the right are small bungalows and chalets built on the edge of Thames-side marshes, occupying small plots of ground, served by unmade roads.

26. Green Belt in the Vale of St Albans

An air view of development plan green belt near London Colney, Hertford-shire.

The use of most of the land shown in the photograph and on the map has not changed since the area was designated as green belt. But three developments have recently taken place. A new dual-carriage-way, A6, has been constructed to by-pass London Colney in the north-west. In the south-west sand and gravel working is spreading. Between London Colney and the new road settlement infilling has been permitted.

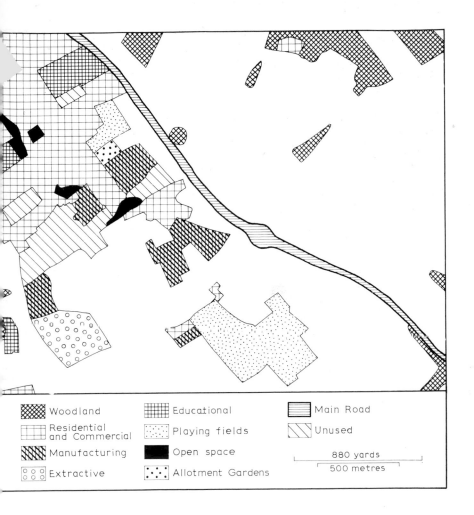

Woodland

Residential and Commercial

Manufacturing

Extractive

Educational

Playing fields

Open space

Allotment Gardens

Main Road

Unused

880 yards
500 metres

A map of the same area showing some non-agricultural uses of land within the green belt.

27. Welwyn Garden City 1939

The well-grown vegetation in this older established New Town gives a maturity to the scene which post-war residential areas inevitably lack at present. The arrangement of streets appears more formal and monumental from the air than when viewed on the ground.

28. HARLOW, ESSEX

A high density New Town. The central area is shown, together with some layouts of high density housing, including tower blocks, and a large wedge of agricultural land and open space separating small neighbourhood units.

29. CRAWLEY, SUSSEX

A medium density New Town. Part of the old town lying between the church and the railway crossing can be seen in the foreground on the left. In the centre of the photograph, close to the church, is the New Town centre. Beyond are residential neighbourhoods, mostly of medium density housing, served by their own schools, shops and open spaces.

30. Cassiobury, Watford, Hertfordshire

The residence of the Earl of Essex on the outskirts of Watford, from an early nineteenth-century painting by J. M. W. Turner. The house, rebuilt in 1800 by James Wyatt in picturesque Gothic style, looks over grounds remodelled by Humphry Repton between 1801 and 1802. In the foreground, a herd of deer placidly watch a barge passing on the Grand Junction Canal. In the middle distance, sheep graze at the edge of the River Gade, enlarged to form a broad artificial lake. Behind the trees on the right stood a rustic cottage for a lock-keeper; in the wood on the left, a wooden chalet was occupied by a gamekeeper. A century earlier this scene had been a stiffly regimented formal garden laid out by Moses Cook. A century later it was to be acquired by the people of Watford for use as a municipal park and recreation ground. Cassiobury is typical of many parks beyond London whose landscapes have often been changed dramatically at the whim of fashion or to meet the stern demands of changing economic conditions.

31. SHARDELOES, AMERSHAM, BUCKINGHAMSHIRE

A modest country estate landscaped by Humphry Repton before 1803. The alterations were designed to extend the range of ornamental prospects beyond the immediate precincts of the house to embrace both sides of the Misbourne valley. The hard edge of beech plantations on the skyline were broken, bare sweeps of grass were diversified with clumps, single trees were planted at the edge of an artificial lake created in the eighteenth century by Richmond. Little has been changed in this landscape since 1803. It is typical of a country estate held for several generations by the same family, where considerations of utility and appearance are nicely balanced.

9

Industrial London: A General View

*

PETER HALL

However large the allotted compass, no account of the industrial geography of London could be completely adequate. In the first place, there is too much of London industry for that. In 1961, according to Ministry of Labour figures, the Greater London conurbation contained 4,671,000 workers: 1,613,000 in manufacturing. So in 1961 the conurbation accounted for some 23 per cent of the employed population of England and Wales, or close upon 20 per cent of those employed in manufacturing. This share had been falling slightly through the 1950s; but only because the conurbation was by then no longer an adequate unit to describe the industrial geography of London. During that decade the largest increases in employment, whether in absolute or percentage terms, were in the so-called 'Outer Ring': outside the conurbation, and between fifteen and forty miles (24 km. and 64 km.) from the centre of London. Adding this ring, we obtain a greater 'London Region' where the employed population in 1961 stood at the six million mark: nearly one in three of all the workers in England and Wales.[1] This is a measure of the concentration of British industry within the metropolitan region, a phenomenon which is paralleled in other big cities of the world.

Secondly, London's industry is too heterogeneous. Of the 24 major divisions into which the Standard Industrial Classification is grouped, in only four does London make a negligible showing. Two —agriculture, and mining and quarrying—are primary industries; the two others—metal manufacture, and textiles—represent early stages in the manufacturing process. In every other division, London's contribution is important enough to merit a separate account. London is not distinguished by a single staple industry, such as cotton in Lancashire; nor even by a recognizable group of associated industries, such as the engineering and metals group of the West Midlands. The observer of London industry then must impose his own order upon the apparent confusion, his own simplicity upon the rich complexities; the more summary the account, the simpler the resultant pattern, and the more schematic and distorted the picture that is presented. That is inevitable.

Thirdly, the internal distribution of London's industry is equally complex. Just as London has examples of most industries, so do most of its constituent areas. Patterns do exist in the geography of London industry, but there are so many different ones, each overlaying the next, that the final picture is confused.

To bring any order to the subject, it is necessary to limit the problem. Here I exclude the whole group of service industries, which have been discussed in Chapter 7 in relation to the place where they are most important—the Central Area. In this chapter I give a general view of the evolution of manufacturing industry in London. It claims no originality; and details and qualifications must be sought in other places. Some of them are described in the account of industry in inner north-east London (Chapter 10); and I have treated them elsewhere.[2]

The first essential is to delimit those areas of London where manufacturing industry is mainly concentrated. Figure 49 at the beginning of the next chapter combines several indices of industrial concentration to give a general view of London industry.

The Victorian Manufacturing Belt

This map reveals what appears to be a clear pattern of manufacturing industry. It is dominated by the great industrial crescent which runs round the north and east sides of central London, from the western edge of the City and the West End, through the southern parts of St Marylebone and St Pancras, through Islington, Finsbury, Holborn, Shoreditch, Bethnal Green and Stepney. It extends to Southwark on the south bank of the river; to the north it throws out two great projections, one north and north-west to Camden Town, Kentish Town and Holloway, one north-east to south Hackney and

Stoke Newington. These projections separate great blank areas of the map: the residential suburbs of north-west London, from Kensington round to Highgate; of north-central London, from Barnsbury up through Canonbury to Highbury; and of north-east London, from Bow Common across Victoria Park to Clapton. Within the belt there are minor discontinuities; and more important, there are major sub-concentrations of industry, in the centre of the West End, in Clerkenwell, in Shoreditch, in Whitechapel, in Fleet Street.

It is evident that this great crescent lies wholly within that area of London which was fully built-up before 1900. Here indeed are concentrated the industries and the types of productive organization which characterized the economy of Victorian London. It is, in a more than formal sense, the *Victorian Manufacturing Belt*, though the term is a convenient misnomer; some of these areas and industries were established before Victoria came to the throne, some have continued to evolve rapidly in the twentieth century. And the term is not meant to suggest that here the industries are stagnant or declining, that their methods are inadequate to the requirements of the mid-twentieth century. The Victorian Belt is still, incomparably, the major industrial area of London. Within it, in 1951, over half a million people were working in manufacturing industry: just over one-third of the total manufacturing labour force in the whole Greater London conurbation.

It is not surprising that the typical industries of this zone show many common features of organization and of location. First, this is the home of the small workshop, often in ingeniously-converted premises: an old house or shop, a former warehouse, even a disused chapel. Because of this fact, the casual observer may easily fail to recognize the area for what it is—one of the most concentrated and important industrial areas of Britain. The industries that have developed here are those where the advantages of small-scale production are most apparent, and where indeed large-scale factory operation may bring positive diseconomies. They use little machinery; they do not need specialized industrial premises; they produce in small quantities, often in very short runs, to particular orders, which may depend on rapidly-changing fashions. All the most typical trades of this area—clothing, furniture, printing and its ancillary trades, precious metals and jewellery, precision engineering and light metal trades—share these features.

Secondly, small-scale production is accompanied by a very typical

227

form of organization: extreme disintegration of the productive process into a number of stages performed by different undertakings, demanding extraordinarily strong and complex linkages among the specialist firms themselves. The simplest type of linkage is vertical, where the goods pass from one specialist contractor to another, almost as along an assembly line, as in sections of the clothing industry. More complex linkages occur, for instance, in the specialized engineering trades, and are discussed in the next chapter. With this type of productive organization, the real assembly line runs through the streets; a journey around the Victorian manufacturing crescent on any typical weekday reveals the extraordinary congestion of goods vehicles, hurrying in all directions about their business. Until the Greater London Traffic Survey publishes its findings we can only guess the densities and patterns of goods movement in London; but within the Victorian belt there cannot be less than a million trips every working day.

The third feature arises out of the second. It is an extreme dependence upon the specialized facilities available within London, and especially within the immediate area of location. In this sort of industry, the traditional type of location analysis, in terms of raw material sources and markets, can only mislead. The material is most usually itself a manufactured or at least a semi-manufactured product, supplied by a specialist supplier, either a manufacturer himself or a wholesaler: the cloth merchant, the timber sawmill, the supplier of specialized engineering components. The finished product may find its way to a retail shop or to a wholesale warehouse; but often, for the individual manufacturer, it will represent only one further stage in a complex productive process. In these circumstances, to unravel the precise economics of location is an unprofitable enterprise. Like a pack of cards, the individual enterprises stand or fall together. No one firm could exist without the external economies offered by the existence of the metropolitan economic machine, and more particularly of the specialized industrial 'quarter' immediately around the workshop. Thus the small furniture maker in Hackney Road finds within walking distance the services of sawmills, specialized accessory shops, tool dealers, upholsterers and polishers. All describe themselves, in their notices, as 'Suppliers to the Trade'; along Hackney Road there is only one trade, and everyone knows its trends, its secrets, its gossip. Only a mile to the south, in Whitechapel, the same notice is seen; but we have passed an invisible boundary, and the nature of the 'Trade' has changed. The trimmings shops and sewing machine depots and specialized employment offices minister only to the garment trades; in streets and cafés the talk is no longer of veneering or polishing, but of machining and buttonholing and overlocking.

The historical geography of the quarters shows that they developed in close proximity to their immediate market. And though today it would almost be as true to say that the market depends on the industries, still in the last resort the real *raison d'être* of the industrial quarters is the near presence of the demand. In historical terms there have been two great metropolitan markets: the West End retail market and the City–East End wholesale market; and this is the basis for what is still the most useful geographical division within the Victorian manufacturing belt today.

The *clothing* trades illustrate this most perfectly.[3] There is a *West End* centre, incorporating two separate but contiguous quarters. One is the highest grade men's bespoke tailoring, traditionally centred on Savile Row north of Piccadilly, but extending east of Regent Street into Soho where much outwork is carried on. This centre has hardly changed, in productive methods or in location, in the century since 1860: suits are individually cut in the Savile Row workshops, and made up by craftsmen who still dispense, to a considerable degree, with the advantages of division of labour or of machinery. The other is the much newer women's ready-made outerwear industry, concentrating especially upon dresses and mantles, in the congested quarter on both sides of Oxford Street. Margaret Street is the 'trade street' for this quarter, as is Savile Row for the other. The industry here developed about 1900 out of a much older bespoke 'Court Dressmaking' quarter to the west of Regent Street (and just north of the Savile Row quarter), in response to the rapid development at that time of mass retail distribution through the shops of Oxford Street. Different though they may seem, for both quarters the critical factor of location is the immediate presence of the purchasers, whose unpredictable and highly personal demands must be met at very short notice.

In contrast the *East End* clothing industry began by producing for a wholesale market: the traders at the eastern edge of the City, who had been dealing in second-hand clothes in the 'Petticoat Lane' area since the sixteenth century, and who developed the manufacture of cheap ready-made clothes about 1850. The impetus was technological innovation: the sewing machine was perfected, and the band saw for cloth-cutting invented, in this period. But this industrial revolution failed to create a factory system: the necessary capital equipment was light and easily acquired, and so the clothing trades of the East End came to be organized on the basis of extreme vertical disintegration of the productive process. From the wholesale warehouse, each stage of production was contracted and even subcontracted among a host of specialists. This, the so-called 'sweating system', reached its apogee about 1890 with the immigration in large numbers of poor, unskilled Jewish workers from Eastern Europe. Since that time, the Jewish clothing quarter of Whitechapel has changed profoundly in character. The power of the wholesaler has weakened; the demands of the market have become more exacting; the skills of the second-and third-generation Jewish population have developed. Those types of production which are more standardized, less subject to fashion, more suitable for factory production, have tended to leave Whitechapel for outer east and north London.[4] Whitechapel, in fact, has become a second West End, highly-concentrated upon fashionable and high-grade clothing. Middlesex Street, E.1, is barely distinguishable from Margaret Street, W.1; there is the same bustle, the same animation, the same extraordinary congestion of goods and people in the streets.

Furniture making, in contrast, had a West End centre, but has almost entirely lost it.[5] This centre served a retail market, both for bespoke and ready-made goods; it migrated north during the eighteenth and early nineteenth centuries from Covent Garden and St Martin's Lane to Oxford Street and finally to Tottenham Court Road, which is still today the main street for furniture retailing. But in furniture manufacture the demands of the market are more predictable, the advantages of factory production greater, the need for a location close to the retailer less urgent; today the West End manufacturing quarter survives only in a few workshops attached to the big stores. Yet the East End quarter still survives, though it clings tenaciously to its traditional small workshop organization. Like the East End clothing quarter it started in close dependence on the wholesalers, who were in this case at the north-eastern corner of the City, around the site of Liverpool Street Station; about 1870, owing to demolitions and the pressure of commerce on space, the quarter moved north to its present centre, the Curtain Road area of Shoreditch. Within the complex, Curtain Road is still the 'trade street' for the wholesalers' showrooms; the small manufacturing workshops crowd into the streets around, and spread eastwards into the converted shops and houses of Hackney Road. In this quarter, the form of organization which had developed by 1880 closely resembled that in clothing to the south in Whitechapel. The wholesaler was the impetus for the whole productive process; timber was obtained in small quantities, already sawn, from a merchant in the neighbourhood; the job would go through the hands of a number of specialists before delivery to the wholesale warehouse. Since 1900 the wholesaler has lost much of his importance; brand names and advertising have aided the more enterprising firms, which have outgrown their congested sites and have migrated outwards in search of cheap land. They went especially to the Lea valley in the inter-war period, but now they are found as far away as the New Towns; paradoxically, though, the small manufacturer continues to hold his own in the Curtain Road quarter, which remains one of the liveliest sections of the great Victorian manufacturing belt.

The *printing* industry comprises a great number of subdivisions; not only the obvious ones like newspaper and periodical work, book printing, advertising, jobbing, and commercial stationery, but also the very important specialist ancillary processes upon which the printer depends, and which technological developments have multiplied and complicated since 1900: process engraving, photo engraving, typesetting, and lithographic plate making.[6] Up to about 1870 all these varied trades found their home in the Victorian belt of London; and within that belt, the key to the location pattern lay far back in history. Printing developed where publication of the medieval written manuscripts had taken place: near the church. This then was the origin of the publishing centre of St Paul's Churchyard and Paternoster Row, which survived from the early sixteenth century to the air raids of 1940; it was the origin also of the newspaper printing area of Fleet Street immediately to the west, in what was at first merely an extension of the book publishers' quarter. By 1880 book printing was being driven out of London by high wages and high rents; later, much periodical printing left central London for the same reason. But the same rule applies as with the clothing trades: those parts of printing, and those processes, which depend upon unpredictable and novel demands, upon detailed specifications and consequently upon close contact between buyer and producer, must remain close to the central area where demand originates. So commercial work for City business houses is still concentrated round the northern edge of the City, from Clerkenwell to Shoreditch; the specialist engravers, typesetters and platemakers are heavily concentrated in Clerkenwell, though their products may be taken out to the provinces for the actual printing process; and the whole of newspaper printing has to remain in the centre, next to the centres of intelligence, despite the large scale of operation and the consequent demands on scarce and valuable land.

The most complex of the quarters is the *precision engineering, light metal, jewellery and precious metal* quarter, which centres on Clerkenwell and spreads north to Camden Town, Kentish Town and Holloway.[7] Despite the great variety of the trades represented here today, which are described in detail in the next chapter, they have evolved from a few common origins; the most important of which lie in Clerkenwell. On the south-eastern border of that district, and actually within Holborn, lay London's traditional centre of jewellery and precious metal work: Hatton Garden. Just as the area immediately east of the city walls had early become associated with Jewish immigrants and the second-hand clothing trade, Hatton Garden on the north-western edge of the City became the centre of immigrants who specialized in precious metals and stones. In the heart of Clerkenwell, stretching east and north-east from the village green on the high eastern bluff of the Fleet river valley, there had developed by the eighteenth century a specialist craft tradition in the manufacture of watches, clocks, specialized measuring instruments like barometers, and surgical instruments. The most important craft, that of watch and clock making, seems to have migrated gradually north out of the City after 1700 as the built-up area spread and as rents (no doubt) became too high in the City itself. By the mid-nineteenth century, at the zenith of its fortunes, this trade was an amazing example of extreme subdivision of skilled crafts, working on the domestic system. A watch would need the combined skills of a score of specialized small masters, most of whom lived above their work within a very limited industrial quarter. Figure 46 shows the trade at that time; ninety years after, in 1951, Figure 47 shows hardly a trace of the industry, save for a few sundries-men; for Clerkenwell watch and clock making suffered a grievous blow in the late nineteenth century from the competition of cheap Swiss goods, and decayed rapidly. Similarly rapid was the decline of the piano manufacture of Camden Town, which developed around 1850 as an

Key (Fig. 46):

- ● Watchmakers (74/018)
- ■ Clock makers (15/181)
- □ Clock case makers (11/15)
- ☆ Watch balance makers (4/8)
- ◠ Watch barrel makers (1/1)
- △ Watch cap makers (7/9)
- ○ Watch case makers (23/43)
- ▼ Watch dial plate makers & finishers (20/021)
- E Watch engravers (9/o)
- ∇ Watch escapement makers (12/21)
- ◇ Watch finishers (7/13)
- f Watch fuzee makers (2/4)
- G Watch case gilders (3/7)
- ⊙ Watch glass makers (4/8)

Key (right, Fig. 47):

- ◈ Watch guard maker (1/2)
- V Watch hand makers (19/2)
- ∨ Watch jewellers (26/33)
- L Watch joint finishers (4/4)
- ⊙ Watch key makers (2/4)
- × Watch material dealers (2/9)
- M Watch motion makers (14/17)
- P Watch pallet makers (5/2)
- ♟ Watch pendant makers (3/3)
- ⚘ Watch pinion maker (V1)
- + Watch secret springers (22/33)
- S Watch spring makers (5/15)
- T Watch tool makers & dealers (7/15)
- W Watch wheel makers (2/2)

FIG. 46 (Left) The Clerkenwell watch and clock-making quarter 1861
FIG. 47 (Right) The Clerkenwell watch and clock-making quarter 1951

The figures in brackets show the numbers of makers engaged in trades listed in Post Office London Directory, 1861. The numbers of makers within the map area are expressed as proportions of the total numbers of makers in the London area.

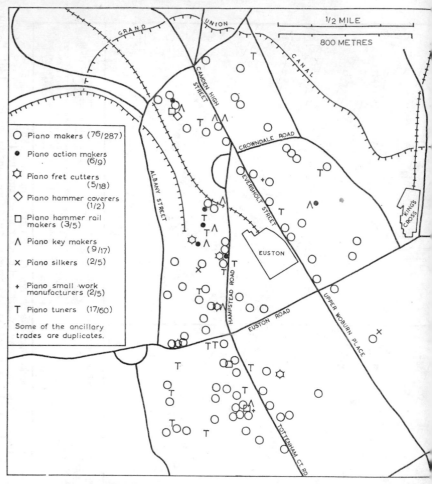

FIG. 48 The Camden Town piano-manufacturing quarter 1861
The figures show the numbers of makers within the map area as proportions of the total numbers of makers listed in the London area.
Based on Post Office London Directory

outgrowth of the Tottenham Court Road furniture district, and which was organized on the basis of a number of 'piano makers'—the final assemblers—served by an army of skilled small masters who performed the specialized operations. Figure 48 shows this trade in its heyday. Unlike the watchmakers the piano makers were always willing to provide a cheap article for the mass market; but after 1918 that

234

market turned to more automatic entertainment, and today this trade, too, has left few traces.

The collapse of such basic industries, though, merely released the available skills, and the tradition of technological innovation, and harnessed them to meet the increasingly complex demands of the twentieth-century industrial revolution. Some of the skills were absorbed very directly, as when watchmakers went into meter making, or the wire-makers and brass-finishers of Clerkenwell went into electrical wire manufacture. The typical products of the quarter today are specialized precision engineering products, often of considerable value in relation to their bulk. The key factor of location, as in the clothing and printing trades, is the necessity for close contact with the buyer and specifier of what is often a custom-built product. Like them also, these trades tend towards specialization in small workshops, with a considerable degree of interdependence. This is an almost self-contained industrial world, where each firm finds just around a few corners a dozen suppliers, half a dozen skilled labourers, a score of markets; and connecting them all, the omnipresent telephone and ubiquitous light van. In the circumstances, the question to be asked is not, why is this industry here?; but, how could it conceivably be anywhere else? There is an old song, often heard in London:

> *We're here*
> *Because we're here*
> *Because we're here*
> *Because we're here.*

That is precisely the *raison d'être* of this type of London industry.

The Riverside Industrial Belt

The second great belt of London industry is separated only by a few street blocks from the first. It runs along both banks of the Thames downstream from London Bridge; on the north it runs from Limehouse through Millwall, Silvertown, Canning Town and Barking to Dagenham, and then less continuously to Tilbury and Shellhaven; it projects up the lower Lea valley (Bow Creek) to Old Ford, and up the lower Roding valley (Barking Creek) to Romford Road; on the south bank it runs from Bermondsey, eastwards through Deptford, Greenwich and Woolwich to Erith and North-fleet, and then discontinuously as far as the exit of the Medway into the Thames at the Isle of Grain. This *Riverside Manufacturing Belt*[8] has enjoyed a long and complex evolution, since the eighteenth century or earlier; it is still expanding downstream, and now reaches some 30 miles (48 km.) below London Bridge. In 1951 that part within the Greater London conurbation—downstream only, that is, as far as Dagenham and Erith—employed some 180,000 manufacturing workers, or 12 per cent of the Greater London total.

The *raison d'être* of the riverside industries is also the existence of London; but the influence is much simpler to trace than with the Victorian Belt. One group of industries locates here because it depends on heavy, low-value goods which are imported by water and need processing at their break-of-bulk point. Most of these industries produce solely or mainly for the immediate London market: grain milling, sugar refining, timber storage and processing, power stations; the cement industry around Dartford, which depends on waterborne coal as well as local chalk and clay; and the paper mills of the Cray valley, which import coal, pulp and china clay. But for some the market is wider: thus the oil refineries which congregate below Tilbury/Gravesend, and the blast furnace which forms the beginning of the integrated productive process at the Dagenham Ford Works. The water-imported materials tend to be more important in the lower stretches of the Riverside Belt: in the innermost zone, upstream from Woolwich Reach, they are not very important at all.

Where these bulky materials are processed in a large plant, and where, in particular, space for holding large stocks is necessary, then cheap open land must be found; and this is if anything more important if the industry is in any way dangerous or noxious, as with some of the chemical industries which migrated out of inner London across the Lea valley into West Ham after 1850. Fortunately the river downstream from London Bridge is lined by alluvial marsh-land, which remained largely undeveloped as late as 1800, and which has been extensively used for industry and dock development since that date. In late Victorian times oil refining was regarded as dangerous, and was banished to remote locations in the Thames estuary; inertia and cheap land for expansion have kept it there, and here is now the greatest concentration of oil refineries in Europe.

Water transport may be necessary also for the transportation of the finished product, if it is sufficiently bulky: for this reason submarine cable manufacture, which catered mainly for an export market, was located at Woolwich where the product could be loaded directly on board ship. This, the first branch of the electrical industries to develop in London—from 1860 onward—was followed by others in the same area.

Other manufacturing industries in the riverside zone are ancillary to the port itself, and locate close to the dock areas they serve, as at Millwall on the Isle of Dogs, and Silvertown. Here are found ship repair, marine engineering, boiler making, constructional engineering, chain and wire rope manufacture.

The industries of the riverside belt are very different in character from those of the Victorian crescent; they are organized in bigger, more self-contained and self-evident plants; to the uninitiated, this is much more evidently an industrial landscape. But in places, especially in the inner, older-developed districts, the plants are smaller and the methods of organization more characteristic of the traditional manufacturing industry of inner London. In Stratford and Millwall, indeed, a veritable 'quarter' exists for the chemical industries, and the firms obtain important external economies from their near proximity to each other.

The West London Industrial Belt

The other manufacturing areas of London are all in the outer part of the conurbation, the suburban ring which was developed almost wholly between 1918 and 1939. So they can collectively be called the *newer manufacturing areas*. But just as the Victorian Belt was a convenient misnomer, so is this: in no area of importance does development start *de novo* after 1918; there were areas of industrial colonization which served as nuclei for later development.

Most important of the newer industrial areas, and most complex in nature, is the *West London Industrial Belt*,[9] which stretches across the southern and western parts of the old county of Middlesex. Like the Victorian Manufacturing Belt, it consists of a series of concentrations which are strung together like beads on a necklace. The belt actually starts in the centre of the old county, with concentrations in Cricklewood, west Hendon and Colindale; it then runs south-west roughly along the line of the North Circular Road, with important industrial areas in Wembley and Willesden, to Park Royal, north Acton and north Hammersmith. Here it turns and throws off three separate westward projections, along the main transport lines. One runs south-west along the Great West Road, an interwar arterial, and can then be traced very discontinuously through Feltham to Staines. A second runs due west along the line of the Great Western Railway to Southall and Hayes. A third follows the line of Western Avenue, another interwar arterial road, to Alperton, Perivale and Greenford.

Altogether, there were about 250,000 manufacturing workers in the West London Industrial Belt in 1951: sixteen per cent of the total for the Greater London conurbation. Over 30,000 of them were in Park Royal alone.

The first obvious feature about this zone is that, compared with the Victorian Belt, the industrial concentrations are much more sharply-defined. With only occasional exceptions of pre-1914 development—such as north Acton, where industry took over converted dwelling houses and where, in consequence, the landscape resembles that of the Victorian Belt—the industrial zones were developed as such from the start, generally by private enterprise in the form of industrial estates. This fact, coupled with the higher standards of mass housing in the interwar period, was enough to ensure as a rule that industry and housing did not mix, even though effective town planning was almost unknown before the 1932 Town and Country Planning Act. The typical industrial estate started with a number of factory buildings left by accident, as with the First World War Ordnance Factories at Staples Corner (Cricklewood) or the British Empire Exhibition halls at Wembley; around them an estate company would put up new prefabricated buildings for rent. The most usual result is a roughly circular concentration of small factories with both road and rail access, as at Perivale and Wembley.

The largest single concentration, at Park Royal, is more complex. The name records that the then Prince of Wales opened the site in 1903, as the permanent home of the Royal Agricultural Society; the project was unsuccessful and was closed in 1906. To the north, adjacent to the main railway line at Willesden Junction, big factories had already arrived by 1914, attracted by rail and canal access. On the former showground, munitions factories were established during the First World War; then, after a considerable delay and almost by accident, they were converted to peacetime use by their owners. The financial success of the move caused them to start building new factories to rent; and Park Royal mushroomed between 1928 and 1935.

So today there is a marked contrast between one area of Park Royal and another. On the edges of the estate, but especially along its northern border, are the giant factories, mainly concerned with food or drink manufacture; in the centre are the homes of the small plants employing less than 100 men, usually occupying general-purpose rented buildings, and most characteristically engaged in general or electrical engineering. The firms here are not very different from those in the specialist engineering quarter of Clerkenwell, St Pancras and Islington. The same industrial groups dominate, there is the same great variety of specialist production, the same dependence on materials and components suppliers and manufacturers, the same tendency for a firm to act merely as one link in a complex productive process; many firms in Park Royal choose the relatively safe course and act as regular subcontractors of small engineered parts for big firms such as Ford Motors.

The most characteristic West London industry, D. H. Smith pointed out as long ago as 1933, is West End type industry. It tends to sell direct, not through wholesalers, and its most typical products are either luxury goods or are destined to be embodied in them. In some cases, indeed, a direct historical connection can be traced between the older type of West End industry, and the West London industry of today: coach and wagon builders, for instance, came to supply the motor industry, and one such firm, Park Royal Vehicles, is a subsidiary of ACV, one of the biggest firms in West London in the 1950s. Just as the old carriage builder had to be located close to his buyers, so as to be in touch with their requirements and even their individual whims, so does the modern body builder: PRV build the bodies for London Transport buses, and close consultation with London Transport officials is imperative at every stage of design and production.

In this case, the market is an immediate and local one. Although nearness to the London market is the most important factor of location for the West London industries in general, the idea may mean different things to different firms. To some, which are links in the chain of processes, the market means the general location of other plants in the Greater London area. Of the goods which reach their final form here, some are capital goods ordered by other commercial organizations, as in the case of the London buses; contact with the officials of these organizations, which may have their head offices in London, may be an important reason for location near the West End. Perhaps the majority of the firms in West London, though, are producing proprietary articles for a consumer market. Here, the market may mean the actual buyers of the product—a mass of people widely scattered, and not easy to conceptualize; it may mean the sales organization, which for a big firm will invariably be localized in the West End; it may mean the firm's own West End showrooms and sales organizations, which represent the first approach to the national and even to the export market.

But it is not only important to be near the market; many of these firms find it imperative to be in close contact with that even more elusive concept, marketing and technical *trends*. Many of these industries are 'science-based':[10] they depend heavily on research, which has to keep in touch with work done elsewhere. London is a great centre of scientific and technical training: certainly the biggest in Britain and probably in western Europe. It is the most important gathering-point and market-place for the skills of those already trained; there is no source of highly-trained scientists, technologists and managers like it. In London there is less chance than elsewhere of falling behind in knowledge of current trends, whether that means real technical innovations or merely trends of fashion which affect sales. For firms making standardized consumer goods for a mass market, it is essential to have good design services, to keep track of people's changing tastes at the point where tastes are apt to change first, to observe current trends in marketing techniques. These sales points are imponderables, and to many they will seem a sad commentary on the state of twentieth-century civilization; why should they matter? The fact is that the economic geographer must record things as they are. Though these factors cannot be given a money value, cannot be recorded as an x per cent cost advantage to the London manufacturer over his counterpart in a Development District, firms believe that they are important; that if they neglect them they will eventually fall behind in the competitive race, and perhaps perish in consequence. Without conclusive evidence—and that, in the nature of things, is not available—it would be wrong to deny them.

London is not merely a specialized labour market for the highest sorts of skill; it is simply the greatest emporium for labour of every degree of training. In the 1890s, the Booth Survey of London Life and Labour commented: 'One has usually but to hold up the finger to secure whatever men are needed'.[11] That is still true; but it is now also true that the employee can similarly get the job he needs. In particular, London has an enormous supply of—and demand for—semi-skilled labour of a quick, adaptable kind. The advantage is not merely one of sheer numbers; labour in London is thought quicker and more responsive in learning than in many provincial centres. Again, this is an imponderable; but certainly it was the experience of London firms which took the plunge after 1945 and located branches in Development Areas like South Wales or North-East England.

It is remarkable to see, then, how similar are the industries of West London, in their organization and their location, to those of some parts of the Victorian manufacturing crescent. In both, the industrial pattern is dominated by the small workshop; there is the same dependence on a host of other plants, which supply the materials or order the product, in what is in fact a complex production process; there is the importance of the London market for goods which depend on innovation, whether in technology or in fashion; the need for access to a large and varied labour pool; the reliance on the general-purpose, ready-built rented factory. Yet the outward expression is very different. There is not much apparent similarity between the densely-crowded, often ill-converted workshops of the Victorian crescent, and the typical industrial estate of the West London Belt. Several factors combined to bring about this change. Both goods and labour became much more mobile after 1900. The motor van was a quicker and a more flexible medium of city goods transport than the old horse-drawn cart; that increased the practicable radius for the sort of small workshop industry which had always flourished in London. The importance of close personal contact diminished somewhat also with the development of the motor-car and the telephone. Better suburban transport services—trams, then buses, electric trains—coupled with cheap fares and steadily-rising living standards, released the working class of London from the densely-peopled slums which ringed the Victorian central area. So those firms, which had traditionally been forced to tolerate inefficient working conditions in the old industrial quarters, were free to demand what had always up to then been a luxury for London industry: space.[12] That space was available at extremely low cost at the edge of the then built-up area; the most heavily-industrialized area of West London had been in 1914 the area nearest to central London which was still undeveloped.

The Lea Valley Manufacturing Belt

The second largest of the newer manufacturing areas—and, indeed, the only other one of any importance within the conurbation—lies in the north-east. It follows the line of the wide, alluvial Lea valley south from Waltham Cross in Hertfordshire to Old Ford, where it merges with an extension of the riverside zone up the lower course of the River Lea. [13] It is separated from the west London zone by the great residential areas which occupy the mainly higher ground of the northern and central parts of the old county of Middlesex. On closer examination the belt divides itself into several quite clearly separate sub-areas of concentration. Some of these, in the valley itself, are part of the early outgrowth of London in this direction, before 1914; they include the areas at Tottenham, at Blackhorse Lane (Walthamstow) and at Enfield Lock. Another sub-area stands apart from these, on the high ground to the west of the valley; it follows the Great Cambridge Road, an arterial of the 1920s.

The Lea Valley belt employed in all about 120,000 manufacturing workers in 1951: some eight per cent of the Greater London total. It was thus the smallest of the four major industrial belts of Greater London.

Compared with West London, the Lea Valley industry shows instructive similarities and differences. The similarities are in organization and scale of production. There are a few big factories, but many small ones. Many of the small firms occupy ready-built factories. They rely on brought-in materials and components; they are here first and foremost because of the presence of the London market—and here the nearness of the Docks for export may be important. They draw on a big pool of semi-skilled labour from the working-class suburbs, which developed from late Victorian times, along both sides of the Lea valley. Nevertheless there are important differences, which largely concern the type of product. General and electrical engineering are well-represented here, as in West London; but the emphasis of production tends towards more basic articles of everyday use, such as electric light bulbs. And there are certain industries hardly represented at all in the west: furniture, clothing,

footwear and stationery. These were distinctively East End industries, characteristic of nineteenth-century Shoreditch and Whitechapel and Hackney. Detailed study indeed shows that many firms
migrated here out of the congested East End districts between the
wars.[14] The driving force was essentially the same which at this time
might drive a West End coach-maker to Acton and a Shoreditch
cabinet-maker to Edmonton, a Clerkenwell precision engineer to
Perivale and a Hackney slipper-maker to Tottenham. But it tended
to drive West End firms westwards, East End firms north-eastwards.
Of course, the traditions of East End industry were changing power-
fully and continuously during these years, whether firms left their
traditional areas or stayed. The wholesaler's power was weakened;
unskilled labour was less depressed; the quality of the product
improved. In this sense East End industry became more and more
like West End industry, and the process has continued, so that it is
less easy to see distinctions between the Lea Valley and West London
than when D. H. Smith looked at them in 1933. Nevertheless, the
fact remains that, by and large in London industry, East has been
east and West west; never the twain have met.

Growth Since 1945: London's Outer Ring

The four industrial areas described here contained, in 1951, nearly
three in four of all the manufacturing workers in the Greater London
conurbation, though they occupied only about a quarter of the total
land area of London. Outside them were some isolated concentrations which accounted together for about eight per cent more of the
manufacturing workers of Greater London: the Kingston By-Pass in
south-west London, especially between Raynes Park and Tolworth;
the Wandle valley in south central London, from the Croydon
By-Pass in the south up through Mitcham and Merton to Wandsworth; and south Hertfordshire around Barnet and Elstree, on the
extreme northern edge of the conurbation. Save for the Wandle
valley, all were creations of the post-1918 age.

Since 1951, though, the main development of manufacturing industry has taken place outside the boundaries of the Greater London
conurbation. Precise figures are not yet available, but during the
decade 1951–61 the manufacturing work-force of the conurbation
increased by perhaps 105,000, of which perhaps 125,000 represented
increase in the suburban ring while the inner (or old London County

Council) area decreased by about 20,000. But in the 'Outer Ring' of the wider London Region, between fifteen and forty miles (24–64 km.) from central London, the increase in the manufacturing labour force was well over 200,000. This increase was dominated by the great 'growth points' of the southern British economy since 1918: engineering, electrical goods and vehicles. Together these three groups accounted for nearly two-thirds of the total net increase in manufacturing employment.

The growth of manufacturing in the Outer Ring has been concentrated in the major centres. But these include not merely the old market towns of the region—towns like Reading, High Wycombe, Luton, Guildford—which are now among the fastest-growing industrial towns of Britain; there are also the eight London New Towns, established between 1946 and 1949 to take overspill industry and population out of the congested inner parts of the conurbation, some of which by 1961 had become major centres in their own right. The growth of manufacturing industry, though, laps over the New Towns belt, and even beyond the boundaries of the London Region as the planners now define it. In the great outer 'fringe zone' which extends outside the London Region as far as the Solent–Wash line— the conventional boundary of south-eastern England—employment in manufacturing industry during 1951–61 increased by over 150,000. This is the zone of such rapidly-growing manufacturing centres as Portsmouth, Oxford, Bedford and Cambridge. Thus, of the total increase of manufacturing jobs in south-east England in the 1950s, the Greater London conurbation got just over one-fifth; a striking measure of the inadequacy of our conventional boundaries.[15]

References

1. Cf. Peter Hall, *London 2000* (1963), Chapters 1 and 3.
2. P. G. Hall, *The Industries of London since 1861* (1962); P. G. Hall, 'The East London footwear industry: an industrial quarter in decline', *East London Papers*, 5 (1962), 3–21. For the origins and development of London industry see also: O. H. K. Spate, 'Geographical aspects of the industrial evolution of London till 1850', *Geographical Journal*, 92 (1938), 422–32; M. J. Wise, 'The role of London in the industrial geography of Great Britain', *Geography*, 41 (1956), 219–32; J. E. Martin, 'Industry in Inner London', *Town and Country Planning*, 25 (1957), 125–8; R. C. Estall and J. E. Martin, 'Industry in Greater London', *Town Planning Review*, 28 (1957–8), 261–77; Jean Chardonnet, *Métropoles économiques*, Cahiers

de la Fondation Nationale des Sciences Politiques, 102 (Paris 1959), Chapter 1.

3. For the clothing trades see especially Hall, *The Industries of London, op. cit.*, Chapter 4; P. K. Newman, 'The early London clothing trades', *Oxford Economic Papers*, 4 (1952), 243–51; Charles Booth (ed.), *Life and Labour of the People in London* (1892–7), IV; V. D. Lipman, *Social History of the Jews in England* 1850–1950 (1954); S. P. Dobbs, *The Clothing Workers of Great Britain* (1928); D. L. Munby, *Industry and Planning in Stepney* (1951), Chapter 5.

4. Cf. Gillian Lonsdale, 'The changing character of the East London industry', *East London Papers*, 5 (1962), 91–102.

5. Hall, *The Industries of London, op. cit.*, Chapter 5; J. Leonard Oliver, 'The East London furniture industry', *East London Papers*, 4 (1961), 88–101; A. Heal, *The London Furniture Makers from the Restoration to the Victorian Era, 1600–1840* (1953); Charles Booth, *op. cit.*, IV.

6. Hall, *The Industries of London, op. cit.*, Chapter 6; P. M. Handover, *Printing in London from 1476 to Modern Times* (1960).

7. These trades are more fully described in Chapter 10.

8. For further detail see James Bird, *The Geography of the Port of London* (1957), Chapter 7, and Munby, *op. cit.*, Chapter 6. An important study of a riverside industry is L. G. Wooder, *The Paint and Varnish Industry of Great Britain*, unpublished M.Sc. thesis (University of London, 1955).

9. For further detail see Hall, *The Industries of London, op. cit.*, Chapter 8, where it is known as the 'West Middlesex industrial belt'; Middlesex disappears as an administrative unit on 1st April 1965. The basic sources for this area are D. H. Smith, *The Industries of Greater London* (1933), Section V; and B. A. Bates, *Some Aspects of the Recent Industrial Development of West London*, unpublished M.Sc. thesis (University of London, 1954).

10. Cf. Scottish Council (Development & Industry), *Inquiry into the Scottish Economy, 1960–1961* (the Toothill Report) (Edinburgh 1961) 35. This report gives a very penetrating analysis of the locational advantages of London and the South-East.

11. E. Aves in Booth, *op. cit.* (1892–7) IX, 181.

12. Cf. Colin Clark, 'Transport – maker and breaker of cities', *Town Planning Review*, 28 (1957–8), 247–9.

13. Hall, *The Industries of London, op. cit.*, Chapter 8; Smith, *op. cit.*, Section III.

14. Hall, *The Industries of London, op. cit.*, Figure 22, 136.

15. For further detail of these changes cf. Hall, *London 2000, op. cit.*, Chapter 3; see also *The South East Study, 1961–1981* (H.M.S.O., 1964), Chapter 4 and Appendix 2, Table 18.

10

Three Elements in the Industrial Geography of Greater London

*

J. E. MARTIN

The industries of Greater London are distributed in patterns of extreme complexity. Figure 49 is a simplified map of the major industrial areas described in the preceding chapter. They are defined as localities where manufacturing is highly concentrated whether in several large plants or in numerous small works. The distribution of major areas in Figure 49 therefore reflects the location of manufacturing employment, as the inset confirms, except where a large labour force is concentrated into single isolated factories. At the heart of London there is an inner, or Victorian, belt of manufacturing. It includes the Southwark and Bermondsey area south of the Thames and a crescent north of the river close around the City. This inner belt is a legacy of Victorian industry and an entity of much less importance than at the beginning of the present century. In 1954, 130,000 manufacturing operatives were employed in the twelve square kilometres (4·6 sq.ml.), represented on the inset to Figure 49, that include the inner belt. An additional 35,000 were found in the four square kilometres (1·5 sq.ml.) that include the West End. An aggregate of 265,000 were employed in the 39 contiguous square kilometres (15 sq.ml.) that are shaded in the inset to Figure 49. All these figures are for operatives only. Total workers in manufacturing, including non-operative staff, were much more numerous.

In this chapter special attention is given to inner north-east London as shown in Figure 50. It includes the part of the inner or Victorian manufacturing belt north of the Thames (extending in a crescent from Fleet Street to the East End), decayed inner suburbs such as

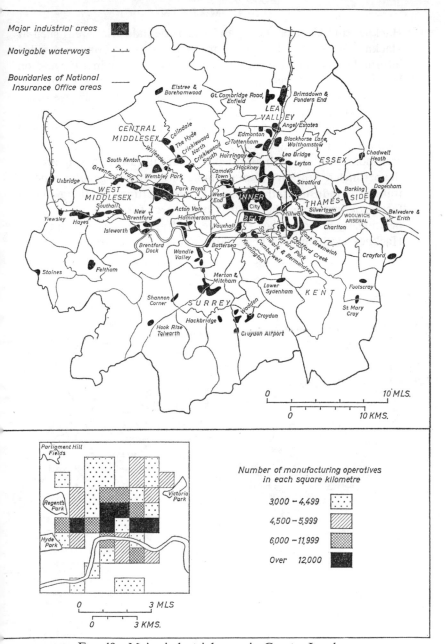

FIG. 49 Major industrial areas in Greater London

Prepared largely from unpublished maps. The writer is particularly indebted to Mr Bryan A. Bates and Dr L. G. Wooder. This is a modified version of a map submitted in a Memorandum of Evidence to the Royal Commission on Local Government in Greater London, Appendix CII, by the Greater London Group, October 1959.

Inset prepared independently from punched card results for 1954, kindly made available by the London County Council.

Hackney and Camden Town and waterside industrial areas such as Hackney Wick and Old Ford. For inner north-east London detailed information is available on the location of industry in 1955 and on locational factors affecting over 150 firms in the late 1950s.[1] Figure 50 summarizes salient features of localization. Where there are dense clusters of factories or workshops in kindred trades industrial 'quarters' have been delimited. There are the clothing factories and workrooms, for example, gathered in the East End quarter in a discrete concentration with an intensity that falls away sharply around the perimeter. Finsbury is an example of an area of general concentration of industry rather than of specialization. Clothing manufacture is important there but is only part of a grouping in which printing, food and other industries are also very significant. The Hackney clothing area (Fig. 50) exemplifies a district of marked

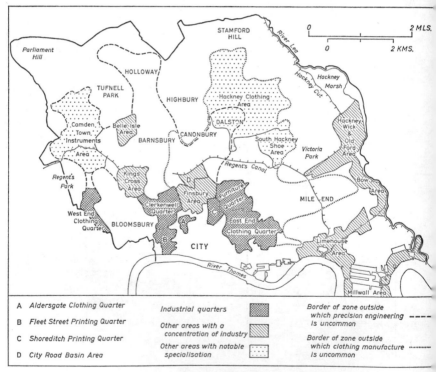

FIG. 50   Distinctive industrial areas in inner north-east London
A modified version of a map by the writer first published in *Town and Country Planning*, March 1957.

248

specialization but with establishments that are too dispersed to justify calling it a 'quarter'. Clear patterns exist in inner north-east London despite the makeshift nature of most of the industrial premises. Ageing factories with a history of varied use, converted shops and houses, cinemas and ballrooms, chapels and church halls, freed by depopulation, are normally in use, as are outbuildings erected on back land and one-time warehouses.

Three groups of industries are to be examined in this chapter. Each of the three constitutes a distinct element in the geography of London manufacturing and each has a component in inner north-east London which will receive closer scrutiny. The three groups are: first, clothing industries; second, precision instrument and electrical engineering industries; third, industries of waterside areas.

Clothing Industries

Areas where clothing industries dominate are highly localized. Tailoring and dressmaking are shown in Figure 51 and other clothing trades show a related though more suburbanized distribution. The East End quarter (Fig. 50) in 1955 grouped over 900 clothing establishments with 17,000 workers in about one square mile (2·6 sq.km.). This quarter specializes most of all in ladies' coat, costume and gown manufacture. Men's tailoring is a subsidiary activity. A predominance of women's outerwear workrooms with less than 50 operatives each is characteristic, though very small plants (less than ten operatives) are not so important here as in the West End. In the late nineteenth century very small workshops in men's tailoring dominated the East End quarter. Today small specialist ancillary producers, such as buttonholers, button and buckle coverers, pleaters and embroiderers are more important in this quarter than in any other district. The Aldersgate quarter and the Finsbury area (Fig. 50) are centres for the millinery and neckwear industries and for women's tailoring. Finsbury is remarkable for having large workrooms despite its central position, usually on upper floors, notably in women's outerwear but also in the lingerie and children's wear branches. Ancillary and accessory production, apart from artificial flower making, are not found there. Extending northward and eastward from the centres already mentioned is a broad zone where clothing manufacture is also important. Figure 50 defines this zone (by a pecked line). It is also obvious in the inset to Figure 51 and

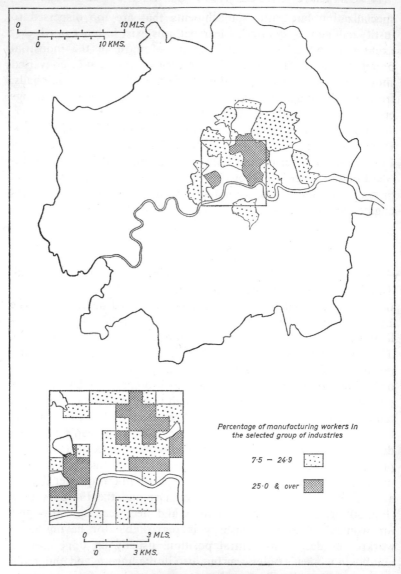

FIG. 51 Tailoring and dressmaking industries in Greater London

The main map shows the percentage of manufacturing workers engaged in tailoring and dressmaking in each National Insurance Office Area in May 1958. Based on statistics supplied by Ministry of Labour, Watford. The inset shows the percentage of manufacturing operatives in these industries in each square kilometre in 1954. (See Fig. 49 inset.)

quite distinct from the separate West End quarter. Within the zone Hackney is notable for the high proportion of its labour force in the clothing industry. In actual number of operatives the Hackney clothing area (Fig. 50) approaches the East End quarter, but the latter has a denser concentration. The ladies' tailoring and dress trades are important in Hackney, but it differs from the East End quarter in having more large factories in men's tailoring and more production of shirts, pyjamas and underwear. Ancillary firms are less numerous than in the East End though production of accessories (such as belts and shoulder pads) is important in Hackney. Such lines as shirts, pyjamas and more standardized dresses are dominant in the clothing trades that spread into the north-east suburbs of Essex and the Lea valley (Fig. 51).

An analysis of the location factors affecting firms in inner northeast London in the late 1950s reveals size and organization of the firm to have been critical. In the women's outerwear industry four or five basic types of firm could usefully be distinguished. First, were larger self-contained firms with, say, more than 50 indoor workers and with their own workrooms in the East End quarter. These were used principally for the ladies' suit branch, said to be very exacting in its skilled labour requirements, especially jacket manufacture; skirt production in the Lea valley and coat making in the Home Counties by the same firms were lower quality work. These firms made use of at least showroom facilities in the West End and stressed the need for liaison with them. Second, there were firms using outdoor 'contractors' in Hackney or the East End quarter to supplement their indoor production elsewhere, for example, the parent company of a multiple store group with its design teams, main production and warehouse in Finsbury. Service to and control of contractors were considered impossible from outside London. Third, there were the outdoor contracting firms themselves, notably in Hackney. Fourth, there were firms with small indoor workrooms in the East End quarter or Hackney, with their own showrooms on the spot or selling to wholesalers mostly in the West End. Commonly they used local domestic outworkers and bought supplies from local merchants. Other types of firm could be distinguished. For example, one that marketed dresses in bulk made only sample and urgent requirements at its West End design centre and subcontracted most of its work to East London. It had affinities with the type known as a 'principal firm' that does no manufacturing itself.

London's attractions as a location for clothing manufacture are enhanced by the contracting system. Outdoor factories are most important for high fashion wholesale production of women's tailored garments.[2] The 'principal firms' giving work to outdoor factories accounted for half the wholesale sales effected in Marylebone (West End) and Stepney in 1950.[3] Outdoor contractors are concentrated in Hackney and the East End. Principal firms specialize in anticipating high fashion demand, contractors in organizing severely fluctuating production. 'A considerable part of a contractor's time is normally spent waiting for orders in the principal firm's office'[4] and ease of access to the Mortimer Street vicinity in the West End is a vital consideration.[5] The flow of gown vans between east London and the West End is everyday evidence of interdependence. In the Finsbury area many of the workrooms belong to large stores and multiples or firms with nationally advertised brand names, a slightly more stable sector of the industry. The Finsbury, Aldersgate and Barbican area concentrated many large workrooms in the women's clothing trades around 1900,[6] alongside the textile merchanting centre which had expanded from an initial centre running from St Paul's Churchyard along West Cheap that existed 500 years before.[7]

The East End quarter and Hackney are centres of Jewish enterprise in tailoring and of skilled male workers such as cutters. In Britain, women's tailoring is the branch of clothing using the highest proportion of male labour, 29 per cent in 1959, but in London 37 per cent and in the East End quarter 43 per cent.[8] There is 'a local pool of highly skilled machinists, tailors and pressers which is found only in London' and 'the sectional system in machining as practised in London depends on an experienced foreman and skilled head machinist on each bench.'[9] The 'lavish use of hand pressing' also distinguishes London tailoring[10] and at Moss Bros.' Harringay factory the amount of skilled hand sewing is an outstanding feature.[11] The advantages of London in securing skilled labour are shared by firms of all sizes if in sufficiently central locations. The clothing industries, however, combine skilled with semi-skilled lower-paid female labour. 'Machining and finishing clothing represent one of the two most common manual occupations among West Indian women in London.'[12] Light clothing manufacture generally is often in suburban factories on account of its bigger use of women workers of slight skill, including housewives with children. In Walthamstow (Essex) there is a concentration of the neckwear industry estimated to produce two-thirds of the British output.[13] In this trade, as in blouse making, home-workers are numerous. By contrast tie cutting, which requires specialist staff, occurs partly in the Aldersgate and West End quarters. The daily flow of female labour comes especially from the north and north-east into Finsbury and from the east into Stepney.[14] The same radial bias appears in the distribution of suburban clothing factories. In daily movements of male labour cross-flows between Hackney and Stepney are considerable.[15]

Advantages of easy contact with ancillary firms, most important for smaller enterprises in tailoring, are best secured in the East End quarter or Hackney. Pleating contractors offer expert services that contribute considerably to the efficiency of London factories as a source of fashion clothing.[16] In the most style-sensitive branches, quick access to firms that will make up fur collars and cuffs or cover buttons and buckles as the market temporarily dictates is desirable. Horizontal linkage, where firms send out work to others nearby when unable to cope with a sudden rush of orders, produces similar economies of agglomeration.

Another common characteristic of small-scale production in clothing is a rapid turnover in ownership. The established areas of specialization have a large stock of workrooms to rent for which there is an organized market. Under post-1947 town planning controls they carry indispensable light industrial use rights. This is a new influence stabilizing location. Size of clothing plant is related to all the critical location factors. Some firms manage to shift production from the London hub, leaving design teams and showrooms there. Typically they are larger, in more standardized branches, rather self-sufficient from ancillaries and with a low proportion of key male labour.

Precision Instrument and Electrical Engineering Industries

The precision instrument and electrical engineering industries (Fig. 52) sharply contrast in distribution with the clothing group. They have gravitated to outer London and are especially important to the north-west and the south, the first being the weightier sector. The engineering and metal trades not represented in Figure 52 include, generally speaking, those of earlier growth and those characteristic of waterside sites. As may be seen (from the heavy line in

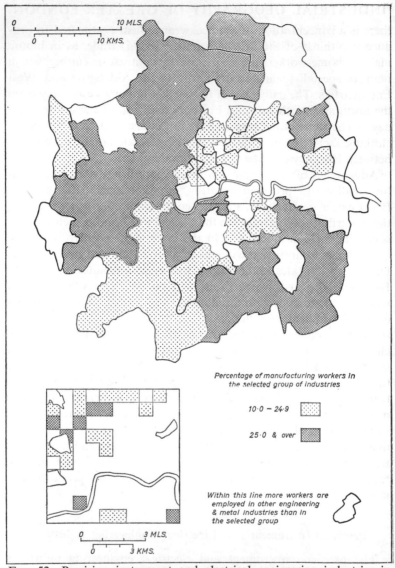

0   10 MLS.

0   10 KMS.

Percentage of manufacturing workers in the selected group of industries

10·0 — 24·9

25·0 & over

Within this line more workers are employed in other engineering & metal industries than in the selected group

0   3 MLS.

0   3 KMS.

FIG. 52   Precision instrument and electrical engineering industries in Greater London

The main map shows the percentage of manufacturing workers engaged in the selected industries in each National Insurance Office Area in May 1958. Based on statistics supplied by Ministry of Labour, Watford. The inset shows the percentage of manufacturing operatives in these industries in 1954. (See Fig. 49 inset.)

The selected group consists of the following Minimum List Headings from the Standard Industrial Classification (1948 edition):—54, 70, 73, 74, 79, 83, 90, 91, 100, 101. Among the headings excluded are 69 (general engineering, not elsewhere specified) which includes industries that properly belong in the group mapped (weighing machinery, gas meters) but also others with a different location pattern.

Figure 52) there is a block of contiguous areas in central and easterly parts of London where these other engineering and metal trades are more important than the precision and electrical group that have been mapped.

The Clerkenwell quarter (Fig. 50) played a crucial role in the development of London's modern precision and electrical industries, a role more decisive than an inventory of its present activities might suggest. These activities include the making of optical and measuring instruments and some production of parts in metal or glass and of cases for these goods. Small foundries, electro-plating and other metal-finishing works are also present. The Hatton Garden jewellery centre lies in the south-west corner of the quarter. The Clerkenwell concentration is dense enough to impress the casual visitor, but more important is a zone of specialization in related trades that extends north and north-west from Clerkenwell into Kings Cross, Barnsbury, Holloway, Camden Town and adjacent areas. Engineering, metal and instrument plants are widespread in these districts, usually too scattered for the distinctiveness of the zone to be obvious on the ground, yet much more common than elsewhere in inner north-east London (see the pecked boundary in Figure 50). Manufactures in this zone include food, drink and tobacco machinery, gas meters, weighing machines, printing machinery, machine tools and wireless. Electrical appliances such as irons, blankets and toasters are manufactured in variety. Metal plating and spraying, sheet metal work and the production of turned and pressed parts and components show a very similar distribution. A Camden Town area has been indicated in Figure 50 with unusual specialization in instruments, including optical and surgical. Such manufactures extend into the West End, as does also, for example, the making of X-ray equipment, motor vehicle accessories and art-metal work.

As has been shown in the previous chapter, Clerkenwell entered the nineteenth century endowed with a cluster of watch, clock and scientific instrument trades. Within a short distance of this nucleus much technical experiment and advanced manufacture occurred in the nineteenth century. John Braithwaite, elder and younger, inventors of diving bells and air pumps, had a factory in Euston Road from 1804[17] and Sir Henry Bessemer used a bronze foundry in Pancras Road for experiments.[18] New trades evolved there. One firm, beginning with the manufacture of thermometers in 1850, evolved gradually into a producer of aeronautical instruments and automatic

255

controls and until very recently had moved only to the King's Cross area.[19] Another firm developed the manufacture of complex surveying equipment from an initial interest in the making of simple wooden drawing instruments.[20] At a scientific instrument factory in City Road in 1878 'long lines of benches' were 'filled by the most intellectual class of skilled workmen among us.'[21] The value of such labour in a new industry in the vicinity, a factory making machinery for the aerated water industry, was summed up by a visitor: 'all the parts are made here and put together with an accuracy resembling first-class watchmaking.'[22] One of the first firms of gear cutters in London produced wheels and pinions in Clerkenwell from 1862 for the watch and clock trade; when it moved to central Middlesex in 1938 it was manufacturing geared electric motors and aircraft components.[23] Ferranti, making his first dynamo in 1881, sold it in the Euston Road and two years later set up on his own in Clerkenwell to begin the manufacture of dynamos, switches and transformers.[24] Johnson Matthey, the precious metal refiners of Hatton Garden, provided electrical contacts, contact bi-metal and other requirements for the new electrical and radio industries.[25] Valve and radio making were built also from the scientific glassware industry. Cossor in 1896 had 'a small workshop employing but a handful of people' in Farringdon Road where experimental and scientific glassware was made. Production gradually expanded to include all kinds of low-voltage lamps 'which were then made by hand throughout, even to the hair-like carbon filaments', X-ray, cathode ray tubes and experimental apparatus for Signor Marconi, and then in the First World War valves and wireless. In 1918 the firm moved to Highbury (Fig. 50) and began the bulk production of valves and later radios.[26] In 1908 Siemens chose a factory at Dalston for manufacturing tantalum lamps, 'a highly specialized and delicate task . . . by processes which were still elementary and which involved a strong element of personal judgement and individual skill.'[27] In the inter-war years Clerkenwell and the zone to its north were the principal nursery for the growth of precision engineering industries of west and central Middlesex, though assisted by other nuclei south of the Thames and in the West End.

In the late 1950s the engineering trades located in Clerkenwell and the zone to the north included three main types. First, there were manufacturers of components including screws, pressed and turned parts, switches and highly accurate tubes for instrument, lighting, radar, aircraft and similar trades. The location factors chiefly stressed by the firms were proximity to the manufacturers served, often with short runs of custom-made parts and mainly in north-west and inner London, and in some cases also the use of specialist labour. Second, there were manufacturers of finished products, usually complex assemblies demanding refined specialization, for example, hydrographic and electronic instruments, cams and tools for automatic screw machines, sterilization equipment and magnetic tape recorders. Skilled labour was much stressed as a location tie and sometimes nearness to London component makers and sub-contracting metal workers, though in other instances component sources were widespread. Third, there were industries partially of a servicing nature. A London centre was maintained where a repair and overhaul service was available at short notice and where replacement parts or selected components were manufactured. The printing machinery makers were organized like this, with their London centres in Clerkenwell and Southwark and their standard production of heavy machinery dispersed to the provinces. The servicing of laundry and food industry machinery and of electrical plant offered similar examples. Experimental engineering based on specialist labour of rare skill also existed in the zone and some firms had moved away their bulk production but retained units for laboratory testing and the occasional assembly of machinery.

It has been observed in the radio industry that where firms chose to establish branches in development areas 'they dared not sacrifice the advantages which a London works gave, by enabling them to recruit skilled labour and by maintaining them in close contact with the centre of the industry. Those few firms which did choose to transfer their entire production activity to development areas nearly all found it necessary to continue to employ some skilled workers in London.'[28] Interestingly, a committee, which in 1907 looked into the possibility of relocating the Post Office Holloway factory, found it manufactured instruments 'of delicate mechanism' and those which were 'for the time being, in an experimental stage.' Of the skilled artisans 86 per cent lived within three miles (4·8 km.) and there were advantages in having the point of inspection near the place of manufacture of instruments by outside contractors.[29]

One factor in the location pattern not yet mentioned is the concentration near Clerkenwell of warehouses and showrooms for certain goods. In 1950 more than half the wholesale sales of 'photographic and scientific goods' and of 'electric supplies and appliances' effected in Greater London occurred in Holborn. This borough, with Finsbury, also had an important share of wholesale sales of 'industrial equipment and supplies.'[30] Considerable stocks of machine tools, non-ferrous screws and fine tubes are held in distribution centres in the vicinity. Significantly, the other notable concentration of such stockholders is in west and central Middlesex.

Industries of Waterside Areas

A third major element in the industrial geography of Greater London is made up by the industries characteristic of waterside areas. They include a wide range of chemical industries, grain milling and sugar refining, constructional engineering and sawmilling. Their greatest concentration is on the Thames from Deptford and Limehouse downstream and in the lower Lea valley (Figs. 49 and 53). Measured by their percentage contribution to local manufacturing employment they are most important in the Stratford and Silvertown areas (Fig. 49).

There is a distinctive range of metal and engineering trades that grew up in proximity to the great shipbuilding industry of mid-Victorian Millwall (Fig. 53). Among products then were marine engine castings, boilers and chain cable and in the later nineteenth century, with shipbuilding already in decline, they included machines for bending armour plates, floating sheers and depositing docks and pneumatic grain elevators.[31] Since 1900 the bulk of London shipwrights have turned to repairing. Some Millwall firms, however, switched from shipbuilding to bridge building and constructional engineering and one, since 1880, has made the transition to the manufacture of fabricated steelwork, including cupboards, lockers and shelving.[32] The submarine cable industry has generated another group of engineering industries. It developed from 1850 at Silvertown and at points on the south bank of the Thames from east Greenwich to Erith (Fig. 49), with shorter-lived works on the Regent's and Surrey Canals.[33] Water transport was important in this industry and at Charlton in the 1880s the long, narrow works 'clung to the river in a fashion which indicated the almost complete reliance of the company upon the sea,'[34] Most of the Thames works still exist but with new emphasis, for example, on switchgear, grid transmission cable and rubber products, though ocean cable is still made

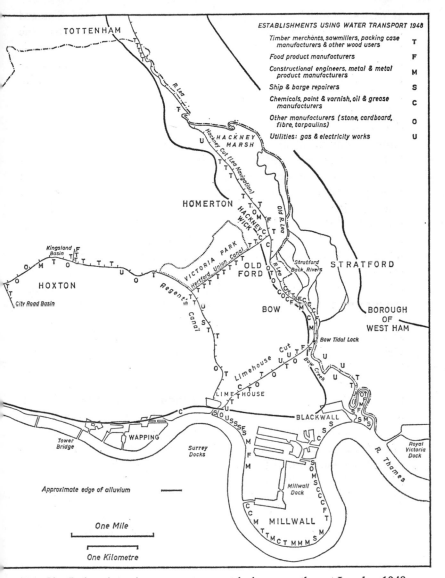

FIG. 53   Industries using water transport in inner north-east London 1948
Note: Dockside establishments as well as those on the south bank of the
Thames and east of the county boundary are not covered here.
Based upon L.C.C. River and Canalside Survey (unpublished).

at east Greenwich and Erith. At Charlton a cluster of Siemens factories now occupies a square of land stretching far back from the river and production includes telephone exchange equipment and is backed by a considerable office and research staff.[35] Such manufacture, distinct as are its origins, comes to have much in common with electrical engineering in west Middlesex.

The need for access to water transport has been only one factor in the evolution of a distinctive group of industries in waterside areas. Another important element has been the search for spacious and isolated sites by industries handling dangerous or noxious substances. In a sense the Royal Arsenal at Woolwich (Fig. 49), which employed 10,000 by the late nineteenth century, was an early example, located where the remote Thames-side marshes had been used initially for proving ordnance.[36] One of the most magnetic areas for such industries in the later nineteenth century was the tract of alluvial land bordering the Lea at Stratford, here about a mile (1·6 km.) wide and a continuing repellent to housing.[37] The channel of the River Lea at this point divides into numerous branches termed the Stratford Back Rivers (Fig. 53). The marshland near the rivers, attractive to industry, fetched a relatively high price.[38] Of the extensive use of water transport by chemical, metal and food works in the vicinity there is ample evidence from the mid-century onwards.[39] The district also gathered a concentration of trades that stored inflammable materials in bulk and generated fumes and effluent. Legislation of 1844 tended to push such industries to sites offering a measure of isolation and in 1867 'the district immediately bordering the tidal portion of the Lea' had 'become a nuisance district, the seat of trades expelled beyond the limits of the better parts of the metropolis.'[40] By the close of the nineteenth century, legislation on industrial premises had become much tighter in the county of London than outside and the concentration of chemical trades in Stratford just over the boundary was considerable. There was a certain grouping of paint and varnish plants similarly in the Wandle valley just outside the county.[41]

At the present time riverside works on the Thames, below the confluence with the Lea, generally use river transport and in some instances have private jetties. Above this point and on the Lea and canals the use of water transport by industry is tending to diminish. In the area shown in Figure 53 a slight, general decline in its use was recorded between 1948 and 1958.[42] Prominent among the users are the timber and veneer merchants and sawmillers that cluster on the canals in the vicinity of Hackney Wick and Old Ford. This cluster has developed only in the present century. The firms generally receive the bulk of their supplies by barge but distribute by road and are centrally placed in relation to the furniture industry of today. Most, though not all, of the chemical works on the Lea and at Millwall make some use of water transport (Fig. 53). They include paint and varnish makers and oil and grease blenders. Across the Lea in Stratford on and near the back rivers there are works producing acids, iron oxide, acetates, soap, paint, varnish and numerous small factories making ink, glue, gum, disinfectants and greases.

Barges distribute imported materials, for example, resins, oils, gum copal to the factories and redistribute products of refineries and riverside coke ovens. Intermediate products, for example, synthetic resins and drying oils, move by road within the local agglomeration of factories and to paint, rubber, linoleum and other industries throughout London and southern England. Constructional engineers and metal refiners, as in Millwall, use river transport. For iron and brass foundries there is also a significant demand in waterside areas from shipping, dock, public utility and chemical concerns.

Availability of water transport is frequently only one among other locational considerations that include large storage areas needed in the forward buying of bulky goods and existing fixed capital equipment. In fact, on the Regent's Canal relatively few plants use barges at all (Fig. 53) and the siting factors for pharmaceutical and engineering works, for example, are the existing enclaves of industrial properties. Rather similarly the Belle Isle area (Fig. 50) is an enclave of substantial premises where the most offensive of nuisance industries were concentrated in the nineteenth century[43] and is now used by diverse producers. In many of the waterside industrial areas land has now been scheduled for 'Special Industry' under town planning law, so that existing patterns tend to be frozen. In the lower Lea valley, however, where sites are now typically cramped and road access poor, the market value of old and substantial factories is relatively depressed and expensive piling may be needed for new buildings on the alluvium.[44]

Conclusion

The distribution of industry in London shows exceedingly complex

261

patterns. Many of the location factors discussed have a vital role in other industries. Linkages with ancillaries are pervasive in the printing industry. Typesetters and engravers, mostly small-scale, are concentrated centrally in the Fleet Street and Clerkenwell quarters (Fig. 50) where they can provide an efficient rush service with advertisements and picture blocks. There is also interdependence between superficially different industries: to take one minor example, the same frame makers serve both the handbag and lampshade trades.

The evident bias to radial axes in the migration of industry in London has its converse in present journeys to work in the inner belt.[45] It is a key to understanding location patterns in a wider context. 'Basildon claims nine clothing firms employing 14·3 per cent of the new labour force (a reflection of the fact that this New Town draws most of its population from a group of east London boroughs where this industry predominates), whereas for comparable reasons, the furniture and cabinet making trades account for 12·6 per cent of Harlow's new employment.'[46] The persistence of established areas of specialization may be illustrated from many industries. There is the furniture quarter (Fig. 50), a declining relic which was the nursery for, among other concerns, Harris Lebus, now occupying 38 acres (15·3 ha.) organized in five main zones at Tottenham.[47] More than half the furniture establishments in the quarter even today have less than five operatives each and they specialize on products where variety, short runs and subcontracting are at a premium, such as glass-fronted cases and occasional furniture of all kinds. Clerkenwell, a Victorian centre for lithography where George Baxter made his reputation as the greatest British colour printer of his day,[48] still has some concentration of litho plate-making, while adjacent Finsbury and Barnsbury are notable in production of calendars, greeting cards and colour lithography. Need for accessibility to central London is illustrated by the shop and office fitting industry, with half its national employment in the metropolis. It is generally sited as near central contract points as possible, though repelled to where sufficiently cheap space can be rented for assembling and finishing larger units. In most cases the factors that influence location of an industry in detail, within London, cannot be dissociated from those that decide its degree of concentration in London at large, rather than elsewhere in Britain.

INDUSTRIAL GEOGRAPHY OF GREATER LONDON

References

1. J. E. Martin, *The Location of Industry in Inner North-East London*, unpublished Ph.D. thesis (University of London, 1961).
2. M. Wray, *The Women's Outerwear Industry* (1957), 263.
3. *Ibid.*, 265 (Table) and Board of Trade, *Census of Distribution 1905*, III, Tables 3, 5, 6, 8.
4. Wray, *op. cit.*, 267, note 2.
5. Borough of Hackney, *Supplementary Evidence Submitted to the Royal Commission on Local Government in Greater London*, February 1959, 8.
6. *Report, Royal Commission on London Traffic*. V, Plate F, P.P. 1906, XLIII.
7. C. T. Caves, 'Market for textiles', *Times Trade and Engineering* (June 1938), supplement, xv.
8. *Ministry of Labour Gazette* (May 1960), 189 and tables for May 1959, supplied by Ministry of Labour, Statistics branch, Watford.
9. Wray, *op. cit.*, 253-5.
10. *Ibid.*, 255.
11. W. Tute, *The Grey Top Hat* (1961), 124.
12. Ruth Glass, *Newcomers* (1960), 29.
13. A. D. Chaplin, *Towards a Plan for Walthamstow*, unpublished paper (1962), 42, cited with the author's permission.
14. *Census 1951, England and Wales, Report on Usual Residence and Workplace*, Table 5, 43-216.
15. *Ibid.*, Table 5.
16. Wray, *op. cit.*, 264.
17. F. E. Hansford, 'John Braithwaite', *St Pancras Journal* (May 1955), 4-5.
18. Sir Henry Bessemer, F.R.S., *An Autobiography* (1905), 77.
19. Negretti and Zambra Ltd., *Centenary 1850-1950* (1950), 4-14.
20. Cecil J. Allen, *A Century of Scientific Instrument Making 1853-1953* (1953), 16-21.
21. Percy Russell, *Leaves from a Journalist's Notebook* (1878), 131.
22. *Ibid.*, 123.
23. *Times Trade and Engineering* (June 1938), supplement, xxx.
24. P. Dunsheath, *A History of Electrical Engineering* (1962), 160.
25. *Times Trade and Engineering* (June 1938), supplement, xxxii.
26. G. A. Willingham, *Half a Century of Progress 1896-1947* (1947), 1-14.
27. J. D. Scott, *Siemens Bros. 1858-1958* (1958), 216-17.
28. D. C. Hague and J. H. Dunning, 'Costs in Alternative Locations: The Radio Industry', *Review of Economic Studies*, 22 (1954-55), 204.
29. *Report of Departmental Committee on Government Factories and Workshops*, 18-20, P.P., 1907, X.
30. Board of Trade, *Census of Distribution 1950*, Vol. III, Tables 5, 6, 7, 8.
31. *Poplar Library Cuttings*, 690.1.
32. S. Pollard, 'The decline of shipbuilding on the Thames', *Economic History Review*, second series, 3 (1950), 83-5 and *Joseph Westwood and Co. Ltd.* (The company, n.d.) (*Poplar Library*).

33. G. L. Lawford and L. B. Nicholson, *The Telcon Story 1850–1950* (1950), 15, 28, 38.

34. Scott, *op. cit.*, 192 and 214.

35. *Ibid.*, 214–5, 266–7.

36. W. Hornby, *Factories and Plant* (1958), 79.

37. A. Rees, 'A growth map for N.E. London during the railway age', *Geographical Review*, 35 (1945), 459.

38. *Second Report, Royal Commission on Pollution of Rivers*, River Lea, Vol. II, Mins. of Ev., Q 4078, 14080, P.P., 1867, XXXIII.

39. Martin, *op. cit.*, 259.

40. P.P., 1867 XXIII, *op. cit.*, Vol. I, Report, xiii.

41. L. G. Wooder, *The Paint and Varnish Industry of Great Britain*, unpublished M.Sc.(Econ.) thesis (University of London, 1955), 203–10 and maps, cited with the author's permission.

42. London County Council, *Development Plan First Review 1960*, II, Table 13, 165.

43. George Godwin, *Town Swamps and Social Bridges* (1859), 10–11.

44. *Milling* (18th Jan. 1958), refers to French and Co.'s silo.

45. Martin, *op. cit.*, 382–399.

46. J. H. Dunning, 'Manufacturing industry in the New Towns', *The Manchester School of Economic and Social Studies*, 28 (May 1960).

47. The British Productivity Council, *A Review of Productivity in the Furniture Industry* (1954), 29.

48. E. Liveing, *The House of Harrild* (1949), 16–17, and Ruari McLean, *Victorian Book Design and Colour Printing* (1963), 33.

11

Dormitory Settlements around London

*

J. T. COPPOCK

Around the conurbation there is a penumbra of partly urbanized land in which settlements of many kinds are located,
from large towns like Luton and Southend, whose populations in 1961 were respectively 131,505 and 164,976, to numerous
isolated houses in areas of attractive scenery, as in west Surrey.
Although these settlements are not strictly part of London and
although the processes by which they have grown are, in many re-
spects, similar to those which have led to the expansion of the conurbation itself, they merit separate treatment on two counts. In the
first place, the sequence of expansion, absorption and infilling by
which London grew has now been broken; for planning control over
house building and the creation of the green belt make it unlikely
that the settlements which now surround London will ever become
part of the built-up area of the conurbation in the way that once-
separate towns, such as Croydon and Kingston, have done. Secondly,
the extent to which their growth can be attributed to the conurbation
varies greatly and is not a simple function of distance. At one extreme,
some dormitory settlements like Gerrards Cross virtually owe their
existence to the presence of London; at the other are towns like
Saffron Walden which act as markets and service centres for the
surrounding countryside and lie outside London's sphere of influence. For most of these settlements London's contribution to
their growth has been both direct and indirect; they have accommodated industries which cramped quarters or higher wage rates have
driven out of London, they have provided homes for those working

265

in, or retiring from, the conurbation and their growth has been stimulated by the arrival of new industries attracted by access to the port of London and to the largest market in the country.

Residence and Employment

These settlements vary greatly in character, but, although they may be broadly classified as industrial towns, dormitories or service centres, the differences between them are not absolute, but relative; for each is a centre of employment, all act to some extent as dormitories for those working elsewhere, and all but the smallest have some manufacturing industry. Dormitory settlements, where a large proportion of the employed population moves out daily to work elsewhere, are generally small, for as they increase in size they tend to attract more industry and to provide a range of services for a wider area. Their location is largely determined by ease of communications and, to a lesser extent, by the attractiveness of their scenery; they are found all round the conurbation, but are most numerous to the north-west and south-west and along the shores of the Thames estuary. Towns with marked concentrations of manufacturing industry are most common to the north-west of London, where they are favoured by good rail and road communication with both London and the industrial Midlands, and along the lower Thames, where industry is less diverse and often tied to riverside locations. Towns with a well-balanced employment structure are more widely scattered and tend to be found at greater distances from the conurbation than dormitory settlements. There are also, of course, holiday resorts around the coasts.

Figure 54, based on the 1951 Census Industry and Workplace tables, shows both the major centres of employment outside the conurbation and the extent to which various administrative areas act as dormitories or draw labour from elsewhere. The picture which it conveys is limited by deficiencies of the data; administrative boundaries do not accurately define towns, for the built-up area often extends into adjacent rural districts, while the latter frequently contain sizeable towns which may themselves attract labour from other parts of the same district. Furthermore, the map shows only the net movements and suggests a much simpler pattern than actually exists. The aggregate of movements in and out is very much larger and, even when these are nearly equal, they may well be of

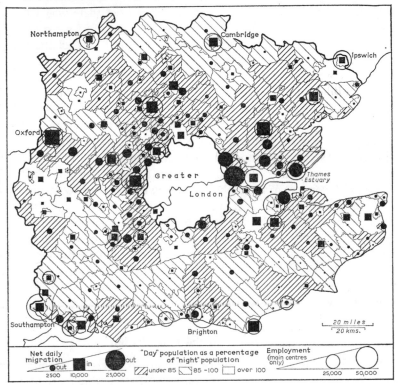

FIG. 54   Net daily migration and employment around Greater London
Based on 1951 Census, Usual Residence and Workplace and Industry
volumes.

quite different kinds, the inward movement, for example, consisting
largely of short journeys by factory and shop workers from adjacent
districts, while an important element in the outward movement
consists of office workers travelling long distances to workplaces in
central London. Thus, 5,319 people moved into St Albans, 2,815
from the adjacent rural district, while 6,808 moved out, 1,637 of
them to workplaces in the county of London.[1]

Nevertheless, the ratio of the occupied population working in each
administrative area (the 'day population') to the resident occupied
population (the 'night population') does give a broad indication of
the character of different areas.[2] With a few exceptions, the rural
districts were dormitory areas, with a net outward movement,
although the scale and relative importance of this varied consider-

267

ably; for example, from Amersham Rural District there was a net outward movement of 5,932 people, the equivalent of 33 per cent of the night population, while from Tenterden Rural District the net movement was only 361, or 13 per cent of the night population. The larger towns were generally employment centres, with a net inward migration, the chief exception being Southend, with a net movement out of 13,870 people, equal to 22 per cent of the night population; but from many of the smaller towns, particularly those on the periphery of the conurbation and on the coast, there was a net outward movement. In some instances this was quite small, both in numbers and relative importance, but in Chorleywood the day population was only 47 per cent of the night, in Canvey Island 56 per cent and in Rickmansworth 61 per cent; such towns clearly have an important dormitory function. Data for most of the smaller dormitory towns and villages, where the ratio of day to night population is likely to be even lower, are unfortunately lost by inclusion in the district totals; in Billericay, for example, 80 per cent of the night population was estimated to have been employed outside the town in 1950, compared with 50 per cent for the district in which it lies.[3]

Employment in the Conurbation

While much of the country around London serves as dormitory areas for those working elsewhere, many of the resulting journeys to work are quite short ones to nearby towns. Similarly most of the journeys to workplaces in the conurbation take place from homes within its boundaries and in 1951 only 242,531 people moved in daily from homes outside, compared with the 4,122,809 who lived and worked in London.[4] The number of people moving into the conurbation has, however, been rising rapidly. It was estimated at a third higher in 1958, while, to take a single example, the number of season tickets from Farnham to London termini increased by 72 per cent between 1954–5 and 1959–60.[5] Moreover, while much of the daily movement from dormitory areas is quite local, it is the exodus to London which is the distinguishing characteristic of many of the smaller dormitory settlements.

The proportion of the night population moving to workplaces in the conurbation varies considerably (Fig. 55). In 1951 it was highest immediately around the conurbation, exceeding 50 per cent in Hornchurch and Romford, and diminishing outwards. Many of these

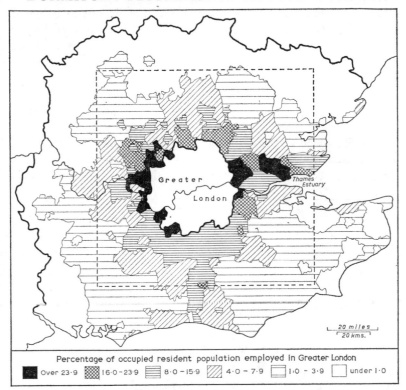

Percentage of occupied resident population employed in Greater London

Over 23·9 | 16·0-23·9 | 8·0 - 15·9 | 4·0 - 7·9 | 1·0 - 3·9 | under 1·0

FIG. 55 Percentage of occupied population resident outside Greater London but employed in the conurbation 1951
The pecked line marks the area shown on Figure 1.
Based on 1951 Census, Usual Residence and Workplace volume.

journeys were to places of work just across the conurbation boundary; considerable numbers of people move daily from south Essex to the industrial areas of Dagenham, Barking and East and West Ham, and from south Buckinghamshire and south-west Hertfordshire to those of west Middlesex. The pattern of movement to places in central London is, however, broadly the same, although the relative importance of central London *vis-à-vis* outer London tends to increase with distance from the conurbation. Thus, while 57 per cent of the night population in Hornchurch worked in the conurbation, 34 per cent of them in the Central Area, the comparable figures for Brighton were 4 per cent and 69 per cent.[6] The proportion employed in the conurbation does not fall off equally in all directions.

269

Three areas beyond the conurbation fringe stand out as being of greater importance: south Essex, from Southend to Hornchurch; the central Chilterns including the dormitory towns of Amersham, Chorleywood, Gerrards Cross and Great Missenden; and a belt of country extending from Surrey across the Weald to Brighton and the south coast.

In view of the great variations in the density of population around London, such maps of percentages can be misleading. Nevertheless, Figure 56, which records the numbers of those moving from each local authority area to work in the conurbation, shows that the greatest numbers did, in fact, come from those districts immediately

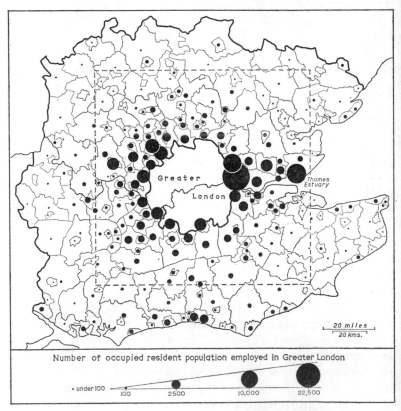

FIG. 56   Number of occupied population resident outside London but
working in the conurbation 1951
The pecked line marks the area shown on Figure 1.
Based on 1951 Census, Usual Residence and Workplace volume.

270

around the conurbation where the proportions of the night population working in London were highest. It also shows that numbers
moving from towns some distance away from the conurbation were
often larger than those from the adjacent rural districts; indeed, at
distances of over 30 miles (48 km.) it was only from the towns that
any considerable numbers travelled to work in London.

While the census data provide the only general view of the relationship of workplace and residence, the picture they offer is necessarily crude; the two surveys recorded in Figure 57 give a better idea
of the daily flow of movement between dormitory settlement and
place of work, although they are only two of many thousands which
might be prepared if suitable data were available.

In 1960, before the staff employed by the Shell International
Petroleum Company in offices in the City were moved to the new
Shell Centre on the South Bank, a travel survey was undertaken to
estimate the effect that such a move would have on journeys to work.[7]
This survey, which excluded senior and part-time staff, obtained
replies from 4,887 employees and can be used to illustrate the wide
scatter of homes from which staff are concentrated at one place of
work. While most of the staff questioned lived in London, 22 per cent
came from homes outside the conurbation; Audley End, Broadstairs
and Winchester mark the furthest limits, but while some staff lived in
most parts of the Home Counties, two areas were particularly important, south Essex and Surrey, both major dormitory areas for the
conurbation as a whole. This pattern of residence is, however,
somewhat different from that of all those working the Central Area,
for comparatively few Shell employees lived in places to the north-
west of London. The survey also illustrates the importance of travel
by train to central London, for 65 per cent of those questioned used
British Railways' services for the main part of their journey and
26 per cent the railway services operated by London Transport;
moreover, 85 per cent of those travelling by British Railways (which
include nearly all those coming from beyond the conurbation)
arrived at four termini, all with easy access to the City, viz., Liverpool Street, Waterloo, London Bridge and Blackfriars.

The inset map in Figure 57 is based on a sample survey of 25 per
cent of the households in the Hertfordshire village of Radlett undertaken in 1963.[8] It illustrates the complementary process of dispersal
from a dormitory settlement and shows the importance of both
journeys to central London and quite local movements to nearby

271

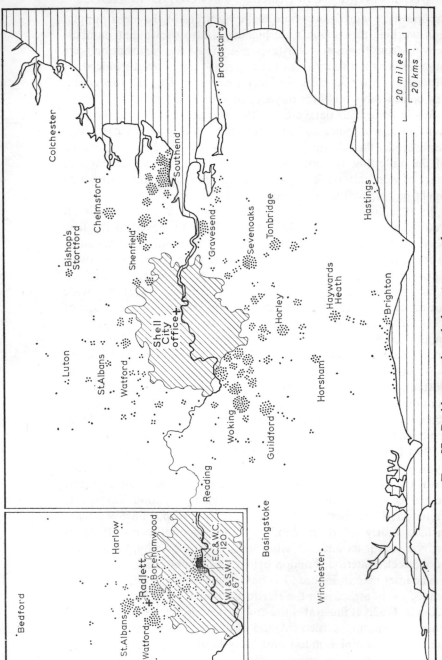

FIG. 57 Residence and workplace: two sample surveys
1 dot represents 1 person. The shaded area represents the built-up area of London.

centres of employment. Five-sixths of those questioned worked outside Radlett and for these central London was the most important place of work, employing 39 per cent of those who left Radlett daily; two-fifths of these worked in East Central postal districts (mainly the City), a quarter in the West End and most of the remainder in Westminster. Places within five miles (8 km.) of Radlett provided the second largest number of jobs, for a quarter of those employed outside Radlett worked in Borehamwood (the most important single centre), Watford and St Albans, or in villages nearer Radlett. Most of the remaining places of work (19 per cent) were in north London, particularly in Edgware, Stanmore, Mill Hill, Hendon and Cricklewood; but Radlett residents made daily journeys to places as far away as Bedford, Stevenage, Harlow, Staines and Amersham.

As in the Shell survey, rail travel was of great importance to those working in the City, for whom through trains are provided to Moorgate; 88 per cent of those employed in East Central postal districts regularly travelled by train, compared with an average of only 38 per cent of all those working outside Radlett. On the other hand, 47 per cent of those employed in the West End travelled by road (although differences in the kind of employment in the two areas are probably a contributory factor). Of those working outside central London, seven times as many travelled by road as by rail, although only a quarter of those using road transport would have had a convenient journey by train. In view of the wide dispersal of workplaces it is not surprising that the length of time spent in travel should vary considerably; the maximum recorded was $3\frac{1}{2}$ hours a day, but 28 per cent claimed to have door to door journeys of two hours or more. On the other hand, many of those employed in other parts of Hertfordshire spent less than half an hour daily in travel.

Dormitory Settlements

The importance of dormitory settlements must not be exaggerated, since most of those who travel long distances to work live in the larger towns which are considerable places of employment in their own right, while many largely residential towns have a high proportion of retired people. Nevertheless, they are often highly distinctive both in layout and in social composition. In the period before 1918 such settlements were largely restricted to the vicinity of a railway station with good passenger services to central London; indeed, in respect of long journeys to workplaces in the conurbation they remain so, although improvements in road transport since 1918 and increasingly widespread car ownership since 1945 have made for greater flexibility of location of both homes and workplaces. As the Radlett survey shows, many daily journeys to workplaces in outer London and in the surrounding towns, which are of increasing importance as places of employment, are now made by car, while the practice of travel by car to a distant station and completion of the journey to central London by train is causing many local problems over the provision of adequate parking space at stations, e.g. at Tonbridge.

Apart from the lines through the Buckinghamshire Chilterns, to Hertford and across the south Essex clay plain, the network of railway lines to London from outside the present conurbation boundary had largely been completed by 1870. There do not seem to have been any striking examples of early dormitory development in these areas, for, although very favourable season ticket rates minimized the effect of distance, there was plenty of land available nearer London. It was only later that those seeking 'the happy compromise between suburban convenience and rural amenities' were forced to look further afield.[9] Nevertheless, the opening of a station did generally lead to the building of some, often substantial, houses for those working in London, e.g. at Sevenoaks, although the kind and number varied with the closeness of the railway net, the cost of travel and the frequency and speed of trains.[10] As Chapter 3 has shown, the railway companies differed considerably in the extent to which they sought suburban traffic and in the kind of passengers they encouraged. On many lines to the north-west the running of suburban trains had to be reconciled with the demands of heavy main-line traffic, although as early as the 1850s the London and North Western company was encouraging low-density development by the offer of a free first-class season for 21 years to those building houses of an annual rented value of £50 or over at places as far out as King's Langley, Boxmoor and Tring.[11] On the other hand, companies serving the counties east of London, such as the Great Eastern, did much to encourage third-class travel. The nature and frequency of the service offered in turn attracted developers of quite different kinds, so that dormitory settlements with distinctive social characteristics grew up; thus inhabitants of Tunbridge Wells presented a strongly-worded petition in 1874 against proposals to reduce railway fares which, they feared, would lower the social tone of the town.[12]

Although it could be claimed in 1910 that there was no reason 'why the City man should not live thirty miles [48 km.] from his work,' it is in the period since 1918 that dormitory settlements have grown most rapidly, encouraged by the rising demand for houses and the difficulty of finding further attractive sites nearer London.[13] The electrification of much of the Southern Railway system to the south and south-west of London played an important part in promoting their growth (cf. Fig. 75); thus, the number of season tickets from Hayward's Heath on the electrified main line to Brighton trebled between 1926 and 1936 and it increased twice as rapidly as East Grinstead, which was nearer London but lay on a branch line and was served by steam trains.[14]

The role of the railway in the creation of dormitory settlements is most clearly demonstrated where an existing town was by-passed and a new settlement grew up around the station, or where the late building of a line led to rapid development. The Buckinghamshire town of Amersham, some 25 miles (40 km.) from London, illustrates the first situation (Fig. 58). In the decades preceding the opening of the railway the population of Amersham parish, of which this small town was the chief settlement, had been falling. The railway line followed a course half a mile (0·8 km.) outside the town, avoiding Shardeloes park which lay to the west. After the opening of the station in 1892, the population of the parish began to increase rapidly as 'a large and growing villa community' developed on the plateau to the north.[15] On one estate plots of between one and five acres (0·4–2·0 ha.) were being advertised in 1910 and, although many smaller houses were built, such low densities were quite characteristic in settlements of this kind.[16] Although post-war building has now linked the two settlements, they remain quite distinct, old Amersham with its eighteenth-century houses fronting directly on the broad main street, and Amersham on the hill, with its twentieth-century detached and semi-detached houses. Other examples abound, such as Borehamwood and Elstree, Hayward's Heath and Cuckfield, Three Bridges and Crawley. The existence of new and old is often not immediately apparent on a map, especially where they have the same name and have fused to form one settlement, as at Beaconsfield; but some remain quite separate, as at Iver and Denham.

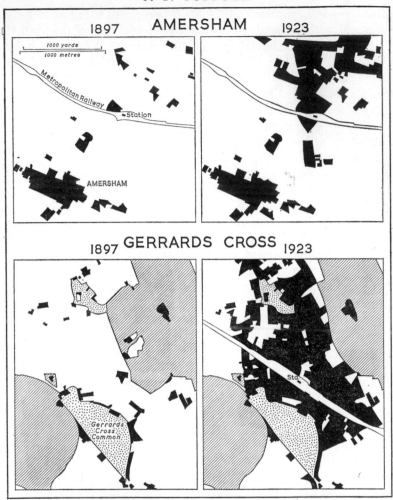

FIG. 58   Amersham and Gerrards Cross 1897 and 1923
The black areas are houses and gardens, the stippled areas are common
land, the shaded areas parkland.
Based on six-inch maps of the Ordnance Survey.

The sudden growth of a dormitory settlement following the
opening of a railway line is well illustrated by Gerrards Cross, which
lies some twenty miles (32 km.) west of London on the plateau between the Wye and Colne valleys. The railway from Marylebone to
High Wycombe was not opened until 1906, at which time Gerrards

276

Cross was a loosely knit hamlet lying around the edge of Gerrards Cross Common (Fig. 58). Within less than twenty years of the opening of the line a substantial settlement of over 400 houses, many of them detached, had grown up around the station, partly on farmland and partly in the grounds of a small park.[17] Gerrards Cross has continued to grow and, although not an urban district, is sufficiently important to have merited a town map in the Buckinghamshire Development Plan.

While most dormitory settlements have grown up as fairly compact towns or villages around a railway station, numerous isolated houses have also been built, particularly in areas of attractive scenery; the substantial houses along the ridge road from Elstree to Barnet provide a good example. Such development was very common before 1939 in the extensive stretches of sandy heathland in west and south-west Surrey, in places such as Frimley, Haslemere and Woking. Figure 59 shows one example on the Wentworth estate between Virginia Water and Sunningdale, where large houses, often with an acre (0·4 ha.) or more of ground, were built on former parkland or heath, both before 1914 and between 1914 and 1939.

In complete contrast were the scattered shacks, bungalows and houses built throughout south Essex after 1880, particularly between 1914 and 1939. Here the stimulus was cheap and easily acquired land, and, on the coast, the attraction of a place by the sea. The agricultural depression of the 1880s and early 1890s threw much of this poor clayland out of cultivation and farms and estates were bought by property speculators; one developer alone bought several thousand acres.[18] Prospective purchasers could acquire land for a small down payment and plots of varying sizes were sold, some as smallholdings, some for permanent residences and others for weekend cottages. Some schemes, like that at Linford, were abortive and only a few houses were built; elsewhere not all plots were sold and great rural slums developed, inadequately serviced and connected only by unmade tracks.[19] Figure 59 shows an example of such development near Pitsea; replacing this legacy of poor housing was one of the major tasks which faced the Basildon Development Corporation.[20]

The existence of a railway station alone was not sufficient to promote the growth of a dormitory settlement; it had to lie at convenient travelling distance from London or other place of work, land had to be available and generally a builder or estate company had to promote development. Building at Gerrards Cross was made possible

To Virginia Water

1934

To Sunningdale

To Virginia Water

1894

To Sunningdale

Pitsea

1920

Pitsea

1895

Parkland   Wood and Heath   Roads

1000 yards
1000 metres

by the fact that several estates were sold, but the early development of Brookman's Park was prevented until the 1920s by lack of available land.[21] The rapid inter-war growth of Amersham was in part due to the acquisition of the Weller Estate by the Metropolitan Railway Estates Company which promoted development by widely advertising the charms of 'Metroland'. Some settlements around stations remain small, as at Bayford or Welwyn North, while much of rural Essex, poorly served by railways, is still little affected by the spread of dormitory settlements. Nor must the growth of dormitories be attributed solely to railway communications. Improved roads and greater use of road transport have also been important, although they have rarely been the cause of new settlements.

Since 1939 planning control has greatly affected the growth of dormitory settlements of all kinds. The building of scattered dwellings has been strongly discouraged and existing settlements made more compact by in-filling. Where land has been available, development has been rapid, but elsewhere, particularly in the green belt where most of the dormitory settlements lie, further expansion has been resisted.

Radlett

While each dormitory settlement has its own distinctive characteristics, the processes which formed them are best illustrated by reference to a specific example, the Hertfordshire village of Radlett, which has grown from a small hamlet in the 1890s to a flourishing settlement of more than 8,000 inhabitants, most of whom depend on employment outside the village.[22]

Radlett lies some fifteen miles (24 km.) north of London where the A5 trunk road (Watling Street) and the main railway line from Bedford and the east Midlands to London (St Pancras) converge to follow the valley of the Tykeswater, a convenient gap through the northern rim of the South Hertfordshire Plateau (Fig. 60). Most of the present village is underlain by Reading Beds or Glacial Gravels which gave rise to agricultural land of only medium quality; but the undulating terrain and the wide views to north, south and west were to provide an attractive setting for modern residential development.

Watling Street has long been an important thoroughfare, but the railway station was opened only in 1868.[23] The first Ordnance Survey 1:2,500 Plans, surveyed in 1871, show that there were then only

279

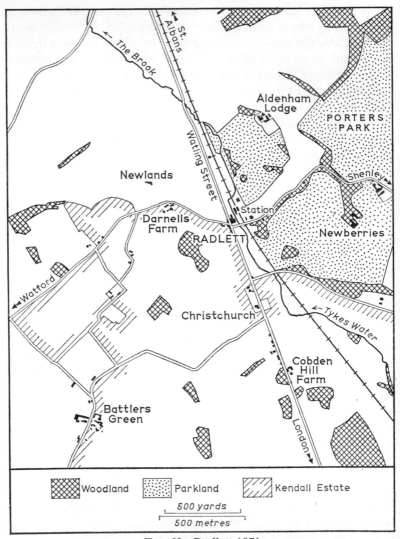

FIG. 60   Radlett 1871
Based on the six-inch maps of the Ordnance Survey and on a map of the
Kendall estate.

some 50 buildings in what is now Radlett, mostly cottages, together
with a few farms, three inns, a newly erected church and vicarage,
and three mansions—Newlands, Aldenham Lodge and Newberries
(Fig. 60). Buildings were widely dispersed, most of the cottages being

strung out for over a mile (1·6 km.) along the main road. In so far as Radlett had a focus, it was the intersection of Watling Street and the Watford–Shenley road, where two of the inns were situated; it was here that the railway station and three railway cottages were built. Half a mile to the south the church of Christchurch had been erected in 1864, reputedly to meet the needs of those working on the railway; for the parish church of Aldenham, in which civil parish Radlett lies, is some two miles (3·2 km.) to the west.[24]

In some ways, the growth of Radlett thus resembles that of Amersham on the hill; for in both instances the main settlement in the parish has been by-passed by the railway, to be overshadowed by the growth of a new centre around the railway station. Yet for nearly 30 years after the opening of the railway to passenger traffic, Radlett changed little in size or character. By 1896, when the Ordnance Survey Plans were revised, a few cottages and a school had been added and a number of buildings destroyed, generally, as in the case of Aldenham Lodge, to be replaced by new structures. But the map also shows the beginning of residential development of a quite different kind; two new roads, Park Road and Station Road, had been cut on land west of Watling Street and a number of new dwellings had already been erected (Fig. 61). Writing in his parish magazine in December 1894, the vicar had commented ruefully on the 'sudden development of a quite innocent looking piece of arable land in the midst of our little village into a barefaced plain of "Eligible Building Sites" '.[25]

Between 1894 and 1914 the village grew comparatively rapidly, although the rate of house building averaged only about twenty houses a year.[26] There were two principal reasons for this residential development: an improvement in railway services resulting from the cutting of the second Elstree tunnel and the building of two additional platforms opened in 1895, and a change of attitude on the part of local landowners who had previously been opposed to house building.[27] This latter change was probably the more important. In 1898 an estate office had been opened on the Kendall estate, which covered most of the land west of Watling Street, and in 1902 the Aldenham Lodge estate was sold to a developer from St Albans.[28] At about the time the Kendall estate was conveyed by Lord Phillimore to his son, Robert Phillimore, who actively promoted its use for residential purposes.[29] The Aldenham Lodge estate was laid out with roads and building plots, although the pattern of building followed was not

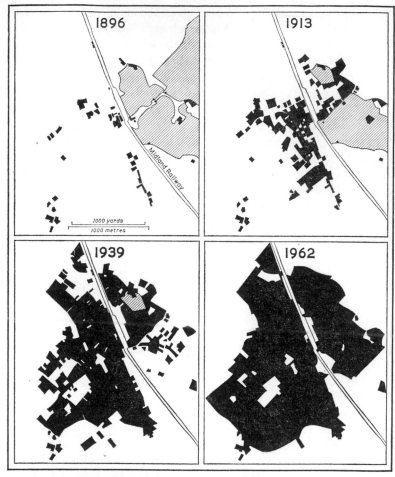

FIG. 61   Radlett 1896, 1913, 1939 and 1962
The black areas are houses and gardens and the shaded areas parkland.
Based on the six-inch maps of the Ordnance Survey, Rating valuations,
a map in the West Hertfordshire Divisional Planning Office and a survey
by the author.

as regular as that planned. A brochure of 1908 mentioned Radlett's
'convenient proximity to Town' and prescribed a minimum value of
£1,000 for houses erected on the estate, although conditions printed
on an undated map of the estate, presumably relating to a few years
later, permitted houses of not less than £500 on sites nearer the railway line.[30]

Yet even these contrasted markedly with the small terrace houses, costing little more than £100, which had been erected along the new roads to the west of the railway. This difference epitomizes a characteristic of Radlett (and of many similar dormitory settlements) which persists in muted form to the present day; although the village gives the impression of being simply a dormitory settlement for professional and business men, there has long been a contrast between low-density, detached houses, generally owned and occupied by those working elsewhere, and the small terrace or semi-detached houses, frequently rented and occupied by those working locally. This dichotomy was particularly marked in the period before 1914. Detached houses accounted for a third of all dwellings in Radlett in 1913, most of them substantial buildings in large gardens of a quarter of an acre (0·1 ha.) or more; on the other hand, terrace houses and cottages, at densities of twenty houses to the acre (50 per hectare) and over, accounted for nearly half the stock of dwellings, although they occupied less than a quarter of the total area under houses.[31] These contrasts were accentuated by the attitude of the principal landowner, Robert Phillimore. A Fabian, he built a number of dwellings for working-class tenants, notably a block of tenements at Scrubbitts Square, which were let at rents as low as 4s. 6d. a week; he is also said to have brought poor Londoners to live in them.[32] For at this time Radlett was less a dormitory settlement than a village with a railway. Many of the inhabitants were employed locally on farms and estates, on the railway, in road haulage, and, more particularly, in numerous sand and gravel pits and at the Kendal Brick and Lime works. The significance of the railway was as much in the transport of goods as in that of passengers; sand and gravel from Radlett and from the hamlet of Colney Street to the north were dispatched by rail and the station, with its extensive sidings and loading ramps, was also used for agricultural commodities, particularly livestock, and for general merchandise for nearby villages which were not served by the railway. On the other hand, it would be wrong to suggest that the village had no dormitory function, and in the absence of other means of transport, those working outside Radlett must have been far more dependent on the railway as a means of travel than are their successors today. The writer of a topography of Aldenham parish attributed Radlett's growth in this period to its improved railway services; yet the slow development of the Aldenham Lodge estate, where only 48 houses had been erected by 1913, suggests that there was no great demand from would-be commuters for housing of this kind.[33]

By the eve of the First World War, Radlett had become a flourishing village of some 450 dwellings (Fig. 61).[34] A parish hall had been built in 1895, temporary Roman Catholic and Methodist churches were erected in 1902, a new school in 1903 and a Congregational church in 1905.[35] In addition to the tradesmen normally found in a village of this size, Kelly's Directory for 1912 names two doctors, an architect, chemist, jeweller, antique-furniture dealer, cycle repairer, motor company and a laundry, indicating the influence of its small but relatively wealthy dormitory population, many of whom must have been numbered among the 164 private residents listed.[36]

Although the rate of development between 1900 and 1914 was comparatively rapid, it was piecemeal. Roads had been laid out on the Kendall and Aldenham Lodge estates, but plots were sold here and there and houses were built both to order and as speculative investments by a number of different builders, some local and some from outside the area. There seems to have been little active promotion of estate development in any systematic way, although Robert Phillimore, by laying out roads, by commissioning building for letting and by his readiness to sell land, did play an important part in the growth of the village.

This piecemeal pattern of development of both speculative and custom-built housing was continued after the First World War, when the village began to acquire more clearly the characteristics of a dormitory settlement. Two-thirds of the dwellings built in the inter-war years were detached houses, generally for owner-occupiers, although the proportion of large houses was considerably lower than before 1914, only a third of these detached houses being at densities of four houses to the acre (10 per hectare) or less.[37] Yet although the emphasis on housing of this kind and the lack of proportionate growth of local employment indicates that the village was increasingly a dormitory, the dichotomy noted earlier was perpetuated, less markedly, by the building of 78 semi-detached and terrace houses to rent by the local authority, Watford Rural District Council, on land to the west of the village.

Apart from a slowing down in the early 1930s, building seems to have proceeded fairly steadily in the inter-war years; by 1928 the number of dwellings exceeded 800 and by 1939 there were nearly 1,300 (Fig. 61).[38] Although further houses were erected on the Aldenham Lodge estate, the great bulk of building was on land west of the railway, a tendency accentuated with the purchase of the Newlands estate to the north-west of the village by a local consortium. This, too, was developed in piecemeal fashion by a number of different builders, mainly local, but there were still many vacant plots at the outbreak of the Second World War. A new chapter was opened in 1935 by the sale of Newberries Park for development, for this had previously acted as a barrier to eastward expansion. Here again roads were laid out and drains dug, but only 37 houses had been erected before war broke out. A prospectus for would-be purchasers on this estate, where it was intended to adopt a density of six houses to the acre (15 per hectare), invited them to live in the garden village with its unrivalled accessibility.[39]

Since 1944 the pattern of development has been somewhat different, its rate faster and the average density of building higher. Local authority housing has played a more important part and private building has been distinguished by generally smaller houses on narrower frontages; for example, much of the Newberries estates has been developed at densities of ten houses per acre (25 per hectare), almost twice that of pre-war building. Thus, over the 70 years of its modern growth, the contrasts in housing types have become progressively less marked. Immediately after the war there was little private house building, but the housing estate built by Watford Rural District Council was greatly enlarged by the addition of 191 permanent houses (mainly semi-detached) and 21 temporary houses, although not all these have been built to house Radlett residents. Since the early 1950s building has been predominantly of detached houses and bungalows for owner-occupiers. The rate of building, averaging more than 50 houses a year between 1953 and 1962, with a peak of 106 houses in 1955, was higher than at any previous period.[40] Nearly half these houses were built by one firm of builders in Newberries Park, where the mansion was destroyed to provide additional sites and where only a few ornamental conifers survive as reminders of its former state. Building on this estate provides the only example of systematic estate development on any scale in Radlett, though smaller estates have been laid out in the post-war period to the north-west and south-west of the village. Other post-war housing has been erected on vacant plots along existing roads (Fig. 61).

Planning control and the position of Radlett in the green belt

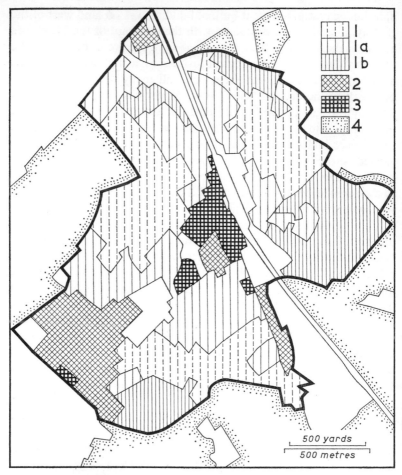

Fɪɢ. 62   Generalized age-of-building map of Radlett

Key: 1, large detached houses at densities of less than six per acre, mainly built 1900–39; 1*a*, detached houses at higher densities, mainly built before 1939; 1*b*, detached houses at higher densities, mainly built since 1945; 2, mainly semi-detached houses built since 1918, including both private and local authority houses; 3, terrace houses and tenements mainly built before 1914; 4, land outside Radlett for which planning permission for residential development has been refused.

The thick line marks the urban perimeter of Radlett; the area outside is green belt.

Based on Ordnance Survey maps, records of the Herts. Planning Department and on a survey by the author.

286

have had a considerable effect upon its post-war growth. It is now an excluded village, i.e. development is generally permitted within the urban perimeter, but strongly resisted outside. As a result, most of the land by-passed or neglected in the early period of expansion has now been built over, while numerous applications for planning consent to develop land outside the present perimeter have been refused, although some of these have probably been made solely with the aim of obtaining compensation (Fig. 62); most of the remaining open land within the village is either public open space or land on which approval for planning proposals is awaited. Rising land values and shortage of land for building have also led to the erection of new houses in the grounds of existing houses, but, despite the low density of pre-war development, frontages are generally too narrow to permit much development of this kind. It is ironical that this situation should arise at a time when demand for housing is so great and when improved rail services have made Radlett more attractive to those working in London. For there can be little doubt that, without planning control, the population of Radlett would now be much nearer the total of 11,000 envisaged in the Greater London Plan.[41]

Figure 62 gives a generalized picture of housing in Radlett in 1962. The different shadings show the predominant type of housing, although houses of other types exist in each area; indeed the variety of housing resulting from the piecemeal development over a period of 70 years is very apparent on the ground. Nearly three-fifths of the houses are detached and the average density of building is low, although this ranges from over twenty to under one house per acre (50 to 3 per hectare). The contrasts in housing noted earlier are also indicated by the 1963 rating valuation. Rateable values of dwellings range from under £20 to over £500, but there are peaks in the distribution of values around £100 and £170, indicating the two kinds of housing, although there is a considerable tail of higher values, representing the large, older houses.[42] Differences between individual roads are even more marked; thus the average rateable value in Cragg Avenue, on the local authority housing estate, is £75, while that on The Avenue, containing many of the large houses built before 1914 on the Aldenham Lodge estate, is £320.

As the sample survey discussed earlier shows, Radlett is now very largely a dormitory settlement. Local employment is confined to shops, schools, a few offices and workshops and a small factory, and part of the labour force employed in Radlett moves daily from surrounding towns and villages. Some 80 shops, mainly along Watling Street, provide a wide range of services, although 89 per cent of the residents also use Watford, St Albans, Borehamwood and central London as shopping centres.[43] Apart from scrap metal collected by a local firm, the railway is now largely concerned with passengers, while the once-quiet Watling Street carries a steady stream of through-traffic. Apart from the church, the three inns, one rebuilt, the railway station and a few cottages, a visitor from the past would find little to remind him of the Radlett of 70 years ago.

The motives which guide people to a particular dormitory settlement are complex. Radlett householders questioned in the sample survey were asked to name the principal reason why they chose to come to Radlett. Nearness or convenience of travel to place of work (the former especially for those working locally) was the most important single reason given and constituted a third of all replies. Probably some of those who gave nearness to London as their chief reason were similarly influenced by ease of getting to work, although not all of them worked in London. Availability of housing or of land for building was the second major reason offered, accounting for twelve per cent of replies, while the rural setting of Radlett was given in nearly as many replies (ten per cent); one informant even attributed his choice to the then bad rail service, which, he hoped, would preserve its rural character. A fifth chose Radlett because of friends or relations already in the village, but, despite the considerable number of children who attend private schools, the presence of schools in the locality does not appear to have played a major part in attracting people, being mentioned in only two per cent of replies. The character of the village and war-time acquaintance with it were other reasons offered. Most of those who felt unable to offer a single reason gave accessibility and rural setting as the chief attractions.

In view of the fact that three-quarters of Radlett's houses have been built since 1914, it is only to be expected that most Radlett householders have migrated into the village. Changes in the occupation of existing houses have also been largely due to migrants; in sample post-war years an average of seven per cent of houses had a change of occupier.[44] Four-fifths of those questioned were not natives of Radlett, and of these more than two-thirds had come since 1945. Exactly half the immigrants had moved from various parts of London and 21 per cent from other parts of Hertfordshire, mainly towns and villages near Radlett. A fifth of those who came from London had previously lived in inner London, mainly in Hampstead, Highgate and Kensington, while 61 per cent had migrated from the newer suburbs of north London, particularly Edgware, Wembley, Harrow, Barnet, Finchley, Mill Hill and Southgate. Other migrants had moved from elsewhere in the Home Counties, more than 80 per cent of all migrants coming from southeast England; only three per cent came from places outside the United Kingdom.

These figures give a somewhat misleading impression of the origin of the migrants, for only fifteen per cent of those who came to occupy houses in Radlett were living in their birthplace at the time of the move and a further eight per cent near their birthplace. A third were Londoners who had been born in other parts of the conurbation; for them, Radlett was often the third stage in a journey from inner to outer London and then beyond the conurbation boundary. As many as 44 per cent of the migrants had been born outside south-east England, ten per cent coming from northern England and eight per cent from the Midlands; yet, for most of these, too, movement to Radlett had been preceded by a period of residence in London.

This picture of Radlett as a dormitory settlement is different in detail from that of other settlements around London. Unlike older towns and villages, such as Beaconsfield, it lacks any considerable pre-railway nucleus, while its slow and steady rate of growth distinguishes it from those settlements like Gerrards Cross, where the late arrival of the railway induced a sudden expansion; residential development was not promoted on any scale by either railway company or private developer, while the nearness of centres of employment, like Borehamwood and Watford, has reduced its dependence on London. Yet many of its features have analogues elsewhere, and, with its lack of local employment, its good rail and road communications, its adequate services, its low density housing and its attractive countryside, it illustrates clearly the dilemma facing many of the smaller towns in the green belt; for although a good case can be made for permitting an increase in population, satisfaction of the great demand for housing would quickly destroy this rural setting and eliminate the narrow belts of largely agricultural land which now separate Radlett from its neighbours, particularly Watford and Borehamwood, the outskirts of which are respectively only one and a half miles and one mile away (2·4 and 1·6 km.). To change the character of the village by greater provision of local employment would not only be difficult, but would similarly imply an unacceptable expansion. At present, many of the migrant families have young children of school age; the dilemma is likely to become even more acute when they, too, require employment and separate accommodation.

References

1. *Census 1951, Report on Usual Residence and Workplace* (H.M.S.O., 1956).

2. See J. Westergaard, 'Journeys to work in the London region', *Town Planning Review*, 28 (1957), 37–62.

3. *Essex Development Plan, Report of the Survey*, Part II, Town Map Areas, South Essex (1952), 52.

4. *Census 1951, Report on Greater London and Five Other Conurbations* (H.M.S.O., 1956), xliii.

5. A. G. Powell, 'The recent development of Greater London', *Advancement of Science*, 17 (1960–1), 79; *Surrey Development Plan*, Part II (15), Report and analysis of survey, town maps, Farnham and District (1963), para. 83.

6. All these figures are based on the 1951 Census Report on Usual Residence and Workplace, *op. cit.*

7. *A Report on a Staff Travel Survey*, conducted in November 1960 by Mr G. H. Harris, Estates and General Services Division, Shell International Petroleum Co. Ltd., February 1961. The writer is very grateful to Mr Harris and the Company for permission to use this material.

8. This survey was undertaken in January 1963 by members of the Radlett Twenties Club. Every third house in Radlett was visited, but refusals and unsatisfactory replies reduced the proportion to one in four. The survey probably underestimates the proportion of local employment.

9. A brochure on the Newberries Estate, by D. C. Houses (Radlett) Ltd., n.d., in the possession of Mr R. B. Holland.

10. *Kent Development Plan*, Part A, 1952, Report upon the survey and analysis of the problem, II (1952), section S2.

11. E. Course, *London Railways* (1962), 199.

12. *Ibid.*, 205.

13. *Country Homes*, official guide of the Metropolitan Railway (1910), 3.

14. S. Vere Pearson, *London's Overgrowth and the Causes of Swollen Towns* (1939), 83, and M. O. Pitt, *New Towns in the London Area*, unpublished Ph.D. thesis (University of Cambridge, 1954), Table III.

15. *Victoria County History, Buckinghamshire*, 3 (1925), 141.

16. *Country Homes, op. cit.*, 53.

17. *V. C. H.*, Buckinghamshire, *op. cit.*, 194.

18. B. E. Cracknell, *Canvey Island*, Dept. of English Local History, University of Leicester, Occasional Papers No. 12 (1959), 52.

19. Course, *op. cit.*, 215.

20. *Basildon Development Corporation, 1st Report*, (H.M.S.O., 1950), 38.

21. Information from Mr P. J. Walter.

22. Despite its size, Radlett is usually referred to as a village. Much of the information in this section has been gathered by observation, from maps and from a number of people who knew Radlett before 1914, particularly Miss W. Watson, Mr J. T. Burrell and Mr W. Wiggs.

23. *Victoria County History, Hertfordshire*, 2 (1908), 149.

24. J. E. Saul, *Radlett Past and Present* (1927), 18–19.

25. Vicar's letter, *Banner of Faith*, January 1895.

26. Aldenham Parish Rate Books. Those relating to years before 1928 have now been deposited in the Hertfordshire County Record Office, the remainder are in the offices of the Watford Rural District Council.

27. Notes and draft article on Radlett by the late J. K. Wainwright and article by Rev. T. Marsden, *Herts. Advertiser and St. Albans Times*, 14th June 1879. The writer is grateful to Miss R. Wainwright for permission to consult her brother's notes.

28. Saul, *op. cit.*, 13 and *V. C. H.*, Hertfordshire, *op. cit.*, 149.

29. Saul, *op. cit.*, 39.

30. Aldenham Lodge Building Estate, Radlett, particulars and conditions of sale, 1908, in possession of Miss Wainwright. Map, n.d. in possession of Mr H. Coward.

31. Ordnance Survey 1:2,500 Plan of Radlett, surveyed 1913, sheets 12 and 16.

32. Saul, *op. cit.*, 39.

33. *V. C. H.*, Hertfordshire, *op. cit.*, 149, and O.S. Plans.

34. Rating Valuation, Aldenham Parish 1913.

35. J. K. Wainwright, notes.

36. *Kelly's Directory, Essex and Hertfordshire* (1912), 189–90.

37. From unpublished 1:2,500 plan of Radlett in South-West Herts. Divisional Planning Office and parish rate books.

38. Rate books, Aldenham parish, 1928 and 1939.

39. Brochure, Newberries estate, *loc. cit.*

40. Rate books, Aldenham Parish, 1945 to 1962.

41. P. Abercrombie, *Greater London Plan 1944* (H.M.S.O., 1945), 198.

42. 1963 Rating valuation, Aldenham parish.

43. Radlett Survey 1963.

44. Rate books, Aldenham Parish.

12

The Green Belt

*

DAVID THOMAS

I t was Sherlock Holmes who observed that 'the lowest and vilest alleys of London do not present a more dreadful record of sin than does the smiling beautiful countryside'. When considering green belts, both journalists and planners have often dwelt upon the sinful —on the shortcomings of planning authorities, on the attempted encroachments of developers, on the struggles between counties and county boroughs and on the questionable motives of some green belt protagonists. But London's green belt is of interest from another standpoint: that it has, by restricting certain kinds of development, affected both the use of land and changes in its use in the zone fringing the urban area. The nature and the aims of green belt proposals have varied greatly over the last 75 years. It is necessary first to trace the confused development of the philosophy of green belts, that is, to study how London's green belt came to be what it is, before examining the consequences of its designation.

The Green Belt Idea: 1890–1939

Chapters 4, 5 and 6 have already described the great expansion of urban London between 1814 and 1939. Towards the end of the nineteenth century the feeling strengthened that, because London was growing so rapidly, there was a need to conserve pleasant open spaces before they were built over. The idea received stimulus from two sources. First, Ebenezer Howard and his followers in the garden city movement were advocating country or rural belts around cities

292

to control their growth and so to preserve agriculture (and hence the city's food supply), to promote amenity and to retain space for recreation (cf. Chapter 13.) They were dissatisfied with the appearance, with the facilities and with the general level of health in the cities which had evolved through the preceding century of industrial expansion and sought to create not only cities with gardens, but cities within gardens, that is, with attractive rural surrounds.[1] The second stimulus was provided by the success of schemes for preserving green girdles around cities both in other European countries and, more particularly, in North America.

The first set of proposals for a green belt round London seems to owe more to the second stimulus than the first. During a visit to the United States, Lord Meath was favourably impressed by the broad boulevards around Chicago, Boston and other cities. On his return in 1890 he suggested that suburban parks and open spaces should be linked by 'broad sylvan avenues and approaches'.[2] Eleven years later William Bull, M.P., published proposals for a green girdle around London modelled on American examples. His plan was to join existing open spaces by a park belt, half a mile (0·8 km.) wide, running a little beyond what was then the outer edge of London. He envisaged 'a circle of green sward and trees which would remain permanently inviolate'.[3] Within a few weeks Lord Meath published his own plan for a green girdle, substantially the same as that of Bull. Like Bull he hoped the London County Council and neighbouring authorities would combine to acquire the land.[4] However, when Bull's proposal came before the Parks and Open Spaces Committee of the London County Council, of which Lord Meath himself was chairman, there seems to have been little enthusiasm for it.[5]

The green girdle schemes of Lord Meath and Bull were based entirely upon the need to preserve amenity and recreational land. They were intended not to regulate London's growth, but to introduce a green ring into that development. Rather different was the intention of the London County Council when in 1891 it required Lord Meath's Committee to consider 'the need of statutory control and direction as to the extension of building in the suburbs of the county of London and in the adjacent parts of neighbouring counties'.[6] The aim, like those of the sixteenth and seventeenth-century green belt proclamations, was to safeguard the health of the growing metropolis.[7]

Yet another concept is exemplified in the plan of George Pepler, published in 1911, which was an attempt to improve communications around London. The proposal was that a quarter-mile (0·4 km.) strip of land should be bought encircling London and linking existing open spaces. In the centre of the belt there was to be a system of roads, railways and tramways, interspersed with grass and trees, while the remaining open land was to be developed as garden suburb or parkland.[8] No action was taken on this, or any other plan put forward at the time. The difficulties and costs were thought insurmountable and the youthful county council was fully occupied with even more pressing problems.

During the 1920s concern was again felt about the growth of London. In 1924 the London County Council carried a resolution asking its Town Planning Committee 'to consider and report whether or not the preservation of a green belt or unbuilt-on zone or zones within the boundaries of or adjacent to greater London is desirable and practicable.' The reports of the committee suggest that the belt under consideration was half a mile (0·8 km.) wide, but nothing was done as it was felt that the statutory powers of the council were insufficient.[9] Eventually in 1927 Neville Chamberlain, then Minister of Health and responsible for planning, created the Greater London Regional Planning Committee. Among other things, the committee was asked to study the benefits of separating London from satellite developments by an agricultural belt. The committee's technical adviser was Raymond Unwin, who had been closely associated with Howard and his ideas while, with Parker, he was designing the first garden city at Letchworth. In a report, published in 1933, Unwin outlined his plan for the development of Greater London, one of the major proposals of which was a green girdle.

Unwin's girdle was not what Howard or Chamberlain had envisaged. He proposed not an agricultural belt, but a park belt which would compensate for the deficiency of playing fields and pleasant open land nearer the centre of London: in effect it was an extension of the ideas of Lord Meath and Bull. The belt was not continuous, though he attempted to make it as nearly so as possible, and it was wider than any suggested earlier—there are sometimes six miles (9·6 km.) between the inner sections, drawn close to the edge of London, and the outer sections. He hoped that the belt would secure 'a break in the outward sporadic spreading of London' and that development beyond it would be planned by reserving large areas temporarily or permanently from building.[10] Unwin's plan was never formally adopted but his green belt ideas had two important results. First, the park belt proposal was soon accepted by the London County Council and secondly, his concept of building against a background of open land rather than planning open spaces within unlimited building land eventually became one of the most widely accepted tenets of town and country planning.

In 1934, the year following the publication of Unwin's report, the Labour Party gained control of the London County Council and immediately adopted more direct methods to prevent the alarming loss of land suitable for recreation. An approach to the government made it clear that no financial assistance was forthcoming and early in 1935 the Council's green belt scheme was launched. Its aim was 'to provide a reserve supply of public open spaces and of recreational areas and to establish a green belt or girdle of open space lands, not necessarily continuous but as readily accessible from the completely urbanized area of London as practicable'. The London County Council offered grants of as much as half the approved cost of an acquisition or preservation to neighbouring county authorities to enable them to 'sterilize' open space and farmland. Doubts arose about the powers of local authorities to undertake such a plan. A bill was therefore introduced into Parliament to ensure that the land was permanently and legally preserved. The Green Belt (London and Home Counties) Act was passed in 1938.

Within fourteen months of the beginning of the London County Council scheme 18,300 acres (78 sq. km.) had been secured against harmful development and today nearly 28,000 acres (113 sq. km.) are protected. The land lies broadly in the zone where Unwin proposed his green girdle. 27 per cent is public open space, 14 per cent will eventually become open to the public and the remaining 59 per cent is mainly agricultural land.[11] The 1938 Act also allowed local authorities to acquire green belt land without assistance from the London County Council. With this land a total of nearly 36,000 acres (146 sq. km.) is now reserved against building.

The Green Belt Idea: Abercrombie and After

During the Second World War a number of committees were planning the post-war use of land and resources in Britain. One of these was the Committee on Land Utilization in Rural Areas (Scott

295

Committee) which, in what must be one of the most influential foot-notes in the history of planning, defined what it conceived a green belt to be.[12] A green belt was not merely an artificially preserved or 'sterilized' ring of commons, woods and fields around a town to off-set its smoke and dirt. Sterility must be avoided. Consequently a green belt was envisaged as a tract of ordinary country, of varying width, round a town where the normal occupations of farming or forestry should be continued so that, as elsewhere in rural areas, the farmer was the normal custodian of the land. But a green belt had a second role. Because of its proximity to a large town it would nor-mally include golf courses and other recreational land for the towns-man's use. The farmer, on his part, would recognize that certain types of farming, such as sheep rearing, were unsuited to such an area, but in essence it would remain an ordinary tract of countryside.

The emphasis upon the importance of agriculture in a green belt was a return to the ideas of Howard and his group, and it was this concept which Patrick Abercrombie accepted. When he produced his plan for Greater London in 1944 it contained proposals for a green belt up to ten miles (16 km.) wide.[13] The intention was to restrict urban growth (provision was made for overspill in New and Ex-panded Towns—see Chapter 13) while actively encouraging agricul-ture, enhancing the natural beauty of the area and fostering recrea-tional possibilities. The method of controlling land under the Green Belt Act of 1938 was impractical on this scale and consequently Aber-crombie proposed to control the actions of owners and leaseholders. The aim was not to replace the London County Council scheme, under which he hoped land would continue to be acquired for public use where suitable for playing fields or of high amenity value, but to supplement it.

In 1946 Abercrombie's green belt proposals were accepted in principle by the Minister of Town and Country Planning, the first formal government recognition of the need for a continuous green belt round London. The decision was confirmed by a Ministry memorandum in 1947 and in the same year the Town and Country Planning Act enabled, *inter alia*, the ideas of Abercrombie to be im-plemented. County and county borough authorities no longer needed to buy land to prevent building, they were empowered to refuse permission for development. Three years later a green belt map, based upon that in Abercrombie's plan, was prepared by the Ministry for the guidance of planning authorities. When submitting their development plans for approval, planning departments in the London area included a further modified version of this green belt. In 1954 and the following years, the development plans for the London area were approved by the responsible Minister (then of Housing and Local Government), and the green belt which they defined, with minor changes, became part of statutory documents.

Then in 1955 came the clearest statement, to that time, of the government's attitude to green belts; one which seemed to focus attention away from the character and viability of the belt itself and on to its effect upon the town or city. In a statement in the House of Commons, Duncan Sandys, Minister of Housing and Local Government, expressed concern that, apart from those around London, no planning authorities had submitted green belt proposals to him, and asked that they should consider the designation of green belts where appropriate. Within a few months the statement was followed by a Ministry circular outlining the official view of a green belt's purpose and nature.[14] A green belt was recommended under three circumstances. First, it could be used to check the growth of a large built-up area, secondly, it could prevent the merging of two neighbouring towns, and thirdly, it could preserve the special character of a town. If possible the green belt was to be of sufficient width to ensure that a substantial rural zone would be preserved. Except in very special circumstances, no new buildings, or changes in the use of existing buildings, were to be allowed other than for agriculture, sport, cemeteries, institutions standing in extensive grounds, or other uses appropriate to a rural area.[15] There is no mention in the circular of amenity and no proposal to encourage agriculture or recreational facilities, except by restricting urban growth. That this was not an oversight was confirmed later by a senior officer of the Ministry who said, 'the designation of the green belt is not a measure for the protection of the countryside'.

The contrast between these official views and those of Abercrombie may be reduced in two ways. First, since Abercrombie's plan was published many powers have become available for protecting countryside and space for recreation. National Parks, Areas of Outstanding Natural Beauty, Areas of Great Landscape, Scientific or Historic Value, nature reserves, and Sites of Special Scientific Interest may all be designated by statutory bodies. All of these can occur within green belts, where they identify and protect land of special amenity or other value. Secondly, as time has passed, greater attention has been paid in planning decisions to amenity, and to the balance between land uses, though agriculture seems to hold no special place in the scheme. In a recent, and highly optimistic, booklet on green belts published by the Ministry of Housing and Local Government the emphasis is upon the green belt's openness, and not upon its agriculture.[16]

The 1955 circular also requested that local planning authorities contemplating the creation of green belts, after consulting with neighbouring authorities, should submit to the Minister a sketch plan showing the approximate boundaries. When any sketch submission was accepted in principle by the Minister county authorities were empowered to treat the area agreed as if it were full green belt, until such time as a formal amendment to the development plan was approved, modified or rejected. Local planning authorities around London took advantage of the instructions and many extensions to the green belt have been proposed. These are now in various stages of approval. A number of small additions appear in approved development plans, for example the Ascot and Chesham Town Map areas; a revised version of the Buckinghamshire extension has been formally approved, though it has not yet become part of the development plan; and considerable areas in most of the Home Counties have been submitted as green belt and are awaiting final decisions (Fig. 63). An extension of the green belt into East Sussex to the south and east of Crawley was accepted provisionally but, following a public enquiry, has since been rejected. The effective green belt at the moment is much wider than ten miles (16 km.). The combined approved and provisional belt is in some places, to the north of London for example, over 30 miles (48 km.) wide and covers nearly 2,000 square miles (5,180 sq. km.).

The most recent development followed the publication of a white paper in February 1963 on employment, housing and land in the London region.[17] In this, and in statements which he made in the House of Commons, the Minister of Housing and Local Government made it clear that the green belt already approved could not be regarded as sacrosanct. Allowing for the houses that could be built within the conurbation, in New and in Expanded Towns over a ten-year period, there still remained the need to find land around London for 200,000 houses. Many of these would have to be built on land at present designated green belt. He proposed asking planning authorities to consider what additional areas, preferably with little

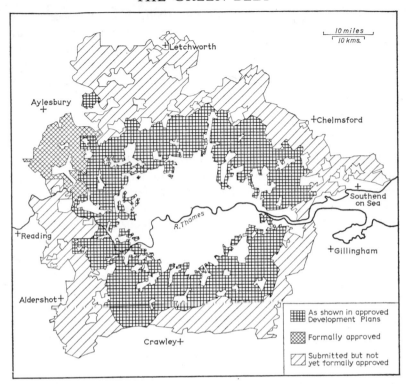

FIG. 63   London's green belt April 1963
Based on maps of the Ministry of Housing and Local Government.

amenity value, would be suitable for housing. Hertfordshire and
Essex were particularly suited to such building because spare railway
capacity existed in these counties to carry commuters. An area of
disused greenhouses in the Lea valley was immediately proposed as
the first development. In the course of time the Minister intended to
add substantially to the area of the green belt, presumably by approv-
ing some, or all, of those areas provisionally agreed with local
authorities.

The white paper seems to indicate a further shift of attitude away
from that outlined by the Duncan Sandys circular. In 1955 the green
belt was clearly regarded as having one purpose: to check the growth
of London. In 1963 the green belt land on which it is proposed to
build is not 'the fine countryside which forms an important part of
the green belt,' it is the land 'of little amenity value' which is not

'essential to the purposes of the green belt.' If the purpose of the green belt is to check growth, that purpose cannot be achieved by allowing building, whether on unattractive country or not. It is clear that the purpose has changed, and changed so as to bring it closer to the amenity and recreational aims of Howard, Unwin and Abercrombie.

The Use of Land

Whatever the aims of the present green belt it is plain that, over a long period, land use on the fringes of London has been modified greatly. From 1935, under the London County Council green belt programme and later with the aid of the Green Belt Act, considerable areas have been reserved against development and much public open space created in a zone ten miles (16 km.) wide beyond the edge of built-up London. From 1939 all developments in the same area have been restricted or controlled. During the Second World War and immediately afterwards all but essential building was prevented by shortage of materials and labour, then in 1947 the Town and Country Planning Act enabled local planning authorities to comply with Abercrombie's green belt proposals. From the middle 1950s green belt control has been in full operation.

But, though the development of the landscape has been modified, and though the green belt is more open than it would have been if economic and social forces had been allowed to operate unhindered over the last 30 years, much of the green belt is still not green. Southeast England has long been the most densely populated part of the country and the one in which agriculture has experienced greatest pressure from other land uses. Together with the officially approved activities there are many other diverse uses of land, most of which persist from before the time when planning permission was necessary and the green belt established. Local planning authorities have no powers, except those of compulsory purchase which incur heavy compensation, are unpopular and are used sparingly, to change the use of land. Occasionally non-conformable uses have been introduced despite green belt control, though usually only where some special reason exists. Intermixed with agricultural land, therefore, are the permitted activities (for example, schools, hospitals, cemeteries, golf courses, playing fields); some uses which are inappropriate but inevitable (for example, gravel digging, sewage disposal works, water

300

TABLE XIV

The use of land in the north-west of London's green belt

Land-use category	Subdivision	Per cent* of development plan green belt	Per cent* of area beyond inner edge of green belt	Per cent* of whole area
Residential and	to 1955	5·9	14.9	21.4
Commercial	1955–1960	0·4	2·1	2·2
		6·3	17·0	23·6
Manufacturing	to 1955	0·3	1·0	1·0
	1955–1960	–	0·3	0·3
		0·3	1·3	1·3
Extractive	——	0·9	0·7	0·6
Transport	road	1·4	1·6	1·6
	rail	0·4	0·8	1·0
	air	0·7	0·9	1·0
		2·5	3·3	3·6
Public Services	public utilities	0·1	0·3	0·4
	service and govt.	0·2	0·5	0·5
	cemeteries	0·2	0·1	0·3
		0·5	0·9	1·2
Institutions,	schools, etc. to 1955	1·8	2·4	2·4
normally with	1955–1960	0·1	0·2	0·2
large grounds	hospitals	0·7	0·5	0·7
		2·6	3·1	3·3
Woodland	——	10·2	8·7	7·6
Water	——	0·9	0·7	0·7
Recreational	playing fields	0·8	0·9	1·0
	golf courses	2·4	2·2	2·2
	open spaces	2·8	2·9	3·0
	others	–	0·1	0·1
		6·0	6·1	6·3
Agricultural	grass and arable	68·7	56·9	50·1
	orchards	0·4	0·4	0·4
	nurseries	0·1	0·1	0·1
	allotment gardens	0·2	0·4	0·7
		69·4	57·8	51·3
Unused	cut over	0·1	0·1	0·1
	other	0·3	0·3	0·3
		0·4	0·4	0·4

* Percentages are rounded to one decimal place.

(Based on O.S. 1:25,000 sheets TL 00, TL 10, TL 20, TQ 09, TQ 19, TQ 29)

pumping stations); and some uses which are undesirable (for example, manufacturing industry, houses, army camps). Roads, railways and airports serving London also occupy large areas. In Plate 26, the entire area of which is designated approved green belt in the Hertfordshire development plan, some of these non-agricultural activities are shown in and near the village of London Colney, to the south-east of St Albans.

To study the components of the green belt in greater detail it is necessary to confine attention to one sector of the belt. In that sector it is necessary to assess quantitatively the importance of each use of land, and to elucidate the pattern of recent development. Such is the diversity within London's green belt that no one part is truly typical of the whole, but the north-west contains all the major elements, though not necessarily in precise proportion to their occurrence throughout the belt. The north-west sector is conveniently represented by the areas of six 1:25,000 Ordnance Survey sheets.[18] They cover an area stretching from Barnet, Edgware and Harrow Weald, in the north-west part of the conurbation, through development plan green belt to provisional green belt (Fig. 64). It is an area which contains not only a wide range of rural and semi-urban uses of land but also includes industrial towns, such as St Albans and Watford, dormitory settlements, such as Potters Bar and Rickmansworth, London County Council housing estates, such as Borehamwood and Oxhey, and New Towns, such as Hatfield and Hemel Hempstead.

The use of the land in the area covered by Figure 64 can be derived from an analysis of air photographs. Using a sampling technique based upon systematic line traverses, it is possible to make accurate estimates of the distribution of the land among eleven major land-use categories.[19] The major categories may be subdivided in order to give a more precise picture of the activities which exist in the green belt, and with a number of categories it is possible, by comparing the air photographs with Ordnance Survey maps, to estimate the amount of land developed for that use between 1955 and 1960. The results of these calculations are shown in Table XIV.

The first column of percentages in Table XIV shows the incidence of each land use in the development plan green belt. In this area, which covers 60·4 per cent of the land represented in Figure 64, the picture revealed seems quite satisfactory. Residential and commercial activities occupy 6·3 per cent of the land, manufacturing 0·3 per cent, extractive industry 0·9 per cent and land devoted to transport

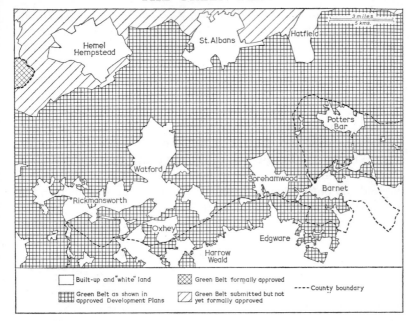

FIG. 64   The green belt to the north-west of London 1963
'White' land is land left between the allocated urban area and the green
belt which may be developed at a later date.
Based on maps in the library of the Ministry of Housing and Local
Government.

and public services 3·0 per cent. Together, the non-conformable
activities cover only 10·5 per cent of the approved green belt. There
is as much land available for recreation as there is devoted to residential and commercial uses, as much woodland as there is land
devoted to the non-conformable uses, and dominating all other
activities is agriculture, which occupies nearly 70 per cent of the
approved green belt.

The picture presented by these statistics, however, is illusory:
it is both unrealistic and inconsistent. The lack of realism lies in the
fact that the development plan green belt contains within it a large
number of urban and industrial areas which have not been scheduled
as green belt. But Borehamwood, Potters Bar, St Albans and Watford cannot be eliminated by draughtsmanship; they are there and
no cartographic artifice will remove them. The inconsistencies stem
from the different principles and motives which have guided local
planning authorities in their drawing of green belt boundaries. This

is seen clearly in an area such as this, which is traversed by a county boundary. For example, Clare Hall Hospital, near Potters Bar in Middlesex, is not scheduled as green belt, but hospitals in the Vale of St Albans in Hertfordshire are. The small village of South Mimms in Middlesex is excluded from the green belt; the larger village of Shenley, two miles (3·2 km.) distant but within Hertfordshire, is wholly included in the approved green belt. An even more striking example is the village of Elstree, through which runs the county boundary. Middlesex Elstree is unscheduled while Hertfordshire Elstree is shown as green belt in the respective development plans. A more reasonable estimate of land use in the zone immediately beyond the outer edge of London would be one that included all land, whether it is designated green belt or not.

The second column of percentages in Table XIV attempts such an estimate. Measurements have been made of all land covered by Figure 64 beyond the continuous inner edge of the development plan green belt, that is, of 87·1 per cent of the area shown. The inclusion of the built-up areas alters greatly the balance between land uses. Residential and commercial land is now seen to occupy 17·0 per cent of the extra-metropolitan area, manufacturing 1·3 per cent, extractive industry 0·7 per cent and transport and public services 4·2 per cent. Together, the non-conformable activities take 23·2 per cent of the total area and, with institutions standing in large grounds, occupy over one-quarter. The figure for woodland is reduced to 8·7 per cent in the new calculation but that of recreational land increases slightly to 6·1 per cent, a result of the higher proportion of the area devoted to playing fields and open spaces within the urban agglomerations. The farmer, it is clear, is not 'the normal custodian of the land'. Little over half the land is devoted to agriculture, and this is dispersed and fragmented among other uses of land (Fig. 65). This can hardly have been the picture which the Scott Committee had in mind when defining its conception of a green belt.

The third column of percentages in Table XIV shows the use of land over the whole area of study to the north-west of London. In addition to the land covered by the second column it includes the outer parts of the conurbation.

The sample statistics also provide estimates for three of the land-use categories of the amount of land which has changed to these uses from 1955 to 1960. Upon the development plan green belt of Figure 64 this does not amount to much. The only important change was the

304

Agricultural land
(including farm buildings, orchards
nurseries and allotment
gardens)

FIG. 65 Agricultural land to the north-west of London 1963
Based on air photographs in the Ministry of Housing and Local Government library.

0·4 per cent of the green belt which became residential and commercial land. While 0·4 per cent is a very small proportion of the green belt it does represent an increase in residential and commercial land of nearly seven per cent. No land was converted to manufacturing use over the period and only 0·1 per cent to institutions with extensive grounds. In the whole area beyond the continuous inner edge of the green belt the changes are more marked. Of the extra-metropolitan area shown in Figure 65, 2·1 per cent became residential and commercial between 1955 and 1960 (an increase in area of over 14 per cent), 0·3 per cent became land for manufacturing industry (an increase in area of over 31 per cent), and 0·2 per cent became institutions with extensive ground (an increase in area of 8 per cent). When the area of the conurbation is taken into account the result is not greatly altered, except that, as might be expected, the rate of growth of residential and commercial land is lower.

The areal distribution of these developments is clear (Fig. 66). Much of the change in use has occurred either within the towns or

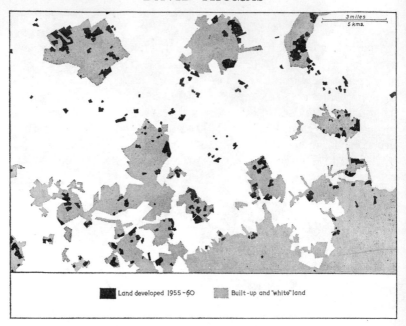

FIG. 66 Land developed for residential, commercial, industrial and educational uses to the north-west of London 1955–60
Based on air photographs in the Ministry of Housing and Local Government library.

villages, where waste or open land has been developed, or on their peripheries, where land left between the edge of town and the surrounding green belt has since been converted to urban or semi-urban use. For example, within Rickmansworth and Watford substantial areas have been developed upon land which was already enclosed by building. In Bushey, to the east of Watford, and in Potters Bar, almost all the peripheral land not scheduled as green belt has now been built up. The developments in the belt itself appear from the map to be scattered. In fact no isolated building has been allowed; all development is designed to 'infill' or 'round-off' existing settlements. For example, to the north-west of Borehamwood the large village of Radlett has substantial additions (Chapter 11) and the same is true of Abbots Langley, to the north-west of Watford. Though 'infilling' and 'rounding-off' are elastic terms, none shown in Figure 66 contributes greatly towards the merging of adjacent settlements or constitutes ribbon development.

Other Controls in the Green Belt

Apart from the approved and provisional green belt there are two other means by which open countryside has been preserved in the area fringing London. First, there exists a number of statutory controls upon land use and changes in land use, which are quite separate from green belt control, and secondly, there is the factor of land ownership, which in a number of instances has effectively prevented urban expansion.

The land-use controls often operate more positively than green belt procedures in preserving attractive countryside. This is to some extent because they are often overseen by statutory bodies which are concerned specifically with amenity, recreation facilities, scientific research or timber production, but also because their purposes are more clearly defined. [20]

The National Parks Commission, created in 1949, has the power to designate National Parks and also Areas of Outstanding Natural Beauty. No National Parks occur within green belts but Areas of Outstanding Natural Beauty do. In the Chilterns to the north-west of London, and in the North Downs, such areas have been proposed in the London green belt. Here local planning authorities are obliged, in consultation with the National Parks Commission, to pay special attention to the preservation of landscape beauty. Local planning authorities themselves have powers under the Town and Country Planning Act of 1947 to outline Areas of Great Landscape, Scientific or Historic Value, and quite extensive areas have been so designated around London. In these areas developments which harm attractive landscape or features of scientific or historic interest are restricted, but with what severity control should be applied has never been clearly defined. The work of local authorities in protecting areas of scientific interest has been extended since 1949 by the Nature Conservancy. This body is able both to buy or lease land for nature reserves and also to notify local planning authorities of sites which, because of their flora, fauna, geology or geomorphology are of special scientific interest. Before allowing any development in a Site of Special Scientific Interest local planning authorities must consult with the Nature Conservancy. In addition to buildings of historical interest which have been scheduled by local planning authorities the Ministry of Works has exercised its powers, over a much longer period, to 'list' monuments of archaeological or historical importance.

DAVID THOMAS

Woodland is often more particularly protected. It is possible for local planning authorities to make a tree preservation order, which has the effect of preventing the felling and trimming of trees or woodland except with the consent of the authority. The order may provide for the replanting of trees after felling. The Forestry Commission is also entitled to enter into a forestry dedication covenant with a landowner. In return for financial assistance the owner undertakes to use the land only for the growing of timber, and in a way approved by the Forestry Commission. The covenant is binding upon future owners of the land though it is possible under certain circumstances to withdraw from the agreement.

Lastly, land use is controlled by arrangements made under the Green Belt Act of 1938. Where the land is not converted to public open space restrictive covenants are included in leases to ensure that it remains rural in character.

In Figure 67 the additional land-use controls which exist in the

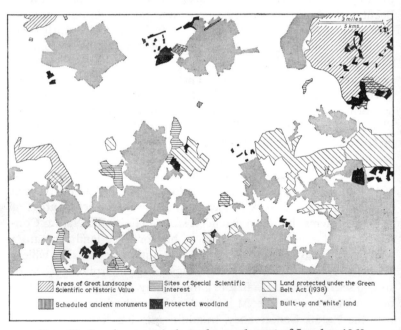

FIG. 67   Land-use controls to the north-west of London 1963
Land protected as green belt is not shown
Based on material in the map library of the Ministry of Housing and
Local Government.

308

selected section of the north-west green belt have been shown. Large areas of Great Landscape Value have been designated in the Broxbourne Woods area to the east of Hatfield, in the lower vale of Chess to the north of Ricksmansworth, and to the north-west of Hemel Hempstead. A number of ancient monuments have been scheduled, the largest of which is Verulamium, on the western edge of St Albans. Sites of Special Scientific Interest have been outlined at Water End, between Hatfield and Potters Bar, and for a number of woodland and water areas such as Bricket Wood and the Colne valley. Tree preservation orders have been issued widely in Broxbourne Woods and on Enfield Chase, north-east of Barnet, while Forestry Commission dedication covenants have been made in respect of woods to the north of Borehamwood and between St Albans and Hemel Hempstead. Land secured by the Green Belt Act of 1938 gives protection to a large number of areas on the immediate fringe of London. A particularly important acquisition under the Act is the section

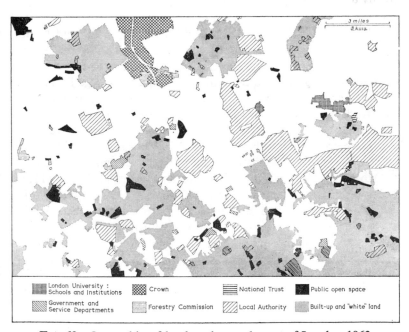

FIG. 68   Ownership of land to the north-west of London 1963
The unshaded area is privately owned
Based on material in the map library of the Ministry of Housing and Local Government.

309

between Barnet and Potters Bar, through which run the Great North Road and a railway carrying heavy commuter traffic. All the statutory controls have prevented urban expansion over the scattered areas to which they apply, but, more important, they have added greatly to the visual amenity of the green belt.

Land ownership operates far more negatively as a factor controlling land use. Urban expansion depends upon the acquisition of sites on the fringes of towns and cities by private individuals or by large-scale developers. The land most readily available will be that which is privately owned, though in a number of instances, such as at Hatfield and Watford, the owners of large estates have tenaciously resisted building. Land not privately owned, on the other hand, often acts as a buffer to urban growth and, particularly where the ownership is by a local authority or government department, may be used as an instrument of public policy.

Some of the land not privately owned in the north-western section of the green belt is shown in Figure 68. Crown and Forestry Commission land forms as effective a barrier between Hemel Hempstead and St Albans as any green belt. Land held by Schools and Institutions of London University, though not extensive, in one instance provides some security against the merging of two settlements. The field station and farm of the Royal Veterinary College lie between Potters Bar and Brookman's Park, one mile (1·6 km.) to the north. Hertfordshire and Middlesex County Councils, by contrast, own large tracts. Apart from land purchased under the 1938 Green Belt Act there are the grounds and farmland of hospitals, smallholdings, reservoirs, agricultural institutes, a golf course, and many schools. St Albans is a clear example of a settlement the expansion of which is being restricted and guided by land owned by the local authority. The National Trust and government departments hold little land in this area, but public open space again serves to modify urban growth. Hadley Common has maintained the distinction between the settlements of Barnet and Hadley Wood, to the north, and Cassiobury Park, landscaped grounds which passed into public ownership between 1909 and 1930, provides a green wedge penetrating to the centre of Watford.

Implications in the London Region

To the geographer the green belt is of interest because it has affected the way in which the landscape has evolved. It has excluded the development of many activities on the fringe of London. It has given a cleaner edge to town and country and it has, to some extent, improved visual amenity.

But from a planning point of view, green belts have been less satisfactory. Their design has suffered because they have been based upon hazy ideas. Many local authorities have operated on the assumption that green belts are to protect countryside. Others have attempted to promote amenity. Of those which accepted that green belts are to prevent town growth, few have had any idea of at what point any given town becomes too big. Green belt design in the London area has also suffered because the Abercrombie green belt boundaries and those later modelled upon them were based upon projections of population and industrial growth which proved to be inaccurate. 'White' land left between the allocated urban area and the green belt is now quite insufficient to satisfy the demand for urban needs. Again, there has been a tendency to look upon the green belt as a policy in itself, rather than as the complement of vigorous decentralization, overspill programmes for population and industry, and New Town building. Lastly, in the eyes of many, the green belt idea has become debased. Roughly one-tenth of England and Wales is scheduled as green belt. This is a large proportion of the total area of the country and is justifiable only if the motives which have prompted its designation are beyond question. The suspicion has grown that in more than isolated instances green belts have become weapons in the battle between counties and neighbouring county boroughs, and, more alarmingly, weapons in the battle between the 'haves' and 'have nots'.

References

1. E. Howard, *Garden Cities of Tomorrow* (1945). This edition is prefaced by essays on the garden city movement by F. J. Osborn and Lewis Mumford.
2. Lord Meath, 'The green girdle round London', *The Sphere*, 6 (1901), 64. Reprinted with some omissions in *The Garden City*, n.s. 1 (1906–7), 59–60.
3. W. J. Bull, 'A green girdle round London', *The Sphere*, 5 (1901), 128–9. For maps of all the green belt proposals mentioned here see D. Thomas, 'London's green belt: the evolution of an idea,' *Geographical Journal*, 129 (1963), 14–24.
4. Lord Meath, *op. cit.*, 64.
5. London County Council Minutes, Parks and Open Spaces Committee, 28th June, 8th July, 26th July, 1901.

6. London County Council Minutes, 28th July, 1891. The resolution is cited in full in Sir I. G. Gibbon and R. W. Bell, *History of the London County Council, 1889–1939* (1939), 503.

7. S. E. Rasmussen, *London: the Unique City* (1937), 67–75.

8. G. L. Pepler, 'A belt of green round London', *Garden Cities and Town Planning*, n.s. 1 (1911), 39–43, 64–8.

9. Mrs Hugh Dalton, 'The green belt round London', *Journal of the London Society*, No. 255 (1939), 70.

10. Greater London Regional Planning Committee, *Second report* (1933), 78–83.

11. London County Council, *Green Belt round London* (1961), 3–9.

12. Ministry of Works and Planning, *Report of the Committee on Land Utilisation in Rural Areas*, Cmd. 6378 (H.M.S.O., 1942), 71.

13. P. Abercrombie, *Greater London plan 1944* (H.M.S.O., 1945), *passim*.

14. Ministry of Housing and Local Government, *Green Belts*, Circular No. 42/55 (H.M.S.O., 1955).

15. Later amplified in Ministry of Housing and Local Government, *Selected Planning Appeals*, 2nd Series, Vol. I (H.M.S.O., 1959), 10.

16. Ministry of Housing and Local Government, *The Green Belts* (H.M.S.O., 1962).

17. Ministry of Housing and Local Government, *London. Employment: Housing: Land*, Cmd. 1952 (H.M.S.O., 1963).

18. TL 00, TL 10, TL 20, TQ 09, TQ 19, TQ 29.

19. J. G. Osborne, 'Sampling errors of systematic and random surveys of cover-type areas', *Journal of the American Statistical Association*, 37 (1942), 256–64; M. J. Proudfoot, 'Sampling with transverse traverse lines', *ibid.*, 265–70.

20. D. Thomas, 'Statutory preservation of the countryside in England and Wales', *Zeitschrift für Wirtschaftsgeographie*, 6 (1962), 34–8.

13

New Towns in the London Region

*

ROBIN H. BEST

The creation of the New Towns has been perhaps the greatest achievement of post-war town and country planning in Britain. Under the New Towns Act of 1946, fifteen New Towns had been designated by 1960 and are now in various stages of construction. Of these, eight are in the London Region, four in the rest of England and Wales, and three in Scotland. Since 1960 a further five sites have also been designated—four in the provinces and one in Scotland.

Not all these New Towns are meant to fulfil the same function. The provincial towns already being built are primarily intended to house people employed in existing factories, works or collieries in the vicinity. They are found, therefore, in widely scattered locations where there has been an exceptional local need for housing and associated facilities. On the other hand, the more typical type of New Town has been designed, initially at any rate, to receive overspill population from large cities and to provide a substantial amount of employment for these people by the establishment of new industrial premises in the towns themselves. Although two such towns exist in Scotland,[1] and the five newly designated towns are also of this character, it is the eight New Towns encircling London, some 25–30 miles (40–48 km.) from the centre of the metropolis, which at present form the only considerable and well-defined regional grouping of this type of settlement. As such they hold a special interest.

313

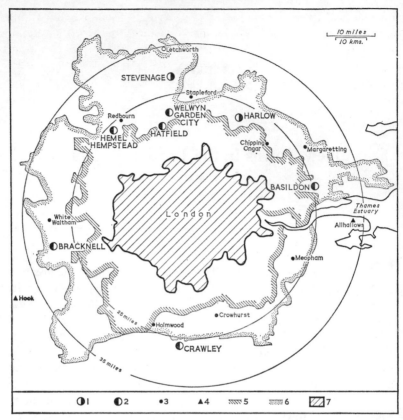

FIG. 69   New Towns in the London Region

Key: 1, New Towns on sites proposed in Greater London Plan 1944;
2, other New Towns; 3, sites of New Towns proposed in Greater
London Plan 1944, but not accepted; 4, other proposals not
accepted; 5, outer boundary of approved green belt; 6, outer
boundary of proposed green belt; 7, built-up area of London.

Based on the Greater London Plan 1944 and maps of the Ministry of
Housing and Local Government.

Historical Background

In many ways, the New Towns can trace their origins from the
model factory villages, such as Bournville and Port Sunlight, which
were built by enlightened industrialists for their employees towards
the end of the nineteenth century. With their fairly open housing for
those days, their individual gardens, and a reasonable provision of

open space, these settlements represented a reaction against the cramped, cheerless and unlovely environment that was the legacy of so much town development during the Industrial Revolution, and which found its particular expression in the dreary streets of 'by-law' housing built on an unrelieved gridiron pattern in many industrial towns.

The more immediate forerunners of the present New Towns, however, were built in the London Region at the beginning of this century. At that time, as indeed at the moment, the idea of starting afresh to build new and separate towns in the open countryside, largely untrammelled by existing development and property interests, held a great and compelling attraction. It was Ebenezer Howard who, in 1898, first advocated a definite policy of constructing so-called 'satellite' towns to remedy the conditions under which so many people lived in Victorian Britain. He detested the great and overcrowded city and envisaged self-contained towns of limited size which could provide urban facilities in a pleasant setting and allow easy access to the open countryside. Each town would, in fact, be separated from the parent city by a green belt and would itself be surrounded and contained by a green belt.

From such conceptions the Garden City movement developed, and it was largely because of Howard's efforts and enthusiasm that these ideals were given a more practical form.[2] In 1903 land was bought at Letchworth in Hertfordshire, some 35 miles (56 km.) to the north of London, as a site for the first Garden City (Fig. 69). A second followed at Welwyn, also in Hertfordshire, in 1919 and, despite rather slow growth, the soundness of these ventures is demonstrated by the fact that both towns are thriving communities at the present day. Designed by Raymond Unwin and Barry Parker on the principles enunciated by Howard, Letchworth was planned to be about 6,000 acres (2,400 ha.) in extent with a population of between 30,000 and 35,000.[3] By 1961 it had not fully attained the intended size, but it was still a substantial settlement with a total area of 4,900 acres (2,000 ha.), including the green belt, and a population of 25,000. Welwyn Garden City also became well established, and after the Second World War the original town provided the nucleus for further planned expansion under the New Towns Act to help in relieving conditions in London.

In the interval between the First and Second World Wars, the relative growth of the total urban area in England and Wales far outstripped that of population, as lower densities of development associated with the semi-detached rather than terrace type of house came securely into vogue.[4] Most of this new development was peripheral to existing settlements, and the mounting public uneasiness and concern in the 1930s about the growing size of cities and towns was reflected in the deliberations and recommendations of the Royal Commission on the Distribution of the Industrial Population which was appointed in 1937. One of the recommendations of the report of this commission (the Barlow Report), for instance, was that a national authority should examine the possibility of moving industry and population from congested areas and consider 'the methods by which such decentralization or dispersal should be encouraged and secured, in the form of garden cities or garden suburbs, satellite towns, trading estates, or by the development of existing small towns or regional centres.'[5] London was singled out for immediate action.

This increasing realization that drastic measures were necessary and, indeed, long overdue to prevent further marked deterioration in the physical environments of cities and large towns, and especially London, was enhanced by war-time privations and the general desire, so prevalent in times of national danger, to tackle social problems with energy and idealism once hostilities are ended. It was against this background that Sir Patrick Abercrombie produced his Greater London Plan in 1944, which provided for the dispersal of about 1¼ million people from the existing built-up area, including some 400,000 persons to eight new satellite towns to be built outside the green belt ring.[6] It was this plan that, for the first time, made positive and detailed recommendations for a group of New Towns in the London Region to assist in solving the problems of the over-crowded metropolis.

In October 1945, shortly after the end of hostilities, the New Towns Committee was appointed 'to consider the general questions of the establishment, development, organization and administration that will arise in the promotion of New Towns in furtherance of a policy of planned decentralization from congested urban areas.' The urgency of the situation was clearly recognized by the members of the committee, and it is to their credit that less than a year later they had produced their final report, as well as two interim ones, covering many aspects of the planning, development and administration of the New Towns.[7] The New Towns Act, embodying many of these recommendations, followed quickly and became law in August 1946.

Within three years, work or planning was in progress on all the London New Town sites to be selected.

Choice of Site

Under the New Towns Act, sites are designated, after a public local inquiry if necessary, by the minister responsible for town and country planning, and a Development Corporation is set up to acquire (and dispose of) land and to plan and implement the development of the town. The first step in this procedure is, of course, to choose a suitable site, and the responsibility for this decision rests with the minister concerned (now the Minister of Housing and Local Government). The finding of a satisfactory open piece of land several thousand acres in extent is no easy matter in a small country like Britain when certain definite requirements have also to be fulfilled.[8] To economize on construction costs, for example, it is desirable that a New Town site should include a large proportion of reasonably level and stable land; it should have satisfactory road and rail access and the possibility of supplying water, drainage and sewerage without undue cost; the locality must be one which industry is likely to find attractive; and lastly, but very important, the town should be located far enough away from the parent city to allow it to maintain a reasonably independent existence, but not so far away as to discourage people from moving out to it willingly and making it difficult, in the case of London, to draw on the special facilities of the metropolis in the field of entertainment, specialized shopping, and certain cultural activities.

Yet, important as these conditions are, perhaps the one that has exerted most influence on the siting of New Towns—and a disproportionate influence in many ways—has been the emphasis placed on the avoidance of 'good' agricultural land. Much of this attitude may have stemmed from the Report of the Committee on Land Utilisation in Rural Areas which was presented in 1942.[9] The majority of the Committee were at pains to emphasize what they considered to be the serious effect of urban encroachment on agriculture and the countryside in general, and they thought it essential that the acreage of agricultural land should be maintained as far as possible and that the better quality land in particular should be preserved from urban development. Consequently, it was not surprising to find that they urged that 'unless there are strong reasons

317

to the contrary, new towns should not be sited on good agricultural land,' and furthermore, that 'in their siting due attention be paid to agricultural considerations.' It is interesting to note that Professor Dennison, in his minority report, took complete exception to these views. Although admitting that the amount of highly fertile land was limited, he maintained that this was not in itself a sufficient reason for giving agriculture a prior claim to it. In his opinion, 'there are, indeed, many more pressing social needs than that of preservation of land for agriculture.'

In practice, however, it was the recommendations of the majority report which were largely accepted in subsequent land-use planning, and in the siting of New Towns the quality or usefulness of the land for agricultural purposes has been a major determinant in the decisions reached. Of the sites suggested by Abercrombie in the Greater London Plan, two—White Waltham in Berkshire and Meopham in Kent—were rejected mainly to avoid valuable farmland (Fig. 69). Not only have whole sites been turned down on agricultural grounds, but there are a number of examples among the eight New Town sites eventually selected where the originally designated acreage was drastically cut in size to minimize the taking of fertile farmland. After public local inquiries had been held to consider objections made to the draft designation orders, 317 acres (127 ha.) were excluded from the area originally proposed at Crawley, 394 acres (159 ha.) at Harlow, 770 acres (310 ha.) at Bracknell and 2,020 acres (810 ha.) at Hemel Hempstead. Most of these reductions were made in order to save agricultural land after representations by the farming community and others with rural interests.[10] More recently, development of a projected 'private enterprise' New Town at Allhallows in Kent was not permitted, very largely on the grounds that it would seriously injure vital agricultural interests in an area of very fertile 'two-crop' land.[11]

The First New Towns

At the end of the war, Greater London presented one of the most urgent problems for land-use planning in Britain. Although it was hoped to establish a green belt around the built-up area and eventually provide beyond it for a large part of the substantial housing needs of the metropolis, it was realized that the immediate post-war demand for housing was so pressing that some housing estates would need to be established by the London County Council within the green belt area as an interim measure. Nevertheless, it was also decided to make a start with the longer term development at a greater distance, and accordingly the first four New Towns to be designated in 1946 and 1947 were all around London.

Ideally, the Ministry of Town and Country Planning would have liked to spread the initial New Town sites evenly around the metropolis, but because of difficulties in finding suitable locations to the west or east this was not possible. In the event, two of these first New Town sites were located to the north of London (Stevenage and Harlow), one to the north-west (Hemel Hempstead), and only one to the south (Crawley) (Fig. 69). The four original New Towns were followed by two more in County Durham, and then, in 1948, two further sites were designated in the London Region—Welwyn

TABLE XV

Population and extent of the London Region New Towns

New Town	Year of designation	Existing population 1960/61	Proposed population*	Designated area 1960/61	Existing urban area 1960/61	Proposed urban area
		number	number	acres	acres	acres
Stevenage	1946	41,800	60,000	6,156	3,015	4,150
Crawley	1947	54,100	56,000	6,047	n.a.	3,535
Hemel Hempstead	1947	51,500	80,000	5,910	4,380	4,980
Harlow	1947	53,500	80,000	6,395	1,750	3,000
Hatfield	1948	20,100	25,000	2,340	1,000	1,400
Welwyn Garden City	1948	34,400	50,000	4,317	2,300	3,500
Basildon	1949	53,700	97,000	7,818	n.a.	4,620
Bracknell	1949	19,900	25,000	1,873	n.a.	1,873
Total London Region New Towns		329,000	473,000	40,856	20,727†	27,058

*As being planned for in 1960/61. A number of these population targets have subsequently been increased.
† Estimated.

Source: New Town Development Corporations. The author is grateful to the New Town Corporations for supplying the information on which these tables are largely based.

Garden City and Hatfield, both in Hertfordshire, again to the north of the metropolis. Basildon and Bracknell, to the east and west respectively, were only designated in 1949 and completed the ring of eight New Towns around London, giving a somewhat better areal distribution of sites (Table XV). It is interesting to note, however, that of the ten possible New Town sites suggested in the Greater London Plan only two, Stevenage and Harlow, were eventually chosen.

At first, the development of these New Towns was a slow and painful process.[12] The proposals often excited strong opposition locally and consequent legal actions resulted in protracted delays before actual development could begin. There were many reasons for these objections by local people, but one of the most important was the fact that land and buildings within the designated area could be compulsorily acquired by the Development Corporation at 1939 values, although there was a 60 per cent supplement allowed for owner-occupiers. This difficulty was subsequently overcome by repeal of the appropriate sections of the Town and Country Planning Acts involved. Even so, technical and administrative problems continued to hinder the progress made in the construction of the New Towns, and, in particular, the national economic crises in 1947 and later imposed severe restrictions on the amount of capital investment that was allowed.

Yet in spite of this unfortunate start, the New Towns began at last to prosper in the 1950s, until, by about 1960, they had not only made considerable headway towards fulfilling their original master plans in many cases, but, financially, were also in a sound position, showing a net surplus on the combined revenue accounts.

Land Use

As in most existing towns, the administrative area of a New Town over which the Development Corporation exercises its jurisdiction (i.e. the designated area) does not usually coincide with the geographical extent of the town, which is expressed by the total or overall urban acreage (Table XV). This distinction is very important, for in most cases it is clearly invalid to equate the designated area of the settlement with its 'urban' land which is usually far less extensive. Such a procedure is particularly irrelevant and dangerous where urban densities are involved as it can lead directly to the calculation of spuriously low density figures for the towns concerned. The contrast is made plain enough by the London Region New Towns in which the aggregate extent of the designated areas amounts to 40,856 acres (16,500 ha.), whereas the combined urban areas being planned total only some 66 per cent of this figure, or 27,058 acres (10,100 ha.), leaving the remaining 13,798 acres (5,550 ha.) undeveloped in rural uses.

Even though this proposed area of urbanization is likely to be increased by new extensions to accommodate larger ultimate populations, the area involved will still represent but a very small proportion of the total urban land in the London Region. This is apparent from the fact that in 1960/61 no more than about 20,727 acres (8,350 ha.) had been developed for all urban uses in the London

TABLE XVI

Main urban land uses and densities in Greater London

Administrative area	Population	Housing (N.R.A.)	Industry	Open space	Education	Four main uses
	'000s			acres		
London A.C.	3,348	31,437	3,743	11,227	1,497	47,904
Metropolitan T.M.As.*	4,647	122,493	9,531	55,558	6,349	193,931
New Towns†	329	9,574	1,908	2,533	1,678	15,693
	'000s			acres p.t.p.		
London A.C.	3,348	9·4	1·1	3·4	0·4	14·3
Metropolitan T.M.As.*	4,647	26·4	2·1	11·9	1·4	41·8
New Towns†	329	29·1	5·8	7·7	5·1	47·7

The figures refer to the situation in about 1951, except those for the New Towns which refer to 1960–61.

* Metropolitan Town Map Areas include the county of Middlesex, Metropolitan Essex, Metropolitan Surrey, West Kent and Thameside Kent.
† Partly estimated.

Source: Ministry of Housing and Local Government and New Town Development Corporations.

New Towns, while the total land used for housing, industry, education and open space alone in the more closely built-up parts of
Greater London[13] in about 1951 amounted to 241,835 acres
(97,500 ha.) (Table XVI).[14] By way of further comparison, the whole
urban area of England and Wales in 1961 extended to about 4 million
acres (16,000 sq. km.), and the aggregate urban area of all New
Towns in England and Wales (and not only those of the London
ring) in this same year was considerably smaller than the current
annual loss of farmland to all urban development, which is averaging
about 35,000 acres (14,000 ha.) These facts perhaps help towards
giving a better perspective to the extent of the areas covered by the
developed portions of New Towns which actually take up much
smaller amounts of land than is frequently assumed.

The total urban area of any settlement is, of course, subdivided
into a number of individual urban uses, and four main urban uses
are conventionally distinguished following the data requirements
specified for Town Map submissions by the Ministry of Housing and
Local Government. These are housing (net residential area), industry, open space and education. The remaining, or residual, urban
uses are many and varied, covering such categories as transport,
commerce (including shopping and business centres), public buildings, government establishments and statutory undertakings. The
proportionate composition of the total urban area proposed for the
London New Towns is shown in Table XVII and is compared with

TABLE XVII

Composition of the proposed urban area in New and existing towns

Urban category	Housing	Industry	Open space	Education	Four main uses	Residual uses
	%	%	%	%	%	%
London New Towns	50·5	9·3	17·4	8·9	86·1	13·9
County Boroughs*	43·9	9·4	19·6	6·1	79·0	21·0
Large Town Map Areas*	44·7	8·9	18·8	6·5	78·9	21·1

* Figures for proposed uses derived from a sample of 79 County Boroughs and
186 large Town Map Areas of over 10,000 population.

Source: New Town Development Corporations and Ministry of Housing and
Local Government.

corresponding proposals for London, the County Boroughs and other large towns of over 10,000 population (large Town Map Areas). The proposed rather than the existing position is taken for the New Towns as the information for this is more complete and the present situation only represents a fairly transitory stage in which the land-use composition of certain New Towns, where development is not in its more advanced stages, may be somewhat distorted. With existing towns the proposals recorded do not differ very materially from the present percentages.[15]

From these data, it is evident that housing is easily the greatest proportionate use of urban land, and in the London Region New Towns it will account for just over one half of the total urban area. This is a distinctly higher percentage than in the other large towns of England and Wales where the proposed proportion lies between 43 and 45 per cent. Open space is the second main use and, at seventeen per cent, takes up a rather smaller proportion of the proposed urban area than in existing large towns. Industry and education cover only a very much smaller percentage of the total area—around nine per cent each.

Taken together, the four main uses in the New Towns will form a greater percentage of the total urban area than in existing towns; and, correspondingly, their residual uses will account for a smaller proportion. This is quite understandable, for much of the residual area in older towns is devoted to land under railways, docks, public and government buildings, and commercial uses and shops, the extent of which may often reflect an important regional orientation. These uses will not usually be so considerably represented in the New Towns, at least in their present phase of development; and the contrast is further emphasized by comparison with the metropolis itself, where national and regional functions reach their highest level of development. Within the administrative county of London the four main urban uses take up only 64 per cent of the total acreage, compared with 86 per cent in the surrounding New Towns, while commercial establishments and offices, railways, waterways and docks make up thirteen per cent, and other urban uses 23 per cent.[16]

Densities

From the acreage figures given in Table XV it is seen that the London New Towns vary appreciably in size, the proposed urban areas ranging from 1,400 acres (570 ha.) in the case of Hatfield to 4,620 acres (1,870 ha.) at Basildon. But the use of acreage figures alone for comparing and contrasting different New Towns, or settlements of any sort, is not always very satisfactory, especially when the populations of the towns concerned differ markedly in size. By referring the acreages to a standard population base, however, comparability of data between settlements can be achieved and contrasts are more readily discernible. For planning purposes, therefore, it is convenient to adopt a measure for the provision of land in terms of acres (or hectares) per thousand population (acres p.t.p.). In effect, this is a density figure, though expressed in a way which is the exact converse of the more usual measure of density in terms of persons per acre. In Table XVIII, land use in the London New Towns is tabulated in this form.

Because most of the New Towns, and especially those in the London Region, have been built over a broadly comparable period of time in the post-war years, they have all naturally tended to adopt the architectural forms and designs current at their time of construction. But this superficial similarity by no means implies that the

TABLE XVIII

Proposed provision of land for the London Region New Towns

New Town	Total urban area	Housing (N.R.A.)	Industry	Open space	Education	Four main uses	Residual uses
				acres p.t.p.			
Basildon	47·6	26·6	4·1	8·0	4·0	42·7	4·9
Bracknell	74·9	39·3	7·0	8·4	4·7	59·4	15·5
Crawley	63·1	31·6	5·4	11·2	6·6	54·8	8·3
Harlow	37·5	21·3	3·7	7·0	3·7	35·7	1·8
Hatfield	56·0	30·4	3·0	5·6	8·0	47·0	9·0
Hemel Hempstead	62·3	29·8	6·5	11·6	7·0	54·9	7·4
Stevenage	69·2	33·2	6·5	13·0	4·2	56·9	12·3
Welwyn Garden City	70·0	30·0	7·0	13·6	4·4	55·0	15·0
Average: London Region	57·2	28·9	5·3	9·9	5·1	49·2	8·0

Source: New Town Development Corporations.

New Towns are all alike in such features as their densities of development, and even a cursory glance at Table XVIII reveals striking differences between the towns in the proposed provisions of land for all uses. The existing provisions for 1960–61 also follow a very similar pattern.

Harlow is planning for the smallest provision of urban land (i.e. the highest density). With only 37·5 acres (15·1 ha.) p.t.p. for all urban uses, it has 20 acres (8·1 ha.) p.t.p. less land than the average London Region New Town and is twice as densely developed as Bracknell (with 74·9 acres, 30·2 ha., p.t.p.), which is the New Town with the greatest overall provision. Similarly, Harlow has a residential allocation of only 21·3 acres (8·6 ha.) p.t.p. whereas Bracknell has one of 39·3 acres (15·9 ha.) p.t.p. This is clearly reflected in the proportion of flats to houses, the lowest percentage of flats being at Bracknell and the highest percentage at Harlow.

Very considerable variations, therefore, are apparent between the extremes of the density spectrum. Closer inspection of the data suggests, however, that the London New Towns fall into two quite distinct density categories. On the one hand, the two New Towns in Essex—Harlow and Basildon—are allocating an appreciably smaller than average provision of land (higher density) for the total urban area and the main urban uses. The remaining towns, on the other hand, are providing for a greater than average provision or lower density of development—with the exception of Hatfield. This particular town is a special case, as a large part of its associated industrial area existed prior to the building of the New Town and lies outside the designated area. The provision of land for industry inside the town is, therefore, the smallest for all the towns in the London ring, and an allocation which was closer to the average would result in the overall urban provision, and that for the four main uses, being raised to slightly above average.

This two-fold density division in the London ring closely reflects the two main density groupings of high and medium density New Towns which have been defined for the whole of Britain.[17] No low density category is recognized, and the reason for this omission (and the adoption of the terminology actually used) is explained by a comparison of the provisions of land being planned for, and achieved, in New Towns with those in existing towns. Consequently, in Table XIX the provisions of land in two of the London Region New Towns—Harlow and Crawley—which are characteristic of the high and medium density categories, respectively, are set out with the corresponding average figures for County Boroughs, the London New Towns as a whole, and other large towns of over 10,000 population in England and Wales. The figures for a group of small towns and villages in East Sussex are also added for comparative purposes. In this instance, the New Town *proposals* are contrasted with the *existing* situation in other settlements as this perhaps allows a better appreciation of the sort of standards which are being envisaged for the New Towns.

TABLE XIX

Provision of land in New and existing towns

Urban category	Total urban area	Housing (N.R.A.)	Industry	Open space	Education	Four main uses	Residual uses
			— acres p.t.p. —				
County Boroughs*	43·3	18·8	3·5	8·1	1·2	31·6	11·7
London New Towns	57·2	28·9	5·3	9·9	5·1	49·2	8·0
Large Town Map Areas*	73·6	31·2	5·7	15·1	2·6	54·6	19·0
Small Settlements in East Sussex*	131·5	83·2	2·8	18·5	6·5	111·0	20·5
Harlow	37·5	21·3	3·7	7·0	3·7	35·7	1·8
Crawley	63·1	31·6	5·4	11·2	6·6	54·8	8·3

* Figures for existing uses derived from a sample of 79 County Boroughs, 186 large Town Map Areas of over 10,000 population, and 39 Small Settlements of under 10,000 population.

Source: New Town Development Corporations and Ministry of Housing and Local Government.

From the comparison it is quite clear that the London New Towns (and, indeed, those throughout the country) can in no sense be regarded as having very open densities of development. Taken as a group, they hold an intermediate position (with 57·2 acres, 23·1 ha., p.t.p.) in the density hierarchy between County Boroughs (with 43·3 acres, 17·5 ha., p.t.p.) and other large towns of over 10,000 population, i.e. large Town Map Areas (with 73·6 acres, 29·8 ha., p.t.p.). Their provision of land for residual uses, however, is lower than that for all the urban categories of cities and large towns, whereas the provision for education is greater.

When the London New Towns are considered on the basis of high and medium density categories, instead of as one undivided group, an even more significant pattern emerges. The New Towns of medium density, represented by Crawley in Table XIX, show a very close similarity in many of their provisions of land with large Town Map Areas. This is particularly noticeable in the figures for the aggregate of the four main uses, although the similarity disguises the fact that, within this total, the greater provision for education in the New Towns tends to be offset, and rather surprisingly, by a smaller provision for open space.

The high density New Town of Harlow shows no similarity at all in its provisions of land with the average large Town Map Area, but instead has a close resemblance to the County Boroughs which are heavily weighted by the densely developed northern industrial towns. Basildon is not so tightly developed as Harlow, especially in its residential area, but its overall provision of urban land is much closer to that of the average County Borough than that of the large Town Map Area.

At the other end of the density scale, Bracknell (Table XVIII) is the most openly developed of the New Towns, particularly in its residential sector. Even so, its provision of land for the total urban area barely exceeds the figure for large Town Map Areas, and falls well short of the overall provision of land which is typical for smaller settlements of under 10,000 population in Lowland Britain.[18] A good example in the London Region of very low densities in this latter category of Small Settlements is provided by data for the small towns and villages of East Sussex (Table XIX).

The figures recorded in Tables XVI and XIX give a quantitative form to the well-known generalization that densities of development tend to decline (i.e. provisions of land increase) from the centre towards the periphery of a large urban agglomeration (cf. Fig. 9). High density development in its more extreme form is found in the London Administrative County with a provision of only fourteen acres (6 ha.) p.t.p. for the four main urban uses. From this lower limit, an outward progression into the adjacent metropolitan areas of Middlesex, Surrey, Kent, and Essex shows a threefold rise in the provision of land to 42 acres (17 ha.) p.t.p. for these same uses. The surrounding New Towns on the outer edge of the green belt show a further, though far more limited increase in existing land provision—or lowering of density—to a figure of 48 acres (19 ha.) p.t.p. which, in most cases, is probably not so very different from older towns of similar population in the same general area. Finally, in the small towns and villages in the predominantly rural areas of East Sussex the lower limits of density are reached with a provision for the main urban uses of as much as 111 acres (45 ha.) p.t.p.

From this analysis, it should now be obvious why no New Town can be classified as a low density settlement. Most of the New Towns composing the London ring are planning for, and already have, a moderate provision of land, or medium density, which approximates to that of existing towns of a similar size. The remainder are being more tightly developed and will have a low provision of land, or high density, which is more akin to that of County Boroughs where space standards are normally considered to be very inadequate. Consequently, the widespread belief that New Towns in general are wasteful of space and have alienated an unwarranted amount of agricultural and rural land for their development compared with existing towns is shown to be completely fallacious. Indeed, the question should not be whether New Towns are of too low a density compared with existing settlements; but rather it should be one of whether their densities are not too high at a time when, in many technically advanced countries, a greater emphasis is being placed on more spacious living conditions.

Trends in Development

The mistaken idea about the excessive openness of New Towns appears to stem in part from the final report of the New Towns Committee (Reith Report) in 1946 which made recommendations on the planning principles and standards to be adopted.[19] It has often been too readily assumed that these proposals were largely carried into effect in subsequent New Town development when, in fact, this was not so.

The building of the first New Towns in the London Region followed very closely upon the publication of the Reith Report, but it was soon evident that the space standards being applied were often significantly less generous than those suggested by the New Towns Committee. From Table XX it can be seen that, in the early master plans, the allocation of land for the total urban area in five London

New Towns amounted to about ten acres (4 ha.) p.t.p. less than the figure recommended. The main reduction was with the provision for housing. As construction of these towns progressed, their master plans were modified to take account of such circumstances as upward revisions in the ultimate population to be accommodated. If, then, the average proposals of the present master plans (as in use in 1960–1) for the same five London Region towns are contrasted with the earlier versions, it is apparent that a general reduction in space standards has taken place over the period amounting to thirteen acres (5 ha.) p.t.p. for the whole urban area (Table XX).[20]

Since 1949 no further New Towns have been designated in the London Region, but the trend towards increasing densities is emphasized by the draft land-use proposals for two projected New

TABLE XX

Trends in New Town space standards

Proposals of:	Date	Designated area	Total urban area	Housing (N.R.A.)	Industry	Open space	Education	Four main uses	Residual uses
						acres p.t.p.			
New Towns Committee	1946	194·0	83·0	40·0	10·0	10·0+	5·0	65·0	18·0
Early Master Plans (5 London Region Towns)*	c.1948–9	106·9	71·7	31·3	8·5	12·0†	5·7	57·5	14·2
Present Master Plans (5 London Region Towns)*	c. 1960–1	88·4	58·8	28·7	5·7	11·0	5·2	50·6	8·2
Hook	1961	75·3	65·0	21·6‡	5·7	16·9	4·6‡	48·8	16·2
Allhallows	1955	60·0	34·9	18·4	1·6§	n.a.	2·5	n.a.	n.a.

* Average of Crawley, Harlow, Hemel Hempstead, Stevenage and Welwyn Garden City.

† Excluding allotments.

‡ Partly estimated. If existing development is excluded, the figure for housing would be about 17·1 acres p.t.p. The figure for education includes some minor residual uses.

§ Excluding nearby oil refinery.

Towns in this period which were not eventually proceeded with—Hook in Hampshire and Allhallows in Kent (which was to be a private enterprise venture rather than a government undertaking under the New Towns Act). Reduced land allocations are particularly noticeable for the residential areas of these two towns (Table XX).

This general decline in space standards, and especially those for housing areas, in the New Towns is a reflection of government policies and architectural fashion since the early post-war years which have put increasing stress on higher densities in all new development.[21] Many factors have contributed to this attitude, which began with the economic crises of the early post-war years and the consequent pressures for economy in land-use planning proposals and the 'saving' of agricultural land. Nowadays, the main factors thought to favour the use of higher urban densities are the desire to achieve so-called 'urbanity', the shortage and high price of building land, and the scale of agricultural land losses. Whether these are legitimate reasons for the restrictions in density that are being encouraged is altogether another matter: many authorities would think not.

As the London New Towns have been under construction for about fifteen years they have all moved out of their early stages of development and, in some cases, are now very substantial settlements indeed. The original intention was that, as the building of the New Towns approached completion, the Development Corporations would be wound up and the appropriate local authorities would take over the administration. However, the government subsequently decided that this plan should be modified, so that a period of consolidation will now be allowed between the end of the major development phase and the time when the towns can be considered to be fully grown.[22] During this time ownership and management of the land and properties of the original Development Corporations are to be vested in another body which is independent of the local authority—the Commission for the New Towns set up in 1961 under the New Towns Act of 1959. Two of the London New Towns—Crawley and Hemel Hempstead—have already been transferred to its jurisdiction (in 1962).

It should not be assumed from this, however, that the London New Towns already existing are all necessarily showing, or are likely to show, a slackening off in their rates of growth. The designated areas of those not yet transferred to the Commission are not immutable, and when circumstances demand it they can be readily extended. Bracknell, for instance, had its designated area increased by 1,080 acres (440 ha.) in 1961 and its population target raised to 40,000: the Development Corporations of Stevenage and Harlow have also been asked by the Minister of Housing and Local Government to examine the possibility of increasing their target populations by some 60,000 or more, which would most probably involve extensions in the designated areas.

Since 1960, the building of further New Towns, as well as the extension of existing sites, seems to have come back into government favour after a lapse of a decade, but all the latest New Towns to be designated have so far been in the provinces or in Scotland. The Minister of Housing and Local Government has stated, however, that a regional study of planning problems and policies in southeast England, to be published in 1964, will examine the need for a second generation of New Towns (and expanded towns) in the London Region.[23] If and when such New Towns around London, or in other parts of the country for that matter, come to be planned and built they will provide the opportunity for more compact and well designed layouts than can readily be obtained in ordinary suburban development which is peripheral to large urban centres. But compactness does not necessarily imply a high density, and the long-term trend towards a reduction in New Town space standards must be halted and even reversed if the legitimate demands for privacy, amenity, lack of congestion, and a healthy environment by the affluent society of the 1960s are to be adequately met.

References

1. The third New Town in Scotland—Glenrothes—is also to take over-spill population now that the modern colliery nearby, in association with which the town was built, is having to be closed down because of unforeseen technical difficulties.

2. Ebenezer Howard, *Garden Cities of Tomorrow* (1902).

3. J. P. Reynolds, 'The Plan', Chapter 6 in *Land Use in an Urban Environment* (1961), Fig. 3.

4. R. H. Best, *The Major Land Uses of Great Britain* (1959), Fig. 6.

5. *Report of the Royal Commission on the Distribution of the Industrial Population* (*Barlow Report*), Cmd. 6153 (H.M.S.O., 1940).

6. P. Abercrombie, *Greater London Plan 1944* (H.M.S.O., 1945).

7. Ministry of Town and Country Planning and Department of Health for Scotland, *Final Report of the New Towns Committee (Reith Report)*, Cmd. 6876 (H.M.S.O., 1946).

8. Ministry of Local Government and Planning, *Town and Country Planning 1943–1951*, Cmd. 8204 (H.M.S.O., 1951), 125.

9. Ministry of Works and Planning, *Report of the Committee on Land Utilisation in Rural Areas (Scott Report)*, Cmd. 6378 (H.M.S.O., 1942).

10. Cmd. 8204, *op. cit.*, 129.

11. W. E. Adams, 'A private enterprise New Town', *Town Planning Review*, 28 (1957), 181–90.

12. Cmd. 8204, *op. cit.*, 126–9. See also: L. Rodwin, *The British New Towns Policy* (1956).

13. Comprising the County of Middlesex and the four metropolitan Town Map Areas of Metropolitan Essex, Metropolitan Surrey, West Kent and Thameside Kent, in addition to the London Administrative County.

14. *Report of the Ministry of Housing and Local Government 1958*, Cmd. 737 (H.M.S.O., 1959), Appendix XXII, 210–24.

15. R. H. Best and J. T. Coppock, *The Changing Use of Land in Britain* (1962), Chapter 7.

16. *Ibid.*

17. For a fully detailed account referring to all the British New Towns see: R. H. Best, *Land for New Towns* (1964).

18. Best and Coppock, *op. cit.*, Chapters 6 and 7.

19. Cmd. 6876, *op. cit.*, paras. 29–39.

20. Best, *op. cit.*, Chapter 4.

21. Ministry of Housing and Local Government, *The Density of Residential Areas* (H.M.S.O., 1952). For a more recent statement of this policy from the same source see: *Residential Areas—Higher Densities* (H.M.S.O., 1962).

22. Central Office of Information, *The New Towns of Britain* (H.M.S.O., 1961).

23. Ministry of Housing and Local Government, *London. Employment: Housing: Land*, Cmd. 1952 (H.M.S.O., 1963).

14

Parks and Parkland

*

HUGH C. PRINCE

For centuries foreign visitors have praised England's spacious parks and park-like open spaces, much as English travellers have admired the broad, tree-lined boulevards and parkways in foreign capitals. A German emissary to the court of Queen Elizabeth expressed his astonishment at the great profusion of parks, and two centuries later another German described the whole country as 'adorned with parks.'[1] In the early nineteenth century Prince Pückler-Muskau reported that 'they swarm whichever way you turn your steps,' and thirty years ago a young Danish architect, Steen Eiler Rasmussen, devoted more than a quarter of his *London: the Unique City* to a description of parks and open spaces.[2]

London Parks

Londoners are apt to take parks for granted, or regard them as recapturing, in the words of the *Economist*, 'some of the seething natural life of the forest and marshes out of which they, like the rest of London, have been created.'[3] By contrast with the evident artificiality of closely packed buildings, parks in the midst of London have all the appearance of being natural. It is not difficult to suppose that their varied and irregular outlines, the informal groupings of trees, the stretches of hard-worn turf, the winding streams and lakes are vestiges of a primitive landscape enveloped by buildings, 'a bit of the *native* country, surprised and fairly taken prisoner by the outstretched arms of this giant of modern cities.'[4] Such a view will deceive no one who conscientiously studies their history.

333

During the past 300 years, they have been formed and managed, unlike public gardens in continental cities, 'with a broad and noble feeling for natural beauty.' At the beginning of the eighteenth century, turning away from the stiff formality of palace gardens, improvers began to copy natural scenery. William Kent, according to Horace Walpole, 'followed Nature, and imitated her so happily, that he began to think all her works were equally proper for imitation. In Kensington garden he planted dead trees, to give a greater air of truth to the scene—but he was soon laughed out of this excess.'[5]

Single trees which appear entirely natural have often been planted and jealously preserved as foils to particular buildings, not only in parks but in architectural settings such as Parliament Square, the churchyard of St Margaret's, Westminster, and along the Thames embankment between Westminster and Blackfriars bridges. Their naturalistic dispositions have been contrived with as much care as the formal sunken garden at the side of Kensington Palace. Every square, burial ground, heath or metropolitan common has also been designed or painstakingly remodelled in an informal manner.

Each open space possesses a distinctive character but almost all are park-like in appearance. Indeed, Clapham Common, a metropolitan common, is more closely planted with ornamental trees than the open football fields of Regent's Park, and one of London's most grotesque folly towers, Severndroog Castle, is situated in the Shooter's Hill woods which are neither commons nor royal parks. On the other hand, few Londoners would consider Hampstead Heath a park. To a casual observer, 'it is a piece of uncultivated land which—for some unexplained reason—still lies there untouched in spite of the development of the town. He lives in the happy delusion that it is a no-man's-land where everybody can do as he likes.'[6] But Rasmussen emphasizes that it is a public park in all but name, administered by the London County Council's Parks Committee, superintended by park keepers. Its trees and shrubs have been planted and thinned to enhance the beauty of the scenery and to conceal buildings which might spoil its views.

In the central districts of London most parks and gardens are open to the public. The largest private enclosures, Buckingham Palace Gardens and parts of the grounds of Lambeth and Fulham palaces, serve occasional functions of church and state. The public are admitted to the secluded gardens of the Temple, to the fields of Lincoln's and Gray's Inns and also to a number of small courts, quadrangles and squares in Bloomsbury and the West End. But by far the largest area of open space in central London lies in five royal parks: St James's Park containing 93 acres (38 ha.), the Green Park 53 acres (21 ha.), Hyde Park 361 acres (146 ha.), Kensington Gardens 275 acres (111 ha.) and Regent's Park 472 acres (190 ha.). Much of the land they now occupy was acquired by Henry VIII from the estate of the dissolved Abbey of Westminster. The Tudor monarchs kept them as private pleasure grounds and hunting preserves on the outskirts of London but they were opened to the public by James I, Charles II and the Prince Regent. They originated as public parks at about the time buildings reached their boundaries. They were laid out in their present form no earlier than the streets and terraces which overlook them. In the broadest sense, they have been created as integral parts of the urban scene.

The designers of the royal parks profoundly changed the character both of London and of the surrounding countryside. John Rose (1629–77), George London (d. 1713), Henry Wise (1653–1738), Charles Bridgman (d. 1738), William Kent (1684–1748) and Lancelot Brown (1716–83), the leading gardeners of their periods, were employed by the Crown in designing and improving the royal parks. Charles II's gardeners, André Mollet and John Rose, were responsible for designing and carrying out formal schemes in the French style at St James's and Greenwich parks. With the support of powerful patrons and friendly writers, such as the Earl of Essex and John Evelyn, they dominated fashions in gardening during the Restoration period. In succeeding generations the prevailing tastes were dictated to a large extent by royal gardeners. The Mall in St James's Park, the Spanish chestnuts at Greenwich, the terraces, avenues and canal at Hampton Court, the sunken garden and ha-ha in Kensington Gardens, the Serpentine and Rotten Row in Hyde Park, the 'dark verdancy' of the Green Park, and the sweeping grass in Regent's Park have been slavishly imitated at different times.[7]

The royal gardeners occupied positions of great respect in eighteenth-century society: their advice was sought by wealthy patrons, they dined with the highest nobility, and, above all, their work was intelligently discussed in books and journals. 'Enough has been done,' wrote Horace Walpole in 1780, 'to establish such a school of landscape as cannot be found on the rest of the globe.'[8] Their prestige lacked only the accolade of knighthood, liberally conferred on botanists, architects and painters but withheld from the most eminent gardeners. After the death of Lancelot Brown in 1783 no other royal gardener exerted such a wide influence on contemporary taste. Humphry Repton (1752–1818), the foremost designer of the Regency period, did not landscape London's royal parks, although as early as 1797 the Prince Regent favoured him with a commission at Brighton.[9]

Many features of the open spaces in outer London have been copied from royal parks in the central districts. Kensington Gardens' round pond is reproduced on Blackheath and at Whitestone Pond on Hampstead Heath. Bandstands and rustic lodges reappear at Peckham Rye and Clissold Park. Sycamores, planes and daffodils are shared by the Green Park and by Kennington and Victoria parks. Dense rhododendrons and limes screen tennis courts and rose gardens. Spreading chestnut trees cast their shade over cricket pavilions and bowling greens.

What gives parks and open spaces in inner London a special value is not only their appearance, nor the unexpected vistas of the City and Westminster seen from distant spots such as the Serpentine bridge or the top of Observatory Hill in Greenwich Park, nor the intricate skyline of Whitehall viewed at close range from St James's Park, but the avenues they provide leading from central districts to the outskirts. A two-mile (3·2 km.) walk across St James's Park, the Green Park, Hyde Park and Kensington Gardens separates Downing Street from Kensington Palace. From there it is a short step through tree-lined streets to Holland Park. Beyond Shepherd's Bush lies Wormwood Scrubs and beyond that the golf courses of Perivale and Greenford. Another green way leads from the West End shopping centres around Oxford Circus up Portland Place through Regent's Park to Primrose Hill whose spacious lawns reach north to the Hampstead boundary. Hampstead Heath, Kenwood and Bishop's Wood extend to Finchley, whence the wooded ridges of Enfield Chase can be seen in the distance. On the south bank of the Thames, overlooking dockland and the Isle of Dogs, is Greenwich Park. From the adjoining tract of Blackheath along Shooter's Hill Road is a short walk to Woolwich and Eltham commons and the wooded summit of Shooter's Hill. London has no formal parkways and the Mall is its only straight tree-lined boulevard, but chains of parks, woods and heaths introduce casually a rural aspect to central parts of the town.

Parks in central London also provide many neighbouring buildings with extensive views. Carlton House Terrace and the ministries in Whitehall command views of St James's Park; the embassies in Palace Gardens overlook Kensington Gardens; houses in Park Lane and Bayswater face Hyde Park; and houses in Croom's Hill look into Greenwich Park. The value of parkland scenery to surrounding buildings has been exploited to the full in Regent's Park, a park designed by John Nash expressly for the benefit of his terraces and villas.

Parks, squares, woods, heaths, commons, cemeteries, football grounds, running tracks, cricket fields, bowling greens and tennis courts occupy about thirteen per cent of the surface in the Central Area (Chapter 7) and no less than fifteen per cent of the area of the county of London.[10] In appearance they reflect the dominant informal style of the royal parks. Most have been created or remodelled since buildings reached their edges and none are of great antiquity. The oldest royal park in London, enclosed in 1433, is Greenwich Park. Above all, they have grown up with the town. They belong to London, not as secret recesses, but as grand open vistas through trees, across grass and over water.

Parks on the Outskirts of London

The peace and solitude of the Green Park in the early morning, a flock of sheep placidly grazing in Hyde Park in summer sunshine, white clouds reflected in the Serpentine, the high open hills of Hampstead on a windy afternoon are fleeting reminders of the countryside. But the open spaces of inner London include no farms. It is not until the River Brent is crossed and the ducal meadows of Syon Park are entered that a herd of cattle may be seen in a yard littered with straw.

The parks and open spaces of outer London, while owing much to the central royal parks and their designers, are more spacious, less restrained and altogether more rural in aspect. The palatial grounds of Hampton Court and the closely planted Royal Botanic Gardens at Kew resemble the stately parks in Westminster, but another royal park at Bushy has the appearance of a large, well-ordered home farm with high hedgerows and deep meadows. The Tudor palaces at Nonsuch and Oatlands have disappeared and most of their grounds have been covered with suburban dwellings.

Richmond Park, a hunting preserve enclosed in 1637 by Charles I, is the largest royal park near London, containing 2,358 acres (955 ha.). Both Charles Bridgman and Lancelot Brown improved its landscape and its now venerable oak plantations once made a contribution to the nation's timber supplies. It still possesses large herds of red and fallow deer, not penned in a small paddock, as at Greenwich Park, but ranging freely over broad expanses of grass and bracken. The attractions of the park are its wildness, its remoteness and its distant horizon. Its rolling surface, diversified by rabbit burrows and reed patches, is unmown and unmarked by gravel paths. In the centre are the Pen Ponds, sheets of clear water that seem miles from anywhere, and from the top of nearby hills extensive prospects spread in all directions.

The view from Richmond Hill embraces a noble sweep of silver Thames, prettily adorned with some of the earliest and most delightful essays in landscape gardening (Fig. 70). It recalls 'the peculiar happiness' felt by R. S. Cambridge in 1755, to see 'regularity banished, prospects opened, the country called in, nature rescued and improved, and art decently concealing herself under her own perfections.'[11] A few early masterpieces have vanished from the scene and many have been reduced in size. But those that remain have lost none of their power to evoke the opposing moods of gaiety and melancholy sought by their creators.

Two street names, Pope's Grove and Grotto Road, and a rock-work subway, are all that survive of the poet's garden at Twickenham. At the time of its creation, between 1718 and 1744, it was perhaps the most famous garden in England. Horace Walpole describes it as 'a singular effort of art and taste to impress so much variety and scenery on a spot of five acres (2 ha.). The passing through the gloom from the grotto to the opening day, the retiring and again assembling shades, the dusky groves, the larger lawn and the solemnity of the termination at the cypresses that lead up to his mother's tomb, are managed with exquisite judgment.'[12] Of all his works Pope was most proud of his grotto

> '. . . *where Thames' translucent wave*
> *Shines a broad mirror through the shadowy cave,*
> *When lingering drops from mineral roofs distil*
> *And pointed crystals break the sparkling rill.*'[13]

It became a museum of shells, stalactites, flints, marble, alabaster and other rocks presented to him by friends and collectors. For his

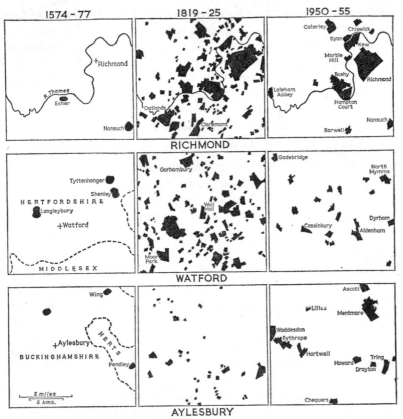

FIG. 70   Parkland in three localities compared 1574–1955
The area of parks is indicated in black.
Based on Christopher Saxton, A. Bryant and C. & J. Greenwood, and
Ordnance Survey.

villa a portico was designed by William Kent; for the garden he
received grafts of choice pears from Philip Miller, small urns for the
laurel circus from the Prince of Wales and lime trees from his friend
Lord Bathurst.[14]

Before he moved to Twickenham Pope helped Lord Burlington to
plan the layout of the gardens for the villa at Chiswick. In the
autumn of 1715, in an epistle to Lord Burlington, the poet writes of
the Chiswick bowers 'where Pope unloads the boughs,' 'while you,
my Lord, bid stately piles ascend.' For twenty years, while fresh
additions were made to the gardens, the poet addressed neighbourly

advice and commendation to his patron at Chiswick. But credit for the authorship of the finished work belongs neither to Pope nor to Burlington. The lines of the first *allées* and plantations were drawn by Charles Bridgman, and the forms of the exedra, its statuary, the Ionic temple, obelisk, serpentine water, cascade and grotto were sketched by William Kent. Kent is largely responsible for the informal arrangement of garden architecture, trees, grass and water, composing an elysium of small dimensions. It is his achievement that inspired Pope to write in 1735:

> '*To build, to plant, whatever you intend,*
> *To rear the column, or the arch to bend,*
> *To swell the terrace, or to sink the grot;*
> *In all let Nature never be forgot.*'[15]

Opposite Richmond, half a mile (0·8 km.) from his Twickenham villa, Pope collaborated with Lord Bathurst and Charles Bridgman to lay out the gardens of Marble Hill for Henrietta Howard. In 1724 Mrs Campbell wrote to ask: 'How does my good Howard do? Methinks I long to hear from you; but I suppose you are up to the ears in bricks and mortar, and talk of frieze and cornice like any little woman.'[16] The house was completed five years later; its grounds, planned by the poet and the royal gardener, planted by Lord Bathurst, are the perfect foil to the box-like house. Gay and informal, they are seen at their best at the edge of the river.

The close circle of artists and patrons who created three elysiums at Twickenham, Chiswick and Marble Hill also contributed to changing the face of surrounding districts. Pope and Bridgman collaborated with Bathurst in making a serpentine lake, raising cascades and planting in the grounds of Richings at Iver in Buckinghamshire. In the same locality, at Iver Heath, Burlington designed a house which has now disappeared.[17] Between 1719 and 1720 Bridgman laid out the grounds of Carshalton House. The decaying forms of a spacious lake, an intricate grotto, a curious water house and fanciful entrance gates are still to be seen there.[18]

William Kent added picturesque embellishments to the palaces of Queen Caroline and Frederick, Prince of Wales. At Carlton House and Kensington he added to the work of Bridgman; in 1732 at Hampton Court he designed a gothick entrance to the Fountain Court, and in 1735 at Kew he built Merlin's Cave, later demolished by Brown. In Gunnersbury Park, later altered by the Rothschilds, he is supposed to have designed some of the castellated sham medieval walls which still stand.[19] At Claremont for Thomas Pelham, Duke of Newcastle, he took up the theme of Vanburgh's gothick belvedere, adding a lake with an island and a grotto. At Esher Place for the duke's younger brother, Henry Pelham, he built a gothick gate house and added wings to the house. Nothing but these rustic architectural fragments now remain in 'Esher's peaceful grove, where Kent and Nature vie for Pelham's love.'[20]

In 1735, beyond Esher and Claremont, at Woburn Farm, Philip Southcote made a pretty landscape of his possessions, creating the first *ferme ornée* in England.[21] It was a pleasant arcadian landscape of meadows, shrubberies and flower beds through which a gravel path wound tortuously. Temples and ruins crowned the highest land, and a picturesque garden near the house was designed by Kent. Again, nothing remains but a fragment of a rustic brick arch beside the entrance drive.

The fashion set by the early essays of Pope, Burlington, Bathurst, Bridgman and Kent was imitated and developed in many other gardens on the outskirts of London. While Kent planted a peaceful grove at Esher Place and Philip Southcote ornamented Woburn Farm, Charles Hamilton at Painshill put into practice Pope's dictum that 'all gardening is landscape painting.'[22] He modelled a landscape in the likeness of paintings by Salvator Rosa and Gaspar Poussin, creating 'that kind of Alpine scene, composed almost wholly of pines and firs, and a few birch, and such trees as assimilate with a savage and mountainous country.'[23] Among the trees, high above the River Mole, he cut cliffs, formed an artificial lake, raised an island, and not only furnished a grotto with Italian rocks but employed a hermit to dwell in it. In this setting Batty Langley built a gothick tent, a flimsy octagon of wood and plaster open on all sides, now sadly decayed. Painshill is no longer 'great, foreign and rude'; it is hemmed in by suburban gardens, its exotic pines are as common as weeds in the surrounding sand country; familiarity has robbed it of its awe-inspiring power and age has softened its air of wildness.

In 1750 Horace Walpole wrote: 'I am almost as fond of the Shara-waggi, or Chinese want of symmetry, in buildings, as in grounds or gardens.'[24] Vanbrugh, Gibbs, Kent and Batty Langley introduced much rustic gothick architecture into their landscapes before Walpole planned his make-believe castle at Strawberry Hill, Twickenham. At the same time, the district around Twickenham, extending south and west to Esher and Chertsey, was endowed with an exceptionally large number of sham medieval gate houses, temples, towers, pavilions and eyecatchers. Surrey took the lead in the variety and extravagance of its follies and sham ruins. Kew possesses the most audacious garden buildings of this period, designed in 1761 by William Chambers. His Chinese pagoda and ruined arch still stand, but a mosque and alhambra have been swept away.

In the second half of the eighteenth century rude and grotesquely ornamented landscapes were smoothed and polished by Lancelot Brown. At Kew he levelled Merlin's Cave and 'transform'd to lawn what late was fairy-land'.[25] At Claremont he treated Kent's work with restraint, and at Hampton Court he preserved a formal layout. At Fulham, Putney, Wandsworth, Wimbledon, Brentford, Hanwell and Richmond he laid out elegant and spacious parks.[26] At Syon, for the Duke of Northumberland, he created one of the most beautiful landscape gardens remaining near London, its lawns sweeping down to the Thames, unconfined by walls and hedges, yet amply planted with rare trees. By contrast, the extensive park at Osterley is bare and desolate. The house, modernized at the same time and by the same architect as Syon, stands on a flat unimproved plain. Without a landscape by Brown it looks unnatural.

Since 1815 no important new parks have been created and London's suburbs have spread relentlessly over many early landscape gardens. Near where Arnos Grove tube station now rises above streets of semi-detached houses, stood a house filled with Italian treasures. Around it spread a picturesque park fashioned in the image of a Tuscan landscape. In 1829 it enjoyed fine prospects across open country, 'the rural character of the scenery scarcely interrupted by any building except the majestic dome of St Paul's cathedral, which, mingling with the grey of the horizon, climbs into notice above the utmost rise of a distant hill.'[27] East of London, Wanstead has lost not only the earliest major Palladian building in England but also most of its park. The remaining avenues, public boating pond and Grecian temple are sad reminders of its past grandeur. Crowding upon it from all sides are the City of London cemetery, golf course and the Victorian streets of Leytonstone and West Ham. Above it, drifts a pall of smoke from Thameside factories and Becton gasworks. Some former private parks in London have suffered less than Wanstead under public management. The London County Council have succeeded in making Kenwood, Holland Park, and Marble Hill attractive popular resorts without destroying their character as landscape gardens.

The most obvious difference between parks in central London and those in outer districts is that the former are, in the fullest sense, public open spaces, whereas the latter are secluded, hidden from main thoroughfares, and some of them are closed to the public. A state procession, a ceremonial occasion, staged in the Mall, against the background of St James's Park, would be out of place in the shaded avenues of Hampton Court, nor would Kew Gardens provide a public meeting place as inviting as Speakers' Corner in Hyde Park. Fairgrounds and fireworks enhance the pleasures of Battersea Park; they would be unseemly in Syon or Richmond parks.

Another distinction is that open spaces in the central districts are overlooked by London's most fashionable residences, such as those of Park Lane, Knightsbridge, the terraces around Regent's Park and the villas facing Wimbledon Common, whereas parks in outer London are bordered by comparatively modest houses. The presence of parks adds grace to well-proportioned houses in the Mall at Chiswick or in Syon and Montpelier rows at Twickenham, but many undistinguished suburban houses defiantly turn their backs towards parks such as Chiswick.

A difference between parks on the outskirts of London and those beyond is that the former have neither farms nor extensive stands of merchantable timber. Most possess well-appointed stables and fine greenhouses, but few keep livestock or grow crops. No cows graze at Chiswick, nor is wheat grown at Marble Hill. They are ornamental gardens, suburban playgrounds for men-about-town, laid out by members of London society. Their charms are rustic rather than rural.

Parkland beyond London

Beyond the suburbs of London numerous plantations of exotic trees, neat lines of avenues, stretches of ornamental water, and, above all, enclosed areas of parks, whose walls, belt plantations and entrance lodges border the main roads out of the metropolis for several miles, offer glimpses of park scenery. A zone which includes both residential areas remote from London and large tracts of parkland extends at least fifteen miles (24 km.) in all directions beyond the boundary of the administrative county of London. It includes most of the green belt.

Until 1920, parks occupied a higher proportion of the surface area in this zone than of any other district in England. Since then, in Middlesex the acreage of parkland has been halved. Building contractors have taken the largest amount, but golf courses have acquired almost as much. Areas of former parkland now occupied by golf courses and by the grounds of institutions such as hospitals, schools and training colleges, retain a park-like appearance.

Of the parks that survive, some originated as medieval deer parks. They are particularly numerous at the edges of former royal hunting preserves in Enfield Chase and Epping Forest. Christopher Saxton's maps of 1574–77 represent them as enclosures surrounded by high wooden palings (Fig. 71). Wooden palings have long disappeared

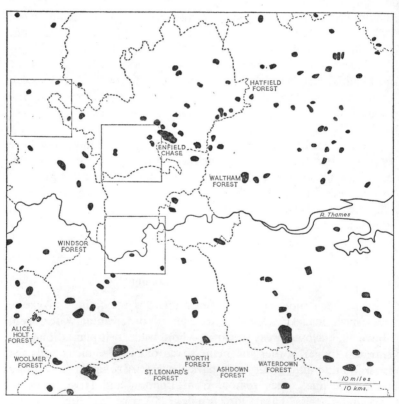

Fig. 71   Parkland in and around London 1574–7
The position of selected localities is shown in outline.
Based on Christopher Saxton.

344

and few parks are now stocked with deer, but old oaks in parks such as Hatfield and Theobalds still bear marks of browsing.

A majority of parks, including some that originated as preserves for deer, were laid out as extensive gardens for the country residences of statesmen, merchants, bankers and officers of the crown who had to live near London. One of the earliest is the royal park at Windsor, but in Tudor times parks at this distance from London were still more than half a day's journey from the court. Between 1563 and 1586 Sir Nicholas Bacon built a substantial house high on the hill at Gorhambury near St Albans, and Francis Bacon who succeeded to the estate in 1601 created the Pondyards, elaborate water gardens, adorned with islands, grottos and a banqueting house.[28] Three broad avenues planted with elm, beech, chestnut, hornbeam and Spanish ash led up the hill from the Pondyards to the house, where another garden occupied thirteen acres (5·2 ha.). Francis Bacon describes in detail his plans for arranging a princely garden, and his correspondence with Robert Cecil, first Earl of Salisbury, expresses interest in the making of the Vineyard at Hatfield, a pleasaunce on the banks of the River Lea, formed at the same period as the gardens at Gorhambury.[29] At Theobalds James I was engaged on a similar project. Adjoining his palace he built an ostentatious terraced garden, divided into courtyards, profusely decorated with statues and clipped shrubs.[30] In 1614 at Moor Park near Ricksmansworth the Countess of Bedford began to construct three lofty terraces, 'with very great care, excellent contrivance, and much cost.' Sir William Temple who saw the place fully matured described it as 'the perfectest figure of a garden' that he had ever seen.[31] The house was built on rising ground half-way up the sandy north-facing slope of the Colne valley. On this inhospitable site a luxuriant garden of eight acres was created. Below it lay the remains of Cardinal Wolsey's residence; above was a much neglected, wild park.

While new beginnings were being made in the layout of gardens, many ancient deer parks fell into disrepair or were devastated during the Civil War. In the second half of the seventeenth century a number of such parks were acquired by wealthy Londoners, some fleeing from smoke, filth and plague, others displaced by the great fire of 1666. The Restoration gardens of Middlesex and Surrey copied the French style of London's royal parks at St James's and Greenwich. In planting they followed the recommendations of John and George Evelyn of Wotton and Deptford, and of the Capel brothers of Kew and Cassiobury near Watford.[32] One of the show-places of the period was created by the Evelyn brothers for their neighbour, the Earl of Arundel, at Aldbury in Surrey.

The fashion set by Londoners for terraces, avenues, canals, rectilinear plantations and neatly clipped yew hedges was an incongruous novelty in the countryside in 1666, but in 1725 Daniel Defoe describes Middlesex completely transformed:

'Let it suffice to tell you that there's an incredible number of fine houses built in all these towns, within these few years, and that England never had such a glorious show to make in the world before.'[33]

In Surrey he observes Carshalton, 'crouded with fine houses of the citizens of London; some of which are built with such a profusion of expence, that they look rather like seats of the nobility, than the country houses of citizens and merchants.'[34] A few miles away he reports:

'we see nothing of business in the whole conversation of Epsom; even the men of business, who are really so when in London; whether it be at the Exchange, the Alley, or the Treasury-Offices, and the Court; yet here they look as if they had left all their London thoughts behind them, and had separated themselves to mirth and good company; as if they come hither to unbend the bow of the mind, and to give themselves a loose to their innocent pleasures.'[35]

By the beginning of the eighteenth century, what was then called a London Box, a square red-brick residence set in 40 acres (16 ha.) or more of ground, had become a familiar sight in London's countryside. In 1757 *The Cit's Country Box* is celebrated in verse by Roger Lloyd:

> '*Some three or four mile out of town,*
> (*An hour's ride will bring you down,*)
> *He fixes on his choice abode,*
> *Not half a furlong from the road:*
> *And so convenient does it lay,*
> *The stages pass it every day:*
> *And then so snug, so mightly pretty,*
> *To have an house so near the city!*'[36]

Lloyd seriously underestimated the distance his contemporaries travelled to and from their homes. Thirty years earlier Defoe counted no fewer than 3,000 Londoners' residences in Middlesex alone, 'not reckoning any of the towns within three miles (4·8 km.) of London.'[37] In 1757 some citizens of London lived as far afield as Oxfordshire and Hampshire, and by 1821 Cobbett noted that London stock-jobbers had reached the south coast and had settled in the neighbourhoods of Brighton, Worthing, Bognor, Cheltenham, Bath, Tunbridge Wells, Ramsgate and Margate.[38]

Since the early eighteenth century most parks within fifteen miles (24 km.) of the boundary of London have been changed beyond recognition. Few have been occupied by one family for more than two generations and few have been occupied by large landed proprietors. The conservative pressures of family tradition and local ties have been weak. In Hertfordshire, for example, the Cecils alone have occupied their seat continuously since 1560 and the landscape of Hatfield has changed much less than that of most parks in the county. Frequent changes of ownership have generally been accompanied by repeated alterations in the layout of parks. At Claremont, the grounds formed by Vanbrugh and Kent were remodelled and the house rebuilt by Brown when Lord Clive moved there; Bacon's gardens at Gorhambury were converted into a landscape garden by the Grimstons; Humphry Repton swept away most of the Restoration layout at Cassiobury. Apart from some fragments of garden architecture nothing remains of the works of Kent and Bridgman, but at Hall Barn near Beaconsfield gardens resembling those described in 1724 by Lord Perceval survive.[39]

In the mid-eighteenth century a Londoner's park had a confident air, fashionable, often ostentatious, sometimes strenuously rustic. Some new owners and designers boldly lowered hills and cut new valleys, some conspicuously neglected to consult the genius of the place. Moor Park in Hertfordshire, for example, had already undergone major alterations at the hands of Cardinal Wolsey, the Countess of Bedford and the Duke of Monmouth before it was acquired by Benjamin Styles, a successful investor in the South Sea Company. In 1720 a fine new house was designed by Giacomo Leoni but its site was ill-chosen. Its intended views across the Vale of St Albans were hidden behind the brow of a hill until a cutting 30 feet deep had been dug at a cost of £5,000. Pope ridiculed the enterprise in his *Essay on Riches*:

> '*Or cut wide views through Mountains to the Plain,*
> *You'll wish your hill or shelter'd seat again.*'[40]

Styles, however, was not to remain at Moor Park long enough to weary of his dearly won vista, 'animated by the meanderings of the Gade and the Colne, rendered beautiful by a luxuriance of verdure, intermingled with noble seats, villages, farmhouses, together with the towns of Rickmansworth and Watford,' nor did he suffer from exposure as Pope predicted.[41] In 1759, a new owner, Lord Anson, commissioned Brown to thin the avenues and to form a small pleasure ground with a lake to the south-east of the house. On the edge of the water stood an Ionic temple dedicated to the Four Winds, commemorating Lord Anson's naval victories. The undulations of the ground were emphasized by clumps of cedars, planted on what Walpole described as 'so many artificial mole hills.'[42] At the entrance to Batchworth Heath a triumphant screen was erected, its laths and brickwork now showing through peeling plaster. In the following century Italianate gardens decorated with urns and busts were added on the west of the house. Moor Park displays magnificent scenery, imposing enough to distract attention from invading golf courses and twentieth-century houses. Among other showplaces, also repeatedly and lavishly redesigned, are Cliveden, Clandon Park, Trent Park, Brocket, Caversham and Stoke Park. Their proud monuments, temples, eyecatchers, their cedars, chestnuts, limes, their impressive approaches and diverted public highways give them a boldly exotic appearance.

Merchants' parks make few claims on the surrounding landscape, but the out-of-town estates belonging to noble landowners assert themselves in different ways. Public houses and almshouses bear the family name; railway stations take their names from the park; war memorials, mausoleums, village churches carry the family crest; farms, cottages, sometimes whole villages have been rebuilt for picturesque effect. Latimers in Buckinghamshire is a property landscaped in this manner by the Cavendish family. At the entrance to the park, beside the lodges, stand an estate office, a school and a carefully contrived group of nineteenth-century Tudor cottages. The present house, with mullioned windows and gables, was completed in 1863, replacing a house built in the mid-eighteenth century.[43] The landscape improved by Brown offended both Walpole and George Mason. Walpole objected to the lake and the house:

'the river stops short at an hundred yards just under your eye, and the house has undergone Batty Langley discipline; half the ornaments are of his bastard Gothic, and half of Hallett's mongrel Chinese.'[44]

Mason condemned the work of Brown as that of 'an egregious mannerist, who from having a facility in shaping surfaces, grew fond of exhibiting that talent without due regard to nature.' At Latimers, Mason complained:

'he had stuffed a very narrow vale by the side of an artificial river with those crowded circular clumps of firs *alone*. The incongruity of this plan struck most of the neighbouring gentlemen, but was defended by the artist himself, under the epithet playful—totally misapplied. Fortunately the soil did not suit the firs; they all died within a twelvemonth and the place was happily rid of them.'[45]

Since Mason wrote, clumps of conifers have been successfully reestablished on the valley side. Above them a flourishing beechwood crowns the summit and the landscape is as picturesque as Brown could have wished.

Much criticism of landscaping at Moor Park, Latimers and other out-of-town parks has been directed towards its failure to appreciate and exploit the capabilities of different sites and situations. A house built behind the crest of a hill, a lake terminated abruptly half way down a valley, clumps planted with little regard for soil or slope are some of the faults mentioned. But in defence of their designers, it may be said that they had to work within the narrow confines of small parks surrounded by unattractive landscapes. They created private landscapes, screened by belt plantations. Roads and settlements have been thrust from sight; pepperpot lodges have been set up to guard the entrances to private property. Most out-of-town parks are not freely accessible to the public. In this they differ from both London parks which are public open spaces, and most country parks which spread unconfined over neighbouring fields and roads.

In London's green belt the contrast between parks and their surroundings is stark and is intensifying. Parks lie within, yet quite separate from, a landscape of poultry farms and piggeries, of wire-netting and bungalows, of gravel pits and scrapped car dumps, of airfields, motorways and filling stations (Chapter 12). The motorist, in particular, travels through a landscape of eyesores; he has few opportunities of seeing park scenery.

Country Parks

In the countryside beyond the green belt are three distinctive

FIG. 72 Parkland in and around London 1819–25
The position of selected localities is shown in outline.
Based on A. Bryant and C. & J. Greenwood.

types of park. A few vast landscape gardens such as Stowe, Woburn,
Luton Hoo and Ashridge contain within their bounds almost every
object to be seen from the windows of the house. Park and garden
embrace the whole landscape. Other smaller parks such as Shardeloes, West Wycombe, Stonor, Beechwood, Knebworth, Knole and
Penshurst are set in landscapes ornamented with clumps and crestline plantations. House, garden and park merge into an ornamented
farming landscape. Finally, there are small out-of-town parks such
as the Prime Minister's residence at Chequers, Disraeli's Hughenden
Manor and parks created or largely remodelled in the nineteenth
century by the Rothschilds at Waddesdon, Eythrope, Aston Clinton,
Tring, Halton, Mentmore and Ascott.

350

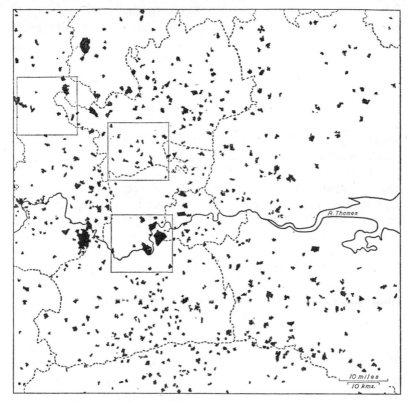

Fig. 73   Parkland in and around London 1950–5
The position of selected localities is shown in outline.
Based on Ordnance Survey one-inch maps.

The great parks at Woburn and Luton Hoo now open their gates
to visitors; Stowe has become a boarding school and Ashridge a
college for adult education. They are spacious enough to absorb
their new activities without losing the essential charms of their
landscapes.

Landscaped estates, especially in the Chiltern Hills, are unobtrusive
and unaffectedly rural. Nestling among the hills are retiring, well
wooded estates such as Stonor, Swyncombe, Watlington, Beechwood, and Knebworth. West Wycombe parades its associations with
the notorious Hell Fire Club in a mausoleum on top of the hill and
in caves beneath. Shardeloes, on the other hand, is a model of pro-
priety and discretion, a modest estate held by the Drake family from

the seventeenth century until the 1950s. In Queen Anne's reign it possessed a walled-in pond garden neatly planted with fruit trees.[46] In 1758 Stiff Leadbetter built a large unpretentious house on rising ground. It was altered and completed in the 1760s by Robert Adam 'in a manner much admired, but it does not seem to make a great figure from the road.'[47] A little-known landscape gardener, Richmond, improved the grounds and dammed the River Misbourne to form a 40-acre (16 ha.) lake.[48] About 1800 Humphry Repton made proposals for landscaping both sides of the valley, to bring the whole estate into the scheme. When Repton visited the estate, extensive stands of mature beeches covered the surrounding hills, but the lawn in front of the house was bare of trees and recent fellings had reduced the edges of the beechwoods to 'the appearance of copses,' lacking 'that venerable dignity which groves ought always to possess.'[49] To give them a firm outline but to avoid the 'unpleasing harshness' of a 'uniform heavy boundary,' they were allowed to form into irregular groupings, leaving some distinctly separated to break the monotony of the lawn. By cutting down a few trees, an immediate improvement was obtained, 'in a better manner than can be expected from a solitary clump a century hence,' and a space through the trees on the horizon was cleared to increase the apparent extent of lawn, 'because the tops of the trees being partly seen over the opening, the imagination will extend the lawn beyond its actual boundary, and represent it as surrounded by the same chain of woods.' Few single trees were planted, so not to produce a 'broken, diffuse and frittered effect,' and new plantations were concentrated in dense masses. The beauty of 'the unequal and varied surface of the ground' was heightened by planting both in the valley bottom and on the crestline:

'whenever the hills are sufficiently bold to admit of ground being seen between large trees in the valley and those on the brow of the hill, it marks so decided a degree of elevation, that it ought sedulously to be preserved.'

Repton also suggested that a pavilion should be built on the edge of the woods, arguing that the scenery, 'seems to require some artificial objects to appropriate the woods to the magnificence of the place.' But considerations of profit and utility outweighed the desire for ornamental trappings, and an ice house was more in keeping with the Drakes' notions of good sense than a pavilion. No higher compliment could be paid to their shrewdness and restraint in carrying out the scheme than William Cobbett's failure to recognize the marks of landscaping.

'Talk of *pleasure-grounds* indeed! What that man ever invented under the name of pleasure-grounds can equal these fields of Hertfordshire?—This is a profitable system too.' Thus reflecting, he rode along the Wendover road and 'went across the park of Mr. Drake, and up a steep hill towards the great road leading to Wycombe. Mr. Drake's is a very beautiful place, and has a great deal of very fine timber upon it. I think I counted pretty nearly 200 oak trees, worth, on an average, five pounds apiece, growing within twenty yards (18 m.) of the road that I was going along. Mr. Drake has some thousands of these, I dare say, besides his beech; and, therefore, *he* will be able to stand a tug with the fundholders for some time.'[50]

Throughout the nineteenth century the Drakes remained prosperous squires, respected local figures in politics and in sport. They built kennels and planted coverts for the Old Berkley Hunt, and, at the end of the century, they managed their woodlands to improve the pheasant shooting. The house has now been converted into flats, but in all else Shardeloes belongs to the Amersham countryside. The park and its surroundings are united.

In a landscape tactfully developed by successive generations of resident landowners such as the Drakes at Amersham and the Verneys at Claydon, the new houses and parks designed in second half of the nineteenth century look harshly alien. In Middlesex, such places as Gunnersbury and Harrow School do not appear blatantly offensive, but in mid-Buckinghamshire, Pevsner views the refronting of Hughenden Manor in 1862 as 'High Victorian originality at its most ruthless (and ugly),' and 'when it comes to self-assertiveness and an intrepid mixture of sources, there is nothing in England to beat Baron Ferdinand de Rothschild's Waddesdon of *c*. 1875–80 and Baron Lionel's, or rather Baron Alfred's, Halton, completed in 1884.'[51]

Between 1850 and 1890, the Rothschild family created seven new parks in the Vale of Aylesbury. In 1851 Sir Anthony de Rothschild moved to Aston Clinton; in 1852 his younger brother, Baron Mayer Amschel de Rothschild began to build Mentmore; and in 1853 his older brother, Baron Lionel, acquired Halton. At Aston Clinton the Rothschild village contains two gothick schools of 1856 and 1862. Mentmore House is surrounded by ornate formal gardens and

350 acres (140 ha.) of parkland. Halton, built 30 years later, is in a French château style with small terraced gardens to match. The other four residences were built by the children of Sir Anthony de Rothschild of Aston Clinton. In 1874 the youngest son, Baron Leopold, bought and enlarged a Jacobean mansion at Ascott, filling its gardens with parterres, ponds, fountains and statuary. In 1874 at Waddesdon, Sir Anthony's son-in-law, Baron Ferdinand, began work on an open site. The top of the hill was levelled and terraced for formal gardens, and its bare slopes were clothed with dense plantations of trees and shrubs. The house is modelled on the Loire châteaux at Chambord and Blois, its gardens are laid out by Lainé, stables and greenhouses in the grounds are also French in style. The grounds are vast, the drives, dark alleys of trees, sunken and circuitous. The view from the bay windows of the house stretches, green and wooded, to the Chiltern Hills; 'the English view, every square yard man-made, and yet with neither a house nor a path in sight'.[52] The village at the gates bears the Rothschild imprint in half-timbered estate houses, village hall, club, reading room, almshouses and the Five Arrows Hotel. At Eythrope Alice de Rothschild's neo-Tudor pavillion, built in 1883, is a lake-side ornament. The park is picturesque, with spidery lake, a fanciful grotto, a restored eighteenth-century bridge and gabled rustic lodges. At Tring Park Sir Anthony's eldest son, Nathan Mayer, the first Lord Rothschild, built palm houses, orchid houses and pineries around his château. At the end of the nineteenth century the park contained a menagerie of zebras, kangaroos, emus, rheas and wild geese.[53] Like other nineteenth-century out-of-town parks it is a private collection, withdrawn from public gaze, enclosed by belts of trees and shrubberies.

In the late nineteenth century railways as well as roads brought places such as Tonbridge, Guildford, Reading, High Wycombe, Aylesbury, Tring and Luton within the orbit of daily travel to London. The coming of the railway to distant rural areas was soon followed by the acquisition of small parks by Londoners, by the restoration or enlargement of old mansions, and by the building of new out-of-town villas and manors set in trim ornamental gardens. A number of small parks at Iver, Gerrards Cross, Chorleywood, Radlett and Brentwood have since been encroached upon by dormitory suburbs (Chapter 11), but the impress of newly established parks around railway stations is evident both in the Vale of Aylesbury and in the Weald. Changes of the kind that began 400 years ago in Middlesex and Surrey have occurred in parts of Buckinghamshire during the past 100 years.

Apart from nineteenth-century residences located along roads and railways leading to London, many country parks lie in remote spots, far from roads or settlements, at the heads of dry valleys in the Chiltern Hills, or deep in Kentish woods. Large areas of parkland occupy light sandy soils such as the Wealden ridges in Kent, Sussex and Surrey, the Woburn sand country of Bedfordshire, the Lower Greensand ridges in Hampshire, Surrey and Kent, the outcrop of Bagshot Sands on the borders of Berkshire, Surrey and Hampshire, and gravel terraces in south Buckinghamshire, west Middlesex and north-east Surrey. Parks are not by any means confined to light soils, but in regions of good farmland, L. D. Stamp observes, 'parks were usually laid out on the poorest land in the neighbourhood.'[54] On the other hand, the medieval village of Pendley in Hertfordshire was destroyed to make room for a deer park.[55] In the eighteenth and nineteenth centuries Luton Hoo, Panshanger, Ashridge and Bayham Abbey were greatly enlarged at the expense of neighbouring farms.[56] At present a few large parks possess home farms, and Luton Hoo, Beechwood, Gorhambury and Mentmore ploughed up part of their grassland between 1931 and 1951.[57] It is also arguable that parks such as Hampton Court, Syon, Chiswick and Kensington Gardens are sited on potentially valuable farmland.

To state that few parks occupy first-class agricultural land is not to deny that much parkland is, or could be, productive as well as ornamental. In addition to the grazing they afford, parks contain much valuable timber, some in well-managed plantations of conifers. On the outskirts of London, the preservation and enlargement of parks may perhaps be less costly and aesthetically more rewarding than maintaining farms as custodians of open spaces. In the green belt, at least, the farmer is neither encouraged nor is he able to perform what Stamp considers 'his unpaid functions as the nation's landscape gardener and steward of the countryside.'[58] The appearance of many pleasant farms has been ruined by unsightly concrete structures and by barbed wire, but the farmer can hardly be blamed for more than a small share in the widespread disfigurement of landscape. It is not, indeed, his responsibility to preserve and enhance the beauty of the countryside, nor to make it accessible to the public. If the Londoner is to enjoy park scenery not only in small patches, in municipal recreation grounds, in cemeteries, or in fossilized private parks, but over large stretches of country, then a new generation of landscape gardeners will have a vital role to play.

References

1. Paul Hentzner, *Journey to England in the Reign of Queen Elizabeth*, translated Richard Bentley (Strawberry Hill, 1757), 32; W. de Archenholz, *A Picture of England*, new translation (1797), 91.

2. Pückler-Muskau, *Tour in England, Ireland and France in the Years 1828 and 1829*, 3 (1832), 192; S. E. Rasmussen, *London: the Unique City*, abridged edition (1960), Chapters 5, 8, 9, 13.

3. 'London's fair fields', *The Economist* (1st June 1963), 905.

4. A. J. Downing, *Rural Essays* (1853), 548.

5. Horace Walpole, 'History of the modern taste in gardening', William Marshall, *Planting and Rural Ornament*, 1 (1796), 233.

6. Rasmussen, *op. cit.*, 238.

7. Richard Church, *The Royal Parks of London* (H.M.S.O., 1956) and Miles Hadfield, *Gardening in Britain* (1960), 124–210.

8. Walpole, *loc. cit.*, 241.

9. Dorothy Stroud, *Humphry Repton* (1962), 105.

10. Robin H. Best and J. T. Coppock, *The Changing Use of Land in Britain* (1962), 178; London County Council, *County of London Development Plan. First Review*, 2 (1960), 3.

11. R. S. Cambridge, *The World*, 188 (1755), cited in H. F. Clark, *The English Landscape Garden* (1948), 1.

12. Walpole, *loc. cit.*, 231.

13. Alexander Pope, *On his Grotto at Twickenham*, also Douglas Grant (ed.), *Poems of Alexander Pope* (1950), xiv–v.

14. Hadfield, *op. cit.*, 185–93.

15. Pope, 'Moral essays IV. Of the use of riches', in Douglas Grant, *op. cit.*, 165.

16. James Lees-Milne, *Earls of Creation* (1962), 80.

17. Nikolaus Pevsner, *The Buildings of England: Buckinghamshire* (1960), 30.

18. Ian Nairn and Nikolaus Pevsner, *The Buildings of England: Surrey* (1962), 114.

19. Nikolaus Pevsner, *The Buildings of England: Middlesex* (1951), 29.

20. James Thomson, *The Seasons* (1730).

21. Clark, *op. cit.*, 40–3.

22. Christopher Tunnard, *Gardens in the Modern Landscape* (1938).

23. Walpole, *loc. cit.*, 237.

24. Pevsner, Middlesex, *op. cit.*, 163.

25. William Mason, *The English Garden* (1772).

26. Dorothy Stroud, *Capability Brown* (1950).

27. Edward Mogg, *Paterson's Roads*, 18th edition (1829), 308.

28. J. C. Rogers, *The Manor and Houses of Gorhambury* (1934), 6–19.
29. J. J. Antrobus, *Bishop's Hatfield* (1914), 56–7.
30. Robert Clutterbuck, *The History and Antiquities of the County of Hertford*, 2 (1821), 94.
31. William Temple, *Upon the Gardens of Epicurus, or of Gardening in the Year 1685* (1692), 126.
32. ed. William Bray, *The Diary of John Evelyn* (1907), Vol. I, 263, 277, 284; Vol. II, 126, 144–5, 193.
33. Daniel Defoe, *A Tour through England and Wales* (1927), Vol. II, 12.
34. *Ibid.*, Vol. I, 158.
35. *Ibid.*, Vol. I, 159.
36. Nairn and Pevsner, Surrey, *op. cit.*, 8.
37. Defoe, *op. cit.*, Vol. II, 12.
38. William Cobbett, *Rural Rides* (1912), Vol. I, 33–4, 160–1.
39. Egmont MS., cited in Alicia Amherst, *A History of Gardening in England* (1896), 240–2.
40. Pope, 'Moral essays IV', in Douglas Grant, *op. cit.*, 166.
41. J. P. Neale, *Views of the Seats of Noblemen and Gentlemen*, 3 (1826), n.p.
42. Horace Walpole, *Journal of Visits to Country Seats*, 5th July 1761, ed. Paget Toynbee, Walpole Society 16 (1928), 24.
43. Pevsner, Buckinghamshire, *op.* cit., 184.
44. Albert J. Foster, *The Chiltern Hundreds* (1897), 120.
45. George Mason, *An Essay on Design in Gardening*, 1768, new edition (1795), 129.
46. George Eland, *Shardeloes Papers of the Seventeenth and Eighteenth Centuries* (1947), 136.
47. Stebbing Shaw, 1788, cited in Arthur T. Bolton, *The Architecture of Robert and James Adam*, 1 (1922), 153.
48. S. and D. Lysons, *Magna Britannia*, 1 (1806), 497.
49. Humphry Repton, *Observations on the Theory and Practice of Landscape Gardening* (1803), 61–5.
50. Cobbett, *op. cit.*, Vol. I, 86, 89.
51. Pevsner, Buckinghamshire, *op. cit.*, 38.
52. C. P. Snow, *The Conscience of the Rich* (1961), 82.
53. 'Tring Park, Herts', *Country Life*, 1 (1897), 604; Joseph Whitaker, *A Descriptive List of Deer Parks and Paddocks of England* (1892), 77.
54. L. D. Stamp, 'Land classification and agriculture', in P. Abercrombie, *Greater London Plan 1944* (H.M.S.O., 1945), 93.
55. M. W. Beresford, *The Lost Villages of England* (1954), 147–8, 205.
56. H. C. Prince, 'The changing landscape of Panshanger', *Trans. East Herts Archaeological Society*, 14 (1959), 42–58; idem, 'Parkland in the Chilterns', *Geographical Review*, 49 (1959), 18–31.
57. Best and Coppock, *op. cit.*, 139.
58. Stamp, *loc. cit.*, 95.

15

The Future of London

*

J. T. COPPOCK

In the post-war period the face of London has continued to change rapidly. Its most obvious expression has been the increase in the number of tall buildings (by London standards) which now break the skyline of Inner London, dramatically symbolized by the slim pencil of the 600-foot (184 m.) G.P.O. tower; between 1956 and 1963 the London County Council gave planning consent for 106 buildings of 150 feet (46 m.) or over to join the sixteen which already existed.[1] In part these contribute to the growth of office accommodation in the Central Area, where nearly a third of all office floor space is in post-war buildings. But others are hotels and a third are blocks of flats. The most widespread change is the construction of new housing, for, despite the shortage of building land in the conurbation, post-war dwellings account for nearly one-sixth of the total stock of housing. New factories, schools and shops, and improved communications, particularly the beginnings of urban motorways, all contribute to the changing face of the capital. Because it is more widely dispersed, building outside the conurbation is less immediately apparent; but, in total, it is even more impressive. These developments foreshadow future changes and, while the purpose of this book has been to describe and analyse what London is and how it has come to be, rather than to present blueprints for the future, this concluding chapter looks forward from the problems which the growth of London has generated to some of the possible solutions.

In essence most of London's problems arise from the continued growth of employment and population in the London Region (Fig. 74). From a national viewpoint this situation raises difficulties, not only because so much of the country's wealth and population is now concentrated here, but also because greater prosperity and rapid expansion in south-east England affect the economies of other parts of the country, especially the industrial areas established on the coalfields. While migration to the London Region is not on the scale of the 1920s and 1930s, it still continues and the London Region enjoys the fastest rate of growth of employment and population in the country; for example, between 1952 and 1958 the Region, which contains 27 per cent of the population, provided more than 40 per cent of new employment.[2] Since the Royal Commission on the Distribution of the Industrial Population reported in 1940, it has become government policy to limit the growth of employment in the London Region and to reduce migration from other parts of the country; but measures to enforce this policy have met, at best, with only limited success.

Problems of London

The more local problems of the London Region, which are the concern of this chapter, are due largely to the increasingly wide separation of the places where people live and where they work; for the conurbation, which houses 65 per cent of the population provides 80 per cent of the employment.[3] As a result, complex transport problems arise from the daily journey to work, expressed most vividly by the $1\frac{1}{4}$ million people who crowd into the Central Area in the morning rush-hours. While this situation is primarily due to the sheer size of London and to the continued growth of employment and population, it is aggravated by the policy of limiting the extent of the continuously built-up area and surrounding towns by means of the green belt, by the outward displacement of population from Inner London, by the concentration of much new employment at the centre of the conurbation in the very area where population is declining and by the inadequacy of the road and rail systems to cope with the resulting flow of passengers and goods. The *County of London Plan, 1943* and the *Greater London Plan, 1944*, which are the basis of post-war planning in and around London, assumed that population and employment would change little and that the essential problem was one of redistribution from the older parts of the conurbation to new and existing towns beyond the green belt. In fact, both population and employment have continued to rise. In recent years employment in the conurbation has been increasing at the rate of about 40,000 jobs a year, or roughly one per cent per annum, and while the resident population of the conurbation has fallen slightly since 1939, that of the remainder of the London Region in and beyond the green belt has risen by approximately a quarter (Table I).[4]

The rise in employment is due to a number of factors, conveniently summed up as 'the magnetic attraction of London':[5] industrial expansion, stimulated by proximity to the London market and the port of London; the multiplication of official and semi-official bodies, each with headquarters in London; and the increase in other office employment, reflecting the prestige attached to a London head-office. Nearly two-thirds of this increase in employment was located in the conurbation which already provides four-fifths of all jobs, a third of them in the Central Area; it is here that the most difficult problems arise from journeys to work and from the concentration of service and industrial traffic in Inner London. New employment in the conurbation has been equally divided between offices and other service industries and manufacturing industry, although more than half this industrial employment has been white collar jobs.[6] But while the increase in employment in manufacturing has occurred mainly in the outer parts of the conurbation where journeys to work are often short and transport problems do not generally arise, and has even declined in Inner London, the growth in office employment has been largely concentrated in the Central Area, where office floor space has increased by a third since 1938 and employment has been rising by about 15,000 jobs a year.[7]

Most post-war planning has been based on the assumption that the location of new economic activities could be controlled; but the rise in employment in manufacturing and service industry in the London Region, despite government intentions to the contrary, shows that the forces making for economic growth in south-east England are too strong to be contained by restrictions on building and employment. It seems certain, therefore, that whatever success governments may have in attracting new employment in the older industrial areas on the coal-fields, population and employment will continue to rise in the south-east. It is true, of course, that there have been weaknesses in the machinery of control. Surprisingly, no attention was at first given to the question of limiting office employment, although this has in fact caused the most acute problems. Planning control over the growth of new offices has also been ineffective; until recently it permitted an increase in floor space of as much as 40 per cent on rebuilding. While these controls have now been strengthened, the government does not feel that other methods of regulating office employment are practicable.[8] Control over new industrial employment through the issue of Industrial Development Certificates has undoubtedly diverted some industrial growth from both London and the London Region, but its effectiveness has been limited. Most new employment has been either in developments which are too small to require a Certificate or in extensions to existing factories for which it is difficult to refuse permission, especially to industries which export a substantial proportion of their products, as many of the 'growth' industries do. It seems unlikely that more rigorous controls could greatly affect the situation and, in any case, industrial employment in the conurbation will probably not increase greatly. On the other hand, the rise in office and service employment, which is most difficult to control, is certain to continue, at least in the short run, because of the building of new offices already approved.

The rise in population within the London Region is largely due to natural increase on a scale quite unforeseen twenty years ago when the Greater London Plan was being prepared; net migration of a quarter of a million people into the region accounted for only a quarter of the total increase in population between 1951 and 1961.[9] Yet these facts hide substantial changes within the region, where there are two opposing currents of migration, the one predominantly of young, single people moving to the centre of London, the other mainly of married couples with children migrating to the suburbs and beyond and of retired people moving from the region altogether; on balance, the latter movement is the stronger and the conurbation experienced a net loss of half a million people through migration, especially from Inner London. Whatever the success of measures to limit migration from other parts of the country, the population will continue to increase and Peter Hall has estimated that it will be at least 35 per cent higher by the year 2000.[10]

If the rise in population and employment cannot be prevented and if population continues to decline within the conurbation while much new employment is located at the centre, it remains true that the essential problem, as Abercrombie showed, is one of redistribution, although on a much larger scale than he envisaged. On the assumption that present policies continue, neither the conurbation nor the green belt will be able to house all those requiring separate accommodation; much of the land for new housing will, therefore, have to be found beyond the outer limits of the green belt.

The Location of New Housing

The number of dwellings required to house the future growth of population will be increased by the trend towards smaller households, while a further demand for housing land will be created by the redevelopment of the older parts of the conurbation where rebuilding cannot provide homes in the same area for all the former residents. In some instances, e.g. the construction of urban motorways, none of those living in the area scheduled for demolition can be rehoused there, but even in purely residential redevelopment, the high densities of much nineteenth-century building, widespread multiple-occupation in existing dwellings, the low provision of land for recreational, educational and other uses and the higher standard of housing now demanded make certain that some of the former residents will have to find homes elsewhere. Even high building is no answer; besides being proportionately much more expensive, it still could not restore gross population densities to the previous level. Such redevelopment will continue, for, while it is true that most of the slums notified in 1955 have now been cleared, large numbers of decaying and sub-standard Victorian housing around the Central Area will have to be replaced over the next 40 years; Peter Hall has calculated that 52 per cent of the dwellings in the county of London were obsolescent in 1961 and it is thought that 150,000 dwellings will be required by 1972 to rehouse those affected by redevelopment in London.[11] Although the L.C.C. expects that population in the county of London will begin to rise again after 1972 as the outer parts of the county are redeveloped, it is not until the great expanses of twentieth-century suburbs come to be replaced in the next century that any substantial increase in densities will be possible.

Allowing for unsatisfied demand at present, a government white paper has estimated that a total of half a million dwellings will have to be found by 1972 to house those who live in the conurbation and require separate accommodation.[12] It is thought that half of these can be provided within the conurbation, 100,000 of them by building on land not at present in residential use. This figure may be raised by the release of land held by the armed services or by British Railways, but it is unlikely that any comparable area will become available to meet further demands arising after 1972. A substantial number of dwellings, estimated at about 500,000 by 1980 and over a million by 2000, will therefore be required outside the conurbation to house Londoners.[13]

Redevelopment of Inner London may be undertaken both by private developers and by local authorities. Commercial redevelopment to provide middle-class accommodation on the fringes of the more desirable residential areas will become increasingly attractive as controls over office building begin to take effect, although rent control, which affects 40 per cent of London's million privately rented dwellings, is likely to be an obstacle.[14] In so far as the new occupiers are likely to work in the Central Area, redevelopment of this kind will reduce the strain on transport facilities, but those displaced will have to be rehoused elsewhere and will add to the demand for local authority housing. Redevelopment of most of the poorer areas will, however, be undertaken only by local authorities. These have already provided dwellings on a substantial scale within the conurbation, many of them in blocks of flats whose high cost is hidden by government subsidies; but, except in areas of comprehensive development, such local authority building has been piecemeal wherever suitable sites could be obtained.

In considering population movement and housing, both within the conurbation and outside, those who can afford to buy or rent accommodation at market values must be distinguished from those who cannot and who must increasingly depend on public authorities to provide housing as the supply of rented, and especially rent-controlled housing declines. Most discussion of the problems of overspill has been concerned with people in this second category and Abercrombie envisaged that 79 per cent of those migrating from the conurbation would move in planned schemes.[15] In practice unplanned or voluntary migration has been more important; between 1952 and 1958, for example, planned migration accounted for only 49 per cent of all migrants. The destinations of those moving to rented accommodation in publicly provided housing have been the L.C.C. out-county estates on the fringes of the conurbation (Fig. 10), as at Borehamwood and Harold Hill, the eight New Towns lying just beyond the outer edge of the approved green belt and the towns which have agreed to receive overspill from London under the 1952 Town Development Act and which lie at distances of between 30 and 110 miles (48 to 176 km.) from the centre of the conurbation (Figs. 69 and 74). Unplanned migration from London, that is, the movement of those who find their own accommodation, has taken place to towns and villages both in and beyond the green belt wherever land

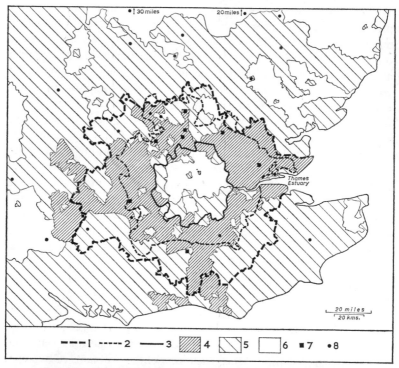

FIG. 74   Population change in south-east England 1951–61

Key: 1, boundary of the London Region; 2, outer boundary of the green belt (approved and provisional); 3, boundary of the Greater London conurbation; 4, local authority areas where population increased by 20 per cent or more 1951–61; 5, other areas gaining population; 6, areas losing population (some small urban areas have not been shown); 7, New Towns (for identification see Fig. 69); 8, Expanded Towns (for identification of those outside the green belt see Fig. 77; the others are Edenbridge, Letchworth, Luton and Luton Rural District).

Based on 1961 Census, preliminary report.

or houses have been available, although the choice has been guided by proximity or accessibility to place of work, by the adequacy of communications generally and by the attractiveness of town and surrounding countryside.

These problems of employment and accommodation do not merely concern the movement of people from London; in the surrounding towns, both population growth through natural increase and migration from outside the London region, and industrial expansion through the development of existing industries, will contribute their quota. Nevertheless, most of the changes will be due to migration. The majority of post-war migrants have been accommodated in the belt of country some 15 to 35 miles (23 to 56 km.) from central London and broadly co-extensive with the extended green belt, where population increased most rapidly between 1951 and 1961 (Fig. 74). The destination of future migrants will depend largely on whether land in the green belt is considered sacrosanct and on the location of new employment. Because of underestimates in the rate of population growth and of private migration, most of the land allocated in the development plans for housing in towns and villages in the green belt has already been used, so that these settlements will therefore be unable to satisfy even the demands arising locally from population increase. While the government envisages that some land at present not zoned for housing will be made available in the less attractive parts of the green belt, other land for unplanned migration can be found only in towns beyond the outer limits of the green belt.

The L.C.C. estates on the outskirts of the conurbation were intended merely to solve an immediate problem after the Second World War and have received 140,000 people from London.[16] The New Towns, too, have rehoused more than 160,000 Londoners and are well on the way to achieving their ultimate population of more than half a million, although the government has suggested that Stevenage and Harlow should be enlarged beyond their planned size.[17] The contribution of the Expanded Towns has been much smaller and the number of migrants totalled only 28,000 at the end of 1962, although 180,000 will eventually move and schemes under discussion will probably raise this figure.[18] But most of these Expanded Towns lie beyond the green belt and, apart from enlargement of New Towns, more land for planned migration can likewise come only from areas beyond the green belt.

365

The Location of New Employment

While the question of land for housing is vital, it is unrealistic to discuss it without reference to the provision of employment. Apart from those L.C.C. estates, such as Oxhey, which have been purely residential, planned migration has generally been linked with the movement of employment so that the New and Expanded Towns should be self-contained communities and not mere dormitories. This policy has been successful in attracting industries, but has failed to provide office employment on a sufficient scale. Unplanned migration has, by its nature, been largely independent of the movement of employment. Some of those who have moved have found jobs in towns in or beyond the green belt, but many migrants continue to work in the conurbation, especially the Central Area. These people, together with those residents from settlements in the green belt who have been attracted by rising employment in Central London, are largely responsible for the increase in long-distance commuting to the conurbation; thus, there was an increase in arrivals at main-line termini during the morning rush-hour of 79,000 between 1953 and 1960.[19] This trend has been encouraged by the improved rail services which have resulted from the electrification of the south Essex, north Kent, Bishop's Stortford and Amersham lines (Fig. 75) and from the introduction of multiple diesel units elsewhere, particularly to the north and west of the conurbation; indeed, it is estimated that these improvements could bring another 170,000 passengers to main-line stations by 1970.[20] Road improvements along the major routeways leading to the conurbation have also facilitated this increase in commuting.

Is it possible to achieve a better balance between the location of new houses and workplaces and so relieve the wasteful congestion in central London? Since sufficient dwellings can be found only outside the conurbation, the answer largely depends on the degree of success in persuading employers to move from the conurbation or to establish new plant and offices outside it. In discussing this question it is important to distinguish both between office and factory employment and between different categories of each. The rise in office accommodation is, in large measure, a result of the value placed upon a central London location; but, while much office employment depends on personal contact between firms or between firms and customer, as in banking and finance, and cannot easily be diverted from the centre, there is routine work, e.g. the keeping of records, which could. Much service employment in medicine and education could also be moved from central London. The government has made some attempt to locate civil service employment outside London and a fifth of all those employed in the headquarters of departments now work outside the conurbation, a proportion which is likely to increase.[21] The scope for similar moves by private firms is, however, more limited, since only a quarter of all office employment is estimated to be in the large firms which alone would find it practicable to move routine work to offices outside London.[22] As a partial solution, it might be possible to divert office employment from the Central Area to accessible suburban centres such as Croydon and Harrow, for this would ease the strain on transport facilities in central London and reduce the length of journeys to work. Indeed, current office building at Croydon, where planning consent has been given for six million square feet (540,000 sq. km.) of offices, foreshadows developments of this kind.[23]

Yet, while it has been shown that costs in locations outside Inner London are considerably lower, rents being as little as a quarter of those prevailing in the Central Area, and while it seems likely that development in telecommunications will reduce the importance of close physical contact, the disadvantages of higher staff costs and rents are clearly not yet sufficient to bring about much migration of office employment from the centre.[24] Perhaps only with the adoption of a transport policy in which users pay the full economic costs of both private and public transport, with a fiscal disincentive such as a differential pay-roll tax to discourage all but essential services from central London, and, as a necessary complement, with the provision of custom-built and standard office accommodation outside the conurbation, will sufficient office and service employment be diverted from central London. Even without such measures the government, both directly as a major employer of office staff, and, indirectly, as paymaster of much other service employment, could undoubtedly play a more important part in providing non-industrial employment in towns beyond the green belt, e.g. by establishing universities, hospitals or branches of government departments. In the short run, at least, it is inevitable that office employment in the Central Area will continue to rise and the Town and Country Planning Association has suggested that at least 300,000 dwellings should be provided by 1981 within commuting range, i.e. within 35 miles (56 km.) of

London.[25] The release of land in the green belt ought therefore to be related to facilities for travel to central London; the most appropriate areas in this respect lie north of the Thames, where there is spare capacity on the railways.

Migration of industrial employment presents rather different problems to firms located in Inner London and those in the outer suburbs. For many industries of Inner London, in which firms are small and contacts with other firms and with their suppliers and markets are important, there are serious difficulties in the way of migration from London (Chapter 10). Unfortunately, many of these industries are located in sub-standard, though cheap accommodation in areas where redevelopment is desirable. Even for those not dependent on rapid changes in consumer demand, migration would be feasible only if it resulted in the establishment of similar industrial quarters in the reception area. For industries in Outer London, which are frequently on a larger scale and require more space, the disadvantages of migration are often less, provided that communications with London and with other industrial areas are good; indeed, if firms wish to expand their factory area greatly, migration is generally the only answer. Such movements have made an important contribution to the industrial growth of New Towns and there should be no major difficulties in attracting industry to towns outside the conurbation if similar provision of factory space and other facilities are made elsewhere.

Such movements of service and industrial employment are essential if planned migration of population is to be possible and if unplanned migration is not to result simply in much longer journeys to work. Yet it is important to notice that such movement of firms does not result in any reduction of employment in the conurbation; since planning consent for industrial or service uses of land can be extinguished only by payment of heavy compensation, the vacated premises are generally occupied by other firms.

The Location of Towns Suitable for Expansion

How migration of population and employment to towns beyond the green belt is best achieved is a matter for debate. In view of the scale of movement which will be necessary, there will have to be provision for matching employment and population and, since such towns will generally be too remote from London for large scale commuting to be practicable, attraction of employment will be the key. Provided that adequate land is made available, the larger towns beyond the green belt, such as Bedford and Colchester, may well be able to attract sufficient employment without further help; but for smaller towns, planned expansion using administrative machinery like that of the New Towns Act or the Town Development Act will be necessary. Although it is probable that the proportion of unplanned migration will rise in view of the trend towards increasing home ownership, there seems no reason why the machinery of either act should not be adapted to provide more houses for sale. Where any considerable expansion of employment and population is planned (and small-scale expansion of small towns seems the least satisfactory approach to the problem) the machinery of the

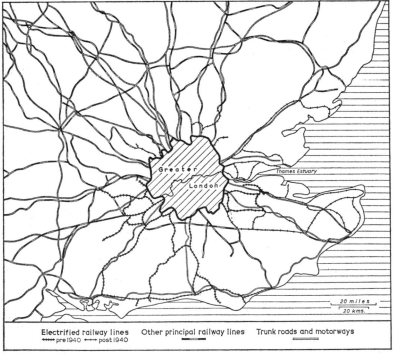

Electrified railway lines   Other principal railway lines   Trunk roads and motorways
pre1940   post1940

Fig. 75   Principal communications of south-east England
Single track unelectrified railways and those scheduled for closing under the Beeching Plan are omitted.
Based on maps of the Ordnance Survey and British Railways and on a map by M. O. Pitt.

New Towns Act will probably be the most appropriate means of achieving it.

The most promising areas for expansion are those with good rail and road communications to central London, to other industrial regions, especially the Midlands, and to the major ports. As Figure 75 shows, road and rail links at present favour the north-west of London which is connected with other major industrial centres by a close network of trunk roads and main-line railways; but, unfortunately, this is already the most urbanized area around London. North-east Essex, on the other hand, which has the poorest communications (but is also the least urbanized of all the areas around the green belt) is likely to remain a backwater until major improvements in communication, promised for the 1970s, are undertaken.

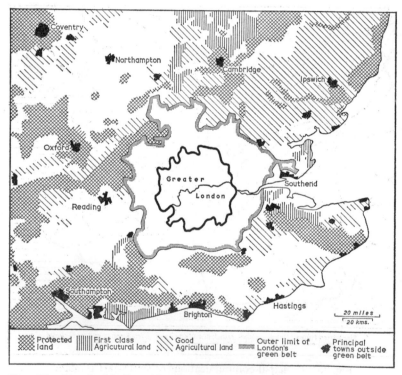

FIG. 76   Good agricultural land and protected land outside the green belt
Based on maps of the Land Utilization Survey, Ministry of Housing and Local Government, National Parks Commission and county development plans.

The situation would, of course, be modified if a Channel bridge or tunnel were constructed, or if Southampton Water were to be extensively developed to reduce the growing demands on the port of London; such changes, together with proposed rail and road improvements, could considerably enhance the attractions of towns south and west of London. Further industrial development along the Thames estuary (Chapter 8) would also act as a powerful stimulus to town expansion there.

The actual choice of towns can be made only after detailed study, although it can never be completely objective. Communications are probably the most important consideration, but the relationship of selected sites to the existing hierarchy of towns, a neglected aspect in the choice of the present New Towns, must also be given due weight (cf. Fig. 10). To conform with government policy, it will be desirable to avoid both good agricultural land and areas of fine scenery (which are often the poorest land); but this cannot be an over-riding consideration. So much of the land beyond the green belt falls into one or other of these categories, while the physical setting of expanding towns has an important part to play in stimulating unplanned migration; some of the flat clay lowlands provide unattractive sites from this point of view.[26] Yet, as far as possible, sites within the unshaded areas on Figure 76 should be chosen. In default of any major schemes to reorganize water supply in south-east England, an important local factor is likely to be the availability of water; proposed developments at Luton have already had to be restricted because of the inadequacy of future water supplies. When these two maps are considered together with Figure 1, they suggest that the strongest *prima facie* case for expansion can be made in respect of towns lying to the west of London.

Figure 77 shows the location of settlements suggested as suitable for expansion by the Town and Country Planning Association and by Peter Hall, together with those towns which have made or are making agreements for expansion under the Town Development Act.[27] They range in size from well under 1,000 inhabitants to over 200,000 and lie at distances of from 24 to 116 miles (38 to 186 km.) from London (Tables XXI and XXII). The differences between the various proposals are interesting and reflect in part different evaluations of the desirability of expanding towns in both the north-west, where the London Region impinges on the industrial Midlands, and the south, where only 55 miles (88 km.) separate London from the

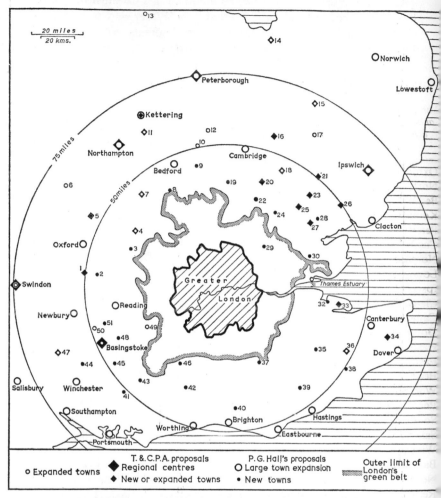

FIG. 77 Proposals for New and Expanded Towns around London
For identification, see Tables XXI and XXII; where appropriate, symbols
are combined.
Based on *Town and Country Planning* 1961 and Peter Hall, *London 2000*

TABLE XXI

Proposals for town expansion: large towns or regional centres

Large towns or regional centres	Sector	Distance from London miles	km.	Population 1961 000's	Town Development Act Agreement	Town and Country Planning Association Proposals	Peter Hall
Oxford	NW	55	88	106			×
Northampton		66	106	105		×	×
Bedford		49	79	63			×
Kettering		75	120	39		×	×
Peterborough		81	130	62		×	×
Cambridge	NE	54	87	95			×
Norwich		111	177	120			×
Lowestoft		116	186	46			×
Ipswich		72	115	117		×	×
Clacton		69	110	28			×
Canterbury	SE	55	88	30			×
Dover		72	115	35			×
Hastings		63	101	66			×
Eastbourne		63	101	61			×
Brighton	SW	55	88	163			×
Worthing		57	91	80			×
Portsmouth		70	112	215			×
Southampton		80	128	205			×
Salisbury		84	134	35			×
Winchester		65	104	29			×
Basingstoke		47	75	24	×	×	
Newbury		56	90	20			×
Reading		38	61	120			×
Swindon		79	126	92	×	×	×

Sources: London County Council, Town and Country Planning Association, Peter Hall.

TABLE XXII

Proposals for town expansion: New and Expanded Towns

New or Expanded Towns	Number on Figure	Sector	Distance from London miles	Distance from London km.	Population 1961 '000s	Town Development Act Agreement	Town and Country Planning Association Proposals	Peter Hall Proposals
Didcot	1	NW	52	83	9		×	
Wallingford	2		47	75	5			×
Princes Risborough	3		40	64	4			×
Aylesbury	4		40	64	28	×	×	
Bicester	5		57	91	6		×	×
Banbury	6		71	123	21	×		
Bletchley	7		47	75	17		×	
Flitwick	8		43	69	3			×
Sandy	9		49	79	4			×
St Neots	10		56	90	6	×		
Wellingborough	11		68	109	31	×	×	
Huntingdon	12		62	99	9	×	×	
Grantham	13		108	173	25	×		
King's Lynn	14	NE	98	157	28	×	×	
Thetford	15		82	131	5	×	×	
Newmarket	16		62	99	11		×	
Bury St Edmunds	17		75	120	21	×	×	
Haverhill	18		56	90	5	×	×	
Royston	19		41	66	6			×
Saffron Walden*	20		45	72	8		×	
Sudbury	21		58	93	7		×	
Quendon	22		38	61	1			×
Halstead*	23		50	80	6		×	
Great Dunmow	24		39	63	4			×
Braintree	25		43	69	21		×	
Colchester	26		54	87	65		×	
Witham	27		40	64	9		×	
Kelvedon	28		44	71	3			×
Ongar	29		24	38	1	.		×
Woodham Ferrers	30		35	56	2			×
Canvey Island	31		35	56	16	×		
Queenborough	32	SE	45	72	3			×
Isle of Sheppey	33		45	72	20		×	
Aylesham	34		64	103	3		×	
Headcorn	35		45	72	2			×
Ashford	36		54	87	28	×	×	
Ashurst	37		32	51	1			×
Ham Street	38		61	98	1			×
Robertsbridge	39		52	83	1			×
Plumpton	40		44	71	1			×
Petersfield	41	SW	54	87	7			×
Billingshurst	42		43	69	3			×
Liphook	43		46	74	1			×
Micheldever	44		59	95	1			×
Alton	45		49	79	9			×
Cranleigh	46		37	59	5			×
Andover	47		66	106	17	×	×	
Hook	48		41	66	1			×
Frimley and Camberley	49		29	46	30	×		
Tadley	50		50	80	3	×		
Silchester	51		47	75	1			×

*Alternatives

coast, with its string of large towns. The Abercrombie New Towns (Fig. 69) were to be fairly evenly distributed around the conurbation, but all save two of the sites actually designated lie north of the Thames. The Expanded Towns, which are further out, also lie mainly north of the Thames, with four in the north-east sector and ten in the north-west; only two are located in the south-east. Most of the Town and Country Planning Association's suggested sites are likewise north of London, with twelve in East Anglia and only five out of 26 to the south of the Thames. Peter Hall's suggestions, on the other hand, like Abercrombie's, are more uniformly distributed around London, with the north-west, where there are only four sites, as the least favoured sector and a majority of sites south of the Thames. While the emptiness of East Anglia is a point in favour of development here, both sets of proposals are clearly contingent on promised improvements in transport.

Whatever the towns chosen for expansion, it is likely that the future map of London will show a built-up area little larger than at present, although its character will have been considerably modified in Inner London which, with more high buildings and open land and fewer people, will contrast with an Outer London, little changed except where new suburban office centres have arisen. Beyond the conurbation, the distribution of urban land in the green belt will look much as now, although the New Towns will show more prominently and there will be a rounding off of other towns; but further out, both the larger towns and selected smaller towns, chiefly tied to the radial pattern of railways and trunk roads, will have expanded considerably.

Administrative Areas

As with other conurbations, one of the difficulties in guiding the growth of London has been the absence of any administrative body responsible for considering either London as a whole or the conurbation in its wider setting. It is true that when the London County Council was created in 1888, most of London lay within its boundaries and that both the Standing Joint Committee on London Planning and the staff of the Ministry of Housing and Local Government have provided some co-ordination; but, while London and the surrounding areas cannot be divorced for planning purposes, they continue to be administered by a large number of separate planning

FIG. 78   Administrative boundaries in the London Region
Key: 1–5, county boroughs; 1, Reading; 2, Croydon; 3, West Ham;
4, East Ham; 5, Southend.
Based on maps of the Ministry of Housing and Local Government and
Ordnance Survey.

authorities, nine within the conurbation itself and fourteen in the rest of the London Region (Fig. 78). The Greater London Council, which is to come into being on 1st April 1965, is an attempt to improve this situation as far as the built-up area is concerned by placing it under one authority for those planning matters which affect the whole conurbation, although some areas, which were originally proposed and which ought properly to be included, have been omitted. Yet, while it is a great gain to have one local authority responsible for virtually the whole of the conurbation, the inevitability of further migration from London and the high probability of continued growth of employment make it clear that the area chosen is quite inadequate for broader planning purposes, where communications, housing and employment must be considered together, not only within the conurbation, but in the surrounding area.

The appropriate area for such purposes can be determined only by further study. Degree of dependence on London is clearly of critical importance, but it is difficult to measure; indices of industrial and commercial linkages would be invaluable, but no suitable data exist for their construction. In default, the rate of population growth, which may be in no way related to London, and the proportion of the employed population working in London can be used (Fig. 55), although neither is a very meaningful or accurate measure of dependence. Certainly it would not be desirable to include every place which has links with London, however tenuous, nor would it be appropriate to include towns more than 100 miles (160 km.) away simply because they have received migrants from London.

Whatever the area defined, it will rapidly become obsolete as the London Region already has. Moreover, while the economically significant unit of the future may well be the city region, it would be a misnomer to call this London. Many places within the region will have only slender links with the conurbation and their inhabitants would not think of themselves as Londoners, any more than do the inhabitants of, say, St Albans today. The London of the future will remain the built-up area and, in a sense, planning control has made it easier to define than at any time since medieval London burst its bounds.

Conclusion

The form that London and its region take in the future will, for the first time in its long history, be conceived as a whole and as a matter of conscious choice. Since few would now question the need to control London's growth, the principal question to be answered is how far regulatory planning of the kind practised since 1947 will be adequate to achieve desired ends. If the two greatest successes of post-war planning, the New Towns and the Areas of Comprehensive Development in Inner London, are any criterion, the best hope lies in similar planned action. For controls can only guide development where there are already strong forces promoting it; they cannot stimulate the growth of towns where these are lacking.

Yet the achievements of post-war planning must not be underrated, although, to the casual observer, its deficiencies are more obvious than its virtues; for what is permitted is seen, but what is refused or modified is not. Both contemporary and future London would be very different if the idea of regulating and modifying the operation of economic forces through land planning had not been generally accepted in the 1940s; for, in the light of pre-war trends and American experience, it can hardly be doubted that the built-up area would have become increasingly diffuse or that, in the absence of planning control, densities of building would have fallen as living standards rose. Post-war planning has made the boundary between town and country increasingly clear-cut; at the same time, the appearance of the countryside has been generally enhanced by a prosperous agriculture and a revived forestry. It is true that, even in specially protected areas, the preservation of this scenery rests on few sanctions except those which control new buildings or mineral workings; the hedgerows and many of the trees which contribute so much to the charm of the countryside could vanish almost overnight if farmers and landowners wished and the land could become neglected and scrub-ridden, as sometimes happens where development is not allowed. Yet, in many ways, the major problem of London's countryside is not so much its preservation or its slow disappearance under bricks and concrete, although these are the issues which attract the greatest attention, but the fact that so little of it is either publicly-owned or land over which there are rights of access for the millions who live in and around the conurbation. Here is an issue almost as important for the well-being of the London of the future as the provision of new towns and motorways.

This book ends, as it began, by reference to those remarkable insights into the future of great cities put forward 60 years ago by H. G. Wells in his aptly-named *Anticipations*, in which he foresaw the key role of transport as 'maker and breaker of cities.'[28] Although planning controls have largely prevented the disappearance of the distinction between town and country which he expected, his analysis is still most apposite and the solution of many of London's problems depends in large measure on how many Londoners will be able to 'abandon the City office altogether, preferring to do their business in more agreeable surrounding.'[29]

References

1. Information from London County Council.
2. A. G. Powell, 'The recent development of Greater London', *Advancement of Science* 17 (1960–1), 81.
3. Town and Country Planning Association, *The Paper Metropolis* (1962), 20.
4. *London. Employment: Housing: Land*, Cmd. 1952 (H.M.S.O., 1963), 3.
5. *Report of the Royal Commission on Local Government in Greater London*, Cmd. 1164 (H.M.S.O., 1960), 89.
6. Peter Hall, *London 2000* (1963), 49, 54; The Paper Metropolis, *op. cit.*, 20.
7. Cmd. 1952, *op. cit.*, 3–4.
8. *Ibid.*, 4–5.
9. Information from Ministry of Housing and Local Government.
10. Peter Hall, 'London revised upwards', *New Society*, 18th July 1963, 7.
11. Hall, *London 2000, op. cit.*, 94; Cmd. 1952, *op. cit.*, 8.
12. *Ibid.*
13. L. C. Kitching, 'Problems of London's green belt', *Journal of the Town Planning Institute* 47 (1961), 35; Hall, *London 2000, op. cit.*, 95.
14. Cmd. 1952, *op. cit.*, 9.
15. P. Abercrombie, *Greater London Plan 1944* (H.M.S.O., 1945), 33.
16. E. C. Willatts, 'Post-war developments: the location of major projects in England and Wales', *Chartered Surveyor* 94 (1962), 361.
17. *Ibid.*; Cmd. 1952, *op. cit.*, 11.
18. Hall, *London 2000, op. cit.*, 77.
19. The Paper Metropolis, *op. cit.*, 23.
20. *Ibid.*
21. Cmd. 1952, *op. cit.*, 6.
22. J. Dunkley, 'Office location in the London Region', *Town and Country Planning* 26 (1958), 34.
23. *Guardian*, 29th August 1963, 19.
24. The Paper Metropolis, *op. cit.*, 48–9.
25. 'The London Region and the development of south-east England: 1961 to 1981', *Town and Country Planning* 29 (1961), 230.
26. But cf. L. D. Stamp in Abercrombie, *op. cit.*, 89.
27. *Town and Country Planning* 29 (1961), 234; Hall, *London 2000, op. cit.*, 135–6, 147.
28. C. Clark's phrase, *Town Planning Review*, 28 (1958), 237–50.
29. H. G. Wells, *Anticipations* (1902), 57.

ADDENDUM

SINCE this book went to press, the Ministry of Housing and Local Government has published a report on the problems that may be expected to arise in south-east England during the next twenty years (*The South East Study, 1961–1981*, H.M.S.O., 1964). This accepts the inevitability of massive population growth in the South East and envisages that up to one million of the increase should be housed in expanded towns. It proposes that Southampton—Portsmouth, the Bletchley area and the Newbury area should be the sites of new cities; that Stansted (to be an additional airport for London), Ashford, Ipswich, Northampton, Peterborough and Swindon should receive large increases in population; and that Aylesbury, Banbury, Bedford, Chelmsford, Colchester, Hastings, Maidstone, the Medway Towns, Norwich, Poole, Reading and Southend should also be expanded. In addition, five of the New Towns, Stevenage, Harlow, Basildon, Crawley and Hemel Hempstead, should be allowed to grow beyond their present target populations. The study thus favours the idea of large expansions of towns and prefers sites north of the Thames to those south of the river. Of the suggested towns, Stansted, the Medway Towns (as such), Maidstone, Poole, Southend and Chelmsford do not appear among the suggestions listed in Tables XXI and XXII.

Index

INDEX

INDEX

INDEX

Millbank, 183, 185
Miller, Philip, 339
Mill Hill, 50, 144, 273, 289
Millwall, 235, 237, 258, 261
Misbourne, River, 352
Mitcham, 243
Mole, River, 341
Mollet, André, 335
Monmouth, Duke of, 347
Montpelier Row, 343
Moorgate, 56, 70, 84, 131, 176, 183, 273
Moor Park, 345, 347, 348, 349
Morden, 71, 73, 74, 147
Mortimer Street, 252
Moscow, 88
Moss Bros., 252
Motor-bus, 66, 73, 83, 125, 138, 150, 151, 191, 240, 241; *see also* omnibus
Motor-car, 150, 151, 199, 241, 274
Motorways, *see* Roads
Mucking:
  Buoy, 221
  Light, 220, 221
Muswell Hill, 91, 131

Napoleonic Wars, 80, 81, 84, 88, 106
Nash, John, 57, 81, 84, 95, 97, 98, 99, 100, 101, 102, 103, 104, 182, 192, 337
National Coal Board, 182
National Insurance, Ministry of, 182
National Parks, 297, 307
  Commission, 307
National Ports Council, 223
National Trust, 310
Nature Conservancy, 307
Nature reserves, 297
Neasden, 134
Netherhall Gardens, 131
Newberries (park), 280, 285
Newbury, 373, 380
Newcastle, 217
New Cross, 62, 174
New Cross Bank, 62
New End, Hampstead, 93
Newlands, 280
  estate, 285
New North Road, 56
New Oxford Street, 54, 184
New River Company, 102
New Road, 56, 59, 62, 68, 84, 86, 87, 88, 95, 101, 107, 109, 115, 116, 121, 123, 171
Newspapers, 187, 189, 231
New Towns:
  area of, 319, 322
  building of, 311, 328–31
  Commission for the, 330, 331

Development Corporations, 317, 320, 330, 331
  densities in, 321, 323–30
  designated area of, 320, 321, 330–1
  examples of, 302
  expansion of, 31, 365, 375, 380
  industry in, 231, 244, 368
  land use in, 320–7
  origins of, 314–17
  overspill in, 296
  population of, 262, 319, 365
  proposals for, 374, 380
  self-contained, 366
  sites of, 39, 40, 317–18, 319, 363, 371
  success of, 377
New Towns Act (1946), 313, 315, 316, 317, 330, 369, 370
  (1959), 330
New Towns Committee (Reith Report, 1946), 316, 328
New York, 190
New Zealand, 218
Nicholas Nickleby, 112
Nine Elms, 199
Nonsuch (park), 337
Norbury estate, 160
Norman Conquest, 169
North America, 213, 293
Northampton, 373, 380
North and South Western Junction Railway, *see* Railways
North Downs, 307
North End, Finchley, 93
North Circular Road, 30, 58, 151, 237
North Downs, 19, 22, 23, 39, 40, 49
North End, Hampstead, 93
North London Railway, *see* Railways
North Sea, 212, 222
North-Western Fever Hospital, 125
Northfleet, 236
Northfleet Hope, 210, 211
Northumberland House, 169
Northern Heights, 22, 54, 56, 60, 64, 80, 91, 92, 115, 124, 125, 129, 131, 132, 134, 136, 138
Northern Heights of London, The, 124
Northern Line, *see* Underground Railways
Northumberland, Duke of, 342
Northwood, 37
Norwich, 373, 380
Nurseries, 92

Oatlands, 337
Observatory hill, 336
Offices:
  building, 182, 183, 184, 197, 198, 363, 367
  bombed, 184, 358

INDEX

INDEX

INDEX

ARTS
&
SS mu